Panamá

1ST EDITION

PANAMÁ

A Great Destination

CHRISTOPHER P. BAKER

The Countryman Press
Woodstock, Vermont

OPPOSITE: *Cloud forest in Parque Internacional la Amistad, Panama*

This book is dedicated to Panama's indigenous people

Copyright © 2011 by Christopher P. Baker

Panamá: A Great Destination

978-1-58157-108-0

Interior photographs by the author unless otherwise specified
Maps by Erin Greb Cartography, © The Countryman Press
Book design by Joanna Bodenweber
Composition by Eugenie S. Delaney

Published by The Countryman Press, P.O. Box 748, Woodstock, VT 05091
Distributed by W. W. Norton & Company, Inc., 500 Fifth Avenue, New York, NY 10110
Printed in the United States of America

10 9 8 7 6 5 4 3 2 1

Recommended by *National Geographic Traveler* and *Travel + Leisure* magazines

A crisp and critical approach, for travelers who want to live like locals.—*USA Today*

Great Destinations™ guidebooks are known for their comprehensive, critical coverage of regions of extraordinary cultural interest and natural beauty. Each title in this series is continuously updated with each printing to ensure accurate and timely information. All the books contain more than one hundred photographs and maps.

THE ADIRONDACK BOOK

THE ALASKA PANHANDLE

ATLANTA

AUSTIN, SAN ANTONIO
 & THE TEXAS HILL COUNTRY

BALTIMORE, ANNAPOLIS & THE CHESAPEAKE BAY

THE BERKSHIRE BOOK

BIG SUR, MONTEREY BAY
 & GOLD COAST WINE COUNTRY

CAPE CANAVERAL, COCOA BEACH
 & FLORIDA'S SPACE COAST

THE CHARLESTON, SAVANNAH
 & COASTAL ISLANDS BOOK

THE COAST OF MAINE BOOK

COLORADO'S CLASSIC MOUNTAIN TOWNS

COSTA RICA: GREAT DESTINATIONS
 CENTRAL AMERICA

DOMINICAN REPUBLIC

THE FINGER LAKES BOOK

THE FOUR CORNERS REGION

GALVESTON, SOUTH PADRE ISLAND
 & THE TEXAS GULF COAST

GUATEMALA: GREAT DESTINATIONS
 CENTRAL AMERICA

THE HAMPTONS

HAWAII'S BIG ISLAND: GREAT DESTINATIONS
 HAWAII

HONOLULU & OAHU: GREAT DESTINATIONS
 HAWAII

THE JERSEY SHORE: ATLANTIC CITY TO CAPE MAY

KAUAI: GREAT DESTINATIONS HAWAII

LAKE TAHOE & RENO

LAS VEGAS

LOS CABOS & BAJA CALIFORNIA SUR:
 GREAT DESTINATIONS MEXICO

MAUI: GREAT DESTINATIONS HAWAII

MEMPHIS AND THE DELTA BLUES TRAIL

MICHIGAN'S UPPER PENINSULA

MONTREAL & QUEBEC CITY:
 GREAT DESTINATIONS CANADA

THE NANTUCKET BOOK

THE NAPA & SONOMA BOOK

NORTH CAROLINA'S OUTER BANKS
 & THE CRYSTAL COAST

NOVA SCOTIA & PRINCE EDWARD ISLAND

OAXACA: GREAT DESTINATIONS MEXICO

OREGON WINE COUNTRY

PALM BEACH, FORT LAUDERDALE, MIAMI
 & THE FLORIDA KEYS

PALM SPRINGS & DESERT RESORTS

PHILADELPHIA, BRANDYWINE VALLEY
 & BUCKS COUNTY

PHOENIX, SCOTTSDALE, SEDONA
 & CENTRAL ARIZONA

PLAYA DEL CARMEN, TULUM & THE RIVIERA MAYA:
 GREAT DESTINATIONS MEXICO

SALT LAKE CITY, PARK CITY, PROVO
 & UTAH'S HIGH COUNTRY RESORTS

SAN DIEGO & TIJUANA

SAN JUAN, VIEQUES & CULEBRA:
 GREAT DESTINATIONS PUERTO RICO

SAN MIGUEL DE ALLENDE & GUANAJUATO:
 GREAT DESTINATIONS MEXICO

THE SANTA FE & TAOS BOOK

THE SARASOTA, SANIBEL ISLAND & NAPLES BOOK

THE SEATTLE & VANCOUVER BOOK

THE SHENANDOAH VALLEY BOOK

TOURING EAST COAST WINE COUNTRY

TUCSON

VIRGINIA BEACH, RICHMOND
 & TIDEWATER VIRGINIA

WASHINGTON, D.C., AND NORTHERN VIRGINIA

YELLOWSTONE & GRAND TETON NATIONAL PARKS
 & JACKSON HOLE

YOSEMITE & THE SOUTHERN SIERRA NEVADA

The authors in this series are professional travel writers who have lived for many years in the regions they describe. Honest and painstakingly critical, full of information only a local can provide, Great Destinations guidebooks give you all the practical knowledge you need to enjoy the best of each region.

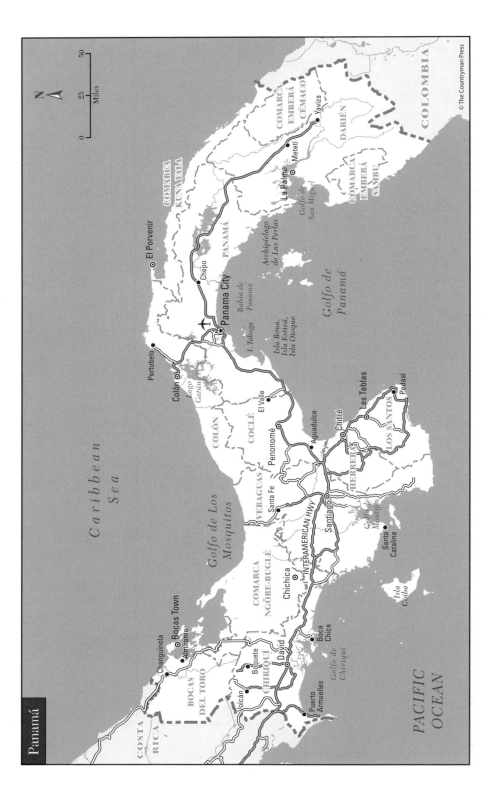

Panamá

N

0   25   50
Miles

Caribbean Sea

PACIFIC OCEAN

COSTA RICA

COLOMBIA

© The Countryman Press

COMARCA EMBERÁ CÉMACO

COMARCA KUNA YALA

DARIÉN

COMARCA EMBERÁ SAMBÚ

PANAMÁ

COLÓN

COCLÉ

VERAGUAS

HERRERA

LOS SANTOS

COMARCA NGÖBE-BUGLÉ

BOCAS DEL TORO

CHIRIQUÍ

Golfo de Los Mosquitos

Golfo de Panamá

Bahía de Panamá

Golfo de San Miguel

Golfo de Montijos

Golfo de Chiriquí

Archipiélago de Las Perlas

Isla Coiba

Lago Gatún

INTERAMERICAN HWY

Yaviza

Meteti

La Palma

El Porvenir

Chepo

Panama City

Portobelo

Colón

El Valle

Penonomé

Aguadulce

Chitré

Las Tablas

Pedasí

Santa Fe

Santiago

Chichica

Santa Catalina

Boca Chica

David

Boquete

Volcán

Puerto Armuelles

Changuinola

Bocas Town

Almirante

Isla Bona, Isla Estivá, Isla Otoque

I. Taboga

CONTENTS

Acknowledgments

I could not have prepared this book without the help of a coterie of other people. Particular thanks go to Brian Rudert, of USAID; Annie Dooner; Barry Robbins and Jane Walker, of the Coffee Estate Inn, in Boquete; Carmen Chen, of Gamboa Tours; Hernán Araúz, of Ancón Expeditions; José Abadi, of La Fortuna (the real 'Tailor of Panama'); Kathy de Guardia, Director of Marketing for the Instituto Panameño de Turismo; Melva Quintero, of Canal & Bay Tours; Octavio Abad, Marketing Coordinator for the Autoridad de Turismo de Panama; Pierre Cruz, of Hotel El Panamá Summit; Romano Orlich, of Finca Lerida; and Teresa Arosemena, of the Autorida del Canal de Panamá. Dozens of others helped me in ways large or small. Thank you one and all.

I'd like to hear from you if you have suggestions for ways to improve this book. Also, please let us know about your experiences, both good and bad, with hotels, restaurants, and other businesses listed.

INTRODUCTION

A Rip Van Winkle of Central American tourism, Panamá's time has arrived. The country has witnessed a phenomenal real estate boom in recent years. And then there's the Canal. Not only is it a tourist draw of mega-importance (as well as the world's most concentrated highway of liquid commerce), it now promises to adrenaline-charge Panamá's glowing stature, as an entirely new canal capable of handling tomorrow's mega-megaships is being built parallel to the existing canal. The $5 billion project can only spell a spectacular future for Panamá, focusing international eyes on the country.

The Canal's importance has traditionally blind-sided potential visitors to the nation's diverse and remarkable treasures. In the past two years, however, tourism has exploded out of nowhere. Folks who have long known about neighboring Costa Rica have suddenly cottoned to Panamá's natural wonders, not least its untapped national parks protecting lowland rain forests, to montane cloud forests teeming with exotic animals and birds (more species, in fact, than in Costa Rica). And whereas Costa Rica is depauperate when it comes to colorful indigenous cultures, Panamá boasts *three* vibrant Indian groups (the Kuna, Emberá, and Ngöbe-Buglé), each as distinct as a thumbprint.

Then there's Panamá City, the capital city combining a fabulous colonial core (now in the midst of restoration) with a thoroughly cosmopolitan modern quarter with casinos, world-class dining, and glittering skyscrapers that scratch the sky. There's no shortage of castles brimming with spine-chilling history. And the Azuero Peninsula—yes, I know, you've never heard of it!—offers a jaw-dropping combination of sleepy colonial villages; world-class surfing beaches; and a string of wildlife refuges protecting species from roseate spoonbills and flamingoes to humpback whales and Ridley turtles, which come ashore in *arribadas*—battalions of 10,000 or more individuals at a time! Plus, the sport-fishing and scuba diving are sublime. And the spectacular beaches that have long been the preserve of moneyed locals are suddenly making international news.

This Lilliputian Central American land is actually a Brobdingnagian just awakening to its vast potential. The nation's reputation was long sullied by its image as a banana republic, much thanks to the excesses of pineapple-faced dictator, Manuel Noriega. Since the U.S. military's Operation Just Cause in 1989 that deposed him, Panamá has evolved into a stable democracy. The lingering perception of Panamá as a backward and dangerous country is now passé. Plus, the long, slender nation is only about the same size as South Carolina, making sightseeing a cinch. The country also offers superb accommodations, including wilderness lodges and an evolving array of boutique hotels.

Tourism grew by an average of 12 percent yearly 2004–2008, with more than 1.6 million visitors in 2008. And the pace is picking up, with tourist arrivals expected to top two million in 2010.

THE WAY THIS BOOK WORKS

This book is divided into 11 chapters. Entries within each regional chapter are broken down geographically according to the names of towns or distinct geographic entities, such as valleys or beach zones. The same order of headings—Lodging, Dining, Attractions . . . etc.—is used for each regional chapter.

Some entries include specific information—telephone numbers, Web sites, addresses, business hours, and the like—organized for easy reference in blocks at the top of each entry.

For the same reasons, we have routinely avoided listing specific prices, indicating instead a range. Lodging price codes are based on a per-room rate, double occupancy during winter months (high season). Off-season rates are often cheaper. Restaurant price ratings indicate the cost of an individual meal, including appetizer, entrée, and dessert but not cocktails, wine, tax, or tip.

All information was checked as close to the publication date as possible. Even so, since details can change without warning, it is always wise to call ahead.

Price Codes

	Lodging	Dining
Inexpensive	Up to $100	Up to $10
Moderate	$100 to 150	$10 to 20
Expensive	$150 to 250	$20 to 35
Very Expensive	Over $250	$35 or more

Credit cards are abbreviated as follows:
AE—American Express
CB—Carte Blanche
D—Discover Card
DC—Diner's Club
MC—MasterCard
V—Visa

1

History

> *It is a real tropic forest, palms and bananas, breadfruit trees, bamboos, lofty ceibas, and gorgeous butterflies and brilliant colored birds fluttering among the orchids . . .*
>
> —President Theodore Roosevelt

Natural History

Panamá lies at the southern apex of the narrow Central American isthmus, where the land is pinched pencil-thin at its juncture with South America. Shaped like a lateral S-curve, the nation is oriented east to west—a source of confusion to many visitors, who assume that Panamá runs north to south. It is cusped betwixt Costa Rica (to the west) and Colombia (to the east) and fringed by the Atlantic (to the north) and Caribbean (to the south). The country lies entirely within the Tropics between 7 and 10 degrees north of the equator.

Blessed with virtually every attribute for which the Central American Tropics is known, Panamá's landscapes are kaleidoscopic. A pivotal region at the juncture of North and South America, Panamá is also an ecological crossroads where the biota of the two continents and the Caribbean and Pacific zones merge to produce a veritable cornucopia of biodiversity.

The region is geologically youthful, having been pushed up from the sea only a few million years ago by the cataclysmic collision of tectonic plates that make up the Earth's surface, like a moveable jigsaw puzzle. Deep below the Earth's crust, viscous molten rock flows in slow-moving convection currents that well up from deep within the Earth's core, carrying the plates on their backs. Panamá rides atop the Cocos plate at its jostling juncture with the Caribbean plate. No surprise, then, that much of the 29,762-square-mile (77,381 sq km) nation is mountainous, rising to 11,401 feet (3,475 m) atop Volcán Barú.

There are only two seasons: wet (May to November) and dry (December to April), though the nation is a quiltwork of regional variations. Despite the republic's location within the Tropics, the extremes of elevation and relief spawn a profusion of microclimates. The arid flatlands of the Azuero Peninsula and the sodden coastal plains of the Caribbean could belong to different worlds, never mind the same nation, notwithstanding their similar elevation. Moist trade winds bearing down from the east spill their water on the windward slopes of the Cordillera Central, the nation's spine, while the lowlands at the base of the leeward slopes are left to thirst. The Cordillera thus forms rain shadows over Azuero, much of which is scrub covered, with cacti poking up from the parched earth. And though temperatures in any one place scarcely vary year-round, the smothering heat of the lowlands contrasts markedly with the crisp cool of the highlands.

OPPOSITE: *Pre-Columbian petroglyphs at Sitio Barriles, Panama*

FLORA

Relatively small it may be, but Panamá is clad in multiple shades of green: from swampy coastal wetlands and mangrove forests to dense lowland rain forest and, high above, cloud forests soaked in ethereal mists. In fact, this tropical Eden has 10 distinct ecological zones, including pockets of dry deciduous tropical forest and even patches of semi-desert in the parched Azuero Peninsula.

Visitors are often shocked at the humidity and year-round high temperatures; so close to the equator that the sun lasers down year-round. The greenhouse effect is aided by drenching rainfall that fuels extraordinarily luxuriant growth. As a result, Panamá boasts astonishing species diversity. More than 10,000 species of flora have been identified locally. The country is especially rich in endemic flora.

Most abundant are the ferns (678 species), found from sea level to the highest eleva-tions. Notable, too, are epiphytes (Greek for air plants), arboreal nesters that festoon host tree trunks and boughs and use spongelike roots to tap moisture directly from the air. Prominent among them are bromeliads. These epiphytes have thick spiky leaves that are tightly whorled to form cisterns that capture both water and falling leaf litter (and the occasional unfortunate bug); the decaying matter releases minerals that feed the plant. Other epiphytes, such as dwarf mistletoe, are parasites that draw nutrients directly from the host tree. Most numerous, though are orchids: About 1,200 species have been cata-logued so far, from the pinhead-sized *Platystele jungermanniodes* and the *Flor del Espiritu Santo,* or Holy Ghost orchid (the beautiful white national flower) to the black, 12-inch

Orchid, Panamá

(30 cm) long, tapering petals of the sinister *Dracula vampira*. These exquisite plants are found at every elevation, from sea level to the cloud-wrapped slopes of the Cordillera.

Silvery gray *Palma real* (royal palm) rise from the lowlands like petrified Corinthian columns. With its slightly bulbous trunk, this graceful palm is beloved for its utilitarianism, including thatch for roofing. At least a dozen other species of palm are used for construction and crafts, including the sabal or *Palma cana* (like the royal, a towering giant), and the more slender silver thatch or *guano*. The shores are lined with gracefully curving coconut palm. Despite its ubiquity, it is actually an Old World species introduced to the Americas by the Spanish in the 16th century. Some palms are even adapted for cooler heights, such as the 13-foot (4 m), mountain-dwelling sierra palm, whose branches unfurl from a cello-like fiddlehead.

Vegetation zones vary with elevation and local microclimates. While it may come as no surprise that much of Panamá is smothered in dense lowland rain forest, upland areas have distinctly alpine climes and vegetation, with pine trees predominant. Higher still wildflowers emblazon soggy meadows atop the tallest peaks, where wind-scoured savannas intersperse with forests of stunted trees skulking low against howling rains.

The forests, dry and moist alike, flame with Cezanne color: Almost fluorescent yellow *corteza amarilla* . . . purple jacaranda . . . snow white frangipani . . . and flame red *Spathodea,* or African flame-of-the-forest, emblazon the Panamanian landscape before littering the forest floor with petals resembling discarded confetti. Many are the species, too, that produce succulent fruits. Familiar to most visitors are bananas, papayas, and mangoes, but you'll also find—and should try—guavas (*guyaba*), plumlike passion fruit (*chinola*), oval-shaped *sapote,* and tamarindo, which is cusped within a long peanut-shell pod and, like *guanábano,* mostly finds its way into drinks.

Rain Forests

Rain forests are defined as ecosystems that receive more than 100 inches (250 cm) of rainfall per year. There are at least 13 types of rain forest, from the dense and truly rainsodden evergreen equatorial jungles such as smother the *llanuras*—flatlands—of Darién and the Caribbean lowlands, to mist-soaked ethereal montane cloud forests—officially known as tropical montane rain forest—above 4,000 feet (1219 m), as on the mid-elevation slopes of Volcán Barú. Panamá has several distinct types (even at a single latitude) according to elevation and local microclimates. These crown jewels of Neotropical biota are rivaled only by coral reefs in their complexity.

The broad-leafed lowland rain forests are multi-layered, with species such as baobabs with trunks like pregnant bellies; *yagruma,* whose silvery leaves seem frosted; and the statuesque ceiba (or silk cotton) and *caoba* (mahogany), which soar skyward for 100 feet (30 m) or more to form umbrellas over the solid forest canopy. To support their great height and bulk, these "emergent" giants grow massive flanges at their base, resembling rocket fins, while roots often snake along the ground for many meters. This is also because dead leaves decompose quickly in hot, humid climes (nutrients are swiftly recycled up to the forest canopy), tropical soils are thin, and trees can't send roots deep into the ground.

Tangled creepers twine up the trunks and hang from boughs high above, much like Tarzan's jungle. The canopy so restricts sunlight that little undergrowth grows on the forest floor, where plants compete fiercely for light. More than 90 percent of a rain forest biota is concentrated in the sunlit canopy, where an entire universe of animal and birdlife exists unseen from below.

Big Bully!

The bully of tropical trees is the giant strangler fig. This exquisite yet murderous tree (there are actually almost one thousand species throughout the Tropics) is like something from *Lord of the Rings*. Birthed on the branches of other trees when birds deposit their guano containing seeds, the sprouting fig sends roots creeping along the branches while long tendril roots drop to the ground and begin to take nutrients from the soil. Over decades the roots thicken and merge, twining in an eerie latticework around the host tree. Eventually the latter is choked to death (the process can take a century) and rots away, leaving a complete yet hollow mature fig. Often several fig plants will grow on the same host tree, eventually fusing together to form a compound organism with genetically distinct branches. Pocked with abundant nooks and crannies, the hollow trunk provides a perfect home for bats and other invertebrates, plus birds and lizards, all of them gifted with an abundant food source in the plentiful fig fruits (galls) that grow in clusters directly from the tree branches.

The tree owes its life to a remarkable symbiotic (mutually dependent) relationship with the tiny gall or fig wasp. Pregnant females are drawn to the tree's fruity galls, each of which has a tiny hole through which the wasp enters. She tears off her wings as she squeezes in to lay her eggs in the stigma of the tiny flowers (both male and female) that grow within the gall; the flowers can't pollinate each other, as they mature at different times. Duty performed, the female wasp dies. The hole seals itself. And the eggs are left to hatch. First to emerge are the males, which crawl from their eggs preprogrammed and ready to mate. They chew open the eggs of the females and inseminate them in their natal sleep. Hatching at the exact moment that the male flowers mature, the already pregnant (and winged) females get covered with pollen as they chew a hole in the gall and fly off to find their own tree. (The males also depart the gall and proceed to die.) Locating their own galls on other trees in the right stage of development, each female burrows in to begin the process anew. The pollen she carries is brushed onto the female fig flowers, completing the pollination. In her sole day of life, the female wasp thus ensures a new generation of wasps and of ficus.

Dry Forests

In pre-colonial days, seasonally dry deciduous forest covered much of the Azuero peninsula, which lies in a rain shadow and witnesses an annual five-month drought. Deforestation has vastly reduced the coverage of this tropical habitat, and only pockets remain in *el arco seco* (the dry arc) of southern Coclé, eastern Herrera, and eastern Los Santos provinces. Far less species-rich than wet forests, the dry forests are home to many endemic bird and animal species that include the Azuero parakeet, Azuero spider monkey, and Azuero howler monkey. The wildlife is relatively easily seen thanks to the relatively sparse distribution of trees, which shed their leaves to save water.

Typical tree species include the steel-strong lignum vitae (*guayacán*), with its mottled peeling bark and winged seed capsules. Guayacán is the most dense of any known wood in the world, so hard and durable that it was once used for bearings. The indigenous people used its resin to treat medical conditions, including arthritis. The logwood (*campache*) they used against dysentery and as a black dye. Favoring the dry forests, too, is the contorted gumbo-limbo, with its stout, massive branches and a spreading, rounded crown; it's also known as "burned tourist" due to its shiny, smooth, reddish exfoliating bark, like the peeling skin of sunburned tourists. The smooth, papery thin bark peels off in sheets to

Dry forest display at Punta Culebra Nature Center, Panamá City

reveal a greenish layer beneath. The oily bark gives off a gummy, turpentine-scented resin that has long been used locally for glues and varnish, handy in the manufacture of canoes. Indigenous people use the gumbo-limbo's aromatic sap for medicinal teas. Intriguingly, the soft, spongy wood, if chopped and planted, easily takes root in the ground, for which reason it is used for fence posts.

These dry forest trees are draped with wispy tendrils of Spanish moss, like Fidel Castro's beard, that draw water from the air during rare rainfalls. Dodder vines also twine up tree trunks like serpents around Eden's tree; they usurp nutrients until they kill their host trees. And orchids are also present, often growing on the tops of cactus pads.

Many flora species lie dormant throughout the dry season before exploding in riotous color with the onset of rain; an hour-long deluge can resurrect flora from sun-scorched torpor.

Mangroves and Wetlands

Dense thickets and forests of mangroves line much of the coast. Five species of these tropical halophytes (salt-tolerant plants) grow along Panamá's shores, thriving at the margin of land and sea on silts brought down from the mountains. Thus they are frequent around river estuaries. These shrubby pioneer land-builders trap sediment flowing out to sea from the slow-moving rivers and form a bulwark against wave action and tidal erosion (by filtering out sediment, they are also important contributors to the health of coral reefs).

Mangroves rise from the dark water on a tangle of interlocking stilt roots that give them a resemblance to walking on water. The dense, waterlogged mud bears little oxygen. Hence the mangroves have evolved aerial roots, drawing oxygen directly from the air through pores in the bark (black mangroves, however, breathe through pneumatophores—

Mangrove seed pod, Panamá

specialized roots that protrude out of the mud like snorkel tubes). The roots of red mangroves, the most common species in Panamá, have evolved to filter out salt before taking up water; any salt entering via the shoot is carried to the leaves, which are then shed. White mangroves even excrete salt directly through special glands for that purpose, hence its name.

Mangals—mangrove communities—are a vital habitat for all manner of animal and marine life. Rich in organic content, the muds are the base in a unique ecosystem in which algae and other small organisms thrive, providing sustenance for oysters, shrimp, sponges, and other creatures higher up the food chain. Small stingrays flap slowly through the shallow waters, while baby sharks and tiny fishes flit about in their tens of thousands, shielded from larger predators by the protective tangle of roots. Tiny arboreal mangrove crabs mulch the leaves and are preyed upon by larger, mostly terrestrial, species. Mangals are also important breeding grounds for ibis, frigatebirds, pelicans, and other waterbirds, which nest here en masse. Herons and egrets pick among the braided channels and tidal creeks. Arboreal snakes slither along the branches. Turtles bask on the mud banks. Crocodiles lurk in the silty waters, while manatees forage for food.

Aggressive colonizers, mangroves have evolved a remarkable propagation technique. The shrub blooms briefly in spring, and from the resulting fruit grows a seedling sprout. The large, heavy, elongated seeds shaped like a hydrometer, or plumb bob, germinate while still on the tree. Growing to a length of 6 to 12 inches (15 to 30 cm), they drop like darts. Landing in mud, they begin to develop immediately. If they hit water, they float on the currents until they touch a muddy floor. The seeds can survive months at sea without desiccation and are thus capable of traveling hundreds of miles to begin a new colony. With each successive generation, the colony expands out to sea, eventually forming a great forest. The oldest mangroves form forests, often soaring 60 feet (18 m) high, that exist high and dry and eventually die on land the mangroves themselves have created.

Panamá has significant (and easily explored) mangrove forests in the Golfo de Chiriquí, Bahía de Panamá, and Golfo de San Miguel.

Many other wetland systems support profuse birdlife. Lago Gatún and Lago Bayano, the swampy freshwater bayous of Refugio de Vida Silvestre Las Macanas and Refugio de Vida Silvestre Cenegón del Mangle, and the Caribbean's seasonally flooded San San-Pond Sak all teem with waterfowl: fulvous whistling duck . . . black-crowned night herons . . . common gallinule . . . pied-billed grebe . . . roseate spoonbills.

FAUNA

Panamá is an A-list destination for international birders. Crocodiles and other reptiles abound and are easily seen, as are mammals, such as monkeys and coatimundis. And life beneath the waves gives snorkelers and divers raptures of the deep.

Birds

Ornithologists' hearts take flight in Panamá. The coos, calls, and caterwauling of avian fauna draw serious birders from far and wide to one of the Western Hemisphere's premier birding locales. Its kaleidoscopic habitats provide a home to at least 972 bird species, including 12 endemics—more bird species, in fact, than neighboring Costa Rica.

Parrots (22 species) are among the most recognizable of Panamá's birds; the forests resound with their squawks and screeches. These intelligent and garrulous creatures range from the tiny Panamá Amazon (relegated to the Pacific coast) to the giant blue-and-gold macaw. The latter, at more than a yard long, is the largest of Panamá's six macaw species

Scarlet macaws

The Endangered Harpy

Most threatened of the nation's endemic birds is the harpy eagle. The largest raptor in the Americas, this lowland rain forest dweller can attain an impressive 7-foot-wide (over 2 m) wingspan (the female outsizes the male). Its massive 5-inch-long (almost 13 cm) talons are designed for seizing monkeys and other prey from the treetops. The harpy is a strikingly beautiful bird, with white belly, legs, and underside; slate black shoulders, head, and upper wings; and a pale gray face mantled in a beardlike double crown topped by tufts, like erect ears.

Harpy eagle

Harpy eagles typically nest in the top of ceiba trees, well over 100 feet (30 m) above the ground. Slow breeders, harpy couples lay two eggs every two or three years; when the first egg hatches the second is neglected and only one chick is raised.

The species is threatened and is locally extinct in much of its former range. The Fondo Peregrino-Panamá (507-317-0350; www.fondoperegrino.org) has a conservation and breed-and-release program aimed at saving this magnificent bird.

(neighboring Costa Rica has only two species), which includes a large population of scarlet macaws on Isla Coiba. Macaws are monogamous for life and are often seen—and heard—flying in pairs overhead.

Other quintessential tropical birds that you're sure to see are the toucans, with their banana-like beaks. Keel-billed and chestnut-mandibled toucans are the most common, along with their cousins, the fiery-billed aracarias. Many birders flock to Panamá simply to spot the resplendent quetzal—the Holy Grail of tropical birds. Beloved for its impossibly iridescent green plumage, this pigeon-sized cloud-forest dweller is relatively easily seen on the mid-elevation slopes of the Cordillera, notably around Volcán Barú. Another cloud-forest inhabitant, the three-wattled bellbird, is now threatened.

Panamá boasts 59 species of hummingbirds, of which 4 are endemics. These tiny, high-speed creatures are named for the buzz of the blurry fast beat of their wings: at 10 to 70 beats per second, so fast that they can hover and even fly backwards. Their metabolic rate (a hummers' heart rate can exceed 1,000 beats a minute) is so prodigious that they must consume vast quantities of high-power nectar and tiny insects. In fact, they typically eat the equivalent of their own body weight in a day (they also choose only flowers whose nectar has a sugar content above about 20 percent)! They're a delight to watch, hovering in flight, sipping nectar drawn through a hollow extensile tongue that darts in and out of their long narrow bills.

Turkey vultures (one of four vulture species here) are common throughout the country. So, too, cattle egrets, easily seen in pastures. In fact, the republic is home to 20 species of herons and egrets, plus 6 species of spoonbills and ibis. There are as 16 species of ducks; 4 species of guans; 7 species of quails; 16 species of coots and rails; 28 species of pigeons and doves; 15 of owls, plus the closely related northern potoo; and 54 species of raptors, including osprey and American kestrel. And still you've barely scratched at the surface.

More than 150 of Panamá's bird species are migrants, the majority of which are water-fowl, shorebirds, and warblers. Most are snowbirds, fleeing the North American winter via the Pacific Flyway. Baikal teal, king eiders, and white-cheeked pintail flood the shallow lakes and wetlands in multitudinous thousands. Northern jacana trot across the lily pads on their oversized widely spread feet. Glossy ibis, white ibis, and roseate spoonbills pick for tidbits in freshwater and briny lagoons, while coastal mangroves are ideal nesting sites for pelicans, Neotropic cormorants, and anhingas, colloquially known as "snake-birds" for their long slender necks cocked in an S-shape, like a cobra. And down by the shore, sand-pipers, whimbrels, willets, and American oystercatchers scurry in search of small crustaceans and similar tasty morsels.

Seabirds, too, are well represented. Red-billed tropic birds grace the sky with their snow-white plumage and trailing tails. Frigatebirds hang in the air like kites on invisible strings. Masked, red-footed, blue-footed, and brown boobies—quintessential maritime birds—nest on various offshore isles where—surprise!—even the Galapagos penguin is infrequently spotted, along with three species of albatross, six species of storm petrels, and two species of tropic birds.

See *Birding*, in the Planning Your Trip chapter, for information on birding, including companies offering birding tours in Panamá.

Mammals

The country has 225 mammal species, of which almost half are bats and 8 are marine mammals (see *Beneath the Waves*, below). The bats range from the Jamaican fruit-eating bat to the giant greater bulldog bat, or fishing bat: Named for its feeding habits, it uses

Ibis

Kleptomaniacs of the Sky

What's that sinister looking black bird with 6-foot (2 m) Stuka wings, a long hooked beak, and a devilish forked tail, hanging over the ocean on warm updrafts? Truly one of a kind, the frigatebird is the pirate of the sky. This kleptoparasite uses its lofty perch from which to harry gulls and terns until they release their catch, which the frigatebird then scoops up on the wing as it falls. However, they catch most of their food by skimming the ocean surface and snatching fish. These pelagic piscivores are not above snatching other seabird chicks from their nests.

Boasting the largest wingspan-to-body-weight ratio of any bird in the world, frigatebirds are supreme aerial performers and expend little energy while gliding the thermals. Thus they can stay aloft for days on end, landing solely to roost or breed. They nest in colonies, usually building rough individual nests atop mangroves in areas with a strong wind for lift on take-off.

Frigatebirds, Isla Iguana, Panamá

Despite its sinister appearance, this eagle-sized bird is quite beautiful due to the iridescent purplish green sheen of the male's otherwise jet-black plumage. The male displays a bloodred gular sac that he inflates into a heart-shaped balloon during mating season, when males sit atop their mangrove roosts ululating and preening as the larger females wing around overhead, inspecting prospective mates. The female wears a bib of white on her abdomen and breast, plus a ring of blue around her eyes, all the better to impress her would-be mate. Each pair is seasonally monogamous. The female lays one or two eggs each breeding season. Weaning takes a full year—the longest of any bird.

Unlike pelicans and other diving birds, frigatebirds lack the small preen gland that produces water-resistant oil for the feathers; thus, they need to stay dry. If they submerge, their feathers get waterlogged and they are doomed.

echolocation to detect water ripples made by fish, which it snatches on the wing with its sharp claws as an eagle snatches salmon. Other bats emerge at night to feast on insects, which they echolocate in the darkness by emitting an ultrasonic squeak whose echo is picked up by their oversize ears.

Of the world's 10 species of Neotropical wild cats, 6 prowl the Panamanian forests. Don't expect to see them. They're shy, elusive, and well camouflaged. The jaguars, margays, ocelots, and oncillas have spotted coats, while the low, slinky jaguarundi has chocolaty fur, and the puma ranges from tan to dark brown, depending on habitat. The massive and muscular jaguar is king of the jungle—a full-grown male can measure 8 feet in length, nose to tail. It requires a huge territory for hunting and is highly susceptible to habitat destruction. Although all the cats are good climbers, the slender margay is arboreal and has developed unique ankle joints for a life in the trees.

Ocelot

Creatures you *are* likely to see are the monkeys. Panamá boasts seven species, ranging from the diminutive endemic Geoffrey's tamarin to a nocturnal monkey (endemic to Bocas del Toro), and the large yet herbivorous howlers. The latter occupy thick forests through-out the nation and range from dark brown to black, according to locale. You'll probably hear them before you see them, as the males vocalize their presence with frightening lion-like roars. Mischievous white-faced (capuchin) monkeys are no less ubiquitous, and long-limbed, copper-colored spider monkeys are commonly seen at such venues as Barra del Colorado Island, in Gatún Lake.

Other commonly seen mammals include the slow-moving two- and three-toed sloths (*perosozos*), which spend most of their day snoozing in the cusp of tree branches. Down below, the adorable coatimundi can often be seen scampering roadside or along forest trails. A dark brown relative of the raccoon, it has a tapered snout and long tail held erect. Capybaras, the world's largest rodents, forage in the wetland sloughs of the Darién (I've even seen them alongside the Panamá Canal), where endangered tapirs similarly prefer watery dense-forest habitats.

Born with a Watertight Skin

Panamá boasts more than 120 snake species, more than 100 frog and toad species, and almost 100 lizard species. Let's start with the snakes, which are ubiquitous throughout the nation—masters of camouflage, they're not always easy to see, however (not least, most species are very small and most are nocturnal, making good use of their infrared eyesight). Only about 20 species of Panamanian snakes are venomous, of which about 10 are poten-tially fatal to humans.

The vipers include various species of small yet highly venomous eyelash pit and palm

Boa constrictor

vipers. Some are lime green. Others are banana yellow. Some are gray, brown, or even rust colored. All are supremely camouflaged according to the habitat (usually arboreal) that they prefer. The most fearsome snake in the country is the fer-de-lance (Panamanians call it the *equis*—"x"—for the marks on its back). This huge viper, which grows to 6 feet (1.8 m) in length, is a relative of the equally deadly bushmaster. Supremely camouflaged, it's hard to spot among the leaf litter, despite its massive size. It's wickedly aggressive and is the cause of the vast majority of fatal snakebites in the country. A mildly venomous, silvery black snake called the mussurana (or *zopilota* in Panamá) feeds on other snakes including the *equis;* remarkably, it is immune to even the fer-de-lance's venom!

Slender, beautifully colored coral snakes are also potentially deadly. They're easily recognized by their red, yellow/white, and black banding (some non-venomous snakes mimic the coral's banding; it's best to treat them all as venomous). And the highly venomous yellow-bellied sea snake is often encountered in large congregations in Pacific waters, notably in the Bahía de Panamá. Fortunately, they are non-aggressive and have only rarely been known to bite humans and then only under duress.

The large boa grows up to 10 feet (3 m) long and is colored with somber tones of chestnut and dusky brown; it feeds primarily on rodents, birds, and bats. Like many boas, its skin displays a remarkable pearly blue green iridescence when seen in sunlight (the sheen results from the molecular structure of the skin cells and is unrelated to the skin's pigmentation). It prefers moist forests and open savannas and surprises its prey with a biting lunge that precedes constricting the poor beast to death. Unlike most snake species, which lay eggs, female boas produce live offspring.

Among the most beautiful species are the slender arboreal vine snakes, ever on the hunt for tasty lizards and frogs, which range from the adorable inch-long red-eyed tree frog to the giant cane toad. The latter, introduced two centuries ago to control pests in sugarcane fields, has flourished by devouring many native amphibian species, and repels predators with toxic secretions.

Panamá is famous for its poison-dart frogs, brightly colored thimble-sized critters that hop about the moist forest floors by daytime secure in the knowledge that nothing will eat them. The colors—strawberry red on Isla Bastimentos; cobalt blue and black on Carro Brujo; green and black on Isla Taboga—are warning signs that spell "Toxic!" These Day-Glo amphibians are members of the Dendrobtidae family, which produces some of the deadliest toxins known to man. The frogs secrete these alkaloid compounds through their skin when they feel threatened. One species, the silvery yellow *Phyllobates terribilis,* is so toxic (250 times more deadly than strychnine) that even in its normal state it is fatal to human touch. This is the true poison-dart frog after which all others are named; it is endemic solely to the rain forests of Darién and northern Colombia, whose Emberá-Wounaan communities have traditionally used the secretions to tip their darts and arrows. The earless and deaf golden frog *(Atelopus zateki),* endemic to the Valle de Ancón region and unique for its ability to communicate by semaphore, is considered a national mascot. Like many frog species, its population has declined markedly in recent years and it is now endangered.

Lizards, too, are everywhere, darting from rock to rock or staring you down from a shady crevice. My favorite is the forest-dwelling Jesus Christ lizard, so-named because it can dash across water on its hind legs. The semi-arboreal green and brown anoles are easily recognizable by the way males bob their heads and extend and retract their throat dewlaps, as if opening and closing a Spanish mantilla fan. You'll fall in love with geckos—undeniably cute, bright green, and almost rubberlike, like the charming Cockney-speaking gecko of the Geico ads. You'll probably hear them before you see them, as they love to vocalize with cheeping sounds. Don't be surprised to find them scurrying across your hotel room ceiling! Geckos feed on tiny insects, such as mosquitoes, for which reason house geckos (which live in thatched roofs or crevices in ceilings) are happily tolerated by Central American families.

Red-eyed tree frog

Iguanas—fearsome-looking, dragonlike lizards—are commonly seen in lower elevation forests. Despite their size (up to 5 feet/1.5 m long) and *One Million Years B.C.* appearance, they're harmless herbivores and frugivores. Panamá has several species, including the green iguana, common throughout Central America. Iguanas have a row of protective spines running down their back and along their whiplike tails, which they use to deliver painful lashes if attacked. Males have large dewlaps that hang below their chins to help regulate their body temperature and for use in courtship displays. Most remarkable is the parietal eye, a rudimentary third "eye," or photosensory organ, atop the head to detect motion from above.

Jesus Christ lizards

Other reptilians include freshwater turtles. They're easily seen basking on logs or mud banks in lagoons and wetland ponds. And five of the world's eight species of marine turtles—green, hawksbill, leatherback, loggerhead, and Ridley—lumber out of the surf to lay the seeds of tomorrow's turtles in Panamá's sugar-fine sands. Most females typically time their arrival to coincide with full moons, when there is less distance to travel beyond the high water mark. Finding an elevated spot in the sand, she digs out a 3-foot-deep (1 m) hole with her rear flippers, drops in her 100 or so golf-ball-sized and -shaped eggs, then laboriously fills in the hole, tamps its down, scatters sand about to disguise it and, exhausted after this hours-long labor, crawls back down the beach and swims off through the surf. All five species are endangered, threatening a demise for creatures that have been swimming the oceans for 100 million years. Unlike its smaller cousins, which have an external skeleton in the form of their calcareous carapace, the leatherback (which can measure 8 feet (2.4 m) long and weigh up to 1,000 pounds) has an internal skeleton and an exterior of leathery, cartilaginous skin. Tapered for hydrodynamic efficiency and insulated by a layer of thick oily fat, it has evolved to survive staggeringly deep cold-water dives and migrations of thousands of miles. Visitors to the Azuero Peninsula are in for a special treat if they can time their visit

Olive Ridley turtles coming ashore to nest

Defying Gravity

Scratch your head as you might, you can puzzle all day and night about how the dickens geckos cling to ceilings and scurry along upside down without falling off. Sticky feet? Nah! Suction cups? Forget it! Surface tension? Getting warmer!

Touch a gecko's foot and you'll find it dry and smooth. No gummy adhesive, clasping hooks, or Spiderman-like suction cups. The gecko's astounding adhesive ability is actually due to pure physics. The feat is accomplished by specialized toe pads covered with millions of spatula-tipped filaments, each a mere hundred nanometers thick—a diameter less than the wavelength of visible light. The spatulae themselves tip millions of microscopic hairs that blanket curling ridges on each toe pad on the gecko's five-toed feet. The nanofilaments are so small that they tap into the van der Waals force, the transient negative and positive electrical charges that draw adjacent molecules together. The attractive force that holds a gecko to a surface is thus an electrical bond between the spatulae and the molecules of whatever surface the gecko nimbly scampers across.

The grip, however, is highly directional and self-releasing. The toes bond to a surface when placed downward and are released when the gecko changes its toes' angle, breaking the geometric relationship of spatulae and surface molecule.

to Refugio de Vida Silvestre Isla de Cañas to coincide with an *arribada*—a synchronized mass nestings of olive Ridley turtles.

Arachnids, Insects, and Relatives

Panamá is abuzz with bees, wasps, and flies. There are tens of thousands of species, including hundreds of species of ant (and still counting). Dragonflies flit back and forth across the surface of pools. Some 1,600 species of butterflies—swallowtails, heliconius, scintillating blue morphos—brighten the landscapes, dancing like floating leaves on the wind. There are mantids. Cockroaches. Venomous centipedes. Big stink bugs. Katydids 3 inches long. Stick insects as long as your forearm. And beetles galore—including the 3-inch-long rhinoceros beetle—in a kaleidoscope of shimmering greens, neon blues, startling reds, and impossible silvers and golds.

Probing around with your hands amid rocks is never a good idea, as scorpions (*alacránes* to Panamanians) spend the daylight hours hiding in shady crevices. They stir around dusk, when they emerge to hunt crickets, cockroaches, and other insects, which they subdue with a venomous sting. With their fearsome-looking claws and sharply curving stinging tail, scorpions should be treated with due trepidation.

Beneath the Waves

The seas around Panamá are a pelagic playpen, prodigiously populated by fish and marine mammals. Coral reefs rim much of the shoreline and offshore isles. Sheets of purple staghorn sway to the rhythms of the ocean current. Leaflike orange gorgonians spread their fingers upwards toward the light. And lacy crops of black coral resemble delicately woven Spanish *mantillas*. A kaleidoscopic extravaganza of fish as strikingly bejeweled as damsels in an exotic harem play tag in the coral-laced waters. The species of the Pacific and Caribbean waters differ.

What a Croc!

The olive green American crocodile (*cocodrilo* to Panamanians), one of four species of New World crocodiles with a lineage dating back 200 million years, is a true giant of the reptile kingdom. Males are capable of attaining 16 feet (5 m) of saurian splendor. Their favored habitat is freshwater or brackish coastal lagoons, estuaries, rivers, and mangrove swamps, but they're also numerous within the Panamá Canal and Lago Gatún. They spend most of their mornings basking on mudbanks, soaking up the sun and regulating their body temperature by opening or closing their gaping mouths. Come nightfall, they slink off into the water for the hunt. The American crocodile exists on a diet of fish (crocodiles are vital to aquatic ecology, for they wean out weak and diseased fish) and the occasional careless waterfowl and small mammals. Crocs cannot chew. They simply chomp down with their hydraulic-pressure-like jaws, then tear and swallow, often consuming half their body weight at one sitting. Powerful stomach acids dissolve bones 'n' all.

Crocodiles may look lumbersome but they are capable of amazing bursts of speed. They're also supremely adapted to water. Their eyes and nostrils protrude from atop their heads to permit easy vision and breathing while they otherwise lurk entirely concealed underwater. A swish of their thick muscular tails provides tremendous propulsion.

They make their homes in burrows accessed by underwater tunnels, much like a beaver's. They reach sexual maturity at about eight years of age. Winter is mating season. The mature males battle it out for harems then protect their breeding turf from rival suitors with bare-toothed gusto. The ardent male

American crocodile

gets very excited over estrous females and roars like a lion while pounding the water with his lashing tail. Mating can last up to an hour, with the couple intertwined like Romeo and Juliet. Females lay their eggs during dry season in a sandy nest covered with moist, heat-creating compost. They guard their nests with gusto. Once the wee ones hatch, mum uncovers the eggs and takes the squeaking babies into her mouth and swims off with the youngsters peeking out between a palisade of teeth. Dad assists until all the hatchlings are in their special nursery, which the dutiful parents guard.

The crocodile's smaller cousin, the caiman, is also numerous; its maximum length is 6 feet (1.8 m).

Spiny lobsters the size of house cats crawl over the seabed while small rays flap by and moray eels peer out from their hideaways. Sharks, of course, are ever-present, though most are harmless nurse sharks and even giant whale sharks, the largest fish on earth. Farther out, the aquamarine oceans teem with gamefish, luring anglers keen to snag dorado, tuna, wahoo, swordfish, and marlin.

The stars of the show, however, are undoubtedly the dolphins and whales (primarily humpbacks, but also sperm whales, minke whales, and even orcas) that migrate from colder northern waters and gather each winter to frolic in the nutrient-rich, bathtub-warm waters of the Golfo de Chiriquí and Golfo de Panamá. Here, they gather for courtship and to mate and give birth. On the Caribbean side, Laguna Bocatorito (near Boca del Toro) is famous for its pod of dolphins.

Social History

FIRST INHABITANTS

The first human occupants of the region now known as Panamá arrived at least 12,000 years ago as part of the great southward migration of hominids that initially crossed the Bering Straits around 4,000 years prior. The peoples of the Panamá region eventually evolved into three distinct cultures, each comprising diverse tribes ruled by *caciques* (chieftains) whose names would later be adopted by the Spanish to name the tribes and their regions.

The most complex culture occupied the central Pacific lowlands, centered on today's provinces of Coclé, Herrera, and Veraguas. The tribes evolved advanced slash-and-burn agriculture as well as large villages that are the oldest and most significant archeological sites yet discovered in Panamá. Two of the principal sites, at Parque Arqueológico del Caño (near Natá) and Sitio Conte (near Penonomé), feature prominent ball courts, rows of stone columns carved with anthropomorphic motifs, and graves that once contained precious gold *huacas* (ornaments), such as bracelets, chest plates, pendants, and animal and fertility figurines buried with powerful caciques when they died (the cacique's wives and servants were also buried, along with practical items such as vases, *metates* [three-legged stone corn-grinding tables], and pedestals with tripod legs painted with elaborate zoomorphic designs, intended to facilitate greater comfort in the afterlife). These cultures were immensely skilled in gold metallurgy using the "lost-wax" technique. Like most cultures of Mesoamerica, they lived in thatched circular huts constructed of timber and cane. Caciques

Emberá girls on Playa de Muerte, Darién, Panamá

Guaymi Indians

occupied the largest huts, alongside the cured bodies of their ancestors. Coastal communities were adept at fashioning felled trees into sleek canoes using fire and stone tools.

Farther west, the Barriles culture of the Chiriquí highlands also left significant remains. Migrating from today's Costa Rica about 3,000 years ago, these simple agriculturalists evolved into advanced societies for whom the cultivation of corn and beans was important. Many of their life-sized stone statues depict humans clutching severed heads in their hands, and others being borne on the shoulders of slaves. The society was destroyed around 500 A.D. by an eruption of Volcán Barú. The eastern cultures of the Darién region were related to Amazonian tribes and spoke a *Chibcha* language. They were less evolved than their westerly counterparts, partly because virtually the entire region was smothered in dense rain forest. Little is known about these hunter-gatherers, who were the first indigenous cultures encountered by Spanish *conquistadores*. They were swiftly decimated. (The Emberá-Wounaan and Kuna who occupy the region today arrived from the Colombian rain forests only within the past 300 years.)

Although the various tribes are known to have traded with other groups throughout Mesoamerica, these cultures did not evolve the sophistication of groups elsewhere in the Americas, such as the Aztecs, Incas, and Maya, and no great temple complexes have been found.

THE SPANISH ARRIVE

On August 3, 1492, Christopher Columbus (1451–1506) sailed from Spain on the first of his four voyages in search of a westward route to the Orient. His three-ship flotilla manned by 90 crew comprised the caravels *Santa Maria, Niña,* and *Pinta.* After 33 days, the cry of

"*Tierra!*" rang out as land shadowed the moonlit horizon. Thereafter, the Americas were laid open to Spanish *conquistadores* searching for fortune and fame.

Rodrigo de Bastidas (1460–1527) became the first European to sight Panamá in 1501, when he sailed along the coast of what is now the Comarca de Kuna Yala. Next year, Columbus arrived during his fourth and final voyage to the New World. Sailing along the coast of the isthmus, he named it Veragua and even attempted to establish a short-lived settlement at the mouth of the Río Belén (midway down the coast of today's rain forest-clad Veragua province). Among Bastidas' crew was Vasco Núñez de Balboa (1475–1519). After settling in Hispaniola, where he got into debt, Balboa stowed away to Panamá as one of the founding settlers of Santa María la Antigua del Darién, the first permanent settlement on mainland American soil. Through subterfuge, Balboa soon had himself appointed as governor of the region. He then set out to explore the region. He managed to

Vasco Núñez de Balboa claims the South Sea. 19th century engraving by unknown artist

baptize two caciques, Careta and Comagre. They allied with Balboa, who displayed relatively even-handed treatment of the indigenous peoples. (Some tribes, however, were vanquished with utmost severity, including the Quaregas, whose public homosexual acts enraged Balboa—he had them killed by ferocious dogs.) On September 1, 1513, Balboa set out in search of a tribe rumored to be inordinately rich in gold. After crossing the isthmus, on September 25, 1513, he spied the Pacific—the first European to do so—and famously waded into the ocean (which he named the *Mar del sur,* or South Sea) clad in his armor and bearing a sword and a cross. Within days he set foot on pearl-rich isles that he named the Archipiélago de las Perlas.

Balboa's discoveries proved his own downfall. During his absence, his rivals moved to have him deposed as governor. In July 1514, a rival *conquistador,* Pedro Arías de Ávila (1440–1531), better known as Pedrarias, arrived with 1,500 men-at-arms as the new acting governor of Panamá. Although Balboa married Pedrarias' daughter, in 1517 Pedrarias had his son-in-law arrested and tried for treason. Balboa and his key supporters were swiftly condemned and executed. Pedrarias had none of Balboa's soft touch. He brutalized the native people, who were enslaved or exterminated using the most brutal methods. Those that survived were forced into the thickly forested mountains and deepest parts of the lowland rain forest.

LA FLOTA ... THE TREASURE FLEET

Balboa's discovery of the Pacific positioned Panamá for a golden future as a transit point for the wealth of an empire. In 1517, *conquistador* Gaspar de Espinosa (1484–1537) began laying out a mule track—the Camino de Cruces—to transport treasure from the Pacific to the Caribbean port of Nombre de Díos, founded in 1510. In 1519, Pedrarias founded Nuestra Señora de la Asunción de Panamá (site of today's Panamá Vieja) at the Pacific end of the trail, and established it as the new capital city of Panamá. The city was positioned at the narrowest point of the isthmus. Francisco Pizarro's (1475–1541) conquest of Perú in 1532 filled the coffers of Nuestra Señora de la Asunción de Panamá. Soon, the plundered

A Brutal Denouement

The arrival of the Spanish was a disaster for many of the region's indigenous peoples. The *conquistadores* were not on a holy mission. They came in quest of gold under the *quinto real* (Royal fifth), in which the Spanish crown licensed explorers in exchange for receiving one-fifth of whatever treasure they brought back to Spain; the king's galleons got priority in the treasure ports of the New World. The "Indians" (the term reflects Columbus' belief that he had reached the East Indies by a westerly route) were seen as pathetic heathen to be slaughtered for their gold, or used as chattel under the *encomienda* system (a modified form of slavery, which the Pope had banned in the New World), in which *conquistadores* received land grants and usufruct rights to Indian labor, ostensibly with the purpose of converting the heathen to Christianity. However, the aborigines were not inclined to harsh labor. They were brutally suppressed. Those not slaughtered by musket and sword succumbed to smallpox, measles, and tuberculosis—Old World diseases to which they had no immunity—while others withered spiritually and committed mass suicides.

wealth of the Incas—emeralds, gold, silver, and pearls—was being transferred to the Caribbean for shipment to Spain. Nombre de Díos' harbor was too exposed to storms and pirates. A new mule trail—the Camino Real (Royal Road)—was thus laid out linking the western port to a new Caribbean port, San Felipe de Portobelo, initiated in 1597.

Ships groaning from the weight of their bullion departed Portobelo on twice-yearly treasure fleets *(flotas)* that arrived via Cartagena and, eventually, departed for Havana and Spain. As hundreds of galleons converged, Nombre de Díos and Portobelo held massive trade fairs. Thousands of merchants, clerics, and royal accountants arrived along with soldiers commissioned to guard the mountains of bullion that quite literally were piled high in the streets.

Pirates weren't far behind. As the 16th century progressed, piracy became the scourge of Spain's New World possessions. Although the majority of pirates were freelancers like Walt Disney's fictional Captain Jack Sparrow, many were corsairs *(corsarios)* officially licensed by Spain's rivals—England, France, and Holland—to harass and plunder Spanish possessions and shipping. No vessel, city, or plantation was safe from these bloodthirsty predators. For example, the image of Sir Francis Drake (1540–96) as genteel hero is pure myth; this slave-trader-turned-pirate was a ruthless cut-throat capable, like his cohorts, of astonishing barbarity befitting the times. In 1572 and 1573, Drake sacked Nombre de Díos and waylaid a silver train on the Camino Real, respectively, prompting construction of the first fortifications.

Sir Francis Drake

Meanwhile, in 1588, King Philip of Spain determined to end England's growing sea power and reinstate Catholicism. A great armada of 160 ships was assembled for an invasion, but the larger and heavier Spanish galleons proved no match for England's smaller, nimbler, and more advanced "racers" under the command of Drake, John Hawkins (1532–95), and Sir Walter Raleigh (1552–1618). The Armada was destroyed.

Camino de Cruces cobbled trail near Gamboa, Panamá

Spain's seafaring abilities were shattered. Her colonies were impotent as piracy and smuggling gained new zeal. Thus, in 1595, Drake and Hawkins set off with 26 ships to plunder Panamá. Alas, both Hawkins and Drake sickened of dysentery and died; Drake was buried at sea in a lead coffin off Portobelo on January 27, 1596. Nonetheless, Drake protégé William Parker (1587–1617) successfully sacked Portobelo on February 7, 1602.

During the 17th century, a new breed of pirate—the buccaneers—swept the Caribbean like a plague. This band of seafaring cutthroats had begun as a motley band of international (mostly Dutch, French, and English) ne'er-do-wells who had gravitated to Tortuga, a small French-held isle off the northwest coast of Hispaniola, where they worked the land, hunted wild boars on Hispaniola, and traded *boucan* (smoked meat, from which the buccaneers took their name) to passing ships. Suppressed by the Spanish, they turned to piracy and eventually set up base in Port Royal, Jamaica, where they were given official English sanction and attained infamy for their cruelty and daring under the leadership of Welsh pirate, Henry Morgan (1635–88). In 1668, Morgan attacked and captured the refortified Portobelo. For 14 days his pirates raped, tortured, and pillaged, departing only after the Spanish governor of Panamá paid a large ransom. Morgan's crowning claim to fame, however, was his sacking of Nuestra Señora de la Asunción de Panamá in 1671. During the attack, the city was burned to the ground; in 1673 a new city—today's Casco Viejo, in Panamá City—was established some 5 miles to the southwest. (The raid on Panamá violated a peace treaty between England and Spain; when he returned to England, Morgan was arrested but exonerated. In 1674 he was knighted and returned to Jamaica as Governor, having renounced piracy.)

Following the Treaty of Ryswick, of 1697, which banned piracy and privateering, the buccaneers were finally hounded out of existence.

THE LATE COLONIAL ERA

The rivalry between England and Spain didn't end with the Treaty of Ryswick. War between them erupted briefly 1718–20 and 1727–29. A decade of relative peace was broken in 1739 after English merchant Captain Robert Jenkins showed up in Parliament brandishing his shriveled ear, severed, he claimed, by Spanish coast guards in 1731. Relations between the countries were extremely strained and responding to public opinion, the House of Commons voted for war. A fleet was provisioned and six warships under Admiral Edward Vernon (1684–1757) set off for the Indies. They aimed straight for Portobelo, which fell to the English on November 20, 1739. Before departing, Vernon destroyed the fortifications.

Thereafter, Spain's New World colonies sank into a century of gradual decline. Despite the immense wealth that they had generated, the Spanish crown disdained its colonies, which were treated as a cash cow to milk. Spain applied a rigid monopoly forbidding manufacture in the Americas, which were forced under threat of punishment to import virtually all their necessities from Spain at inflated prices. Even exports to Spain were taxed. Panamá gradually became a neglected, backwater province. Nationalist sentiments swept through Spain's weakened Latin American empire, culminating in September 7, 1821, in liberation leader Simón Bolívar's (1783–1830) creation of Gran Colombia, a federation covering newly liberated Venezuela, Colombia, and Ecuador. On November 10, 1821, residents of La Villa de los Santos issued a letter—the *primer grita de la independencia* (first call for independence)—calling for independence. On November 18, the Panamanians declared independence and joined Gran Colombia. The territory proved too large to govern; a congress hosted in Panamá City in 1826 to unify all the newly freed republics into one nation collapsed. In 1830, Gran Colombia disintegrated. Panamá was press-ganged into union with the República Federativa de Colombia, of which it became a backwater province cut off from Bogotá by the impenetrable rain forests of Darién. It was an unhappy marriage and more than 50 revolts were subsequently ruthlessly suppressed.

The discovery of gold in California in 1848 resurrected Panamá's fortunes. A transcontinental railroad across the United States had not yet been built and argonauts sought a passage across the Panamanian isthmus via the old Camino de Cruces as the quickest route to California. Untold thousands were felled by disease, while others perished at the hands of venomous snakes or ruthless bandits during the grueling weeklong trek. (Even the cholera-stricken U.S. Fourth Infantry, under the command of future Civil War hero and U.S. president, Captain Ulysses S. Grant, 1822–85, were charged extortionate fees for the pack-mule passage en route to their new base in California.) Another 5,000-plus lives were lost in building the Panamá Railroad, completed in 1855 by visionary entrepreneur William Henry Aspinwall (1807–75), whose Pacific Mail Steamship Company provided the boat service between Panamá and the United States.

In 1869, French engineer Count Ferdinand de Lesseps (1805–94) completed construction of the Suez Canal, in Egypt, to grand acclaim. He was soon inspired by something grander—the dream of building a canal across the Panamanian isthmus. In 1880 Colombia sold de Lesseps the exclusive right to build a canal; he launched his Compagnie Universelle du Canal Interocéanique financed by a wildly successful public stock offering.

The Prestán Uprising

One of the most tragic events of the 19th century—the so-called Prestán Uprising—consumed Panamá in March 1885 following a revolt against Colombia by Rafael Aizpuru (1843–1919), former president of the department of Panamá. Upon hearing the news, Colombia dispatched troops from the Caribbean port of Colón to quell the uprising. With Colón now unguarded, on March 16 a group of desperados led by former Colón councilor Pedro Prestán seized control of the city. A U.S. merchant ship carrying arms was in port, but the captain refused Prestán's demands to hand over the armaments. Prestán then took hostage the U.S. consul, the ship's captain, and two sailors from the U.S. gunboat *Galena*, which was anchored in port (and which had taken possession of the munitions). Prestán demanded that the armaments be released in exchange for the lives of his hostages. It is unclear whether the arms were turned over to Prestán, although the prisoners were released. Next day, Colombian troops arrived from Panamá City. Prestán and his hoodlums were routed and fled after putting torch to Colón, which, consisting of wooden houses, was burned to the ground. Prestán was later captured and eventually hanged on August 18, 1885.

Unfortunately, de Lesseps conceived of a sea-level canal—*La Grande Tranché* (great trench)—and stubbornly de Lesseps refused to countenance a dam-and-lock system as proposed by more thoughtful engineers. The task proved too much given the cost and technical challenges of cutting through solid mountain and jungle, and overcoming the mighty Río Chagres. Even more formidable were malaria and yellow fever, which claimed 20,000 lives as black Caribbean laborers toiled in abominable heat and humidity. In 1889, de Lesseps' company collapsed, causing financial ruin throughout France. Revelations of political bribery and financial fraud soon caused the French government itself to collapse, and de Lesseps and his son Charles were each given five-year prison terms for their roles in *la grande enterprise*.

"SPEAK SOFTLY AND CARRY A BIG STICK."

The French attempt to build a canal caused consternation in Washington, which was angling to build its own canal. The United State's evolving sea power made critical the need for a link between the Atlantic and Pacific Oceans. Nicaragua was the favored route. However, one man was determined that Panamá would prevail. Parisian-born engineer Philippe Bunau-Varilla (1859–1940) had worked for the Compagnie Universelle du Canal Interocéanique. After de Lesseps' company went bankrupt, Bunau-Varilla acquired the rights to build a canal and in 1893, he organized the Compagnie Nouvelle to do so. However, his plan faltered and in 1904 Bunau-Varilla sold the rights to the United States for $40 million. The indefatigable little Frenchman then campaigned, successfully, to convince President Theodore Roosevelt (1858–1919) and the U.S. Congress that Panamá was the preferred route. After an arm-twisting, conniving campaign that was a masterpiece of public relations, Bunau-Varilla prevailed. On June 19, 1902, Congress voted for Panamá.

Panamá was still Colombian territory, however. When the Colombian Senate rejected Washington's proposed terms—the Hays-Herran Treaty—for the canal, the ever-wily

Bunau-Varilla and President Roosevelt conjured up a plan to gain Panamá's independence. Bunau-Varilla conspired to incite Panamá's elite, led by Manuel Amador, to declare independence on November 3, 1903. "We were dealing with a government of irresponsible bandits," Roosevelt stormed. "I was prepared to . . . at once occupy the isthmus anyhow, and proceed to dig the canal. But I deemed it likely that there would be a revolution in Panamá soon." Not uncoincidentally, the battleship USS *Nashville* (with 500 Marines aboard) had already arrived off Panamá City to thwart any attempt by Colombia to land troops to suppress the separatist rebellion. Meanwhile, when Colombian troops were dispatched from Colón to Panamá City, Panamá Railroad officials arranged for the officer corps to sit up front; then they uncoupled the rear carriages, leaving the troops stranded in Colón, while the officers were arrested upon arrival in Panamá City.

The United States immediately recognized Panamá's independence. Although he was a Frenchman, Buneau-Varilla (who wrote the Constitution for the new nation in a New York hotel room; his wife even stitched together the first flag in anticipation of the event) had already got himself appointed Panamá's ambassador to the United States. Despite lacking the authority to do so, in Washington he negotiated a treaty granting the United States sovereignty over a 10-mile-wide Canal Zone in perpetuity at a cost of $10 million, plus an annual payment of $250,000; the U.S. was also granted rights to intervene in Panamanian affairs as it saw fit. Days later, an official Panamanian delegation arrived to find that they had been delivered a fait accomplit.

Formal work on construction of the canal by the U.S. Army Corps of Engineers (most of the laborers came from the English-speaking Caribbean islands) began on May 4, 1904, using dynamite and clumsy steam shovels. With the hindsight of the French experience; U.S. engineers concluded that a dam-and-lock system would be far easier to build than a sea-level canal. An ingenious plan was devised to dam the Chagres River to create a vast 23-mile-long lake, 85 feet above sea level; this, in turn, would feed three separate and mammoth locks that would raise and lower ships to sea level. Two key elements were fundamental to success. First was the brilliantly conceived flatbed train system established by Chief Engineer John F. Stevens (1853–1943) to haul out the rock excavated during creation of the 9-mile-long Culebra Cut through the continental divide. Second, and perhaps the true key to success, was medical officer Colonel William C. Gorgas' (1854–1920) far-sighted campaign to eradicate malaria and yellow fever by an all-out extermination effort against mosquitoes (Cuban doctor Carlos Finlay, 1833–1915, had laid the groundwork by his discovery that the *Aëdes aegypti* mosquito was responsible for yellow fever).

George Washington Goethals

When Stevens resigned in 1907, Roosevelt (who visited the construction in 1906 and was famously photographed wearing a white suit and Panama hat) determined to give the U.S. Army Corps of Engineers complete control of canal construction. He appointed Colonel George W. Goethals (1858–1928) as Chief Engineer. Construction was completed two years ahead of schedule. The first passage, by the French crane-boat, the *Alexandre La Valley,* was made on January 7, 1914. On August 15, 1914, the canal was formally opened with the passage of the merchant ship, the SS *Ancon.* More than 5,000 workers died during the decade-long effort, which reduced the sea journey from New York to San Francisco by 9,000 miles.

THE U.S. ERA

The mammoth U.S. presence in Panamá during and after canal construction was an economic godsend for Panamá, which benefited from installation of a modern infrastructure throughout the country. However, a pluralist democracy failed to take root. The next few decades were marked by political instability and corruption among a revolving door of Panamanian leaders. The U.S. invoked its right to intervene in national politics in 1908, 1912, and 1918. Then, on February 8, 1925, the Kuna people revolted, expelled Panamanian officials, and declared independence for their territory along the eastern Caribbean zone of San Blas. The Panamanian government acted forcefully to suppress the revolt, and 22 policemen and 20 tribesmen were killed before U.S. Marines again intervened and the U.S. government brokered a truce. In 1938 the Kuna were granted semi-autonomy of their own *comarca* (region).

Panamanian society was deeply divided over the U.S. presence, which in 1918 included 14 military bases, complete control of the Canal Zone, and even the overseeing of the Panamanian police force. Governments switched between those in favor and those that considered the U.S. presence a humiliation. In 1927, the Panamanian congress appealed to the League of Nations to abrogate the U.S. right of interference. The following year, President Herbert Hoover (1874–1964) agreed to a Good Neighbor Policy of non-intervention. It was ill timed. In 1931, a radical right-wing nationalist group called Acción Comunal overthrew the government of Florencio Harmodio Arosemena (1872–1945), and the party's vehemently racist, anti-U.S., and pro-Nazi leader Arnulfo Arias Madrid (1901–88) took power. Arias' *panameñismo* (Panamá for Panamanians) philosophy hit a chord with the populace and in 1939 he successfully negotiated the Hull-Alfaro Treaty, which revoked the right of U.S. intervention. Although he established Panamá's progressive social security system, he ruled by authoritarian means. In 1941, the National Police deposed him. Arias' overthrow inaugurated a turbulent period in which the militarized police force became arbiters in national politics. Arias was elected by popular mandate on two subsequent occasions (1949–51 and 1968); each time he was deposed by the police. His archenemy was the progressive yet corrupt General José Antonio Remón Cantera (1908–55), an ardent anti-*arnulfista* who was himself elected to the presidency in 1952 (in 1955, Remón was murdered by machine gun at the Panamá City racetrack).

The rising anti-U.S., pro-Spanish *hispanidad* movement then sweeping through Latin America caught hold in Panamá. The continued U.S. presence increasingly stung Panamanian pride. In 1947, the pot boiled over when Panamá's national legislature debated a new treaty that extended the U.S. military's use of bases outside the Canal Zone. More than 10,000 armed and angry Panamanians stormed the Assembly, and one person died in the mêlée. Understandably, the Assembly voted against the treaty and the following year the U.S. military abandoned some of the bases. Meanwhile, the ensuing decade witnessed increasing clashes between demonstrators (primarily middle-class students) and Remón's ever more brutal police, which he renamed the National Guard.

In 1951, the U.S. reformed its canal operations. New austerity measures hit hard upon the 10,000 Panamanians employed within the Canal Zone, where U.S. residents enjoyed a privileged life. Relations between the two nations continued to worsen. Egypt's nationalization of the Suez Canal in 1956, and Fidel Castro's communist revolution in Cuba in 1959, added fuel to demands for Panamanian sovereignty over its canal. President Dwight Eisenhower (1890–1969) attempted to mollify growing militancy in Panamá with reforms that included "titular sovereignty" over the canal. It was too little too late. President John F. Kennedy (1917–63) went further under his "Alliance for Progress," which poured monetary aid into Panamá as a counterweight to the fear of spreading communism. Any goodwill was negated, however, when the U.S. established the School of the Americas within the Canal Zone as an anti-communist training center for military elites from throughout Latin America. (Inevitably, it produced some of the most thuggish military dictators of future years.)

Panamanian flag

Meanwhile, the right—or lack of it—to fly the Panamanian flag next to the Stars and Stripes within the U.S. Canal Zone had sparked several riots, prompting Kennedy to expand the right to fly the Panamanian flag at non-military sites. When President Lyndon B. Johnson (1908–73) proposed reducing the number of Stars and Stripes flown in the Zone, Zonians (U.S. residents of the Canal Zone) protested. On January 9, 1964, students at Balboa High School raised the U.S. flag in defiance of the governor's orders. This incensed Panamanian students. When students from the Instituto Nacional attempted to raise their flag alongside the Balboa flag, they were prevented by irate Zonians and the Canal Zone police. Angry crowds soon formed. Riots broke out. The police fired into the crowds. And Panamá City erupted. Panamanians of every stripe took to the streets and stormed the Canal Zone fence. U.S. businesses and homes were burned. Bullets flew from both sides and many people were shot in clashes against the U.S. Army's 193rd Infantry Brigade, which took over defense of the Zone. The Flag Riots continued for several days and left 27 people dead, including an 11-year-old girl, Rosa Elena Landecho, shot by a U.S. Army sniper.

Relations between Panamá and the United States were forever changed. President Johnson stated his willingness to renegotiate the canal treaty.

THE DICTATOR DECADES

Arnulfo Arias returned to power in the 1968 presidential elections. However, only 11 days into his term, he was ousted by a National Guard coup, following which Lieutenant Colonel Omar Torrijos Herrera (1929–81) gained power. Torrijos ruled over nominal presidents as actual head of government for the next 21 years. This charismatic and handsome left-winger is fondly remembered as a champion of Panamá's poor, Spanish-speaking, mixed-blood majority. He initiated a series of progressive socio-economic reforms that expanded health and education, redistributed land to impoverished peasants, and modernized the nation's infrastructure through massive public works projects. However, Torrijos brutally suppressed political opposition, including censoring the press.

Torrijo's crowning moment came on September 7, 1977, when he and President Jimmy Carter (1924–) signed the Torrijos-Carter Treaty, at Fort Clayton, Panamá (Torrijos was noticeably drunk during the ceremony). Panamanians exulted that the U.S. had agreed to cede gradual control of the canal to Panamá, leading to complete control in December 31, 1999, when all U.S. military bases would also close. (The United States nonetheless retained the right to protect and guarantee the permanent neutrality of the canal.) In an outburst of *soberanía*—sovereignty fever—the Panamanians adorned the canal administration building with a digital clock, which ticked down the seconds until the Panamá Canal Authority assumed command of the waterway.

Torrijos was killed on July 31, 1981, when his DeHavilland Twin Otter aircraft mysteriously exploded over the Cordillera Central. A series of military figures competed to fill the void. In 1983, National Guard Commander Rubén Darío Paredes stepped down to run for the presidency. Darío handed command of the guard—which had been renamed the Panamanian Defense Forces—to Manuel Antonio Noriega (1934–), a Torrijos protegé with whom Darío had struck a deal. Noriega, however, reneged and seized power for himself. For the next seven years he subjected the country to a brutal reign of corruption, intimidation, and terror while fraudulent elections and puppet presidents maintained a pretense of democracy.

Noriega had been trained at the School of the Americas and had joined the CIA payroll in the early 1970s (CIA director George H. W. Bush authorized an annual payment of $110,000 for Noriega). The U.S. government initially gave tacit support to Noriega (he granted the U.S. expanded military rights in Panamá), despite his involvement with drug trafficking, money laundering, and terror. Disgust with Noriega—nicknamed *cara de piña* ("pineapple face") for his pockmarked features—among educated Panamanians crystallized in September 1985, when a political opponent, Dr. Hugo Spadafora (1940–85), was kidnapped, tortured, and murdered while returning to Panamá from exile in Costa Rica. Then, in 1987, Colonel Roberto Díaz Herrera (1937–), Noriega's second-in-command, publicly denounced Noriega, accusing him of drug trafficking and the murders of both Torrijos and Spadafora. Panamá's middle class launched a Civic Crusade demanding that Noriega step down; their peaceful demonstrations were brutally dispersed by Noriega's barbarous paramilitary Dignity Battalions. Instead, the dictator declared a state of emergency, suspended constitutional rights, and

Statue of Omar Torrijos

"NO NOS ESTAMOS DES-
COLONIZANDO A MEDIAS.
ESTAMOS DESCOLONIZAN-
DONOS RESPONSABLEMENTE."
GRAL. OMAR TORRIJOS H.

A Potpourri

The 3.36 million Panamanians are a potpourri—an exotic blend of various shades from white through mulatto to black. Pure "whites" are extremely rare. Almost everyone carries DNA passed down by miscegenation of Spanish (and French) colonialists with Amerindians, African slaves, and English and Dutch pirates during three centuries. Chinese and Indian indentured laborers (imported to work on the Panamá Railroad); Afro-Caribbean laborers and French immigrants (imported to work on the Panamá Canal); American craftsmen, engineers, technicians, military, and administrators (the Zonians); Swiss, German, and Italian farmers who settled the Chiriquí highlands; Hindu and Middle Eastern merchants; and prostitutes from around the globe . . . all added their unique characteristics to the *sancocho* stew.

Mixed-blood *mestizos* officially comprise 70 percent of the population, including *moskitos:* the mixed offspring of *cimarrónes* (runaway African slaves) and indigenous Amerindian people, found mostly in Darién province.

INDIGENOUS PEOPLE

Panamá's bouillabaisse is spiced by the nation's still thriving indigenous cultures: seven distinct tribes display relatively pure bloodlines and together make up almost 10 percent of the Panamá populace. The three largest groups occupy their own *comarcas indígenas*—semi-autonomous districts that equate to provinces. General Omar Torrijos empathized with the plight of Panamá's indigenous people; he created an office for indigenous affairs and, in 1972, rewrote the Constitution to give indigenous peoples their own comarcas and political rights.

Most numerous are the Ngöbe-Buglé (165,000), who live primarily in the highlands and foothills of the Bocas del Toro, Chiriquí, and Veraguas provinces. They are also known as the Guaymí and speak their own Ngäbere language. Their comarca, created in 1997, takes up almost one-tenth of Panamá's territory and was granted after a long (and occasionally violent) campaign to establish their rights. Short of stature, they are easily recognized by the ankle-length dresses (called nagua) of brightly colored fabric edged with zigzag motifs worn by the womenfolk (the men adopt Western fashion). Few Ngöbe-Buglé are assimilated into mainstream Panamanian society, and they are reticent when dealing with "whites"—understandably so given the abuse this once fierce warrior tribe received during five centuries of colonization; and, during the past century, at the hand of cattle ranchers and banana companies, which forced them from their traditional lands. The vast majority live in poverty, practicing slash-and-burn subsistence agriculture or hiring out seasonally for subsistence wages as coffee pickers or plantation workers, including in neighboring Costa Rica. The women make beautiful bags from plant fibers, plus sophisticated hand-beaded bracelets and necklaces (known as *chaquira*)

organized counter-demonstrations by his supporters from the impoverished *zambo* (nonwhite) underclass. Noriega's opponents then called a national strike, paralyzing the nation's economy.

Noriega's handpicked candidate for president, Carlos Duque, was sure to lose the May 1989 elections, as Noriega's political opponents banded together to support Guillermo Endara Galimany (1936–). Noriega tried to rig the vote, but Duque lost by such a wide margin that he refused to play along with the fraud. Noriega therefore annulled the vote. Former President Jimmy Carter, present as an observer, denounced Noriega for stealing the election. Endara set out to stake his victory with a motorcade through Panamá City. His

incorporating sacred motifs of snakes.

Occupying the rain forests of Darién (and extending into Colombia) are 30,000 Emberá-Wounaan tribespeople descended from Amazonian Choco tribes. Their two-part comarca (set up in 1983) takes up much of the north-east and southwest parts of Darién province. Although identical in vir-tually every other regard, the Emberá (21,000) and Wounaan (9,000) speak distinct tongues. They live in scattered villages along the watercourses, and sub-sist from fishing, hunting, and slash-and-burn agriculture.

Emberá indigenous family at Playa de Muerto, Panamá

Encouraged by the Panamanian government (and no doubt influenced by the brutality imparted by Colombia guerrillas, paramilitaries, and drug traffickers that have infiltrated Darién), only in recent years have these traditionally nomadic people coalesced into permanent villages. Evangelical missionaries have made considerable inroads in recent years, adding to the cultural decay of this proud, friendly, and gentle people. The Emberá-Wounaan traditionally wear, solely, loincloths (for men) or grass skirts (for women); under pressure by evangelists, they are increasingly adopting Western wear. They adorn themselves with necklaces and with tattoos made of the black juice of the tagua nut, which they also carve into lovely animal fig-urines. Most famously, they have traditionally hunted with blow darts tipped with the deadly toxins of poison-dart frogs. The Emberá-Wounaan are superb carvers of traditional wooden canoes (*piraguas*), and their exquisitely woven and sewn baskets display inordinate skill—the largest and finest baskets can take an entire year to complete.

The most visually striking and well-known group is the Kuna, numbering around 65,000 concen-trated in the Kuna Yala comarca, which incorporates the San Blas archipelago and eastern Caribbean seaboard. See the sidebar *The Kuna* in the Kuna Yala chapter.

car was waylaid, however, by Noriega's pipe-wielding thugs. The world watched, appalled, on television as Endara and his vice president, Guillermo Ford, were beaten bloody.

Noriega named a trusted associate, Francisco Rodríguez, as acting president. President Bush, however, recognized Endara, canceled the canal lease payments, imposed economic sanctions on Panamá, and sponsored an abortive coup on October 3, 1989, led by Major Moisés Giroldi. The U.S. military in Panamá also began to flex its muscles, and an escala-tion of military exercises (the Torrijos-Carter Treaty guaranteed U.S. forces freedom of movement in defense of the canal) resulted in increased clashes with Noriega's own forces. On December 17, 1989, a U.S. Marine, Second Lieutenant Robert Paz, was stopped and

Flames engulf a building in El Chorrillo during
Operation Just Cause

harassed by Noriega's goons, who shot and killed him. Paz's death was a pretext for the U.S.'s Operation Just Cause—launched by President George H. W. Bush on December 20, 1989. The full-scale assault involved 57,684 U.S. troops and over 300 aircraft, including the first parachute infantry drops since WWII. Noriega sought refuge in the Vatican embassy, which the U.S. military bombarded with raucous music to drive him out! After 10 days, he surrendered. Noriega was extradited to the United States and in April 1992 was convicted of drug trafficking, racketeering, and money laundering, and sentenced to 40 years in prison. His term was later reduced to 17 years; Noriega completed his sentence but at press time he remained jailed while awaiting extradition to either France or Panamá to face new charges. Noriega's headquarters, La Comandancia, was in Panamá City's impoverished residential district of El Chorrillo, which was bombarded in Operation Just Cause. Both the Organization of American States and the United Nations condemned the operation, in which as many as 30,000 Panamanians were rendered homeless and up to 4,000 killed, according to an independent inquiry by former Attorney General Ramsey Clark (23 U.S. servicemen also died).

THE PAST TWO DECADES

After two decades of corrupt dictatorships, the tormented nation has settled into a period of calm as a pluralist (albeit corrupt) democracy. Guillermo Endara Galimany had been sworn in as president during Operation Just Cause. Endara, a pro-business lawyer, demanded $1 billion aid from the U.S. for the damage caused by the operation; famously he went on hunger strike on the steps of the Metropolitan Cathedral. He was succeeded by a Torrijos protegé and the People's Nationalist Party founder, Ernesto Pérez Balladares (1946–), who oversaw a pro-market administration. Charges of corruption against Pérez were set aside by the Panamá Supreme Court, several of whose judges were personal friends appointed by Pérez. His successor, Mireya Elisa Moscoso Rodríguez (1946–), widow of former president Arnulfo Arias and Panamá's first female president, was at press time facing corruption charges following a five-year term tainted by extreme cronyism; for example, shortly after taking office she gave expensive Cartier watches and earrings to all 76 members of the Legislative Assembly.

On December 31, 1999, Moscoso oversaw the proceedings in which the Panamá Canal was finally handed over to the Republic of Panamá. At noon that day, the Autoridad del Canal de Panamá (Panamá Canal Authority, ACP) assumed control. All 14 U.S. military bases were also handed over as 11,000 U.S. troops departed the country.

Omar Torrijos' son, Martín Torrijos Espino (1963–), won the May 2004 presidential election for the Democratic Revolutionary Party (PRD), after having served as Minister for the Interior and Justice in the Ernesto Pérez Balladares administration. Torrijos' term is considered the cleanest Panamanian administration on record. His approval has been assisted by having named the Grammy-winning salsa singer, actor, and lawyer Rubén Blades (1948–) as his effective and popular Minister of Tourism. Nonetheless, Torrijos has been controversial. For example, in November 2006 he publicly called for independence for Puerto Rico. He has developed close ties with Cuba. And in September 2008 he issued a highly contentious presidential decree widening his power to enact security measures. Nonetheless, his administration has been ardently pro-business, culminating in a successful public campaign to promote construction of a new set of locks to handle post-Panamax ships (those too large to fit through the current canal locks). A national referendum October 22, 2006, overwhelmingly approved the Expansion Program. On September 3, 2007, thousands of Panamanians crowded surrounding hills to witness a huge explosion that launched the massive construction effort, estimated to cost $5.25 billion. The new locks are expected to be completed in 2015. The century-old original locks will continue to operate. Together they will permit more than twice the current traffic.

On March 3, 2009, Ricardo Martinelli, of the Democratic Change Party, won the election. That year, unusually, two large earthquakes struck Panamá, followed by devastating winter rains that caused extreme flooding throughout the western provinces.

2

PLANNING YOUR TRIP

The Checklist

Panamá covers 29,157 square miles (75,517 sq km), about one-third larger than neighboring Costa Rica and the same size as South Carolina. Main tourist sites are highly concentrated. Having the basics at hand provides peace of mind and goes a long way to helping you explore and enjoy the country without worry. Providing information running the gamut from weather reports to visitor bureaus, this chapter covers planning and everyday practical matters, as well as emergencies.

CLIMATE

The winter months (ironically, called *verano*, or "summer," in Panamá) coincide with a dry season, (November through April) in most of the country, although certain areas still receive plenty of rain during this period. Summer months (called *invierno*, or "winter" by locals) are the "rainy season," when humidity increases until a half-hour walk can leave you dripping wet. While prolonged thunderstorms and severe tropical storms are common, rains typically fall in middle to late afternoon following clear mornings. Regional variations in rainfall abound. Plan accordingly.

Temperatures average a steamy 90 degrees F (32 degrees C) during the daytime

> **In an Emergency**
> The following numbers are good for most, but not all, of the country:
>
> Ambulance (private): Alerta 507-269-1111; SEMM 507-264-4122
>
> Ambulance (Red Cross): 507-228-2187
>
> Fire (*bomberos*): 103
>
> Police (policia): 104 or 507-511-7000; www.policia.gob.pa
>
> Police (Policía Técnica Judicial, criminal investigation): 507-212-2222; www.ptj.gob.pa
>
> Tourism police: 507-211-3811
>
> Canadian Embassy: Calle 53E, Marbella, Panamá City; 507-264-9731; www.dfait-maeci.gc.ca
>
> U.S. Embassy: Avenida Balboa and Calle 38, Bella Vista, Panamá City; 507-207-7000; www.panama.usembassy.gov
>
> U.K. Embassy: Calle 53, Panamá City; 507-269-0866; www.britishembassy.gov.uk/panama

OPPOSITE: *Dugout canoe on Isla de los Perros, San Blas Islands, Panamá*

in Panamá City and the lowlands, falling to an average of 70 degrees F (21 degrees C) at night, with virtually no seasonal variation. The mountain regions enjoy milder temperatures: Boquete (with a mean temperature of 67 degrees F/14 degrees C) is blessed with a springlike climate year-round. Higher still, on the upper slopes of Volcán Barú, the climate is distinctly alpine: You'll want warm clothing and raingear for hiking! Meanwhile, the lowlands of the Azuero Peninsula lie in a rain shadow known as the *arco seco* (dry arc). Here, the climate is much drier than elsewhere in the country and in summer, residents broil under a sun that beats down hard as a nail. By contrast, Darién province has a thunderous wet season, although torrential rains can fall throughout the year. On the Caribbean coast (which is wetter, in general, than the Pacific) trade winds blow steadily from the Atlantic all year long, but most pronounced in summer, helping take the edge off the pirate sun.

Panamá lies outside the hurricane belt and only very rarely is it affected by the outer perimeters of hurricanes in the Caribbean (where June through October is hurricane season) or, more rarely, the Pacific. A rare exception was Hurricane Mitch, which caused three deaths in Panamá in October 1998.

When to Go
Apart from factoring the weather, consider prices and availability when choosing when to go. Since winter months are high season, many hotels sell out and rental cars can be in short supply. Airfares, hotel rates, and even car rental rates are also generally higher in prime travel season. However, as tourism is still relatively nascent, this is not so much of a problem in most of the county as it is in, say, neighboring Costa Rica. You can save money

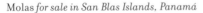
Molas for sale in San Blas Islands, Panamá

by traveling off-season. Christmas and New Year are considered peak weeks, and prices are spiked. Panamanians take to the beaches en masse for Lenten week, when much of the country shuts down; this is especially true for the towns of Azuero peninsula that host *car-navales* and *patronales*—patron saint festivals.

Heading to the San Blas? Go in spring, when ocean visibility is at its best for snorkeling. Birders will find winter months a perfect time, as migratory birds are at their peak.

Weather Reports

A good resource is the World Meteorological Organization Web site (www.worldweather .org/076/m076.htm), which shows real-time weather, short-term projections, and climatological patterns for six locations in Panamá.

The Weather Channel (www.weather.com) has a similar service.

TRANSPORTATION: GETTING TO PANAMÁ

Panamá is served by the main international airport in Panamá City, and regional airlines also fly into several local airports. The country is also a major throughway for cruise ships, although very few actually begin or end in Colón or Panamá City.

Panamá has the best-paved roads in Central America. Panamá City is linked to Costa Rica via the well-maintained Interamerican Highway (or *interamericana*, the Central American portion of the Pan-American Highway stretching all the way from Alaska to the southern tip of Argentina). Well-paved highways link the main towns and beach resorts.

There are numerous ways to get to and around Panamá.

By Air

Panamá has several international airports. Where you land will depend on which part of the country you wish to visit. However, by far the most important airport is Panamá City's modern and efficient **Tocumen International Airport** (Aeropuerto Internacional de Tocumen, PTY; 507-238-2700), 15 miles (21 km) and a 30-minute taxi ride east of the city.

Air Canada (888-247-2262, www.aircanada.com), American Airlines (800-433-7300; www.aa.com), Continental Airlines (800-231-0856; www.continental.com), Delta Airlines (800-221-1212; www.delta.com), Grupo Taca (800-400-8222; www.taca.com), and Spirit Airlines (800-772-7117; www.spiritair.com) all offer regular service from North America, as do numerous charter airlines. However, Panamá's own Copa Airlines (800-359-2672; www.copaair.com) has the most frequent service, with more than 20 weekly flights from Miami, 12 flights weekly from Orlando, plus daily flights from New York City, Los Angeles, and Washington, D.C. It also flies to Panamá from more than 25 other destinations throughout the Americas. Only Iberia and KLM fly from Europe, but you can also fly via other Central American nations, the Caribbean, or Miami.

Air Panamá and Sansa both fly from Costa Rica to **Enrique Malek International Airport** (507-721-1072), in Davíd, handy for vacationers intending to begin or end their Panamá visit in Boquete; and to **Isla Colón International Airport** (507-757-9208), at Bocas del Toro, also served by Costa Rica's Nature Air (www.natureair.com).

Relatively few international flights arrive and depart the **Marcos A. Gelabert International Airport** (507-501-9272), on the former Albrook Air Force Base, in Panamá City.

The Web site of the Civil Aeronautic Authority (Autoridad Aeronaútica Civil; www.aeronautica.gob.pa) has information on the individual airports.

Licensed tourist taxis charge $25 for one person ($14 per person for two people, and $10 each for three or four people) between Tocumen International Airport and downtown. Local taxis are not allowed to service the airport from outside the downstairs arrival area, but you can go upstairs to the drop-off area and catch a local taxi there; negotiate your price (perhaps as low as $15), but note that these taxis are often badly beat up and usually take more than one client (about $11 per person for a shared ride). Local taxis can deliver you *to* the airport, however. For further information, call the Panamá Taxi Driver Union (Sindicato Industrial de Conductores de Taxis de Panamá; 507-238-4176).

Exiting the airport, expect to be hustled by any number of individuals offering to carry your bags or even open the door to your taxi. If you accept, you'll be expected to tip.

Car rentals are available at all the international airports, as are taxis.

By Sea

To be borne on the seas to the former Spanish Main or Panamá City can only add to the drama of your arrival. Yet despite the popularity of the Panamá Canal on the itineraries of cruise ships (at least 18 cruise lines feature the canal), relatively few ships actually dock in Panamá. A few companies operate Canal cruises year-round, but the majority of trips are September through April; trips are typically 10 to 25 days. If your ship docks (or departs) in Panamá City, you can participate in daylong excursions (or occasionally an overnight in port) before sailing off to the next destination.

Cruise ship passing under Centennial Bridge, Panamá Canal

Passengers go ashore from the Sea Voyager, *Panamá*

For information, contact the **Cruise Lines International Association**; 212-921-0066; www.cruising.org.

Two companies specialize in educational nature-focused adventure cruises of Panamá and Costa Rica, both **Cruise West** (507-888-851-8133; www.cruisewest.com) and **Lindblad Expeditions** (1-800-EXPEDITION; www.expeditions.com), using the 100-passenger *Pacific Explorer* and 60-passenger *Sea Voyager,* respectively; the latter's voyages are run in association with **National Geographic Expeditions** (1-888-966-8687; www.nationalgeographicexpeditions.com/expeditions/costaricapanama), with myself as guest lecturer.

By Bus

If you're traveling elsewhere in Central America, you can take a bus from as far away as Mexico. In Panamá City, buses arrive and depart the Gran Terminal de Transporte (Corredor Norte, Albrook; 507-232-5803). Reserve well in advance of your journey. The following three companies offer service:

Panaline 506-256-872 (Costa Rica) or 507-314-6383 (Panamá); www.panalinecr.com /english/index.htm. Between Panamá City and San José, Costa Rica.

Tica Bus 507-314-6385 (Panamá) or 529-62-626-2880 (Mexico); www.ticabus.com. Between Panamá City and Tapachula, in Mexico.

Tracopa 506-2222-2666 (Costa Rica) or 507-775-7269 (Panamá). Between David and San José, and Guabito/Sixaola and San José.

By Package Tour

A few companies sell air/hotel packages that are all-inclusive and focus exclusively on the beach resorts of the Coclé province. The key advantage is their low cost. However, relatively few companies offer motorcoach sightseeing tours as you might find in, say, Europe.

The exception is special interests tours, such as for birders and scuba divers. The Panamá Tourism Authority (Autoridad de Turismo Panamá; www.visitpanama.com) publishes a list of recommended tour companies that offer such tours from North America and Europe.

TRANSPORTATION: GETTING AROUND

By Air

Panamá has about two dozen regional airports throughout the country, and getting around by domestic flights is a viable option. Two domestic airlines compete using 20- to 46-passenger aircraft: **Aeroperlas** (507-315-7500; www.aeroperlas.com) serves the more than two dozen airstrips around the country. A newcomer, **AirPanama** (507- 316-9000; www.flyairpanama.com) competes and also has service from San José, Costa Rica. You can also charter small planes (or join other passengers) with private companies such as **Air Charter Panamá** (507-6633-1156; www.aircharterpanama.com).

Most domestic flights out of Panamá City depart Aeropuerto Marcos A. Gelabert, in Albrook, just a few minutes west of the city center.

Renting a Car

Although aircraft and ships will bring you to Panamá, a car is a good idea once you arrive if you seek flexibility and wish to explore far beyond the capital city and Canal Zone. Most roads are well paved (with the occasional pothole) and you'll only need a 4WD vehicle (carro con doble) if you plan on heading to Darién and into many national parks. However, driving in Panamá is not for the faint of heart, and extreme caution is required. Panamanians are extremely reckless and aggressive drivers, and pay little heed to traffic rules. Running through red traffic lights is common! And a dog-eat-dog mentality often snarls traffic in cities, where drivers block junctions in their jostling for an advantage. Avoid driving at night, as the many hazards include poor (or no) lighting, unmarked verges, other vehicles lacking headlights or taillights, lots of stray animals and pedestrians, and the possibility of a nighttime highway robbery.

Most major international car rental companies have offices at Tocumen International Airport and in downtown Panamá City (and other major cities nationwide). Local information and reservations numbers are listed below. Advance reservations are recommended for the winter high season. You'll need to be 25 years of age (21 for some companies if you have a credit card) and hold a Canadian, U.S., or European driver's license, plus a credit card. Expect to pay a $500 (or more) deposit and at least US$50–125 daily (depending on type of vehicle) for an automatic, with unlimited mileage and compulsory Loss Damage Waiver (enuncia a daños o perdida) and liability insurance. Don't park under coconut palms, as your rental insurance does not cover damage caused by falling coconuts. Local firms' vehicles aren't always as modern or well maintained as the major companies' (you don't want to break down in the boondocks), but rates are often cheaper. Rental cars cannot be taken into Costa Rica, and some agencies may request that you not drive to Darién east of Metetí. Some provincial gas stations close after sundown; and many don't accept credit card payment.

The main highways are patrolled by traffic police, and radar guns are in use to enforce the 50 mph (80 kph) limit. Thank goodness Panamá is about the only Central American country where it would be extremely rare for a corrupt traffic cop to attempt to extract a bribe. Paying on-the-spot fines is not permitted: If a cop asks for a "fine," request a traffic ticket and official identification (police are required to wear a name tag on their uniform). Such incidents should be reported to the police (507-212-2222) and your nation's consulate.

Alamo Rent-a-Car 507-238-4142; www.alamopanama.com.
Avis 507-278-9455 or 238-4056; www.avis.com.
Budget Rent-a-Car 507-263-8777 or 1-866-495-2722; www.budgetpanama.com.
Dollar Rent-a-Car 507-270-0355 or 1-866-700-9904; www.dollarpanama.com.
Hertz 507-263-8777; www.hertz.com.pa.
National Rent-a-Car 507-269-0221 or 1-866-961-3133; www.nationalpanama.com.

By Boat

Scheduled ferries connect Panamá City and Isla Taboga, departing Amador Causeway. Ferry service to Isla Contadora, in the Archipiélago de las Perlas, has been erratic in recent years, but at press time a "ferry" operated by National Tours (507-314-0572, US$80 round-trip) was departing from the Balboa Yacht Club, on Amador Causeway, daily at 8 AM; arrive 30 minutes before departure to buy your ticket. It's a choppy 90-minute journey.

Each comprising dozens of islands, the Bocas del Toro and San Blas archipelagos are a preserve of boat travel. The same goes for much of Darién, where the rivers are a main means of transport. Three modes are *lanchas* (powerful motorized watertaxis), *piraguas* (slender motorized canoes), and *cayucos* (short dugouts powered by paddle). Regular scheduled lanchas connect Boca del Toro town to the mainland and to neighboring islands; elsewhere, service is irregular and open to negotiation.

Colorful Kuna water-taxis and fishing boats on Wichub-Huala, San Blas Islands, Panamá

Mula at Miraflores Locks, Panamá Canal

By Bus

For independent travelers, the easiest (and safest) means of long-distance travel between cities and resorts is by bus. Several private companies compete. Most depart Panamá City from Gran Terminal de Transporte (Corredor de Ancón, Albrook; 507-303-3030; www.grantnt.com), with a choice of fast *(directo)* and slow *(regular)* service to Colón and David aboard modern, air-conditioned buses with reclining seats. Bring a jacket and earplugs—the buses are invariably overly air-conditioned and loud (the piped-in music is deafening, in typical Latin fashion). Most destinations in the country cost less than US$15 to reach (Panamá City to Changuinola is the most expensive route: about $25 one-way). Book your ticket in advance for express buses.

Within Panamá and between large regional towns, service is usually by retired U.S. Bluebird school buses, usually painted in exorbitant fashion. Short-haul service between other towns is by Toyota Coaster minivans; they stop anywhere along their route, dropping off and picking up passengers. Departure time is usually whenever the van is filled to over-flowing, and not before. You pay upon boarding (typically about $1.50 per hour of travel). The rural areas are served by pickup trucks and flatbed trucks with a roof and benches in the back, and called *chivas* (older people may still use the term to refer to a regular bus). They're usually crowded, uncomfortable, and often unsafe as you hang on for dear life on rugged mud and mountain roads.

In March 2010, Panamá City's first stage of phasing out the *diablos rojos* buses began. A new Metrobus system was to be introduced, to be fully functional by 2011, with a single company operating modern buses using a prepaid smartcard system.

Keep a close eye on your luggage, as theft is rife. And beware of pickpockets.

By Rail

The **Panamá Canal Railway Company** (507-317-6070; www.panarail.com) operates trains between Panamá City and Colón, departing the Estación de Corozal, in Albrook, at 7:15 AM. Return trains depart Colón at 5:15 PM. It's a scenic journey, as the trains run alongside the Panamá Canal for most of the way, using the original Panamá Railroad route.

By Taxi

Licensed tourist taxis operate in all towns and cities, and can be found around central plazas and outside most hotels. The safest bet is always to opt for a radio taxi, or a modern, air-conditioned tourist taxi (the ones with green license plates) hailed from outside your hotel. They don't use meters—instead, fares are based on zones, which are required to be displayed in the cab and are also usually posted at taxi stands and in tourist hotels. Ask your concierge for the going rate and agree in advance with your taxi driver (some drivers try to overcharge tourists). If you're dining, your restaurant will call a radio taxi for you.

Local cabs hailed on the street come in all colors, shapes, and sizes, although they all have numbered markings. Fares are generally cheap—typical fares within most cities average between US$1 (the base fare) and US$3, with a US$0.40 surcharge for each extra person. Expect a thrill ride. Taxi drivers up their cash flow by maximizing the number of fares they make during their shift—the faster they go, the more money they make! They often pick up multiple passengers. Most drivers carry very little change, so have the correct change and plenty of bills (either U.S. or Balboas) at hand.

In Panamá City try Radio Taxi America (507-223-7534), Radio Taxi America Libre (507-269-1601), or Radio Taxi Libertad (507-267-7515).

Women should use only radio taxis or tourist taxis connected with a hotel. *Never* take an unmarked (and therefore unlicensed) taxi. Many tourists have been robbed. In all events, ask your driver for his taxi number and jot it down. No number? No go! And even if there's a problem with a licensed taxi, you'll be able to present the police or other authorities with

Panamá Canal Railway, Panamá

Panamá Access

Panamá's "Kilometer 0," from which all other points are measured, is on the north edge of town at the junction of the Pan-American Highway (Transístmica, or *interamericana*) and Corredor Norte. Approximate mileage and times by car between towns and cities:

PANAMÁ CITY TO:	TIME	MILES/KM
Almirante	8.5 hrs	340/567
Antón	2 hrs	84/135
Boquete	6.5 hrs	299/480
Cerro Punta	7.25 hrs	319/514
Chitre	3.75 hrs	147/252
Colón	1.5 hrs	49/80
David	6 hrs	274/438
El Valle	2 hrs	78/126
Las Tablas	4.5 hrs	175/282
Los Santos	4 hrs	159/256
Metetí	4 hrs	134/215
Natá	2.5 hrs	115/186
Ocú	3.5 hrs	152/245
Parita	3.5 hrs	149/240
Paso Canoa (Costa Rican frontier)	6.5 hrs	307/493
Pedasí	5 hrs	203/324
Penonomé	2.5 hrs	94/151
Portobelo	1.75 hrs	65/105
Río Hato	2 hrs	77/123
Santiago	4.5 hrs	155/249
Volcán	7 hrs	309/498
Yaviza	5 hrs	165/266

the driver's ID. Most Panamanian taxi drivers have a good reputation, although many may try to overcharge you. However, few drivers speak English, so a smattering of Spanish plus handwritten directions to your destination will help.

By Excursions

Once you arrive in Panamá, it's easy to explore the country by stitching together a series of excursions. There are a handful of reputable tour operators to choose from, many of which are local to specific resort areas.

The largest company, and also one of the most respected, is **Ancón Expeditions** (507-269-9415; www.anconexpeditions.com), which is perhaps the best operator for birding and nature-related tours. It also has its own nature lodges in Darién and a hotel in Bocas del Toro. One of the best companies specializing in half-day and daylong excursions, including within Panamá City, is **Panamá Travel Experts** (507-6671-7923; www.panama travelexperts.com).

See regional chapters for other tour and excursion operators.

Entry and Exit Formalities

All visitors, including those from the United States, Canada, and Europe, need a valid passport to enter Panamá. No visas are required. As of January 1, 2010, Panamá ended its tourist visa requirement. You can now arrive for up to 90 days without a tourist card. You can request an additional 90 days by applying to the Dirección Nacional de Migración (Avenida Cuba and Calle 29, Panamá City; 507-207-1806), or to regional offices in Chitré, Changuinola, David, and Santiago.

A US $20 tax is payable upon departure.

Recreation

Panamá is replete with exciting recreational activities, many of which make the most of the nation's natural endowments. The scenery is breathtaking, and far more diverse than you might imagine, ranging from the desertscapes and wetlands of Azuero to the cloud-draped Chiriquí highlands and the rain forests of Darién, all of them teeming with wildlife. The birding is out of this world (the nation has far more species than neighboring Costa Rica, which has stolen the ecotourism limelight). Hikers are blessed with options, including mountain highs in Parque Nacional Volcán Barú and Parque Internacional La Amistad. Water sports are off the hook: Surfers are finally discovering the unsung possibilities of the Azuero peninsula, Chiriquí, and Bocas del Toro. You can even go whale-watching off the Archipiélago de las Perlas. Offshore, big game fish seem to line up to get a bite of your hook. And the scuba diving is simply astounding.

Most upscale hotels have swimming pools and tennis. There are golf courses. And canyoneering, kayaking, motorcycling, mountain biking, rock-climbing, sailing, white-

Sunset appetizers aboard National Geographic Sea Voyager, Panama

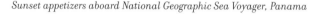

The Beach Scene

Panamá is not renowned as a beach destination, although it *does* have sensational beaches (*playas*) and resort hotels. Panamá's middle class have for many years flocked to the resort hotels of the central Pacific coast, beginning about one hour west of Panamá City and extending along a 40-mile stretch of coast from Punta Chame to Farallón. Unfurling like silver lamé, these beaches are served by large all-inclusive resort hotels. The main beach, Playa Blanca, is suddenly making headlines on the international scene also as a destination *par excellence*. The opening in 2009 of SuperClubs' 300-room family-focused Breezes Playa Blanca (www.super clubs.com) and the soon-to-open and sizzlingly sexy Nikki Beach Playa Blanca (www.nikkibeach panama.com) has infused the scene.

Surfer at Playa Venado, Azuero, Panamá

Farther west, the Azuero peninsula is blessed with dozens of sensational beaches, many of which are within coastal nature reserves. Hotels, however, are few.

For talcum-white sands, Panamanians know to lay their towels on Isla Contadora and other isles of the Archipiélago de las Perlas. The tiny coral cays of Kuna Yala archipelago are similarly ringed with blazing white beaches shaded by towering palms, but here accommodations are limited and generally motley (visit Kuna Yala for the cultural experience, and the snorkeling). The isles of Bocas del Toro also have lovely beaches and a range of accommodations catering mostly to surfers and to visitors seeking offbeat charm.

water rafting, and even zipline canopy tours are all offered. Boquete is the main center for adventure activities. The best all-round company for active adventures is **Panamá Explorer Club** (507-215-2330; www.pexclub.com). In the USA, **Austin-Lehman Adventures** (800-575-1540; www.austinlehman.com) offers a nine-day, multi-activity "Boquete to Bocas Adventure" that should satisfy the Indiana Jones within you.

ATV and Jeep Tours

Exploring by ATV or Jeep is a popular option, especially out of Boquete, where Boquete ATV Adventures (507-6678-5666) and Boquete Mountain Safari Tours (507-6627-8829; www.boquetemountainsafaritours.com) offer trips.

Bicycling

Although the republic's paved highways are no place for cyclists (they're *far* too dangerous), the rugged off-road terrain is tailor-made for mountain bicycles, which can be rented in main tourist centers, including Boquete and Bocas del Toro. **Aventuras Panamá** (507-260-0044; www.aventuraspanama.com) offers rugged mountain bike trips through Parque Nacional Soberanía.

U.K.-based **Exodus** (www.exodus.co.uk) offers a two-week cycling trip from Nicaragua to Panamá. In the U.S., book through **Adventure Center** (1-800-843-4272; www.adven turecenter.com). And **Backroads** (510-527-1555 or 800-462-2848; www.backroads.com) includes bicycling on its multi-activity family trip in Panamá, as does Canadian-based **Bike Hike** (604-731-2442 or 888-805-0061; www.bikehike.com).

Birding and Nature

No other Central American destination can compete when it comes to birding, at least in terms of species abundance. Panamá is home to at least 1,000 bird species. The country is replete with great birding spots. Quetzals are a dime a dozen in the Chiriquí cloud forests. Frigatebirds and boobies nest on the isles of the Golfo de Panamá and Golfo de Chiriquí. Macaws, toucans, and parrots abound in virtually every type of forest. And waterfowl and other migrants on the Pacific flyway flock to the wetlands of the central Pacific. February through April is the best time, when the weather is good and migrant species are still present.

I strongly urge that you go birding with a competent guide. Consider freelancer **Ariel Aguirre** (507-228-0523; www.arielbirding.com).

The **Panamá Audubon Society** (507-232-5977; www.panamaaudubon.org) is a fabulous resource and offers regular half- and full-day field trips ($5 for members, $10 for non-members).

Ancón Expeditions (507-269-9415; www.anconexpeditions.com) specializes in guided birding and nature trips. **Birding Panamá** (507-393-5728; www.birdingpanama.com) also has birding trips from 4 to 10 days. In the U.S., **Exotic Birding** (303-325-5188 or 877-247-3371; www.exoticbirding.com) has seven- and nine-day trips each February.

Blue-footed boobies at Isla Bona, Panamá

Must-have resources include *A Guide to the Birds of Panamá* (Robert S. Ridgely and John A. Gwynne; Princeton University Press) and *The Panamá Canal Birding Trail* map and guide (Panamá Audubon Society/USAID).

In the USA, **Austin-Lehman Adventures** (800-575-1540; www.austinlehman.com) offers a nine-day, nature-focused "Panama Family: Reef and Rainforest Adventure" trip. And **International Expeditions** (800-633-4734; www.ietravel.com) has a nine-day "Panama: Wildlife Bridge of the Americas" trip led by renowned Panamanian naturalist, Richard Cahill.

Canyoneering, Caving, and Rock-Climbing

Boquete is a center for canyoning and rock-climbing. Basaltic eruptions created dramatic columnar formations. Local climbing expert César Meléndez (507-6764-7918; boquete climbing@yahoo.com) offers freelance guide services. Read more about him, and book tours, at www.hablayapanama.com/ecotourism/rockclimbing.

Panama Outdoors (507-261-5043; www.panamaoutdoors.com) offers rappelling, canyoneering (also known as waterfall rappelling), and caving at various locales close to Panamá City. And **Panamá Explorer Club** (507-215-2330; www.pexclub.com) has rappelling.

Golf

Panamá has about 10 courses, concentrated near Panamá City and the beach resorts of the central Pacific. Additional courses are in the planning or laying out stage, including at Red Frog Beach, on Isla Bastimentos. Here are your options:

Cielo Paraíso (507-720-2431; www.cieloparaiso.com) Due for completion in 2011, this private course at Boquete offers stupendous views.

Coronado Golf and Beach Resort (507-264-3164; www.coronadoresort.com) George and Tom Fazio-designed course beside the Pacific shore.

Manta Raya Golf Club (507-993-2255; www.decameron.com) At the Royal Decameron Beach, Golf and Casino Resort and the Costa Blanca Golf and Villas, at Playa Blanca.

Quebrada Grande (507-720-2893; www.valleescondido.biz) Part of the Valle Escondido residential complex at Boquete, "Big Creek" has nine holes.

Panamá Golf Club (507-266-7068; www.clubgolf.com.pa) Private 18-hole club at the members-only Panamá Country Club, in Tocumen, outside Panamá City.

Radisson Summit Golf and Resort (507-232-4653; www.radisson.com/hotels/pangolf) Recently redesigned by Jeffrey Myers, this rolling 18-hole, 6,626 yard, par-72 championship course was laid out in the 1930s on the East bank of the Panamá Canal. Newly reopened in 2009 under Radisson, it has a golf academy.

The Tucán Country Club and Resort (507-211-3472; www.tucancountryclub.com) Surrounded by rain forest at EcoParque Panamá, 20 minutes west of Panamá City, this private 18-hole residential course opened in 2008.

Vistamar Resort (507-215-1111; www.vistamarresort.com) An 18-hole, 6,800 yard, par-72 course at Coronado, one hour west of Panamá City.

Hiking

Hikers are in their element in Panamá, where more than a dozen national parks offer premium trails from easy to extremely challenging. Some trails are true endurance tests, such as those that lead over the *cordillera* and that link with the Caribbean coast of Veragua

Man on horseback at Tonosi, Azuero

province; those in Parque Internacional La Amistad; and some in the Darién, where most of the region is best avoided due to infiltration by Colombian guerrillas and ruthless narco-bandits.

Among the companies to consider are **Coffee Adventures** (507-720 3852; www.coffee adventures.net), **Eco Circuitos Panamá** (507-314-0068; www.ecocircuitos.com), and **Iguana Tours** (507-226-8738; www.nvmundo.com/iguanatours).

Horseback Riding

Horseback riding is a popular activity in a nation where many people in rural regions still rely on the horse for getting around. Rides are offered at most beach resorts, and around the El Valle de Ancón, Boquete, and Cerro Punta (a major horse-breeding center).

More serious equestrians will find superb facilities at the **Club Equestre Coronado** (507-264-3164; www.coronadoresort.com), at the beach resort of Coronado; and at the **Club de Equitación de Clayton** (507-232-6071), at Clayton, on the northern outskirts of Panamá City.

Motorcycling

Given the popularity of organized motorcycle touring in neighboring Costa Rica, Panamá is sadly deficient. **Moto Tour Panamá** (507-6685-6580; http://mototourpanama.com) has dirt bike trips around Boquete. **Costa Rica Motorcycle Tours and Rental** (506-2225-6000 or 888-803-3344; www.costaricamotorcycletours.com) offers guided 14-day trips of Costa Rica and Panamá. And Texas-based **Moto Discovery** (830-438-7744 or 800-233-0564; www.motodiscovery.com) has a 29-day motorcycle trip from Panamá to Texas.

Go-it-aloners should refer to the **ADVrider** Web site: www.advrider.com/forums /forumdisplay.php?f=57.

Scuba Diving

Scuba aficionados get figurative raptures of the deep when talk turns to dives in Panamanian waters, which abound with coral formations, huge swarms of pelagic fish, plus the possibility of diving with whales. The best diving is around Isla Coiba and the Archipiélago de Perlas, renowned for their many manta rays, whale sharks, etc. On the Caribbean side, the wrecks of Spanish galleons litter the seabed around Portobelo (for experienced divers only, due to the deep waters), while Bocas del Toro is known for its coral reefs. The spectacular coral formations of the San Blas archipelago, alas, are off-limits to diving.

Dive outfitters on the Caribbean include **Caribbean Jimmy's Dive Resort** (www .caribbeanjimmysdiveresort.com), at Nombre de Díos, and **Starfleet Scuba** (507-757-9630; www.starfleetscuba.com), in Bocas del Toro. On the Pacific, consider **Scuba Panamá** (507-261-3841; www.scubapanama.com) and **Scuba Coiba** (507-832-2171; www.scuba coiba.com).

Sportfishing

Anglers are hooked big-time on sportfishing in Panamá. The offshore waters teem with feisty gamefish—tuna, wahoo, marlin, sailfish, etc.—that give a rod-bending fight you'll remember. The Pacific waters of the nutrient-rich Gulf of Panamá and, more so, those of the Hannibal Bank and Zane Grey Reef (a seamount where the upwelling of nutrients sustains a phenomenal population of fish) offer sportfishing as good as anywhere in the world.

Charter sportfishing vessels operate from major marinas. Charters typically cost about $375 a half day, $575 a full day for up to four people. Stick with accredited charter operators rather than local fishermen, whose boats often lack shade and may not meet adequate safety standards.

On the Pacific, recommended outfitters include **Gone Fishing Panamá** (507-6573-0151; www.gonefishingpanama.com), at Boca Chica. The **Tropic Star Lodge** (407-839-3637 or 1-800-682-3424; www.tropicstar.com) is a classy sportfishing lodge on the Darién coast focusing its fishing trips on the Zane Grey Reef. You can even opt for a live-aboard dedicated sportfishing vessel, the M/V *Coral Star* (985-845-0113 or 1-866-924-2837; www.coralstar.com), which offers four- to six-day inshore and offshore fishing in Panamá's Pacific waters. On the Caribbean, try **Drago Adventures** (507- 6832-2834; www.dragoadventures.com), at Bocas del Toro.

Inland, Lake Gatún is renowned for peacock bass; the Río Bayano for tarpon and snook; and the Caribbean coastal flats for bonefish. The bass is a non-native species; it is considered a pest in Lake Gatún—no license is required, and there is no limit on the number you can catch. Expect to catch dozens a day! I recommend Rich Cahill's **Panama Canal Fishing** (507-6699-0507; www.panamacanalfishing.com), who uses a Hurricane FunDeck 201 boat to fish the canal.

Sailing

There are excellent anchorages along the Caribbean and Pacific coastlines, although most marinas are on the Pacific. If you're looking for chartered sailing trips, the following companies offer boating adventures: **Naylamp Panamá Sailing and Diving Adventures** (507-6668-6849; www.panamasailing.com), which has 1- to 7-day trips on a trimaran; and **San**

Private yacht in the San Blas Islands, Panamá

Blas Sailing (507-232-7598; www.sanblassailing.com), which has 4- to 21-day adventures in the paradisiacal San Blas archipelago.

Folks with deep pockets can charter luxury motor-yachts through **Panamá Yacht Tours** (507-262-5044; www.panamayachttours.com).

Water Sports

Bring your boards! Along the Caribbean (principally off Bocas del Toro) and Azuero penin-sula (particularly Playa Venado) brisk trade winds whip up the excitement for surfers, who also flock for the waves that wash ashore along the Golfo de Chiriquí, centered on Boca Chica and Playa Santa Catalina. **Panamá Surf Tours** (507-6671-7777; www.panamasurf tours.com) offers surf trips to both destinations. Among the most respected surf camps is **Morro Negrito Surf Camp** (www.panamasurfcamp.com), near Playa Santa Catalina. The **Bocas Surf School** (507-6852-5291; www.bocassurfschool.com) has learn-to-surf pack-ages at Bocas del Toro.

Many resort hotels of the central Pacific provide free use of Hobie-Cats, aqua-bikes, kayaks, and other non-motorized equipment, while commercial outfitters rent Jet Skis and/or offer paragliding, and windsurfers and kiteboarders can also be rented.

Inlets and coves and the waters surrounding the coral cays of the San Blas archipelago are perfect for sea kayaking. **Expediciones Tropicales** (507-317-1279, www.xtrop.com) offers sea-kayaking trips in the San Blas archipelago, as well as on the Chagres River. **Boquete Outdoor Adventures** (507-720-2284; http://boqueteoutdooradventures.com) specializes in single and multi-day sea-kayaking trips in Golfo de Chiriquí.

Surfea Panamá (www.surfeapanama.com) is a great resource for Spanish speakers.

Kayaking at Isla Granito de Oro, Panamá

Whitewater Kayaking and Rafting

Panamá's river runs are considered among the best in Central America for kayaking and whitewater rafting—the ultimate combination of beauty and thrill. The best runs cascade from the mountains of Chiriquí province.

One of the main outfitters is **Chiriqui River Rafting** (507-720-1505; www.panama-rafting.com), based in Boquete, where **Boquete Outdoor Adventures** (507-720-2284; http://boqueteoutdooradventures.com) and **Panamá Explorer Club** (507-215-2330; www.pexclub.com) also offer trips.

Ziplines

Zipline canopy tours are all the rage in neighboring Costa Rica, where at least 20 such cable-systems let you whiz between treetops and across canyons. Don't expect to see much wildlife—the experience is all about the adrenaline rush. Panamá had three such systems in operation at press time: **Boquete Tree Trek** (507-720-1635; www.aventurist.com), on the slopes of Volcán Barú; the **Canopy Adventure** (507-264-5720; http://panamabirding .com/adventure), at El Valle de Antón; and **Canopy Río Piedras** (c/o The Adrenaline Factory; 507-6645-1872; http://theadrenalinefactory.com), between Colón and Portobelo, on the Caribbean coast.

Meanwhile, if you really want to see and learn something about the rain forest, I recommend the **Gamboa Rainforest Aerial Tram** (507-314-9000; www.gamboaresort.com), an open-air tram suspended at treetop level; you'll makes a 0.75-mile (1.2 km) loop, accompanied by a naturalist guide. It operates Tuesday through Sunday; 90 minutes; US$50.

Panamá's National Parks

Panamá's national parks and reserves are administered by the **Autoridad Nacional de Ambiente** (National Environmental Authority, ANAM, 507-229-7885; www.anam.gob.pa). Unfortunately its Web site is abysmal as a resource for visitors.

PANAMÁ CITY

Parque Natural Metropolitano Although only 265 hectares, this park on the north edge of Panamá City has an environmental education centre, and nature trails guarantee fantastic birding and wildlife viewing. Panoramic views of the city.

Refugio de Vida Silvestre Islas Taboga y Uraba Protects 635 acres (257 ha) of marine habitat encompassing several small islands that are important nesting sites for boobies, pelicans, and frigate-birds.

Reserva Natural Isla San Telmo Formed in 1996 to protect this island (in the southeast of the Archipiélago de Las Perlas) and the surrounding waters, which are a prime breeding area for whales in winter months. Marine turtles nest on the beaches, and many endemic bird and animal species occupy the moist premontane forest.

CANAL AND THE CARIBBEAN

Monumento Natural Isla Barro Colorado Located in Gatún Lake and formed during construction of the Panamá Canal), this 3,865-acre (1,564 ha) island is operated by the Smithsonian Institute as a research station to study local flora and fauna. It has trails and is open to visits by arrangement.

Crocodile at Barra del Colorado Island, Panamá

Parque Nacional Camino de Cruces Protects part of the east bank of the canal and forms an eco-logical corridor between Parque Nacional Soberanía and Parque Natural Metropolitano, in Panamá City. Trails include sections of the old Camino Real treasure trail. Excellent wildlife viewing.

Parque Nacional Chagres Spanning the Panamá Canal, this 333,585-acre (135,000 ha) park pro-tects the rain forest watershed upon which canal operations depend. Hiking trails, river rafting on the Río Chagres, and Emberá indigenous villages are highlights. Sensational birding and wildlife viewing.

continued on next page

continued from previous page

Parque Nacional Portobelo Enshrines 97,676 acres (39,529 ha) and marine habitat, including coral reefs and coastal and estuarine wetlands, plus the fortresses and colonial structures of Portobelo—a UNESCO World Heritage Site.

Parque Nacional Soberanía Immediately north of Panamá City and bordering the canal, this 54,619-acre (22,104 ha) park is renowned as a premier site for birding, notably along the Pipeline Road. Excellent hiking trails include the Camino de Cruces—the cobbled colonial-era treasure trail. More than 400 bird species have been counted.

Kuna Yala

Área Silvestre Corregimiento de Narganá Within the autonomous comarca, it protects 244,629 acres (99,000 ha) of coastal lowland rain forest, wetland, and marine habitat along the western shores of Kuna Yala.

Darién

Corredor Biológico Serranía de Bagre Biological corridor linking Parque Nacional Darién and Reserva Natural Punta Patino. Spans 74,130 acres (30,000 ha).

Parque Nacional Darién The largest national park in the nation, 1,423,296 acres (576,000 ha), and a UNESCO World Heritage Site and biosphere reserve. Primary tropical rain forest (including lowland and montane ecosystems), plus freshwater marshes, mangroves, swamp. Sensational birding and wildlife viewing. Limited accessibility. Much of the park is unexplored and/or off-limits due to infiltration by Colombian guerrillas and narco-traffickers. Explore with a professional guide or nature company.

Reserva Forestal Canglón A 78,207-acre (31,650 ha) wetland and lowland rain forest reserve (also known as Humedal de Matusagaratí) on the north bank of the Río Tuira. Protects marshlands and mangroves. Crocodile and capybara are common.

National Geographic Expeditions passengers exploring mangroves, Panamá

Reserva Hidrológica Serranía Filo del Tallo Remote "hydrological reserve" in northern Darién; 61,088 acres (24,722 ha) protect remnant moist tropical forest.

Reserva Natural Punta Patino A coastal reserve of 74,130 acres (30,000 ha), abundant in wildlife. Protects mangroves, marshland, rain forests. Capybaras are frequently seen, and jaguars, tapirs, monkeys, and harpy eagle are among the many other species. Trails and accommodations.

CENTRAL PANAMÁ AND AZUERO PENINSULA

Area Natural Recreativa Salto de las Palmas In Veraguas province, this 2.5-acre (1 ha) recreational site has a waterfall and swimming pool fed by springwater.

Humedal el Golfo de Montijo This Ramsar Internationally Important Wetland protects some 345,940 acres (140,000 ha) of coastal mangroves, wetlands, and tidal mudflats, plus an offshore archipelago and surrounding waters. Migratory shorebirds include many threatened species.

Monumento Natural de Los Pozos de Calobre Natural thermal springs within volcanic canyons good for hiking. Near the communities of El Potrero and Chitra, in Veraguas province.

Visitors looking down to the Pacific Ocean at Parque Nacional Alto de Campaña, Panamá

Parque Nacional Altos de Campaña Preserving four forest habitats, including montane cloud forest, the 11,923-acre (4,825 ha) park is the habitat of the endemic golden frog plus 267 bird species. Trails lead to lava fields.

Parque Nacional Cerro Hoya Covering 80,448 acres (32,557 ha) in the southwest corner of Azuero, it protects rare dry tropical forest and many endemic plant and animal species. Scarlet macaws can be seen.

Parque Nacional Omar Torrijos Herrera Straddling the continental divide in Coclé province, it protects 62,455 acres (25,275 ha) of primary forest of four distinct types. Wildlife ranges from poison-dart frogs to jaguars and tapirs, plus more than 300 species of birds. It has trails and accommodations.

Parque Nacional Sarigua This 19,768-acre (8,000 ha) park provides an exemplar of the devastating effects of over-grazing. Dramatic desertified landscapes, plus pre-Columbian archaeological sites. Also protects coastal wetlands and pockets of dry tropical deciduous forest. Extends out to sea.

Reserva Forestal la Laguna de la Yeguada In the mountains of Veragua province, this reserve protects 17,519 acres (7,090 ha) of the Río San Juan watershed, comprised of native forest and reforested pines on the Pacific slopes. Reminiscent of Colorado's mountain landscapes atop Cerro Verde. Hot springs, waterfalls, and lakes. Horseback rides available.

Reserva Forestal la Montuoso A 25,637-acre (10,375 ha) forest reserve created to stabilize a disturbed watershed of the Azuero peninsula. Rises to 3,239 feet (987 m) atop Alto del Higo, accessed by trail. Humid tropical and premontane forest. Limited facilities.

continued on next page

continued from previous page

Reserva Forestal la Tronosa At 50,851 acres (20,579 ha), this reserve protects the dry forest watershed of the Río Tronosa, in Los Santos province. Contiguous with Parque Nacional Cerro Hoya. Limited access and facilities.

Refugio de Vida Silvestre Cenegón del Mangle This wildlife refuge protects some 2,471 acres (1,000 ha) of coastal lagoons, wetlands, and offshore marine environment—together a prime nesting site for migratory and endemic waterfowl, shorebirds, and seabirds.

Refugio de Vida Silvestre El Peñon del Cedro de los Pozos A 74-acre (30 ha) wildlife refuge in Los Santos province.

Refugio de Vida Silvestre Isla de Cañas Panamá's most important marine turtle nesting site: olive Ridley turtles uniquely arrive en masse during *arribadas*. Also green, hawksbill, leatherback, and loggerhead turtles. Its 62,845 acres (25,433 ha) also protect mangrove forests. Many bird species, plus caimans. Bioluminescent lagoon.

Isla Iguana visitor center, Panamá

Refugio de Vida Silvestre Isla Iguana A 131-acre (53 ha) wildlife refuge centered on Isla Iguana—Panamá's largest nesting site for magnificent frigatebirds, plus pelicans and other seabirds. Also protects marine waters and mainland shore. Five species of marine turtles nest. Humpback whales breed in the warm waters. Coral reefs. The island has trails; camping permitted.

Refugio de Vida Silvestre Pablo Arturo Barios Coastal wildlife refuge protects an important nesting site for sea turtles. Many migratory and resident waterfowl, shorebirds, and seabirds; 74 acres (30 ha). Los Santos province.

Refugio de Vida Silvestre Peñon de la Honda Almost 37,065 acres (15,000 ha) of coastal wetlands, mangroves, and mudflats, plus marine environments. Offshore, Isla Peñon de la Honda is a nesting site for blue-footed booby, black-crowned night heron, and magnificent frigatebird. Vast numbers of shorebirds and waterfowl. Marine turtles nest. Los Santos province.

CHIRIQUÍ

Parque Internacional La Amistad Spanning the border between Panamá and Costa Rica, this massive park ranges from almost sea level to more than 13,000 feet (3,962 m) in elevation, protecting 10 distinct ecosystems. Huge tracts of rain forest and cloud forest. Well-developed trail system near Boquete and Cerro Punta; also accessible from Changuinola. Good for spotting quetzals.

Parque Nacional Isla Coiba Protects 149 miles (240 km) of coastal habitat and offshore marine environment. Habitat hosts many endemic species, plus is a rare refuge of scarlet macaws. Superb snorkeling and diving, and whales breed in these waters.

Islands in Parque Nacional Isla Coiba, Panamá

Parque Nacional Marino Golfo de Chiriquí This 36,423-acre (14,740 ha) marine park enshrines coastal wetlands, marine waters, plus the Archipiélago de las Islas Parides. Pristine coral reefs. Beaches are nesting sites for marine turtles Superb birding and whale-watching.

Parque Nacional Santa Fé De Veraguas This 179,484-acre (72,636 ha) park, created in 2001, protects montane wet forest harboring a gamut of precious wildlife, including all 6 big cat species, plus tapir and more than 400 species of birds.

Parque Nacional Volcán Barú Encircles the dormant Barú volcano (11,400 feet/3,475 m), Panamá's highest peak. Laced with well-maintained trails. Superb scenery, plus hiking, birding, and rock-climbing. Easily accessed from Boquete.

Refugio de Vida Silvestre Playa de la Barqueta Agrícola At the extreme west end of Panamá, this 14,665-acre (5,935 ha) wildlife refuge protects coastal wetlands, mangrove forests, and beaches, plus ocean waters. Important marine turtle habitat and nesting site for seabirds.

Refugio de Vida Silvestre Playa Boca Vieja West of Las Lajas, this remote 9,242-acre (3,740 ha) wildlife reserve protects coastal mangrove forests, inland wetlands, and beaches that are marine turtle nesting sites.

Reserva Forestal Fortuna Protects 48,185 acres (19,500 ha) of cloud-forest and other montane rain forests on the upper Pacific slopes of the Cordillera Central. Superb birding.

BOCAS DEL TORO

Bosque Protector Palo Seco A rugged 602,924-acre (244,000 ha) zone of protected primary forest between Parque Internacional La Amistad and the Caribbean coast. Six different forest types. Home to many Ngöbe-Buglé communities. Limited access.

Humedal Lagunas de Volcán An important stop on the Pacific Flyway, these three lagoons and surrounding wetlands encompass 352 acres (142.5 ha) of montane habitat for such waterfowl as masked duck and wattled jacana.

Humedal de San San-Pond Sak Extending from the Río Sixaola to Bahía de Almirante, this 39,845-acre (16,125 ha) Ramsar Internationally Important Wetland refuge protects mangroves, lagoons and seasonally flooded habitat, plus shoreline and marine environments. Manatees, river otters, and freshwater dolphin are among the fascinating creatures to be seen.

Parque Nacional Marino Isla Bastimentos A marine park covering 32,682 acres (13,226 ha) incorporating Isla Bastimentos, adjacent cays, and surrounding tropical waters. A breeding and nesting site for marine turtles and many seabirds. Coral reefs offer superb diving and snorkeling. Wildlife includes poison-dart frogs, and monkeys.

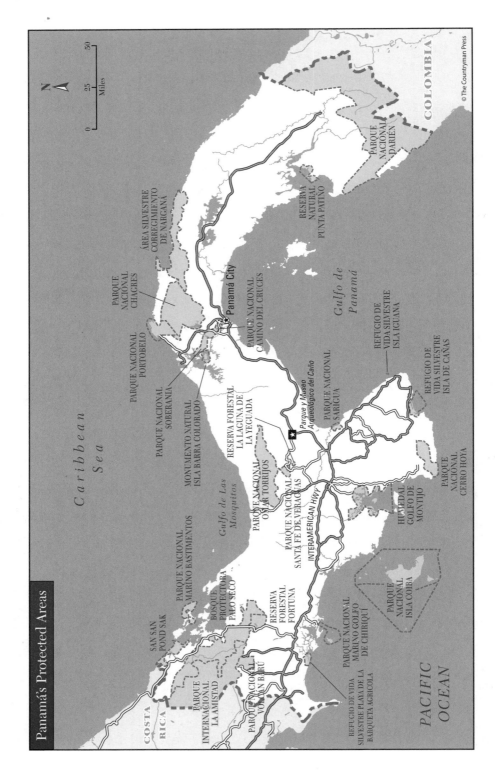

Panamá's Protected Areas

N

0   25   50
Miles

© The Countryman Press

COLOMBIA

Caribbean
Sea

PACIFIC
OCEAN

Gulfo de
Panamá

Gulfo de Las
Mosquitos

COSTA
RICA

Panamá City

PARQUE NACIONAL
DARIÉN

RESERVA
NATURAL
PUNTA PATIÑO

ÁREA SILVESTRE
CORREGIMIENTO
DE NARGANÁ

PARQUE
NACIONAL
CHAGRES

PARQUE NACIONAL
CAMINO DEL CRUCES

REFUGIO DE
VIDA SILVESTRE
ISLA IGUANA

REFUGIO DE
VIDA SILVESTRE
ISLA DE CAÑAS

PARQUE NACIONAL
PORTOBELO

PARQUE NACIONAL
SOBERANÍA

MONUMENTO NATURAL
ISLA BARRA COLORADO

RESERVA FORESTAL
LA LAGUNA DE
LA YEGUADA

Parque y Museo
Arqueológico del Caño

PARQUE NACIONAL
SARIGUA

PARQUE
NACIONAL
CERRO HOYA

PARQUE NACIONAL
MARINO BASTIMENTOS

BOSQUE
PROTECTORA
PALO SECO

PARQUE NACIONAL
OMAR TORRIJOS

PARQUE NACIONAL
SANTA FE DE VERAGUAS

INTERAMERICAN HWY

HUMEDAL
GOLFO DE
MONTIJO

PARQUE
NACIONAL
ISLA COIBA

SAN SAN
POND SAK

PARQUE
INTERNACIONAL
LA AMISTAD

PARQUE NACIONAL
VOLCÁN BARÚ

RESERVA
FORESTAL.
FORTUNA

PARQUE NACIONAL
MARINO GOLFO
DE CHIRIQUÍ

REFUGIO DE VIDA
SILVESTRE PLAYA DE LA
BARQUETA AGRÍCOLA

WHAT TO EAT AND DRINK

As a global crossroads of cultures, it's no surprise that Panamá has absorbed the culinary influences of the world. No town is without its Chinese and Mexican restaurants, an Italian pizzería, and South American *parrillada* (steakhouse). And Panamá City ranks right up there with many international cities for the plethora of superb fine-dining outlets that span the globe, from sushi to chic fusion options.

The country's cosmopolitan images fade with distance from Panamá City. Despite the ubiquity of gourmet international outlets tempting deep-pocket Panamanians, your average local prefers to stick with *comida criollo*—local fare. That means simple dishes that hark back to the land. Call it peasant fare, if you will. Think fried food, sparingly spiced. The staple dishes, found on menus throughout the country, are roast pork (*cerdo asado*) and fried or roast chicken (*pollo frito* or *pollo asado*), invariably accompanied by white rice (*arroz*), black beans (*frijoles negra*), fried plantains (*plátanos*), and sometimes a starch vegetable such as cassava (*yuca*), yam (*malanga*), or sweet potato (*boniato*). Yuca is also the staple of *carimañolas*—the vegetable is boiled and mashed, then stuffed with meat and cheese and deep-fried.

Panamanians seem never to tire of these basic yet tasty dishes. Otherwise there's no such thing as a national dish. One contender, however, might be *sancocho,* a heavily spiced stew that also features beef, chicken, and pork along with various vegetables, including corn and yuca. Regional variations exist—in Bocas del Toro, a pig's tail is often included.

Squeezed between two great oceans, the nation is fulsome with the bounty of King Neptune's larder. Be sure to try *ceviche*—chopped-up fish marinated with diced onions and peppers—found on almost every seafood restaurant's menu. Lobster (*langosta*) and shrimp (*camarones*) are great dishes, buttered with lots of garlic. When it comes to fish, you usually can't go wrong with the local fave: sea bass (*corvina*), also best enjoyed with butter and garlic (*ajo*). Snapper (*pargo*), swordfish (*emperador*), and dolphin fish (*dorado* or mahi

Starfruit

mahi) are other popular species. The Afro-Caribbean community has its own dishes, heavily reliant on the use of coconut milk and hot spices. Meanwhile, Boquete and Cerro Punta are centers of trout farming, the fish finding its way onto many a menu.

While the middle class have adopted North American habits at breakfast, the hoi polloi typically start the day with *arroz con pollo* (rice and chicken), perhaps accompanied with crumbled hard-boiled egg yolk, and seasoned with onions and garlic, plus thick, corn *tortillas* with fresh cheese. *Tamales* (cornmeal pastries filled with chicken or pork and stewed garlic, onions, and peppers) are wrapped in a banana leaf and then boiled. Corn also finds its way into desserts, as in the *chiricanos* (baked ground corn sweet doughs with shredded coconut and either sugarcane juice or honey), popular in the Azuero peninsula. Local sugar sweetens other delicious puddings *(dulces)*, including rice with milk *(arroz con leche)*, *flan* (custard), and *chicheme* (a ground corn drink made of milk sweetened with vanilla and cinnamon).

Tropical fruits abound. Many you'll be familiar with, such as bananas, papayas, pineapples, and mangoes. And there are strawberries and other berries, grown in the cool Chiriquí highlands. But you should try local fruits rarely seen in North America or Europe, such as *carambola* (starfruit), *guanabana* (soursop, which is popular in iced shakes called *batidos*), and *marañon* (cashew fruit). Coconuts are used mainly for the refreshing water *(agua de pipa),* drunk to quench thirst on hot days If that doesn't work, opt for a local lager-style brew, such as Balboa or Soberana. *Campesinos* (country farmers) favor *vino de palma,* a crude alcohol made from palm sap; the urban underclass drinks *seco,* an equally crude sugarcane liquor sometimes mixed with milk.

Lodging Price Codes:	
Inexpensive:	Up to $50
Moderate:	$500 to l00
Expensive:	$100 to 200
Very Expensive:	Over $200

Dining Price Codes:	
Inexpensive:	Up to $l5
Moderate:	$15 to 30
Expensive:	$30 to 50
Very Expensive:	$50 or more

Far more subtle and enjoyable are Panamá's excellent rums, especially the *añejos* (aged rums) of Carta Vieja. And nothing gets a day off to a great start like a fresh cup of locally grown *arabica* coffee. However, note that the best beans are usually exported, and that locals tend to drink their coffee American-style or *espresso* style and heavily sugared.

WHAT TO BUY

Leave some room in your suitcase for souvenirs. Panamá is a veritable potlatch of art and crafts, especially that produced by the nation's indigenous peoples. Then there are the fabulous rum and cigars. No matter where you are, you'll find plenty of fulfilling things to buy.

In Panamá City, the focus is on fashions, electronics, and the like, with the benefit of low prices passed down from the low freight costs of items purchased wholesale in the duty-free Colón Free Zone. You'll also find bargains on designer labels, including cosmetics and jewelry, in the malls of Marbella and El Cangrejo, in Panamá City. There are also plenty of jewelers selling Colombian emeralds. Sartorially minded males might splurge on a lovely *guayabera* shirt, while women will undoubtedly fall in love with the nation's national female dress—the exquisite *pollera.* By the way, Panamá hats originate in Ecuador, not Panamá, which has its own, simpler straw hat style.

Molas for sale in San Blas Islands, Panamá

When buying music CDs and DVDs of *merengue* and *salsa,* avoid the ubiquitous roadside stalls as the recordings here are usually bootleg and often poor quality.

Arts and Crafts

Undoubtedly, the best buys are in indigenous crafts. Stores selling Kuna *molas* (colorful stitched appliqué fabrics) abound in Panamá City; expect to pay anywhere from $15 to $500, depending on size and quality. Every touristy destination has at least one artisans' market or crafts outlet selling everything from a *sombrero montuño,* straw hats from Penonomé or the Azuero peninsula; spectacular woven baskets that are a forte of the Emberá-Wounaan tribes; wooden carvings (animals and nude female figurines are the most popular items) made of lignum vitae and other precious hardwoods; small animal figures carved of tagua nuts by the Emberá-Wounaan; and gorgeous bead jewelry (*chaquiras*) and patterned knitted bags (*chácaras*) crafted by the Ngöbe-Buglé.

The best quality crafts are usually found in the luxury hotel gift stores or other high-end stores. Prices here are fixed, however. It's far more fun to bargain for crafts at stalls and artisans' markets, where you're often buying directly from the artisans themselves. If you can, buy at source in the San Blas archipelago, or an Emberá village, or even a Ngöbe-Buglé community. And if you fancy an exquisitely carved (albeit perhaps grotesque) devil mask as worn during carnival, head to the Azuero peninsula where you can buy directly from famous artists.

The tourist boom, however, has spawned a great deal of kitsch. Avoid the tacky and politically incorrect products made of marine turtles, sharks, frogs, black coral, etc. Buying these items only contributes to the decimation of already endangered creatures.

Kuna woman selling molas with Punta Paitilla behind, Panamá City

Panamá's fine-art world is also quite vibrant and avant-garde. Panamá City (and many of the deluxe beach resorts) features galleries selling fantastic works by leading artists.

Rum and Smoke

Other good buys are delicious Panamanian rum. Stick with the quality rum brands, such as Carta Vieja. The older the rum, the higher the quality—*añejos* aged for seven years are best. *Remember that you will not be allowed to pass through airport security with a bottle of rum if you have to transit aircraft in the U.S.A. or Europe!* Pack your liquors in the checked baggage.

Panamá also produces fine cigars. However, it's a relatively small industry compared to Nicaragua (which competes with Cuba and the Dominican Republic in quantity and quality). When it comes to cigars, you're best to avoid buying from artisans' stalls, as it rarely pays to go cheap: They're usually the lesser brands or fakes, and/or they've been sitting out in the heat. Stick with quality brands that have been properly stored in a humidor. Best yet, visit a cigar factory where you can enjoy learning about the production process. Serious aficionados should look for, or head to, **Joyas de Panamá Cigars** (www.joyasdepanamacig ars.com), which makes five classic varieties: Churchill, Especial #1, Torpedo, Robusto, and Coronita. (Cuban cigars are also sold; it is illegal for U.S. citizens to purchase them here).

Another good buy is delicious Panamanian coffee from the highlands.

MAJOR HAPPENINGS THROUGHOUT THE YEAR

Whatever time of year you visit Panamá, there's sure to be some festival or other fun event going on. The big bash nationwide is the Mardi Gras-style *carnaval*, usually (depending on city) held over the four days preceding Ash Wednesday and featuring fearsome performers in devil masks and costumes, as well as female beauty contests, plus sexy Las Vegas–style cabaret dancers. The biggest carnivals are held in the Azuero peninsula, also the setting for the most important cultural festivals.

Daily newspapers such as *La Prensa* list local festivals and events. For a complete list, see the Biblioteca Nacional (National Library) Web site: www.binal.ac.pa/buscar/calendario.php. The following are among the major happenings to know:

January

Feria Agropecuario de Tanara-Chepo: Chepo. Annual agricultural fair.

Fiesta de Los Reyes Magos: Macaracas, January 6. Traditional Epiphany celebration; the Three Kings (Wise Men) arrive on horseback.

Los Congos: Escobál, 15 miles SW of Colón, throughout January and February. Afro-Caribbean culture and heritage honored with music and dance and reenactments of the slave era.

Panamá City Jazz Festival: Panamá City. International performers headline this four-day festival.

Feria de las Flores y el Café: Boquete, mid-January. Glorious displays of flowers.

February

Carnaval: four days preceding Ash Wednesday. The carnival in Las Tablas is considered to be Panamá's most colorful and crowded carnival. Other towns hosting popular carnivals during this period include Bocas Town and Río Azucar; Isla Grande, where *its* carnival features lots of calypso; and Penonomé, where the Carnaval Aquático begins with the carnival queen floating downriver on a raft.

Commemoration of the 1925 Kuna rebellion: San Blas archipelago, February 15. Lots of *chicha* (corn liquor) flows during this celebration held throughout the archipelago.

March

Feria Internacional de San José de David: David, mid-March. Rodeos and folkloric performances are highlights at this agricultural fair.

Panamanian carnival costumes and folkloric dress, Museo de Herrera, Azuero, Panamá

Feria de Santa Fé: Santa Fé. Annual agricultural fair.

Festival de Azúcar: Pesé. Celebration of the sugarcane harvest, with folkloric dancing.

Festival de Los Diablos y Congos: Portobelo, March 20 (also New Year's Eve). Afro-Caribbean culture and heritage honored with music and dance and reenactments of the slave era.

Fiesta Patronal de San José: Davíd, week of March 19. Locals honor the town's patron saint; folkloric music and dance.

April

Feria Internacional de Azuero: Villa de Los Santos, April and May. This fair promotes the agricultural, industrial, and cultural products of Herrera and Los Santos provinces.

Festival de las Orquídeas: Boquete, April. A celebrated four-day orchid festival.

Festival de Tomate: Natá, mid-April. A three-day agricultural fair honoring the humble tomato, grown locally.

May

Festival de Corpus Christi: Villa de los Santos, May and June. The town bursts to life for two fun-filled weeks of parades, fireworks, and devil dances.

Palo de Mayo: Bocas Town, May 1. Traditional maypole dance.

June

Festival de San Juan Bautista: Chitré, June 24. This religious procession traditionally ends with bull-baiting.

July

Festival de la Pollera: Las Tablas, July. Tribute to the national dress, with young women competing to be the National Queen.

Festival de Santa Librada: Las Tablas, July 20. Religious procession and merrymaking.

Fiestas Patronales (La Peregrinación) de la Virgen del Carmen: Isla Colón (Bocas del Toro); Isla Taboga; Jaqué (Darién); Río Hato and El Harino (Coclé province); third Sunday in July. Religious pilgrimage and celebration.

August

Feria de las Orquídeas de Santa Fé: Santa Fé. Local orchid festival.

Festival de Manito Ocueño: Ocú, third week of August. Three-day folkloric festival.

Festival de Santa Domingo: Parita, August 3–6. Patron saint festival.

Fiesta de Carlos Inaediguine Robinson: Narganá, Kuna Yala. August 20. The Kuna celebrate the birthday of their hero.

September

Fería del Mar: Bocas Town. Four-day beach festival.

Festival Nacional de la Mejorana: Guararé. Considered Panamá's main folkloric festival. Includes an oxcart parade.

October

Día de la Raza: Viento Frío, October 12. Celebrates Columbus' landing.

Festival del Cristo Negro: Portobelo, October 21. Religious pilgrimage with music and dancing.

Festival Nacional de Ballet: Panamá City. International ballet festival.

Festival del Toro Guapo: Antón. Three-day festival featuring beauty contests, bullfighting, rodeos, and dancing.

National Holidays
January 1: Año Nuevo (New Year's Day)
January 9: Día de los Héroes Nacionales (National Heroes Day)
February 28: Martes de Carnaval (Carnaval Tuesday)
May 1: Día del Trabajo (Labor Day)
August 15: Día de Panamá (Panamá Day)
November 3: Día de la Independencia (Independence Day—from Colombia)
November 5: Día de la Independencia (Independence Day—only in Colón)
November 10: Conmemoración de la Primera Reclamación de Independencia (Commemoration of Declaration of Independence from Spain).
November 27: Día de la Independencia (Independence Day—from España).
December 25: Navidad (Christmas)
Easter Friday, which varies annually, is also a national holiday. Most banks and government offices close during national holidays.

Fiesta Cívica del 19 de Octubre: Chitré, October 19. Locals celebrate the founding of Chitré province.
Fiesta Cultural del Emberá-Wounaan: Emberá Purú, Darién. Celebration of indigenous culture with traditional music and dance.

November
Día de Bastimentos: Isla Bastimentos, November 23. Afro-Caribbean music and dance, beauty contest, and parade.
Día de Bocas del Toro: Bocas Town, November 16. Festive events celebrate the founding of Boca del Toro province.
Día de la Independencia: Boquete, November 28. Independence Day celebration.
Festival de Tambor: David, November 28. Independence Day celebration with traditional drumming.
La Grita de La Villa: La Villa de los Santos, November 10. Festival celebrating the nation's demand for independence.

PRACTICAL DETAILS

Banks, Money, Etc.
Panamá's official currency is the *balboa*, often denoted as "B/," which is exactly equivalent to the U.S. Dollar, which can also be used freely. The balboa is divided into 100 *centavos*. Coins are printed in the same size and value as U.S. coins and bear the Panamanian shield and a portrait of Spanish *conquistador* Juan Vásquez de Balboa, or the indigenous *cacique* Urrucá (one centavo coin).

Most hotels will change Canadian dollars or Pounds Sterling or Euros for balboas, as will the few foreign-exchange booths *(casas de cambio)* and most banks. Private banks tend to be more efficient than the state-owned Banco Nacional. Larger bank branches usually

have foreign-exchange counters. Elsewhere antici-
pate possible long lines and waits for service.
Never change money on the streets—many people
are robbed or scammed!

Major credit cards (*tarjetas de crédito*) are
accepted everywhere, and you can use them at
banks and larger hotels to get cash advances.
However, many places (including some banks) will
only accept Visa. Most shops refuse to accept traveler's checks due to the high incidence of fraud, for
which reason banks often put a long hold on such
checks; a surcharge may apply.

Most banks have 24-hour ATMs; a small charge
applies and you will need your PIN (personal identification number). Check with your bank to see
what limit applies for withdrawals. Don't rely on
ATMs having cash, as many will run out, especially
on weekends. And if possible, use them only during banking hours in case there's a problem, such
as your card not being ejected. Banks are usually
open Monday through Friday 8:30–4; some also
open Saturday 8:30–noon.

You'll need to operate on a cash-only basis
when visiting the San Blas Islands and Darién. The
former has only two banks in its entire 150-mile
span, and Darién has barely a handful. Take lots of
small bills, not least because in the San Blas you'll
be expected to pay $1 per photo of people!

Torre BBVA, Panamá City

Communications

Postal Service

The **Dirección General de Correo y Telégrafo** (507-212-7600; www.correos.gob.pa) operates post offices throughout the country. They're typically open Monday through Friday
7–5. However, many hotels sell postage-prepaid letters and postcards, which you can also
mail at your hotel reception. Service is unreliable and slow. It takes between one week and
10 days for mail to North America (US$0.35) and usually at least 10 days to Europe
(US$0.75). The postal service offers express service, which is faster.

Theft is common, so if you're going to mail anything of value, use a private courier service such as DHL (507-271-3451; www.dhl.com.pa), FedEx (507-271-3838; www.fedex.com
/pa), or Airbox (507-269-9774; www.airbox.com.pa), which have offices throughout the
republic.

To receive mail, you can use a mail-forwarding service, which gives you a post office box
in Miami and then transports your arriving mail from there to Panamá. Alternately, rent a
postal box (*apartado postal*, abbreviated *Apdo.*) or have mail addressed to at [your name],
Entrega General, [city], [province], República de Panamá. There's no home delivery in
Panamá.

Telephone Service

The republic's telephone system is efficient. There's no shortage of public phones, which in the most backwater districts often serve the entire community, as in the remote islands of the San Blas archipelago. Many public phones still accept coins, but most use prepaid phone cards, sold at hotels, stores, gas stations, and call centers, and from touts selling them roadside. You insert the card into the phone; the cost of your call is deducted. Cable and Wireless "Telechip Total" (for local calls) and "Telechip Internacional" phonecards (for international calls) cost B/1, B/3, B/5, B/10 and B/20 and can be used in any public phone.

Local calls cost $0.10 for the first three minutes and $0.05 per minute thereafter. Tourist hotels typically charge exorbitant fees for direct calls from in-room phones. The cheapest way to call home is from a call center, found in most cities and usually attached to Internet cafés.

The Panamá code is 507. To dial the republic from North America, dial 011, then 507 and the local seven-digit number. There are no regional area codes within the country. Cellular phone numbers are preceded by the number 6. Four companies provide cellular access: **Claro Panamá** (507-800-9100 or from cellular phones 611; www.claro.com.pa), **Digicel Panamá** (507-306-0688 or 507-306-0600; www.digicelpanama.com), Cable and Wireless's **Mas Movíl** (507-800-2102 or 507-210-7400; www.masmovil.com.pa), and **Movistar** (507-304-7000; www.movistar.com.pa). They have call centers nationwide.

From within Panamá, dial 00 then the country code, area code, and telephone number. Dial 106 for operator-assisted calls, and 102 for directory inquiries.

To make free international calls using the Internet, register with Skype (www.skype .com).

Internet Service

Tourist hotels usually have some form of Internet service. Most upscale hotels have Internet modems and/or Wi-Fi reception in guest bedrooms, although many charge for use. All towns have Internet cafés at reasonable rates, typically no more than B/1 or B/2 per hour.

Electricity

Panamá utilizes 110 volts AC and outlets use U.S. two-prong or three-prong plugs (European visitors will need to bring adapters); however, 220 volts (usually marked as such) is still the norm in some boondock communities. Power outages (*apagones*) are common. Fortunately, most restaurants and hotels have their own back-up generators. Bring a surge protector or transformer to protect against power surges.

Handicapped Services

Panamá is far behind developed nations in terms of handicap accessibility. Few sidewalks have wheelchair ramps, for example. And few buildings have special toilets. Nor are buses adapted for wheelchairs. However, things are changing. Wheelchair ramps are being gradually installed on major avenues in Panamá City, and many new public buildings are handicapped-equipped. So are most major tourist hotels and upscale restaurants built in recent years. Handicapped travelers should factor in the added difficulties of traveling between the Bocas del Toro and San Blas islands, and in Darién, where local transport is typically by small boat.

The **Society for Accessible Travel and Hospitality** (212-447-7284; www.sath.org; 347 5th Avenue, Suite 610, New York, NY 10016) is a handy resource for disabled travelers, as is **Gimp on the Go** (www.gimponthego.com). In Panamá, two good resources to know are the **Instituto Panameño de Habilitación Especial** (Panamanian Institute for Special Rehabilitation; 507-261-9982; www.iphe.gob.pa) and **Unión Nacional de Ciegos de Panamá** (National Union of the Blind of Panamá; 507-268-0526; E-mail uncp@tutopia .com).

Health and Safety

Medical Services

Panamá has a public health system and most towns have *centros de salud* (health centers), although standards are well below those of North America and Europe, and they're often good solely for immediate first aid. However, there are plenty of private clinics (*clínicas*) and hospitals of very high standard, especially in Panamá City and David—a direct legacy of decades of U.S. involvement that inspired generations of Panamanian physicians to train abroad. In the capital, two top private facilities are **Centro Médico Paitilla** (Avenida Balboa and Calle 53; 507-263-6060) and **Hospital Nacional** (Avenida Cuba and Calle 38; 507-207-8110; www.hospitalnacional.com).

The large beach hotels of the Central Pacific usually have a nurse on-site, and all hotels maintain a list of recommended doctors and health facilities nearby.

Most towns have well-stocked pharmacies, and many drugs sold as prescription-only in North America and Europe are available over the shelf (however, the name of a specific drug may be different).

Travel Insurance

Travel insurance that covers health service and medical evacuation is a wise investment. Keep receipts for insurance claims. The following companies are recommended: **American Express** (800-234-0375; www.americanexpress.com); **TravelGuard International** (800-826-4919; www.travelguard.com); and **Travelers** (800-243-3174; www.travelers.com).

Assistcard (305-381-9959; www.assist-card.com) offers comprehensive insurance packages and has a regional assistance center in Santo Domingo (809-683-3433 ext. 24).

Health Issues

Your biggest enemy is the climate. The tropical sun is intense. Many foreign (and especially first-time) visitors underestimate the power of the sun and get badly burned. Use lots of sunscreen with a minimum UV rating of 15. And build up your exposure to the sun gradually. Otherwise you risk getting potentially fatal sunstroke as well as sunburn.

You'll be constantly sweating and may not even notice, as your sweat may evaporate instantly. Avoid alcohol by day, and replenish your body fluids by drinking *lots* of water.

In a tropical climate, bacteria breed profusely. Wash cuts and scrapes with bottled water and rubbing alcohol, and use antiseptic creams.

Stomach ailments are common. To avoid them, avoid food from cheap food stalls, as well as uncooked seafood, unwashed salads, unpeeled fruits, and any meats that have been exposed to flies or left in the heat too long (as at many resort buffet counters).

Water from the faucet is safe to drink in most large cities. However, to be on the safe side, drink bottled water. Ensure any ice you drink is made from bottled water. Don't drink water from streams—a sure way to become infected with the Giardia parasite.

Woman in bikini on Isla de los Perros, San Blas Islands, Panamá

And don't drink or brush your teeth with tap water in Bocas del Toro, the San Blas Islands, Darién, and anywhere along the Caribbean coast.

Mosquitoes are prevalent in humid lowland areas, especially near coastal mangroves. Malaria is present along the Caribbean coast and in Darién, and outbreaks of dengue fever (an excruciating and debilitating disease) often occur. Both are spread by mosquitoes. Ask your doctor for prophylactics against malaria (there is no medication or cure for dengue). To reduce the chance of being bitten, use insect repellent liberally and wear light-colored clothing, ideally long-sleeve shirts and pants. The other biting pest is the "no-see-um" (Panamanians call them *chitras*), a minuscule flea with a nasty bite that itches like hell and leaves you looking like you have chicken pox. They're active on beaches at dawn and dusk. Insect repellent doesn't stop them, but Avon Skin-so-Soft supposedly does. Chiggers (*coloradillas*) live in tall grass and like nothing better than to bore into your skin—remarkably they're almost impossible to feel; once in your flesh their presence can cause serious medical problems. Get medical aid to extract them.

Alas, Panamá is a smoker's paradise and no non-smoking laws apply, even in restaurants, where smokers light up with no consideration for other guests—even No Smoking signs in public venues are not heeded. Many upscale restaurants have no-smoking sections.

Safety Issues

Let's start with traffic—the biggest safety issue you'll face. Panamanians are lousy drivers! Aggressive . . . Devil-may-care . . . Lawless . . . And just plain dangerous. If you rent a car (or even cross a road as a pedestrian), use utmost caution. And pedestrians should use extreme caution at all times; don't expect a Panamanian driver to stop for you just because you're in the street.

Otherwise, overall, Panamá is a safe destination. However, in towns be guarded at all times against snatch-and-grab theft and/or muggings. Avoid lonely places and impoverished areas, especially at night. Guard your belongings closely in crowded areas, such as buses and markets. Don't drive alone at night. And never leave any possessions in a parked vehicle, or unattended on a beach. To reduce the risk of theft, never carry your camera loose on your shoulder; don't wear fancy jewelry; wear clothing over a money belt; and keep the bulk of your valuables in a hotel safe.

Use extra precaution when exploring Colón and the national parks of the Canal Zone, where numerous robberies have taken place. Places to avoid entirely include the impoverished and drug-riddled El Chorrillo area (bordering Casco Viejo) and Curundú (northeast of Ancón), in Panamá City; and the eastern half of Darién, where left-wing guerrillas, right-wing paramilitaries, and all manner of lawless drug trafficking bandits have infiltrated from Colombia. The heavy presence of Panamanian military is no guarantee of safety.

Venomous snakes are common. Usually they're well camouflaged. Never put your hand under rocks or in crevices, never walk around barefoot at night, and wear closed-toed shoes (ideally with ankle protection) whenever walking outside towns. Also, shake out your shoes and clothes in the morning before putting them on—twice I've found scorpions in my clothing. Don't swim in river estuaries, where crocodiles are likely to be found. And when wading in sandy ocean shallows, shuffle your feet through the sand to scare away any stingrays—if you step on one, their slashing tail can inflict an awesome and excruciating wound.

Don't swim if you've been drinking alcohol. And beware riptides, which are prevalent on beaches receiving high surf. They cause many people to drown every year. These narrow and ferociously fast currents drain incoming water back to sea. If you get caught in one, swim *parallel* to the shore to escape the current, otherwise you're sure to tire yourself out and panic in a vain effort to swim back to shore. Check local conditions before swimming.

And as for coconuts . . . there's a reason coconut trees at beach resorts are harvested for their nuts before they fall, and it isn't simply for fresh juice for your *piña colada*. A falling coconut can seriously ruin your day!

Time Zones

Panamá operates on Eastern Standard Time (EST), the same as New York and Miami, and is five hours behind Greenwich Mean Time (GMT) and one hour ahead of neighboring Costa Rica. Daylight Savings is not observed.

Tourist Information

The Panamanian government's **Autoridad de Turismo de Panamá** (Panamá Tourism Authority, or IPAT; Avenida Aquilino de la Guardia and Calle Gerardo Ortega, Edificio Central, Panamá City; 507-526-7000; www.atp.gob.pa) maintains a toll-free number in North America—800-231-0568—plus a Web site for visitors: www.visitpanama.com. You can request literature, published by the authority.

In Panamá, look for *Focus Panamá,* a twice-yearly tourist-oriented publication, and *The Panamá Visitor,* a twice-monthly newspaper. Both are widely available in hotels.

The authority's regional tourist information bureaus include:

Bocas del Toro: Calle 1, Bocas Town, Isla Colón; 507-757-9642.

Boquete, Chiriquí Province: 507-720-4060.

Chiriquí, Chiriquí Province: Avenida Domingo Díaz Don Yobe between Calle 5ta and 6ta; 507-775-2839.

Chitré, Herrera Province: Parque Industrial La Arena; 507-974-4532.

Colón, Colón Province: Colón 2000; 507-475-2300.

El Valle de Antón, Coclé Province: Mercadeo Artesanal; 507-983-6474.

La Palma, Darién Province: 507-299-6337.

Los Santos, Los Santos Province: Vía Playa El Arenal; 507-995-2339.

Panamá City: Aeropuerto Internacional de Tocumen, 507-238-3686; Aeropuerto Marcos A. Gelabert (Albrook), 507-526-6990; Avenida Central and Calle 3, Casco Viejo, 507-211-3365.

Paso Canoa, Chiriquí Province: 507-727-6524.

Pedasí, Los Santos Province: 507-995-2339.

Portobelo, Colón Province: Calle Principal Frente a la Alcaldía; 507-448-2200.

Río Hato, Coclé Province: Calle Principal de Farallón; 507-993-3241.

Veraguas, Veraguas Province: Plaza Palermo, Vía Héctor Alejandro Santa Coloma; 507-998-3929.

Villa de Los Santos, Los Santos Province: Calle José Vallarino; 507-966-8013.

3

PANAMÁ CITY

A World-Class City

The first sight of Panamá City *(Ciudad de Panamá)* causes a double take. Skyscrapers claw at the sky. In fact, as the major banking center south of New York, Panamá City truly is a Manhattan in the Tropics. Sophisticated and edgy, this humming financial center at the Pacific entrance to the Canal has everything you'd expect of a capital at a major crossroads to the world. Fine-dining restaurants. Ritzy casinos. Sizzling nightlife. And top-class hotels. All this, and more, combines with a historic quarter teeming with intimate plazas hemmed by ancient churches and colonial buildings in an amalgam of styles.

Blending old and new, Panamá City—called simply Panamá by locals—captivates with its sentimental allure wed to a cool, contemporary, and cosmopolitan Latin vibe. It is at once both laid-back and seething. And no wonder. For five hundred years, it has served as a conduit of commerce linking two continents and two oceans.

Originally founded at the mouth of the Río Abajo in 1519, the early city—Nuestra Señora de la Asunción de Panamá (site of today's Panamá Viejo)—flourished as the treasures of the Incas arrived for transportation to Caribbean ports via the *camino real.* In 1671 the city was devastated by a pirate raid led by Welsh cutthroat Henry Morgan. The charred ruins were abandoned and a city was founded a few miles west on a rocky promontory, with thick fortress walls. Within a century, however, Panamá sank into decline. The forlorn city's fortunes revived with the California Gold Rush in 1848. Tens of thousands of argonauts flocked to make the passage across the isthmus, aided in 1855 with completion of the Panamá Railroad. Many of the international *arrivistas* stayed to patch their national traits to the cultural quilt of the city. Today, a Parisian architectural influence is noticeable in Casco Viejo (the colonial core of the city)—a legacy of the massive influx during the 1880s of French engineers, technicians, and craftsmen employed by the Compagnie Universelle du Canal Interocéanico in their ill-fated quest to cut a canal through the isthmus.

The failed French enterprise cast Panamá City back into a decade of desuetude and decay. The United States' bully-boy manipulation of Panamá's independence as a prelude to construction of the Canal was a down payment on a glittering future. Panamá City's astronomic rise from relative obscurity to international stature is owed entirely to the Canal. Billions of dollars of investment poured in. U.S. military administrators established 20th-century infrastructure based on the U.S. model: paved highways, electric streetlights,

OPPOSITE: *Fishing boats in Panamá bay*

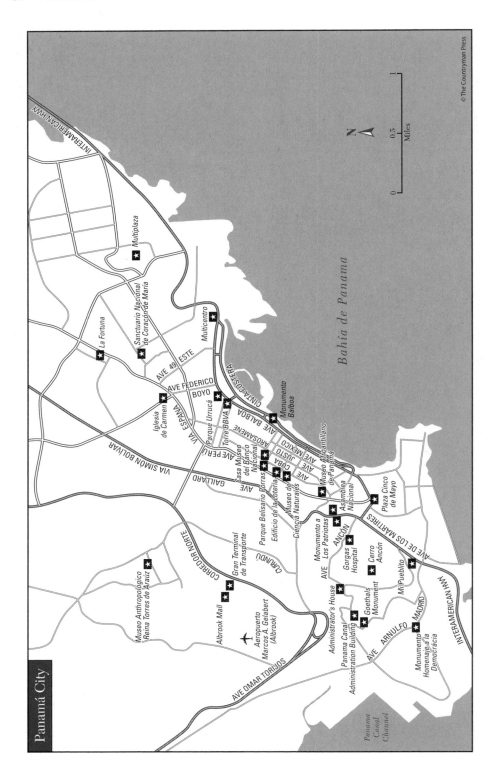

Panamá City

Bahía de Panama

Panama Canal Channel

INTERAMERICAN HWY

INTERAMERICAN HWY

Multiplaza

Santuario Nacional de Corazón de María

La Fortuna

Multicentro

AVE 49 ESTE

AVE FEDERICO BOYD

CINTA COSTERA

Iglesia de Carmen

VIA ESPAÑA

Parque Urracá

Torre BBVA

AVE BALBOA

AVE ROSAMENE

Monumento Balboa

VIA SIMÓN BOLÍVAR

AVE PERÚ

Casa Museo del Banco Nacional

AVE CUBA

AVE JUSTO AROSAMENE

AVE MÉXICO

Museo Afroantillano de Panamá

GAILLARD

Parque Belisario Porras

Edificio de la Lotería

Museo de Ciencia Naturales

Asamblea Nacional

Plaza Cinco de Mayo

CORREDOR NORTE

Gran Terminal de Transporte

CURUNDU

Monumento a Los Patriotas

AVE ANCÓN

Gorgas Hospital

Cerro Ancón

AVE DE LOS MÁRTIRES

Mi Pueblito

Museo Anthropológico Reina Torres de Araúz

Albrook Mall

Aeropuerto Marcos A. Gelabert (Albrook)

Administrator's House

Panama Canal Administration Building

Goethals Monument

AVE ARNULFO MADRID

INTERAMERICAN HWY

Monumento Homenaje a la Democrácia

AVE OMAR TORRIJOS

Panama Canal Channel

N

0   0.5   1
Miles

© The Countryman Press

Ruins of Panama Viejo, Panamá

efficient water treatment and dispersal systems. And new districts in a distinctly vernacular U.S. "colonial tropical" style sprouted overnight in the Canal Zone to the northwest of the colonial city. Here for eight decades, in Ancón, Balboa, and Quarry Heights, U.S. residents (Zonians) lived a quintessential bubblegum American colonial life of Coke and cookies, like residents of the perfect little community of Seahaven (ironically, partially shot in Panama City, Florida) in the Jim Carrey movie *The Truman Show*.

The modern metropolis (population 813,000) is spread along the Bahía de Panamá and is framed inland by forested hills. Every year sees a handful of new skyscrapers needle the sky on the peninsula of upscale Punta Paitilla. But Panamá's ancient side also shines through, not least thanks to a gentrification of recently rundown Casco Viejo. Today it hums with bohemian life. Formerly decrepit colonial buildings have metamorphosed as jazz clubs, ritzy restaurants, and intimate boutique hotels and cafés.

Centrally located, with roads radiating from here to the main sites of touristic interest, Panamá City truly is a crossroads superbly positioned for sightseeing. And the downside? Hot and steamy, Panamá City can feel like a sauna. At times, a five-minute walk will leave you dripping in sweat.

TOURING THE CITY

Panamá City's transportation is hectic. The road network is convoluted and the metropolitan city is not easily navigated beyond the core, which can be walked. A little planning goes a long way.

Getting Your Bearings

Panamá City spreads over 106 square miles (275 sq km) to the east of the Canal, on the southern or Pacific coast of the country. **Casco Viejo**, the historic heart of the city, occupies a small peninsula (San Felipe) offering views west across the Bahía de Panamá towards the man-made Amador Causeway (Calzada de Amador), a breakwater connecting three small islands (Isla Naos, Perico, and Flamingo) to the mainland. Immediately north of Casco Viejo, the working-class district of **Calidonia** butts up to Cerro Ancón (Ancón Hill), a freestanding hulk of a mountain west of which lies the former Canal Zone enclaves of Ancón, Balboa, Quarry Hill, and Albrook.

View over Bella Vista toward Punta Paitilla from Cerro Ancón, Panamá City

East of Casco Viejo, Avenida Balboa (westbound) and Cinta Costera (eastbound) run along the bay between the middle-class **La Exposición** district to the more upscale residential zone of **Bella Vista**, the commercial zone of **El Cangrejo** and **Marbella** (the financial center)—together boasting the city's greatest concentration of upscale hotels, restaurants, and nightclubs—and the peninsula of **Punta Paitilla**, the ritziest real estate in town, pinned by dozens of glittering high-rise condominiums. Most places of touristic interest are located in these zones. Avenida Balboa continues east (as Vía Israel) to the Centro de Convenciones Atlapa and beyond, as Vía Cincuentenario, to **Panamá Viejo**, the ruins of the original city.

Avoid the impoverished and crime-ridden districts of **Santa Ana** and **Chorrillo**, immediately west of Casco Viejo.

NEIGHBORHOODS TO KNOW

Amador This region comprises the former U.S. military site of Fort Amador, the islands of Naos, Perico, and Flamenco; and the scenic Calzada de Amador—a man-made tombolo built as a breakwater using landfill excavated during construction of the Panamá Canal. It has upscale restaurants, nightclubs, a marina, a branch of the Smithsonian Tropical Research Institute, and the city's main cruise ship port. It's also the site of the Frank Gehry-designed Museo de Biodiversidad (Museum of Biodiversity), scheduled for completion in 2011. The www.amadorcausewaypanama.com Web site is a good resource.

View over Balboa and Panamá Canal from Cerro Ancón, Panamá City

Ancón/Balboa/Quarry Hill Surrounding Cerro Ancón (the city's highest hill), the former administrative and residential center for the Canal Zone during U.S. tenure today comprises a bucolic retreat a world apart from the rest of the city in aspect and feel.

Balboa, to the west of Cerro Ancón, is still the center for Canal operations, centered on the Panamá Canal Administration Building, with its fascinating murals open to public view. The serpentine roads on neighboring Quarry Hill are lined with venerable wooden houses and make for delightful exploring. And there are numerous fascinating monuments, churches, and even Art Deco structures. Cerro Ancón offers a 360-degree view of the city.

Bella Vista/El Cangrejo/Marbella This zone of three regions bordering one another in the center of the city forms an upscale and compact triptych that is a veritable forest of glass-concrete-and-metal skyscrapers. Most of the city's hotels are here. So too its fine-dining restaurants (especially in tree-lined Bella Vista's Zona Rosa, or "pink zone"), nightclubs, and casinos and shops (in El Cangrejo). Marbella, to the east, hosts the banks (hence its moniker, Área Bancara, or Financial District) and upscale shopping malls. Laid out in a grid, the area is easily walked: everything is within walking distance of the hotels.

Calidonia/La Exposición These adjoining low-income residential districts form a warren of narrow, traffic-thronged streets lined by apartment blocks and condominiums. Several streets are difficult to navigate due to the hordes of street vendors and impromptu markets. The city's budget hotels are here. The region has several leafy parks and some fascinating buildings, including the Congress building and several museums. City officials have plans to transform much of this region into another high-rise zone.

Casco Viejo Known to locals as San Felipe, the Old City—a UNESCO World Heritage Site—is a delightful enclave of cobbled streets and intimate plazas lined with delightful colonial homes and grandiose structures, most of which went up in the 19th century. The 17th-century cathedral is one of several beautiful colonial churches. The Presidential Palace and Teatro Nacional can be toured, and the zone has plenty of intriguing museums. Recently restored, it's full of charming cafés, globe-spanning world-class restaurants, and a lively bohemian culture.

Ruins of Iglesia y Convento La Merced, Panamá Viejo, Panamá

Panamá Viejo On the eastern edge of the city (take a taxi or guided excursion), the original 16th-century city is today in ruins, preserved much as they were left after Henry Morgan, the pirate, finished destroying the city. A wide and well-maintained path links the main sites, and there's a splendid museum plus an indigenous crafts market.

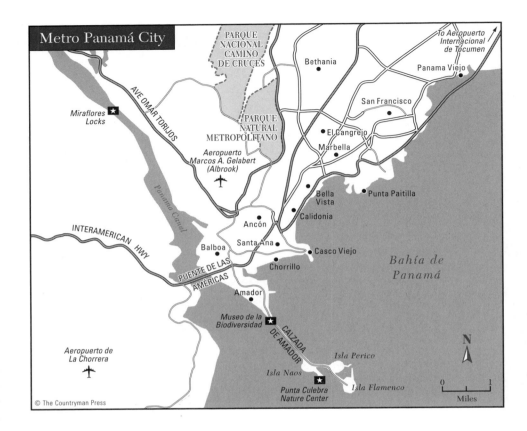

By Bus or Público

In general, taxis are a better bet than buses for getting around in Panamá City, which lacks a printed timetable or route map. Traditionally, hundreds of privately owned *diablos rojos* (red devils) have competed along main routes; these old U.S. school buses are usually tarted up to the max with stunning electric-psychedelic graffiti art, flashing lights, and assorted knick-knacks. The destination is written atop the front windshield. A fixed fare of $0.25 applied at press time. However, the *diablos rojos* are to be phased out and replaced by modern buses under a municipal authority; as of 2010, the long-awaited change had yet to happen (the sooner the better say I, as *diablo rojo* drivers are renowned for dangerous and inconsiderate driving). The main bus station is the Gran Terminal de Transporte (Corregimiento de Ancón, Albrook; 507-303-3030; www.grantnt.com), in Albrook; long-distance buses arrive and depart the top deck floor; local city buses arrive and depart the lower level.

Guard your belongings closely. Pickpockets and thieves work these buses.

By Car

A car can be a liability in the narrow streets of Casco Viejo. And the maelstrom of inner-city traffic in other zones can cause consternation, as can the lack of street signs. The

Panamanian driving style is aggressive: for example, at junctions Panamanians nudge out into streaming traffic.

The main highway for sightseeing is the seafront Avenida Balboa (westbound) and, parallel, the Cinta Costera (eastbound), which link the hotel, shopping, and entertainment zone of Bella Vista/El Cangrejo/Marbella to Casco Viejo. In 2009, the shorefront was extended into the bay with landfill and Avenida Balboa (previously two-way) was widened and turned into a divided expressway—the Cinta Costera—separated by a broad median with a newly laid-out park with bike paths. Impressive . . . except you can no longer cross Avenida Balboa by car; there is only one car access point to the Cinta Costera; and there are no pedestrian crosswalks or bridges for the lowly walker. Talk about lousy planning!

Parque Legislativo, in Calidonia, is the central node from which main arteries span out through the city to suburbs and farther afield. From here:

Avenida de los Mártires runs west to the Puente de las Américas (Bridge of the Americas), which crosses the Canal and (as the Pan-American Highway) leads to the Costa Rican frontier.

Avenida Ascanio Arosemena leads northwest to Aeropuerto Marcos A. Gelabert and connects to Avenida Omar Torrijos Herrera (which leads to the Miraflores Locks and Parque Nacional Soberania) and to the Corredor Norte, a freeway that runs around the northern edge of the city.

Avenida Central España parallels Avenida Balboa and runs east through the heart of Bella Vista and El Cangrejo.

Avenida Simón Bolívar runs northeast past the Universidad de Panamá (Panamá University), crosses the Corredor Norte, and continues as the Transístmica northward to Colón and the Caribbean.

Diablo rojo *bus in Panamá City*

Aeropuerto Internacional Tocumen

To find your way into Panamá City from the main airport, choose either of two options. If you don't fancy paying a series of tolls, take **Vía Tocumen** (the exit road at the airport), a broad expressway that skirts the northern outskirts and eventually becomes Avenida Ricardo J. Alfaro, which runs into Bella Vista. Just west of the airport, you can turn off Vía Tocumen and take the **Corredor Sur**, an *autopista* (toll freeway) with two tollbooths. It leads directly downtown, depositing you at the junction with Avenida Balboa, in Bella Vista. The 10-mile trip to downtown will take 20 minutes minimum, depending on traffic conditions.

By Foot

Casco Viejo and the hotel, shopping, and entertainment zone of Bella Vista/El Cangrejo/Marbella are easily navigated on foot, as they are laid out in grid format. The old city's narrow streets are also shaded by tall buildings. However, those of the more modern Bella Vista/El Cangrejo/Marbella region are broader and more sun-exposed. Always be cautious when crossing streets: Panamanian drivers do not stop for pedestrians!

By Taxi

Taxis are the default mode of transport for many Panamanians, and they sure are the logical choice for tourists. Fortunately, taxis are plentiful (except when it rains); they're also inexpensive. Penny-pinchers should opt for local taxis. They charge considerably less than tourist taxis, which await custom outside large tourist hotels and are allowed to charge about three times the local taxi rates. Tourist taxis are designated by "SET" (for *Servicio Especial Turística*) on their *chapas* (license plates). Local taxis may pick up one or more passengers going your way.

Taxis don't have meters. Instead, official point-to-point rates for local taxis within the city range from $1.00 to $3.10 for fares within and between seven zones, depending on your beginning and end points and the number of zones you pass through (an extra $0.25 charge applies for each additional person). Taxi drivers are required to keep a chart—colored-coded by zone—in their vehicles. Ask to see it. However, it's best to know the fare in advance; taxi drivers often try to rip off clients who show ignorance about the zones. Radio taxis charge $0.50 more. Call Radio Taxi América (507-223-7534), Radio Taxi América Libre (507-223-7342 or 296-1601), or Radio Taxi Libertad (507-267-7515). Either way, tipping is not an expectation in Panamá: a 25- or 50-cent tip is deemed sufficient.

Never take an unmarked pirate taxi, or one with a co-driver, for reasons of safety. Crimes are frequent.

You can also hire a taxi on an hourly ($10–15) or daily basis.

By Tours

The **Oficina del Casco Antiguo** (507-209-6300; guias@cascoantiguo.gob.pa; www.casco antiguo.gob.pa) offers three free guided tours of Casco Viejo in English and Spanish. The tours depart Plaza de la Catedral (Plaza de la Independencia) each Friday and Saturday at 10 AM, 10:30 AM, and 11 AM.

Rudy Ariani (507-671-7165; www.pattyscasitas.com/panamatours.htm) is recommended for personalized guided tours of the city, including by night.

Most local tour agencies also offer city tours, among them **PanamaTours** (507-832-7679; www.panamatours.com.pa).

LODGING

Panamá City's hotel scene is wide-ranging. There's something for everyone, from inexpensive hostels to intimate boutique hotels, and ritzy high-rise hotels with every amenity from tennis and disco to casinos and spas. Most of the latter are found in the El Cangrejo and Marbella districts, a 40-minute walk from Casco Viejo, which has a few—but surprisingly few!—small boutique hotels. Most of the budget options are in Calidonia and La Exposición.

Bed and Breakfast Inns /Boutique Hotels

ALBROOK INN

507-315-1789
Fax: 507-315-1975
www.albrookinn.com
Calle Las Magnolias #14, Albrook
Inexpensive
Perfect for travelers who shun big hotels in favor of small properties with personality, this 30-room bed-and-breakfast started life as part of the U.S. military command center at the base of Ancón hill. Today it's a charming and peaceful spot away from the city hubbub and perfect for exploring Ancón and Balboa. Recently refurbished in a more upscale vogue than before, it's now elegant, with stylishly modern furnishings in its 30 air-conditioned bedrooms, all with TVs, direct-dial phones, and Internet modems. The lush garden features a lovely pool and Jacuzzi.

ARCOS DE BELLA VISTA B&B AND PATTY'S CASITA RENTAL STUDIO

507-6713-7165 (cellular)
www.pattyscasitas.com
Calle 49, Bella Vista
Moderate
Fancy staying in a Florentine mansion in Bella Vista? Dating from 1940, this lovely building has only one two-bedroom junior suite with rather modest furnishings, including a king-sized bed and meagerly furnished lounge plus caged patio with hammock. The owners, Patty Polte and Rudy Ariana, live here, too.

Patty also rents out an exquisitely furnished apartment on Calle 10, in Casco Viejo. The decor mixes chic contemporary with period pieces atop gleaming hardwood floors. It has a king-sized bed with orthopedic mattress, flat-screen TV, and free computer with Internet and Wi-Fi. A lovely space! At press time, Patty had an additional loftlike unit in the works in the same building, with venerable redbrick walls.

Plus she has a one-bedroom condo in a modern high-rise on Calzada de Amador . . . a perfect base for visiting the Museum of Biodiversity when it finally opens.

THE BALBOA INN

507-314-1520
www.thebalboainn.com
2311 Calle Cruces, Balboa
Inexpensive
The past few years have seen an explosion of bed-and-breakfast accommodations open in the Ancón and Balboa districts—perfect for a walking tour of this fascinating historic district. This one is a winner with its airy, spacious lounges. Although not luxurious, all nine air-conditioned rooms are comfy and have delightful wall murals plus satellite TVs, DVDs, Wi-Fi, safes, and—a big plus—ceiling fans. The Dutch live-in owners, former KLM flight attendant Saskia Swartz and her husband Thorwald Westmaas, run this place with aplomb.

B&B LA ESTANCIA

507-314-1581
www.bedandbreakfastpanama.com
Calle Amelia Denis de Icaza #35,
Quarry Heights
Inexpensive
This no-smoking bed-and-breakfast on the west slopes of Cerro Ancón is another former military property to metamorphose

as a charming little hotel. It has seven rooms, and two suites with kitchens. Furnished in a homey fashion, including some rattan pieces, it's a pleasantly comfy and cozy, albeit no-frills, option. A bonus: heaps of hot water in the spacious showers. The lounge has a small library and a piano, and guests get free use of Internet.

HOTEL BRISTOL

507-264-0000
Fax: 507-265-7829
www.thebristol.com
Calle Aquilino De La Guardia between
Calles 51 and 52
Expensive

A member of The Leading Hotels of the World, this gracious boutique hotel—my favorite hotel in the city—is a stand-out offering a rare combination of intimacy and elegance. Heck, it feels like it's been transported from London's fashionable Chelsea district. Behind the Neo-Classical façade, it exudes class with its mahogany old-world wood paneling, shiny marbles, and tasteful contemporary art. The 56 deluxe guest quarters also combine sensibilities of yesteryear and today, with classy chocolate, cream, and gold tones; four-poster beds, and—a nice touch—*mola* pillows that are a sole nod to a Panamanian theme. Butler service 24/7 is another lovely touch. The gracious wood-paneled Baranda restaurant serving award-winning nouvelle dishes is among the city's finest, and the adjacent bar gets lively on weekends, when the city's youthful sophisticates flock.

CANAL HOUSE

507-228-1907
Fax: 507-228-6637
www.canalhousepanama.com
Calle 5ta and Avenida A, Casco Viejo
Expensive

This non-smoking boutique hotel in the heart of Casco Viejo is *the* place to rest your head if you're seeking sophistication and intimacy. A fabulous remake of a century-old house, replete with red-tile roof and wrought-iron balconies. Well, it's not really a hotel. It has only three bedrooms. Actually, they're suites. Two are over-sized, each with a king bed, day bed, separate live-work space (one is a loft), and an enormous wrap-around balcony. The place has been souped up with modern accouterments, such as flat-screen TVs and iPod docking stations, and can you imagine 600-thread-count sheets? I had no idea such luxury existed! Canal House also has a gracious living-dining room, and bookworms will appreciate the library. Bring your laptop—Wi-Fi is throughout. The style throughout is straight out of *Vogue*. In a word . . . *classy!* Individual rooms can be rented, depending on availability. Usually the house rents out complete. This is where actor Daniel Craig laid his head while filming *Quantum of Solace.*

LOS CUATROS TULIPANES

507-211-0877
www.loscuatrotulipanes.com
Avenida Central between Calle 3 and
Calle 4, Casco Viejo
Moderate

For sophisticated digs in the heart of Casco Viejo, this property management company can't be beat. It rents more than a dozen boutique apartments in the historic quarter. Choose from a studio or one-, two-, and three-bedroom apartments, all of which differ in layout. Although many of the units rent long-term, short-term vacationers are welcome. My favorite units are in the beautifully restored 17th-century Casa de Las Monjas (House of Nuns), with two units that open to a lovely courtyard exposing rustic stone walls—a prominent feature inside the rooms too. The furnishings are regal and the autumnal color schemes enhance the sense of sophistication. A real bonus is its location next to Manolo Caracol, the old quarter's top restaurant; and diagonal to Casa Góngora, a venue for live jazz at night. All Los Cuatros Tulipanes units come equipped with high-speed Internet, and there's daily maid service, and attentive staff are on hand 24/7. I consider it a bargain, with many units offered below $150 nightly.

LA DULCE COLMENA B&B

507-6799-1375
www.ladulcecolmena.com
El Avance, Betania
Inexpensive

Wow! Talk about a honey of a bed-and-breakfast. La Dulce Colmena (sweet bee-hive), which opened in 2008, is a colorful and stylish charmer in the quiet residential suburb of Altos de Betania, on the north side of the city. Colonial tilework, gorgeous hardwood furniture, and tasteful fabrics combine in the three individually styled bedrooms. Discerning travelers know that it's all about the small details, and here the owners don't disappoint. And the prices are an absolute bargain. It has Wi-Fi in the common areas. Strictly no smoking. I love it!

HOTEL DEVILLE

507-206-3100
Fax: 507-206-3111
www.devillehotel.com.pa
Avenida Beatriz Cabal and Calle 50
Expensive

A steadfast favorite of travelers seeking deluxe old-world digs, the DeVille harks back to the era of DeLesseps in mood and style. The exterior, with its mansard roof, seems a transplant from Paris. The eclectic decor is more international, melding Oriental rugs with mahogany antiques and contemporary art. Each of the 33 rooms is distinct, though most sparkle with marble underfoot, and orthopedic mattresses and Egyptian cotton linens guarantee contented slumber. The highly ranked Ten Bistro restaurant is here. While not quite up to the superb standards of the Bristol, this boutique hotel in the thick of the dining and entertainment district makes a fine choice.

Budget Hotels

HOSTAL LA CASA DE CARMEN

507-263-4366
www.lacasadecarmen.net
Calle 1ra, El Carmen #32
Inexpensive

This quaint home on the east side of the city offers some of the more simple digs in the city. In addition to a six-bed dorm, it has seven small bedrooms individually styled with their own color schemes. While frugally appointed, they're quite charming and perfect for cost-conscious travelers. There's a library with Internet, a colorful communal kitchen, and a laundry.

HOSTEL MAMALLENA

507-6676-6163
www.mamallena.com
Calle 38 Oeste, La Exposición
Between Avenida Simón Bolívar and Avenida Peru, in a leafy middle-class area, this Australian-owned backpackers' hostel gets high marks for cleanliness and security. It has three dorms and 12 private rooms, all air-conditioned. Amenities include Wi-Fi, Skype, plus free Internet, movies, and coffee.

LUNA'S CASTLE HOSTEL

507-262-1540
www.lunascastlehostel.com
Calle 9na Este 3-28, Casco Viejo
Inexpensive

The choice spot of backpackers, this hostel occupies a creaky old colonial mansion close to the shore. It's the best of all worlds for impecunious and gregarious travelers seeking Spanish-colonial quaint and laid-back, youthful vibes. A bed in the dorm room costs a mere $12, including pancake breakfast, free coffee, free Internet, and

Wi-Fi 24/7. It has lockers and storage, plus laundry, and you can ease back in three "chill rooms" where movies are shown. The place is adorned with colorful retro-style groovy art.

Generic Hotels

COUNTRY INN & SUITES PANAMÁ CANAL

507-211-4500
Fax: 507-211-4501
www.countryinns.com/panamacanalpan
Avenida Amador and Avenida Pelicano, Amador
Inexpensive to Moderate
The best of both worlds sums up this hotel's location on the Amador peninsula. Take your pick of rooms looking west over the Bridge of the Americas and Canal entrance or east towards Casco Viejo and the sky-scrapers of modern Panamá City. All 150 rooms have balconies for better enjoy-ing the views. Decor is homey: this *is* a Country Inn & Suites, so don't expect lavish styling. All have high-speed Internet, plus coffeemakers, hair dryers, and other to-be-expected mod-cons. It has an Internet room, plus gym, and a TGI Friday's restaurant.

CROWNE PLAZA

507-206-5555
Fax: 507-206-5557
www.ichotelsgroup.com
Avenida Manuel Espinosa. Bautista
Moderate
This high-rise hotel is perfectly positioned for business folk, being in the midst of the commercial zone. It's as you would expect a Crowne Plaza to be, with comfy furnishings and plenty of essential ameni-ties, such as hair dryers and Wi-Fi (for a fee). The rooftop pool is a good spot for laz-ing, and there's a sport bar plus business center. It was most recently renovated in 2008.

HOLIDAY INN

507-317-4000
Fax: 507-317-4001
www.hinnpanama.com
Avenida Oma Torrijos Herrera, Ciudad del Saber, Clayton
In the "City of Knowledge," just minutes from the Miraflores Locks, this rather institutional, eight-story hotel is handy for all manner of sightseeing beyond the city. The 137 rooms and suites are actually quite delightful and have sufficient amenities (from 29-inch cable TVs to Wi-Fi) to com-pete with the far more expensive big boys in town. Still, if it's the city itself you're seeking this hotel is a bit far out to make sense. Nor does it have a restaurant: your options are a bar and a café.

INTERCONTINENTAL MIRAMAR PANAMÁ

507-206-8888
Fax: 507-223-4891
www.miramarpanama.com
Miramar Plaza, Avenida Balboa
Expensive
This is by far my favorite of the city's upscale high-rise hotels. First, its situa-tion, close-up to the bay in Miramar, offers spectacular views. Needless to say, the higher up, the better: it soars 25 stories. Walls of glass in guest rooms guarantee that every one (and everyone) is a winner. The 183 contemporary-themed guest quarters are luxurious and fitted with DVDs, Wi-Fi, and other mod-cons. The full-service busi-ness center and banqueting facilities impress, and you get a splendid restaurant, plus Turkish bath, spa, gym, and outdoor pool.

PANAMÁ MARRIOTT HOTEL

507-210-9100
Fax: 507-210-9110
www.marriott.com
Calle 52, Calle Ricardo Arias
Expensive

Soaring 20 stories over downtown El Cangrejo, this business-oriented hotel offers elegance, heaps of amenities, and a great location for visitors keen to partake of the city's nightlife. It has its own casino and huge convention facilities. I like to hang by the lovely outdoor pool. Its 287 rooms and eight suites are graciously appointed and offer sensational views from upper levels. Hair dryers and robes are standard.

PLAZA PAITILLA INN

507-208-0600
Fax: 507-208-0619
www.plazapaitillainn.com
Vía Italia, Punta Paitilla
Moderate
Competing with the Intercontinental for high-rise style, this modern, circular skyscraper boasts 272 air-conditioned bedrooms that each features an entire wall of glass. Hence, stupendous panoramic views. Decor is moderately elegant. It has a pool, gym, business center, and café, and restaurants and a casino are a stone's throw away.

RADISSON DECAPOLIS

507-215-5000
Fax 507-215-5175
www.radisson.com/panamacitypan
Avenida Balboa-Multicentro
Expensive
Reflecting Panamá City's 21st-century chic, this towering Space Age hotel rises 29 stories over the Multicentro complex. From outside, the structure appears to be made almost entirely of green-tinted glass. Inside makes you do a double take. Is it a hotel or a museum of modern art? A massive stainless steel sculpture inspired by the statues of Easter Island guards the lobby. Decor throughout is minimalist. The mood hip. The slick martini bar is *the* place to be for city sophisticates. The sushi bar is no less stylish. There are two other restaurants, plus a casino, and impressive business and meeting facilities. And the 300

bedrooms—done up in clinical whites, jade greens, and chocolates, and replete with all necessary amenities, from coffeemaker to high-speed Internet—are perhaps the most youthful and trendy in Panamá City.

SHERATON PANAMÁ HOTEL & CONVENTION CENTER

507-305-5100
Fax: 507-265-3550
www.starwoodhotels.com
Vía Israel and Calle 77
Expensive
Formerly the Caesar Park Hotel, this highrise is a city landmark. Rising over the Atlapa Convention Center, it relies heavily on conventioneer business, but is popular with tour groups. You're too far out, however, for sightseeing by foot; if you plan on exploring Panamá City, you'll ring up quite some fares using cabs. A major plus are the sweeping city views: make sure you get a west-facing room. The 362 formerly weary rooms (including 18 suites) have recently been upgraded and this hotel now shines. Furnishings are contemporary and classy, though the Sheraton retains its mock-Spanish colonial elements, such as the indoor fountains and arched doorways. Potted palms abound. Shopaholics will appreciate its numerous boutiques, plus there's a spa, an excellent café, and choice of restaurants. And the spacious pool area, surrounded by palms, is a lovely spot to relax and bag some rays. However, we don't like having to pay for the Wi-Fi service in bedrooms, which have flat-screen TVs, in-room safes, and comfy beds.

VENETO HOTEL & CASINO

507-340-8686
Fax: 507-340-8899
www.venetocasino.com
Vía Veneto between Cía España and El Cangrejo
Moderate
With its 24-hour casino dominating the

ground floor, there's no doubt what this hotel's main raison d'etre is. Nonetheless, the 301 guest rooms are classy, even luxurious. Flat-screen TVs, Wi-Fi, chocolaty leather sofas and tawny color schemes, and marble-clad bathrooms make these among the most desirable rooms in town. The hotel's numerous restaurants include sushi and steak outlets. There's a spa. And its location in the heart of the financial and shopping district is a bonus for business folk and shopaholics.

Resort Hotels and Spas

INTERCONTINENTAL PLAYA BONITA RESORT & SPA

877-800-1690
Fax: 507-206-8870
www.playabonitapanama.com
Playa Kobbe, 4 miles west of Panamá City
Moderate to Expensive
Just a few minutes' drive west of the city, this sprawling beach resort has a lovely location, despite its rather mediocre brown sand beach and (it is claimed) polluted ocean waters. The facilities impress, not least the 20 acres (8 ha) of forest-fringed lawns with four swimming pools. I love the classy contemporary sophistication of the 300 bedrooms, which have king beds, orthopedic mattresses, and Wi-Fi. Another highlight: a 10,000-square-foot spa.

NIKKI BEACH HOTEL PANAMÁ CITY

c/o 786-515-1130
www.nikkibeachpanama.com
Avenida Balboa, Punta Paitilla
Very Expensive
Slated to open in 2011, this 52-story condo-hotel promises to take Panamá City's hotel scene to whole new heights. In fact, the first city hotel of Miami's renowned Nikki Beach group, it's billed as Panamá's "first six-star condo hotel" and is intended to woo the sexy moneyed Miami crowd with its sensual contemporary decor and hotter than hot day-and-night party scene. It will have 200 rooms and suites with state-of-the-art fixtures, such as free Wi-Fi and flat-screen HDTVs, and panoramic views through walls of glass. Rising over Multiplaza, it will feature signature restaurants, a swimming pool, luxury spa, rooftop heliport, plus the Casa Nikki Night Club, 46 floors above Panamá City.

DINING

The capital city is a veritable potlatch of fine dining, with something for every taste. Many of the nation's best restaurants are here, spanning the globe with their international flavors, as appropriate for a city that plays such an important role on the world stage. In addition to the full-on restaurants, including those in the upscale hotels, consider eating at simple *fondas*, small kiosk-type restaurants that serve filling meals to go.

CAFÉ CAPPUCCINO

507-264-0106
Avenida Balboa and Calle Anastacio Ruíz, Marbella
A popular lunch stop for the local business crowd, this airy place is also one of my favorite spots for an inexpensive lunch, to be enjoyed in the well-lit, clinically clean interior, or outside on the shaded patio. The eclectic menu includes ceviche, sandwiches, chicken *flautas*, delicious fresh fruit *batidos* (shakes), plus scrumptious baked desserts, and coffees. Open: Monday through Saturday 7 AM–9 PM. Inexpensive to Moderate.

EGO

507-262-2045
Calle Antonio J. de Sucre, Plaza Bolívar, Casco Viejo
Cuisine: Panamanian/Spanish

A cosmopolitan bar facing into Plaza Bolívar, this sexy little space serves delicious tapas such as spicy ceviche, cilantro beef skewers, and delicious shrimp brochette. Tables spill onto the cobbled street, but you can dine in the air-conditioned interior on hot summer days. The cocktails are killer, but it's de rigueur here to savor a chilled pitcher of hearty sangría. This is a great place to romance a date or rekindle a long-lost love. Ha, ha . . . next door, the same owner runs Narciso (get it? ego and narcissism!), serving Italian dishes. Open: Monday through Saturday 5–11:30 PM. Inexpensive to Moderate.

EURASIA

507-264-7859
eurasia_restaurant@hotmail.com
Edificio La Trona, Calle 48, Bella Vista
Cuisine: Oriental fusion
Unique among Central American restaurants for being the only one to receive a five-diamond rating from the American Academy of Hospitality, this marvelous option has gourmands salivating over its stylishly presented French-Asian fusion dishes. I, too, left enraptured after a dinner of shrimp rolls, followed by grilled tuna fillet with caramelized onions in Dijon mustard sauce, and the decadent house chocolate soufflé called *fondant.* The setting is perfect: hosts Kim and Gloria Young's fine-dining restaurant is housed in an aged mansion furnished in quasi-Vietnamese fashion and enlivened with eclectic works of art. Conscientious service. Open: Monday through Friday noon–3 PM and 7–10 PM, Saturday 7–10 PM. Moderate to Expensive.

HABIBIS

507-264-3647
www.habibispanama.com
Calle 48 and Calle Uruguay, Bella Vista
Cuisine: Lebanese
Young bohemian types gather here to smoke the shisha pipes and carouse. The Levantine fare seems like an afterthought! The mellow venue is a converted colonial mansion in the epicenter of the city's most popular party strip. Now infused with a contemporary motif, Habibis is a two-fer venue. Choose the open downstairs patio for dining on such staples as hummus, shish kebab, and shaslik, or *arañitas* (breaded baby octopuses) and more Western fare. Upstairs, the tented lounge resembles a sultan's tent, assisted by a belly dancer who usually performs on weekend nights, when it's one of *the* happenin' spots in the city. In June 2009, it began offering live jazz on Thursday and Friday nights. Open: Tuesday through Sunday 6–midnight. Moderate to Expensive.

INDIGO

507-228-1822
Avenida Central between Calle 2 Oeste and Calle 3 Oeste
www.indigopanama.com
Cuisine: Indian-Moroccan fusion
Opened in July 2008 and inspired by an Indian-Moorish aesthetic, this contemporary restaurant is a veritable Aladdin's cave of *salas* inspired by Moroccan gardens, Andalucian patios, and hip European lounge-bar themes. Sexy. Stylish. *Muy romántico!* It even screens Bollywood movies while you dine to ethnic music such as tribal drums (live!) and Middle Eastern chants. Start and end your night with mojitos and martinis at the Buddha Bar. Chef Liz Araúz is a wizard in the kitchen, where she oversees creation of delicious falafels and samosas, and such entrées as green chicken curry served Thai style with Japanese rice, and lamb cubes Caribbean-style with caramelized onions and couscous. The artistic presentation is museum standard. Open: Monday through Wednesday 6 PM–1 AM; Thursday through Saturday 6 PM–3:30 AM. Expensive to Very Expensive.

LIMONCILLO PONY CLUB

507-270-0807
www.limoncillo.com
Calle 69 Este, San Francisco
Cuisine: Fusion

Occupying new digs since 2008, this remake of one of the city's foremost restaurants reflects the evolving tastes and styles of Chef Clara Icaza and co-owner/designer Jennifer Spector. Jennifer is responsible for the sophisticated contemporary decor that also plays up the past with blond woods, slates, and earth-toned walls festooned with black-and-white prints of yesteryear Panamá City. Icaza taps her broad experience as a chef in New York City, Northern California, and Panamá to create Mediterranean-inspired tropical dishes highlighted by unusual pairings. You'll start, though, with the restaurant's signature basket of fresh-baked breads. Appetizers? Try an East Indian *paratha* flatbread with yellow pea purée, or a Portobella Napoleon with goat cheese and pesto. Main course? A creamy seafood risotto, or grilled sea bass with white bean purée and spicy lemon preserve. Reservations essential. Open: Monday through Friday noon–2:30 PM and 7–10:30 PM (Friday until 11 PM), Saturday 7–10 PM. Moderate to Expensive.

MADAME CHANG

507-269-1313
madamechange@cableonda.net
Calle 48, Bella Vista
Cuisine: Asian fusion

Patrons make the trek from many a mile to savor the delights at what has been acclaimed as Central America's finest Oriental restaurant. Madame Sui Mee Chang and her daughter Yolanda oversee this sophisticated place (the dress code is smart casual), where a classy peach and beige decor proves inviting. The menu features Mandarin classics such as roast duck, and other dishes with a local twist, such as seafood dishes using corvina (sea bass)

with mustard leaves, clams in black-bean sauce, and róbalo (snook) steamed with ginger and green onions. Thai dishes are also there for the asking. Open: Monday through Saturday noon–3 PM and 6:30–11 PM, Sunday noon–10 PM. Expensive to Very Expensive.

MANOLO CARACOL

507-228-4640
www.manolocaracol.net
Calle 3ra and Avenida Central, Casco Viejo
Cuisine: Spanish

Take a tumbledown colonial structure. Spruce it up. Enliven it with eclectic artistic decor and an open kitchen. Then create a scintillating Spanish-inspired menu using the freshest of local ingredients. The result is sure to be a hit with discerning gourmands. And so it is with Manolo Caracol, the genius of Spanish-born owner-chef Manolo Madueño. It serves from prix fixe lunch and dinner menus featuring a variety of tapas, such as green mango ceviche, and delicious gazpacho Andaluz with cucumber and sorbet. Its art gallery features religious artifacts and changing exhibitions. Open: Monday through Saturday noon–3 PM and 7–10:30 PM. Expensive.

NIKO'S CAFÉ BALBOA

507-228-8888
www.nikoscafe.com
Steven's Circle, Balboa

Occupying the former Balboa bowling alley, this popular cafeteria-style restaurant was founded by Niko, a Greek immigrant who went from rags to riches. Today Niko's has six other outlets citywide, but the original is still the best. The seemingly endless buffet options please locals, who've cottoned to good, filling fare served 24/7 at fair prices. Whether you're seeking American breakfasts or T-bone steaks, Greek lunches or local staples, you'll find it laid out to heap on your tray. Open: 24 hours. Inexpensive to Moderate.

PALMS

507-265-7256

www.palmsrestaurant.net

palmsrestaurant@cableonda.net

Calle 48, Bella Vista

Cuisine: Fusion

This chic restaurant impressed me mightily when I dined here shortly after its opening in 2007. It still does. First, I love the suave avant-garde decor that makes great use of glass walls, brushed steel rails, and halogen lighting. No wonder it draws a sexy mon-eyed crowd! The fusion menu spans the globe. My recommendations include a mesclun salad with pear, nuts, and goat cheese, or grilled octopus *escabeche* with capers and sweet red peppers for starters; and perhaps the pumpkin ravioli in sage butter sauce, or beef medallions in three-pepper-and-coffee sauce, served with vegetables and mashed potatoes. Extensive wine list. Impeccable service. Open: Monday through Friday noon–2:30 PM and 6:30–10:30 PM, Saturday 6:30–11 PM. Expensive to Very Expensive.

S'CENA

507-228-4011

www.scenaplatea.com

Calle 1ra, Casco Viejo

Cuisine: Mediterranean

The city's bohemian crowd flocks to this atmospheric restaurant, upstairs in a beautifully restored colonial mansion in the heart of Casco Viejo. Exposed brick walls adorned with oversize prints of yesteryear Casco Viejo infuse this gem with tremendous ambience, assisted by live jazz in the downstairs bar (Platea). Spanish Chef Luis Losa is in charge of the kitchen, which delivers creative Mediterranean classics, such as paella, and broader ranging fare such as shellfish sautéed in Pernod, and filet mignon with portobello, shiitake, and cremini mushrooms. The place gets packed on weekends; reservations essential. Large wine selection. Open: Tuesday through Sunday noon–4 PM and 7:30–11 PM. Expensive.

SUSHI ITTO

507-265-1222

www.sushi-itto.com

Plaza Obarrio, between Calle Samuel Lewis and Calle 55

Cuisine: Japanese

Sure, it's a Mexican chain restaurant, but that doesn't mean squat. This stylishly contemporary restaurant featuring glass walls and blazing-white halogen lighting does a reasonable (although far from gourmet) job with fresh seafood, including teppanyaki and sushi, with plenty of fancy rolls to choose from. Oddly, the menu even has some pasta dishes. The prices here represent a solid value. Open: Daily noon–1 AM. Expensive.

AL TAMBOR DE LA ALEGRÍA

507-314-3380

Calzada de Amador, Isla Perico, Amador

Cuisine: Panamanian

True, it's touristy, but this colorful restaurant (the name means Drum of Happiness), in the Brisas de Amador shopping center near the tip of the Amador Causeway, gives you value for money if you don't mind (or are seeking) a schmaltzy "play up the native theme" experience. It serves traditional *típico* (Panamánian) dishes. Waitresses dress in *polleras*. And it hosts an hour-long folkloric dinner show on Tuesday through Saturday. Reservations essential. Open: Monday through Saturday 6–midnight, Sunday 9–11 AM, noon–3, and 6–midnight. Expensive.

TEN BISTRO

507-213-8250

www.tenbistro.com

Calle 50 and Beatriz Cabal, El Cangrejo

Cuisine: Fusion

Affixed to the Hotel DeVille, acclaimed Chef Fabien Migny's trendy bistro plays the "ten" theme to the max. For example, the menu features 10 meat dishes, 10 seafood dishes, and 10 desserts. All supposedly priced at $10 (actually, some dishes are considerably more). Migny was a co-founder of the Eurasia restaurant, and the French-Asian fusion is paramount on the menu. Prawn spring rolls into a tropical sauce, and saffron crab soup in puff pastry typify the starter list. And imagine beef tenderloin Indochine (with Chinese mushrooms and mustard leaves), or grouper poached in coconut milk, for main course. Decor is chic and contemporary, with a surfeit of whites and tangerines. Progressive house music adds to the trendy vibe. Open: Monday through Saturday noon–3 PM and 6–10 PM, Sunday noon–10 PM. Moderate to Expensive.

LAS TINAJAS
507-263-7890
www.tinajaspanama.com
Calle 51, Bella Vista
Cuisine: Panamanian
More or less copying the theme of Al Tambor de la Alegría, but handily right in the midst of Bella Vista, this tourist-oriented, country-themed restaurant is known for its traditional fare (think of ceviche, fried calamari, and roast pork with yuca) and folkloric shows, held each Tuesday through Saturday nights, when an optional fixed menu is offered. The broader menu is actually wide-ranging. Reservations essential for dinner shows. Open: Daily 11:30 AM–11 PM. Expensive.

Food Purveyors

BAKERIES/COFFEE SHOPS

Café Coca Cola (507-228-7687; Avenida Central and Calle 11, Salsipuedes) Okay, it's not *really* a café, but this is as good as it gets for a slice of working-class Panamanian life and a hearty *pintao* (a demitasse of thick black coffee splashed with a few drops of cream). You can even get pancakes and eggs. Also delicious desserts. However, I'm not sure what to read into the dentist's sign on the upper window.

Petit Paris (507-391-8778; Via Argentina and Calle Jose Marti, Bella Vista) An intimate French-owned pastry shop selling delicious breads, cakes, pastries, chocolates, and desserts including tiramisu. Also prepares salads and sandwiches. Indulge yourself on the patio seating with a strawberry cheesecake and gourmet coffee.

BURGERS, PIZZAS, SANDWICHES, AND FAST FOOD

Boulevard Café (507-225-0914; Avenida Balboa and Calle 33 Este, Caledonia) Unpretentious Panamanian 1950s-style diner that draws local politicos for cheap sandwiches, especially with roasted meats. Also serves *sancocho* stew and local dishes. Not a tourist in sight. Open: Monday through Saturday 7 AM–1AM.

Burgues (507-394-1102; Calle 47, off Calle Uruguay, Bella Vista) Glamorous minimalist decor and gauche chandeliers—perhaps a play on the Spanish word *burgues*, for bourgeois!—in this tiny but trendy burger joint also serving chicken wings, chili con carne, and Levantine dishes such as babaganoush and hummus. But you come for the 6- or 8-ounce burgers, which here reach heights of excellence for Panamá. Try the Swiss cheese, or the cheese and bacon whopper. They come with waffle fries. Bargain priced. Open: Monday through Wednesday 11 AM–12:30 AM, Thursday through Saturday 11 AM–3 AM, Sunday 11 AM–midnight.

Casa Vegetariana (507-269-1876; Center Calle Ricardo Arias and Avenida 3 Sur) Operated by Taiwanese immigrants, this sparsely furnished hole-in-the-wall serves tofu, soy meat, and other vegetarian dishes buffet style, all at a mere 50 cents per portion. Four portions fill your plate for $2. One extra order gets you a free miso soup. Homemade natural juices, such as passionfruit (*maracuay*) and pineapple nectar. Also has outlets off Vía Veneto (in El Cangrejo) and Plaza New York (in Marbella).

Market Steak House and Wine Bar (507-264-9401; Calle 47, off Calle Uruguay, Bella Vista; www.marketpanama.com) This copycat to Burgues (actually, Market got here first) with a cool, upscale ambience and a broad menu that spans tapas such as ceviche and crab cakes; seafood and steaks, including Black Angus filet; and divine desserts, not least chocolate brownie with vanilla ice cream. But if it's a fat melt-in-your-mouth gourmet burger you're seeking, opt for any of six types, including a chili burger. My favorite? The blue cheese burger. Open: Monday through Friday 11–11, Saturday 10:30–11, Sunday 11–9:30.

Ristorante y Pizzería Romanaccio (507-264-9482; Calle Anastacio Ruíz and Calle 53 Este, Marbella) Perhaps the best pizzería in town, although certainly not gourmet. Your choices are many, and portions are huge. Also serves Italian staples, including risotto with porcini mushrooms—the house special. Decor is quintessentially Italian.

SWEETS AND TREATS

Granclement (507-208-0737; www.granclement.com; Avenida Central and Calle 3ra, Casco Viejo) When the heat gets to you while exploring Casco Viejo, you'll be thankful to stumble upon this gourmet ice cream store with flavors ranging the spectrum of tropical fruits. There are also some strange homemade flavors, such as delicious Earl Grey tea. Also sells sorbets and meringues. Open: Monday through Thursday 11:30–8 PM, Friday and Saturday 11:30–11, Sunday 12:30–8.

CULTURE

Architecture

ARCHIVOS NACIONALES AND EDIFICIO DE LA LOTERÍA

Avenida Cuba and Calle 31 Este, La Exposición

Occupying much of Plaza Victor Julio Gutiérrez, in the midst of the La Exposición district, this building is the headquarters of the national lottery. The twice-weekly drawing is held on the north side, in the roofed plaza on Avenida Peru, and features folkloric music and dance.

On the north side of Avenida Peru, opposite the plaza, the neoclassical national archives—**Archivo Nacionales** (507-501-6150; www.archivonacional.gob.pa)—is fronted by Corinthian columns.

ADMINISTRATOR'S HOUSE

107 Heights Road at Quarry Road, Quarry Heights

Although not open to the public, from the road you can view the palatial two-story former mansion of the commanding U.S. generals for the Canal Zone, between 1914 and 1997. It occupies a strategic location on the northern slope of Cerro Ancón, and was placed here (after originally being built near the Culebra Cut) so that the governor would have a grandstand view of the Canal. It is now used as a VIP guesthouse.

GORGAS HOSPITAL

Calle Culebra, Ancón

Whereas the U.S. built its Canal Zone administrative and residential headquarters on the west side of Cerro Ancón, the French had established their settlement on

Casco Viejo

Known also by the moniker Casco Antiguo, and more colloquially by locals as San Felipe, Casco Viejo (Old District) was originally founded in 1673 by survivors of Henry Morgan's sacking of Panamá la Vieja. It was erected with fortified walls (of which only small remnants remain) and covered 109 acres (44 ha). Its more than 900 structures blend architectural styles from Spain, France, and the United States, reflecting the influence that each had on the city through the centuries.

Earthquakes toppled many of the earliest buildings. Other were destroyed in devastating fires, notably that of 1878, which destroyed one-third of the city. Yet enough remains that in 1997 the entire historic district was declared a UNESCO World Heritage Site of Historic Importance. Today a world (and centuries) apart from the glittering skyscrapers of Marbella and Bella Vista, this lived-in museum is by far the most fascinating part of Panamá City. That year an ambitious restoration project was conceived, under the care of the **Oficina del Casco Antiguo** (507-209-6300; www.cascoantiguo.gob.pa), which provides *asistentes de turismo* (licensed guides).

The quarter is a time warp, still timeworn in parts, yet vibrant from an influx of entrepreneurs that have turned Casco Viejo into a South Beach-style hotbed of bohemian cafés, restaurants, nightclubs, accommodations, and other colonial confections in stone. There are also dozens of fascinating historic buildings and eclectic museums facing onto cobbled plazas. And the mood is exquisite, like a tropical version of New Orleans, with its wrought-iron balconies, cascades of colorful flowers, wrought-iron street lamps, and colonial façades painted in various tropical ice cream pastels. Walking these narrow brick-paved streets brings the history books to life.

While the gentrification continues to inch through the district, caution is still required, as pockets of poverty and high crime remain, and the increase in camera-toting tourists and snazzy cars with iPods on the front seat has spawned an increase in opportunistic crime. No longer do you have to follow the prescriptions of yesteryear guidebooks that warned against entering Casco Viejo unless armed with a weapon, but the area immediately west of Plaza Herrera and extending into the truly scary Barrio Chorrillo is to be avoided.

You may recognize many of the venues as settings in the James Bond movie, *Quantum of Solace* (2008).

the northeast side, where in 1881 they erected the wooden L'Hôpital Notre Dame du Canal. The hospital expanded rapidly after 1907, when the U.S. military took over, turning the sprawling complex into a major center for research and treatment of tropical diseases. In 1928 it was renamed Gorgas Army Community Hospital in honor of Major General William Crawford Gorgas (1854–1920), the U.S. military's Chief Sanitary Officer (and later Surgeon General of the U.S. Army) whose efforts to eradicate yellow fever and malaria ultimately made construction of the canal possible. In 1999, after passing into Panamá's hands, it was renamed the Hospital Oncológico, dedicated to cancer.

The original concrete Renaissance-style building, with its flanking staircases (engraved with the words GORGAS HOSPITAL), is suitably monumental in scale, and features a two-story portico topped by green copper domes. Several dozen other buildings have since been added in various styles. Sprawling up the flanks of Cerro Ancón, they include the Ministry of Health and the city morgue. Immediately north and uphill of the hospital, is the **Palacio de**

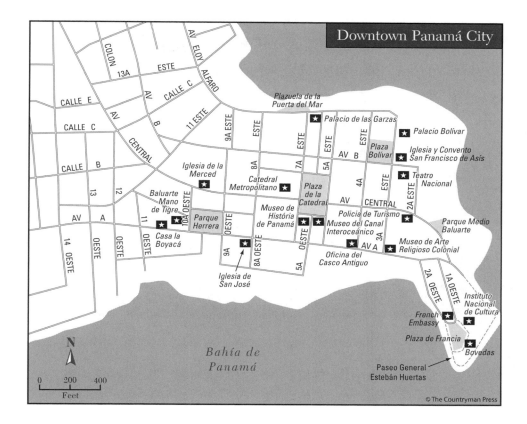

Downtown Panamá City

Plazuela de la
Puerta del Mar

★ Palacio de las Garzas

★ Palacio Bolívar

Plaza
Bolívar

★ Iglesia y Convento
San Francisco de Asís

Iglesia de la
Merced ★

Catedral
Metropólitano ★

Plaza
de la
Catedral

★ Teatro
Nacional

Baluarte
Mano
de Tigre ★

Museo de
História
de Panamá ★ ★

Policía de Turismo ★

Parque Medio
Baluarte

Parque
Herrera ★

Museo del Canal
Interoceánico

Museo de Arte
Religioso Colonial ★

Casa la
Boyacá ★

Oficina del
Casco Antiguo

Iglesia de
San José

Instituto
Nacional
de Cultura ★

French ★
Embassy

Plaza de Francia ★

★ Bovedas

*Bahía de
Panamá*

Paseo General
Estebán Huertas

N

0   200   400
Feet

© The Countryman Press

Justicia Gil Ponce, housing the **Corte
Suprema de Justícia** (507-212-7300),
Panamá's Supreme Court.

   Just below the hospital, peek in at the
lovely **Cathedral of St. Luke** (507-262-
1280), built in 1923 in Romanesque fashion
and graced by Corinthian columns.

PALACIO DE LAS GARZAS

507-227-9740 (Oficina de Guías del
Despacho de la Primera Dama)
Fax: 507-228-2521
gbernal@presidencia.gob.pa
www.presidencia.gob.pa/ver_nodo_
palacio.php?cod=95
Avenida Eloy Alfaro, between Calles 6 Este
and 7 Este, Casco Viejo
By appointment only, with 24 hours written
notice; tours three times daily, Tuesday,
Thursday, and Friday A dress code applies.

Admission: Free
Also known as the Palacio Presidencial, and
taking up the entire block north of Plaza de
la Catedral, this beautiful Moorish-styled
building is the official residence of the
Panamanian President and First Lady,
whose office oversees visits. The palace was
initiated in 1673 as the residence of the
Spanish governor. It gained its current
styling in 1921 and has served through the
centuries as a customs house, courthouse,
college, and bank, finally becoming the
presidential residence in 1855. Its name—
Palace of the Herons—derives from the
herons that strut around the marble Patio
Andaluz, a tradition dating back to 1922
when white herons were given to President
Porras. Note the mother-of-pearl inlay in
the patio fountain.

   A tour is well worth arranging.

Roberto Lewis murals in Palacio de las Garzas

Highlights include an upstairs gallery of life-sized bronze statues of the *virtudes* (Virtues); the Sala Cabinete, where the president's weekly cabinet meetings are held; the Salón Amarillo, where all the most important acts of State are performed; and the Salón Los Tamarindos, the official State dining room. Together the latter salons boast a series of incredible ceiling and wall murals in the style of Maxfield Parrish, by Panamanian artist Roberto Lewis (1874–1949).

The surrounding streets are closed to traffic, and pedestrians are subject to search at the guard posts.

PANAMÁ CANAL ADMINISTRATION BUILDING

507-272-1111
www.pancanal.com
101 Heights Road, Balboa
Daily 24 hours
Admission: Free
Inaugurated on July 15, 1914, the monu-mental headquarters of Canal operations commands a hill at the northwestern foot of Cerro Ancón and offers fine views over Balboa township and the distant Canal. It was built in the shape of an E by New York-based architect Austin W. Lord in a somber classical Roman style. It still serves as the headquarters of the Panamá Canal Authority (ACP). The two-story domed rotunda lobby is encircled by eight marble columns that were accidentally installed upside down. Note the busts of Ferdinand DeLesseps, Theodore Roosevelt, and Emperor Charles V in the alcoves. The upper level is surrounded by the **Panamá Canal Murals**. These four magnificent and enormous paintings depict the stupendous accomplishment of Canal construction (the individual themes depict workers toiling at the Gaillard Cut, the Gatún dam spillway, a lock miter gate, and the Miraflores Locks). They're by New York artist William B. Van Ingen (1858–1955), famous for his murals in the Library of Congress in Washington,

Mural by William Van Ingen in the Panamá Canal Administration Building, Panamá City

D.C. He actually made only charcoal sketches while in Panamá in 1914; the murals were painted in his New York studio.

When sated, nip up the marble-and-mahogany staircase to view 3-D relief maps from the construction era and to admire additional canal-related paintings in an art gallery devoted to the theme (most works are by noted Panamanian artist Al Sprague; www.panamaart.com).

PUENTE DE LAS AMÉRICAS
Interamerican Highway
The cantilevered Bridge of the Americas was the first bridge to span the Canal, when completed in 1962 as the Thatcher Ferry Bridge, prior to which a ferry transported automobiles across the southern mouth of the waterway. The gracefully arched span is 5,425 feet (1,654 m) long in 14 spans, and rises 384 feet high (118 m). Originally it carried the Interamerican Highway, which since 2004 now crosses the Canal via the

Centennial Bridge, opened in that year. The Bridge of the Americas cannot be appreciated by driving over it. You have to view it front on, as it were, from either the Calzada de Amador or the water.

Puente de las Americas, Panamá

A Walking Tour of Balboa

Laid out at the western base of Cerro Ancón, the city's highest point, the leafy district of Balboa occupies the land immediately east of the Canal and was laid out as the administration center and a residential district for Zonians (U.S. Canal workers and their families). Today this district makes for a delightful stroll along palm-shaded boulevards and streets lined with U.S.-colonial-style buildings in tropical vernacular style.

Begin your walk with a tour of the **Panamá Canal Administration Building** (see separate entry). Then, descend the flight of 110 steps that leads west to the **Goethals Monument**. This cubist monolith of gray marble was erected in

Goethals Monument, Balboa, Panamá City

1954 to the memory of Colonel George W. Goethals (1858–1928), the chief engineer in charge of Canal construction from 1907 to 1914. The upturned oblong rises from a circular pool and features a water cascade comprising three salient flanges representing the three sets of Canal locks.

Next, turn north and walk 328 feet (100 m) to Avenida Roosevelt. On the far side, peruse the 95-ton **Bucyrus steam shovel**—one of dozens of similar shovels used during Canal construction. Betwixt monument and shovel you'll pass the **Centro de Capacitación Ascanio Arosemena** (507-272-9249 or 272-8550; Edificio 704; Monday through Friday 9–5; free), the training center for Canal employees. Formerly it was the Balboa High School—the Alma Mater for thousands of students during the existence of the now extinct U.S. Panamá Canal Zone. On January 9, 1964, the school became the ignition point for the Flag Riots after high school students from Panamá's Instituto Nacional got into an altercation with students and parents from the school. Violence erupted and spread throughout the Canal Zone, resulting, during the ensuing four days, in the death of 21 Panamanians. The school's entrance is now a pantheon—the **Monumento a los Mártires**—commemorating those Panamanians killed on the Day of the Martyrs. It is surrounded by 21 columns, each inscribed with the name of one of the deceased. The flagpole that sparked the initial riot is no longer here. After perusing the monument, nip inside the Center, where two floors displays memorabilia relating to the Canal construction, on two levels.

TORRE BBVA

Calles 42 and 43, Avenida Balboa
In a city remarkable for its dramatic contemporary skyscrapers, this graceful edifice built in 1979 is hard to beat. The headquarters of the Banco Bilbao Vizcaya Argentaria, its form is very simple and comprises an upended oblong sheathed in blue-tinted glass. The beauty derives from its sweeping

side panels, curved and layered like onion rings.

Art and Art Galleries

Centro Cultural Casa Góngora (506-212-0388; Avenida Central and Calle 4 Oeste, Casco Viejo; free) The oldest house in Casco Viejo, dating from 1756, was once the home of a Spanish pearl

Return to the Goethals Monument and follow palm-lined **El Prado** Boulevard (formally named Avenida 9 de Enero), westward. Exactly 110 feet (33.5 m) wide, this broad boulevard extends symbolically a full 1,000 feet (305 m)—the exact dimensions of a lock chamber.

About halfway down, on your left, at Edificio 714, pop into the **Centro de Información Propuesta Tercer Juego de Esclusas** (507-272-2278, closed Sunday) to learn about the Canal Expansion currently underway. It has superb audio-visual exhibits. Then continue south to **Stevens Circle**, a small rotunda with a small monument honoring John F. Stevens (1853–1943), Chief Engineer of the Canal project 1905 to 1907. You're now facing the Art Deco **Teatro Balboa** (507-228-0327). Cross the road and enter this architectural gem, which opened as the Electric Theater movie house in 1946. Catercorner, on the northeast side of Stevens Circle, the former Balboa bowling alley is today the original **Niko's Café** (507-228-8888); it's worth popping in for great food and to view the historic photos of the Canal Zone and old Panamá.

Bucyrus steam shovel outside the Panamá Administration Building

Continue by turning south onto Avenida Arnulfo Arias Madrid (formerly Balboa Road). Dominating the skyline ahead, on your right, is the pink-and-white Gothic **Union Church** (507-314-1004), consecrated in 1926. Climb the stairs to view the beautiful stained-glass windows. Crossing Calle La Boca, you arrive at the **Monumento Homenaje a la Democracía**. This huge Homage to Democracy by avant-garde Colombian artist Hector Lombana (1930–) was erected in 2002, replacing the ruins of the old Balboa police station, which the U.S. military blasted into oblivion in 1989 during Operation Just Cause. The somewhat grotesque sculpture—in the form of a spearlike sliver piercing a circular fountain—honors three-time (and thrice deposed) Panamanian President Arnulfo Arias Madrid (1901–88), who allegorically stands atop the pointy tip greeting at the Panamanian people rushing toward him. It was dedicated by scandal-plagued President Mireya Moscoso, Arias' wife.

End your walk by crossing the road south to enter the **Centro Artesanal** (507-6529-0688), where indigenous people sell crafts.

merchant and is today the Casa de la Cultura y del Artista Panameño—a cultural center hosting art exhibits and live music on Wednesday and Thursday nights.

Museo de Arte Contemporaneo (507-262-8012; www.macpanama.org; Avenida de los Mártires, Calle San Blas, Ancón) Housed in a 1930s former Masonic hall, this privately owned museum displays paintings, sculptures, photographs, and ceramics by many leading Panamanian and international artists since the 1950s. More than 400 works are displayed. It hosts a month-long Bienal de Arte plus lectures and music recitals, and you can sign up for art classes.

A Date with Lady Luck

Caribe Hotel and Casino 507-227-8814; Avenida Perú and Calle 28, La Exposición

Casino Internacional 507-212-1749; Hotel Internacional, Avenida Peru and Plaza 5 de Mayo, Calidonia

Crown Casino 507-226 0729; Caesar Park Hotel, Vía Israel, El Dorado

Fiesta Casino 507-215-9000; Hotel El Panamá, Vía España and Vía Veneto, Bella Vista
507 227 1133; Gran Hotel Soloy, Avenida Peru and Calle 30, La Exposición

Majestic Casino 507-215-5151; www.cirsa.com/casinos/majestic_panama; Multicentro, Avenida Balboa, Paitilla

Royal Casino 507-210-9100; Marriott, Calle 52 and Avenida Ricardo J. Arias, Bella Vista

Veneto Casino507-340-8888; www.venetopanama.com; Veneto Wyndham Grand Hotel, Via Veneto and **Avenida Eusebio Morales** Okay, it's not a casino, but the Hipodromo Presidente Remón (507-300-2600; www.hipodromo.com; Avenida José Agustín Arongo, Barrio Juan Díaz) is the setting for nighttime racing and gambling every Thursday.

Historic Buildings, Plazas, and Religious Sites

IGLESIA DEL CARMEN

Vía España and Avenida Manuel E. Bautista, Bella Vista

This neo-Gothic cement confection painted white and gray could have been transported from Medieval Europe. Initiated in 1947 by the congregation of the Carmelites and completed in 1953, it features thin and elaborate twin spires. Inside you'll find a Byzantine altar and interesting murals.

IGLESIA DE LA MERCED

Calle 9 Oeste and Avenida Central, Casco Viejo

With its striking baroque façade, this church is among the city's most imposing ecclesiastical structures. The façade, which is graced by pilasters, actually graced the original Church of Mercy in Panamá Viejo and was rebuilt, stone by stone, during construction of the current church in 1680. It is flanked by twin whitewashed belltowers and an exquisite little chapel venerating the Virgin of Mercy. The interior was gutted by fires in the 19th century, and the restoration a century ago utilized tasteless early 20th-century elements.

The church's simple beauty is echoed by that of the **Casa de la Municipalidad**, across the street to the west. This partly neoclassical building houses the town hall.

Iglesia del Carmen, Panamá City

IGLESIA DE SAN JOSÉ
Avenida A and Calle de San Blas, Casco
Viejo
Dawn to dusk
Admission: Free
This charming little church is quite
unassuming when seen from the street.
However, it boasts within the spectacular
altar de oro (gold altar). According to legend, this baroque masterpiece was moved
from the Iglesia de San José, in Panamá
Viejo, following Henry Morgan's sack of that
city. Supposedly it survived because local
residents had painted it in ash to disguise
the gilt. (How the wooden altar survived the
fire that ravaged the city is a 64-million-
dollar question.)

PANAMÁ VIEJO
507-226-8915
www.panamaviejo.org
Vía Cincuentenario, 4 miles (6 km) east
of downtown
Tuesday through Sunday 9–5
Admission: $3 adults ($6 including
mirador), $0.50 children
The ruins of the original city cover 57 acres
(23 ha) of shoreline and are a must-visit. In
1976 the site was named a *patronato*
(national monument) and restoration was
begun. The various individual sites are
linked by well-maintained trails, and the
museum here is superb.

The site, on a promontory overlooking
the Pacific Ocean, was already occupied by
indigenous peoples when an expedition led
by *conquistador* Pedro Arias d'Ávila arrived
on August 15, 1519. The Indians were
swiftly defeated and enslaved, and the
foundations of the first city on the Pacific
shores of the Americas were laid.
Expeditions set out from here to conquer
Peru. In ensuing decades, the settlement
became a marshaling point for treasure
fleets and was linked by the *camino real* to
Nombre de Dios and, later, Portobelo, on
the Caribbean. The city was partially

A Night at the Movies
To see what's playing while you're in town,
visit www.cinespanama.com.

Cinemark Albrook Mall 507-314-6001;
Albrook Mall

Cinépolis 507-302-6262;
www.cinepolis.com.pa; MultiPlaza Pacífica

Extreme Planet 507-214-7022; Avenida
Balboa.

Kinomaxx 507-208-2479; Multicentro

destroyed by a fire in 1644 but had grown to
a population of 10,000 when on January 28,
1671, pirates led by Henry Morgan attacked
the city. It was consumed by a devastating
fire and abandoned for a new site—today's
Casco Viejo.

The site can be explored on foot in about
two hours.

Begin at the **Centro de Visitantes de
Panamá La Vieja** (Visitors Center), at the
western extreme of the site, where you can
buy a booklet for self-guided tours, and
explore the excellent **Museo de Sitio de
Panamá Viejo**, with a scale model of the
city as it was in 1671. Other highlights
include Spanish armaments and a pre-
Columbian skeleton laid out as unearthed
in a fetal position. Signs are in English
and Spanish, and you can rent an English-
language taped narration. Immediately west
of the Visitors Center, the arched **Puente
de Matadero** (Bridge of the Slaughter-
house) marked the old city's western
entrance, guarded by the ruined **Fortín de
la Navidad** (Nativity Fort).

From the center, a graveled, tree-
shaded trail leads east past the main sites.
Initially it runs along the shoreline of
Panamá bay, where the mudflats are picked
upon by plovers, storks, roseate spoonbills,
and dozens of other bird species in the
thousands.

Pre-Columbian skeletons in Museo de Sitio de Panamá La Vieja, Panamá City

First up is the **Iglesia y Convento la Merced**, which though it survived the pirate attack was thereafter torn town and rebuilt in Casco Viejo. Another 328 feet (100 m) brings you to the ruins of the Franciscan **Iglesia y Convento de San Francisco**, then those of the **Hospital de San Juan Dios**. The trail diverts left to the well-preserved ruins of the **Iglesia y Convento de la Monjas de Concepción**, with its belltower and *aljibe* (well) intact. The trail then continues past the **Iglesia y Convento de la Compañía de Jesús**.

Crossing Vía Cincuentenario, which turns inland, you reach **Plaza Mayor**, the town's ancient and now grassy main square. On its far side, the recently restored bell tower of **La Catedral de Nuestra Señora de la Asunción** beckons you to climb the modern interior staircase for a view over Panamá Viejo from the *mirador* (lookout). The 90-foot (30 m) tower is more or less all that remains of the cathedral, which when completed in 1626 had three naves.

To the rear of the tower you'll see the skeletal ruins of what was the fortified heart of affairs in the ancient city. Here, on a well-guarded promontory separated from the rest of the town by a moat, were the **Cabildo de la Ciudad** (the former town hall) and **Casas Real** (Royal Houses) comprising the courthouse, governor's residence, jail, and main administrative buildings.

Continuing north of Plaza Mayor, scant remains exist of the **Casa del Obispo** (Bishop's House) and various noblemen's houses, plus the Dominican **Iglesia y Convento de Santo Domingo**. To its east, on the shore, the **Casa de los Genoveses** once belonged to Genoese merchants who controlled the slave trade. Another 1,312 feet (400 m) or so brings you to the last of the major ruins: those of the **Iglesia y Convento de San José**, which originally contained the famous Altar de Oro now found in the Iglesia de San José, in Casco Viejo. End your tour at the northern gate to the ancient city: the **Puente del Rey** (King's Bridge).

PARQUE BELISARIO PORRAS

Avenida Peru between Calle 33 Este and
Calle 34 Este, La Exposición

A delightful space studded with statues
and fringed by late 19th-century Spanish-
colonial buildings, this park is pinned by
the **Monumento Belisario Porras**, a dramatic monument (by Spanish sculptor
Victor Macho, 1887–1966) to three-time
Panamanian President Belisario Porras
(1856–1942). The life-sized statue of
Porras is backed by twin granite columns
topped by life-sized nude bronze females—
representing Democracy and Liberty—
holding a torch.

The Cuban embassy, facing the south

Monumento Belisario Porras, Panamá City

side of the park, also looks over busts and
monuments to Cuban nationalist heroes
José Martí and Antonio Maceo. The park is
flanked on its east and west sides by the
beautiful, gleaming white **Gobernación
de Panamá** building and its twin, the
Procuraduria Administración. While
here, step north one block to admire the
1950s yet Romanesque-style **Iglesia de
Don Bosco** (Avenida Central and Calle 34),
which has an exquisite, almost Moorish,
interior.

Parque Francisco Arias Paredes, one
block east of Parque Belisario Porras, is
named for the eponymous Panamanian
politician (1886–1946) who led the coup
that toppled corrupt U.S.-backed President
Florencio Arosemena in 1931. He is there,
in bronze.

The park is a setting for political meetings and, amazingly, the city's annual
Carnival, when it plays venue for *comparsas*
(processions) featuring women dressed
in traditional *polleras* and, in sensual coun-
terpoint, G-string bikinis, sequins, and
feathers.

PARQUE MEDIO BALUATE

Calle 1 and Avenida Central

This small triangular plaza giddy with
bougainvillea is named for a watchtower
that guarded the site during the early colonial era. It looks over a small beach. Ruben
Blades, Panamá's salsa singer-turned-
Minister of Tourism, lives in the lovely
three-story colonial building on the park's
south side.

The eyesore ruins running along the
waterfront (east side) of Calle 1 are those of
the once revered Club Union, the city's
snootiest social club for *rabiblancos* (elitist
whites). It was built in 1917 with designs by
U.S. architect James Wright. After the club
moved to Paitilla in the 1960s, it became
the Club de Clases y Tropas—an officer's
club for the Panamanian army. It became
General Manuel Noriega's favored hangout,

for which reason the U.S. military bombed it during the 1989 Operation Just Cause. It remains a burnt-out shell but there are plans to build a 137-room deluxe hotel that maintains the original structure's façade.

Pedestrian-only **Paseo General Estebán Huertas** leads south from Calle 1 and runs atop the former seawall to Plaza de Francia.

PARQUE URRACÁ
Avenida Balboa and Calle 45 Este, Bella Vista

One of very few green spaces in Bella Vista, this tree-shaded park allows a bucolic escape from the mayhem of traffic on nearby Avenida Balboa. It has a few busts and statues but isn't worth the visit in its own right, except perhaps for the Parade of Torches (November 2), when firefighters set out from here for Plaza de la Independencia bearing the first flag of the Republic in a glass case; and the annual Parada de Navidad (Christmas Parade), which begins here on Christmas Day and features women in *polleras* and other elements of traditional folkloric life.

PLAZA BOLÍVAR
Avenida B between Calle 3 Este and Calle 4 Este

The most intimate and pleasant plaza in Casco Viejo, this tiny square is also its liveliest thanks to the chic cafés and bars that vibrate to bohemian music and chatter at night. It is surrounded by colorful buildings (most dramatic is the salmon pink, Spanish Revival, former Hotel Colombia, dating from 1937, on the west side) and neatly trimmed trees and palms that frame the dramatic **Monumento a Simón Bolívar** (1783–1830), the Great Liberator who led the struggle for South America's independence from Spain.

In 1826, in his quest of unifying the independent nations, the Venezuelan convened the Congreso Anfictiónico in a convent schoolhouse on the park's northeast corner. Today the Antiguo Instituto Bolívar—colloquially called **Palacio Bolívar**—is home to the Ministerio de Relaciones Exteriores (507-211-4100; Calle 3 Este), the Foreign Ministry. Pop inside to admire the Plaza de Los Libertadores, a

Monument to Simón Bolívar, Plaza Bolívar, Panamá City

skylit courtyard with a mosaic floor (inset with a huge compass) and walls bearing the coats of arms of the republics that participated in the congress. To the far side, a bronze bust of Bolívar looks over an excavated portion of the original convent. Here, too, is the **Museo Bolívar** (507-228-9594; Tuesday through Saturday 9–4, Sunday 1–5; admission $1), on two floors. The Sala Capitular (Meeting Room), on the ground floor, is where the congress convened; it shows a replica of Bolívar's gold ceremonial sword encrusted with 1,374 diamonds. Upstairs you can peruse original congress documents in a chilly air-conditioned room.

To the Ministry's south, facing west onto the plaza, is the **Iglesia y Convento de San Francisco de Asís** (507-262-1410; Calle 3 Este and Avenida B). Completed in 1761 and restored in 1988 following a series of near devastating fires, this Romanesque church and convent is topped by a see-through Italianate belfry; inquire in the office to the rear of the church for permission to climb the campanile's spiral staircase for the splendid views. No doubt the sparkling of mother-of-pearl will draw your eye towards the diminutive **Iglesia San Felipe de Neri** (Avenida B and Calle 4), on the park's southwest corner. The city's oldest church dates from 1688. Recently restored, its magnificent highlight is its pyramidal spire adorned with nacre. The church is normally closed to the public.

PLAZA DE LA CATEDRAL

Avenida Central between Calles 5 and 7, Casco Viejo

Casco Viejo's most important square is the setting for the district's key buildings and occupies the very heart of the old city. Although officially known as Plaza de la Independencia, it derives its popular name from the **Catedral Metropolitana**, towering over the square on its west side. The cathedral was initiated in 1688 but not com-

pleted until 1796, using stones from the ruins of the Convento de la Merced in Panamá Viejo. Its baroque façade is topped by a Moorish pediment and flanked to each side by triple-tiered whitewashed belltowers that glitter due to inlaid bands of mother-of-pearl. The interior is somewhat austere. It was here, on November 3, 1903, that the declaration of independence from Colombia was signed.

Boasting an octagonal pergola and ablaze in spring and summer with flame-red *malinche* (royal poinciana), the square is surrounded by intriguing colonial buildings. Among the most striking is the Beaux Art Antigua Mansión Arias Feraud, today the **Casa de la Municipalidad** (507-262-0966; Calle 5 Oeste), or town hall, on the park's southwest corner. Designed by Italian architect Gennaro Nicola Ruggieri and completed in 1881, but twice remodeled, it houses the tiny **Museo de História de Panamá** (507-228-6231; Monday through Friday 8–5; admission $1). Its rather motley two-room collection profiles Panamá's past from the 16th century through the signing of the Canal Treaties in 1977. Since signage is in Spanish only, non-Spanish speakers can only guess at the importance of its various old maps, documents, firearms, and miscellany, which have no chronological order.

To its east, on the next block, the imposing Parisian-style three-story structure with mansard roof is the Museo del Canal Interoceánico (see separate entry)—a must visit! Stroll south 50 yards (46 m) down Calle 7 Oeste to view the ruins of the **Iglesia y Convento de la Compañia de Jesús**, completed in 1749 and which briefly served as a university—the Universidad Javeriana— until destroyed by fire in 1781. Its baroque façade is supported by pilasters but the interior is just a shell.

On the plaza's south side, the historic **Hotel Central** lay derelict for several decades but was slated to reopen in 2009 as

Mercado de las Pulgas fish market, Panamá City

a deluxe 134-room phoenix arisen from the ashes. Alas, the builders gutted the entire building, including an invaluable metal staircase, leaving nothing but the bare walls, which in May 2009 promptly collapsed!

Each first Sunday of the month the square hosts the **Mercado de las Pulgas** (Flea Market), where vendors of souvenirs, trinkets, and foods are joined by clowns, dancers, and other performance artists (9–4 PM).

PLAZA CINCO DE MAYO
Avenida Central and Avenida Balboa, Calidonia
Tiny it may be, but this triangular plaza (at the north end of the Avenida Central pedestrian precinct) is a whirligig of activity. It's pinned by an obelisk—the

Monumento a los Caidos (Monument to the Fallen)—with angels and a fountain at its base. The plaza's name and the monument commemorate six firefighters killed on May 5, 1914, while fighting a blaze in a fireworks factory, which exploded. Each Cinco de Mayo Panamá's firemen, or Cuerpo de Bomberos, don their dress uniforms and march to the plaza to commemorate *"el desastre del Polvorín"* (the gunpowder disaster). And the *bomberos* also pass by each November 27 during a torchlit parade on the anniversary of the creation of the fire brigade in 1885.

The squat neoclassical building on the east side of the plaza began life in 1912 as the Pacific railroad station. Between 2000 and 2005 it housed the nation's anthropological museum. Tucked behind the station is the little-visited **Mercado de Buhonerías y Artesanías** (Avenida 4 Sur and Calle 23 Este; daily 8–6), a small open-air crafts market that was renovated in 2007. It has *fondas*—cheap food stalls.

PLAZA DE FRANCIA
Calle 2 Oeste and Paseo General Esteban Huertas
Casco Viejo
Occupying the triangular tip of the peninsula, this charming little plaza shaded by jacaranda and palms was laid out in 1926 to honor the French entrepreneurs and laborers who pioneered construction of the first and failed attempt to build a canal. The space was once part of an 18th-century fort—the Fuerte Chiriquí—long since demolished. On the eastern side, however, nine vaults—**Las Bóvedas**—today house a restaurant, jazz club, galleries, and the Oficina de Casco Antiguo tourist information office, built into the seawall beneath the Paseo General Esteban Huertas esplanade.

Towering over the plaza is an Egyptian-style obelisk topped by a cockerel. At its base, note the bronze busts of Ferdinand de

Plaza Cinco de Mayo, Panamá City

Lesseps and four other key personalities of the era. Behind, a half-moon gallery is engraved with stone tableaux that regale the story of the Canal's construction, while another rightly honors Carlos J. Finlay, the Cuban physician who discovered that the *Aëdes aegypti* mosquito was the vector of yellow fever.

Appropriately, the **French embassy** (507-211-6200) is here, in a charming robin's-egg blue building on the plaza's north side. Outside, on the east side, your presence is noted by a life-sized bronze likeness of Pablo Arosemena (1836–1920), president of Panamá (1910–1912, and 1920). If you're here on July 4, make a beeline to the plaza for the fireworks hosted by the embassy.

To the northeast side of the plaza, the domed **Instituto Nacional de Cultura** (National Institute of Culture, 507-211-4000; www.inac.gob.pa; closed Saturday and Sunday) houses the agency in charge of Panamá's cultural institutions. You may

recognize it as the Grand Andean Hotel in the James Bond movie, *Quantum of Solace.* The tiny **Teatro Anita Villalaz** (507-211-4020) is here.

PLAZA HERRERA
Avenida A and Calle 9na, Casco Viejo
On the western fringe of Casco Viejo, this somewhat unkempt and seedy plaza honors General Tomás Herrera (1804–54), a governor of Panamá and president of Colombia who died fighting for Panamá's independence from Colombia. He's there in bronze, mounted on his steed atop a plinth. On the west side of the plaza, the **Baluarte Mano de Tigre** watchtower is the only part of the old city wall still extant. Behind, the empty space formed a dry moat. About 55 yards (50 m) farther west, the remarkable building shaped like a prow of a ship is the **Casa La Boyacá**. Built in 1890, this Caribbean-style wooden structure was restored in 2006 as low-cost housing. Don't wander any farther west, as the area isn't safe.

PLAZA JOSÉ REMÓN CANTERA

Avenida Central and 9 de Enero, Calidonia
A broad elevated plaza laid out in front of
the nation's Asamblea Nacional (507-512-
8300), Panamá's legislative assembly, it is
surrounded on two sides by thrumming
traffic. At its heart, rising from a fountain,
is a soaring black granite column erected to
honor assassinated President José Antonio
Remón Cantera (1908–55). Unveiled in
1957, it is engraved with his words: NEITHER
ALMS, NOR MILLIONS, WE WANT JUSTICE. The
plinth supporting the plaza is fronted by
the **Friso Alegórico a la Justicia**
(Allegorical Frieze to Justice), a frieze by
Peruvian sculptor Joaquín Roca Rey (1923–)
showing 17 bronze life-sized figures cavort-
ing in a water cascade.

Cross Calle 9 de Enero, east of the plaza,
to tiny **Plazuela Mahatma Gandhi** where
the city's Hindus maintain a statue of
Gandhi freshly garlanded in flowers.
The modernist building housing the legislative assembly is closed to the public.

Libraries

The nation's principal library is the **Biblioteca
Ernesto J. Castillero National** (506-221-
8360, www.binal.ac.pa; Monday through
Friday 9–6, Saturday 9–5), in Parque
Recreativo Omar.

The Smithsonian Tropical Research
Institute's **Earl S. Tupper Research and
Conference Center** (507-212-8000;Tupper
Building, 401 Roosevelt Avenue, Balboa) has
a research library, plus a small arboretum
(open Monday through Friday 8–5; guided
tours Wednesday and Friday 12:30 PM; free).

The **Instituto Geográfico Nacional
Tommy Guardia** (507-236-1844; www.ign
panama.gob.pa; Calle 57 Oeste and Avenida
6a. A Norte), a great source for information
on Panamá, is on the campus of the sprawling
Universidad de Panamá (506-223-1361;
www.up.ac.pa; Avenida Manuel E. Bautista).

PLAZA SANTA ANA

Avenida Central and Calle 11,
Salsipuedes
This tree-shaded plaza (and Avenida
Central, which runs north from it) with a
domed bandstand is as good as it gets for a
taste of *real* life in Panamá City. Before setting off to walk the pedestrian-only boulevard, prime yourself with a coffee or *trago*
(shot) of rum at the diner-style **Café Coca
Cola** (507-228-7687), a local institution
since 1883 and thick with genuine working-
class atmosphere, such as old men slapping
down dominoes. Che Guevara supposedly
ate and supped here when passing through
Panamá in 1954.

Brick-paved Avenida Central is usually
thronged with shoppers. It's a calliope of
commotion. The crowds usually include
plenty of Kuna women in traditional costume. Shops blare out salsa tunes and other
numbers, played at glass-shattering decibel
levels on bassy speakers. Somehow the
noise-loving Panamanians don't seem to
mind this assault on one's senses and san-
ity. Curiously, most of the stores are owned
by Gujarati Hindus who arrived from India
decades ago and thrived.

Don't go wandering west of the plaza and
Avenida Central into the no-good Chorrillo
area, or east through only slightly less seedy
Salsipuedes, which has a small Chinatown—
Barrio Chino—around Calle 15 Este, with a
Chinese Arch.

PLAZUELA DE LAS PUERTE DEL MAR

Avenida Eloy Alfaro between Calle 7 Este
and Calle 8 Este
This tiny triangular plaza on the north side
of Casco Viejo overhangs fishing wharfs
and the Bahía de Panamá. Several nearby
buildings are of note. The sepia **Casa de
los Monogramas**, on the south side, was
once a convent and exemplifies classic
18th-century Spanish colonial architecture
with its lovely wooden balustrades and *rejas*
(window bars).

SANTUARIO NACIONAL DEL CORAZÓN DE MARÍA

507-263-9833
www.santuarionacional.net
Calle 53 Este between Avenida 2a Sur and Avenida 3a Sur, Bella Vista
Among the most beautiful of all Panamá's churches, this one was only dedicated on August 22, 1949, despite its lovely part Romanesque and part Spanish-colonial façade, topped by a statue of Pope Pius crowning the Virgin Mary. Most striking is its juxtaposition in the shadow of towering skyscrapers. Step inside to admire the stained-glass windows and, in the court-yard to the side, a fountain circled by free-roaming peacocks.

Sanctuario Nacional de Corazón de María, Panamá City

Teatro Nacional, Panamá City

TEATRO NACIONAL

507-262-3525
www.teatronacionaldepanama.com
Avenida—and Calle 3 Este, Casco Viejo
A source of pride and joy, Panamá's recently renovated neoclassical National Theater was designed by Italian architect Genaro Nicola Ruggieri and inaugurated in 1908 with a performance of *Aida*. The exquisite interior is liberally adorned with rococo motifs, like a reduced-scale tropical La Scala. The horseshoe-shaped auditorium is graced by red velvet seats, original gilt, and two tiers of balconies beneath a dome adorned with a magnificent mural by Panamanian artist Roberto Lewis. The painting features the muses, nymphs, and classical figures such as Apollo in an alle-gory symbolizing the birth of the republic. In the lobby, note busts of Lewis and of famous British ballerina Dame Margot Fonteyn (1919–91), who often performed here as a long-term Panamá resident.

Museums and Monuments

CASA MUSEO DEL BANCO NACIONAL

507-225-0640
www.banconal.com.pa/museo.html
Calle 34 Este and Avenida Cuba

Casa Museo del Banco Nacional, Panamá City

Tuesday through Friday 8–noon and 1:30–4, Saturday 7:30–noon
Admission: free
Housed in a two-story mansion dating from 1925, this museum will delight numismatists and philatelists with its exhibitions on stamps, coins, and money bills dating back centuries. It also boasts large photo archives relating to Panamá.

MONUMENTO BALBOA
Cinta Costera/Avenida Balboa between Calles 35 and 36
The dramatic main feature of the city shorefront, this must-see monument features a large marble plinth topped by a larger-than-life bronze sculpture of

Spanish *conquistador* Vasco Nuñez de Balboa standing atop a globe supported by four figures representing Panamá's main ethnic groups. In his hands, he holds a sword and the flag of Spain.

MONUMENTO Á LOS PATRIOTAS
Avenida de los Mártires, between Calle 9 de Enero and Calle J, Calidonia
The 27 students and nationalists killed during the Flag Riots of January, 1964, are memorialized at this monument, comprising a flagpole being climbed by three life-sized bronze human figures. Each January 9, nationalists march past to commemorate the tragic four-day riots.

MUSEO AFROANTILLANO DE PANAMÁ
507-262-5348
Calle 24 and Avenida Justo Arosemena, Calidonia
Tuesday through Saturday 8:30–3:30
Admission: $1
Interested in the story of the Afro-Caribbean contribution to Panamanian culture? Then this tiny museum, in a two-story wooden structure one block east of Plaza José Remón Cantera, fits the bill. Much of the displays are dedicated to the story of the 20,000 or so West Indian laborers—the majority from Barbados—who toiled (and died) to build the Panamá railroad and Canal.

MUSEO ANTROPOLÓGICO REINA TORRES DE ARAÚZ
507-262-8338
Calle 4ta Este and Avenida Ascanio Villalaz, Llanos de Curundú
Tuesday through Friday 9–5, Saturday and Sunday 10–5
Although somewhat out of the way on the north side of the city, on the eastern edge of Parque Natural Metropolitano, visitors interested in Panamá's pre-Columbian culture will find the journey well worthwhile. The more than 14,000 exhibits in this

recently opened museum, named for Panamá's pioneering anthropologist and spanning some 37,660 square feet (3,500 sq m) on four levels, include stone and ceramic figurines, stone *metates* (curved ceremonial tables), and all manner of gold *huacas*—tiny ceremonial figures—plus amulets to half-moon-shaped nose-pieces, sparkle under halogen lighting. It has a ramp for wheelchairs, and a laboratory was slated to open with a glass wall for public viewing.

MUSEO DE ARTE RELIGIOSO COLONIAL

507-501-4127
Avenida 4 at Calle 3, Casco Viejo
Tuesday through Saturday 8–4; Sunday 1–5
Admission: $1
This small museum houses some 200 or so religious icons, including silver chalices, church bells, paintings, and sculptures dating back four hundred years. The venue is what remains of the **Iglesia y Convento de**

Santo Domingo, completed in 1756. Star attraction is the convent's original gilt baroque altar. Stepping back into the harsh light, note the ruins at the corner of Avenida 4 and Calle. Here was the iconic **Arco Chato** (Flat Arch)—a brick-and-mortar arch that survived numerous earthquakes while surrounding parts of the convent toppled. The gravity-defying arch finally succumbed one night in 2003.

MUSEO DE LA BIODIVERSIDAD

507-215-3015
www.biomuseopanama.org
Calzada de Amador
Panamanians and the world have been holding their breath for years in anticipation of this long-touted museum finally opening. The on-again, off-again project finally caught wind and at press time the sensational Frank Gehry-designed Puente de Vida (Bridge of Life) building was nearing completion. This highly controversial structure is a jumble of multi-layered tilted

Monumento Balboa, Panamá City

boxes, like multi-faceted quartz crystals, topped by a twisted and jagged roof. It's a far cry from Gehry's far more elegant titanium Guggenheim Museum in Bilbao, Spain. Hopefully the exterior won't actually be painted in the gaudy primary colors, as planned.

The Museum of Biodiversity is a collaboration of the Smithsonian Tropical Research Institute, the University of Panamá, and the Interoceanic Regional Authority, who came together to form the Fundación Amador. It will feature eight halls, each with innovative multimedia exhibitions that showcase the astonishing biodiversity of Panamá and the Neotropics, plumbing the deepest ocean to the depths of the rain forest canopy. One salon will profile the geological forces that have shaped the world.

MUSEO DEL CANAL INTEROCEÁNICO

507-211-1649
www.museodelcanal.com
Calle 5 Oeste, Plaza de la Catedral
Tuesday through Sunday 9–5 (ticket office closes at 4:30)
Admission: $2 adults, $0.75 children under 12
One of my favorite sites in the city, this superb museum on the southwest corner of Plaza de la Catedral traces the history of the conception and building of the Panamá Canal. Appropriately, it is housed in the former headquarters of the Compagnie Universelle du Canal Interocéanique, the company founded by Ferdinand De Lesseps. Previously it had been the Grand Hotel (where de Lesseps was fêted in 1879). Later it

housed the U.S. Canal Commission 1904–12. On three levels, the exhibits follow a logical chronological path that begins with that of Balboa (exhibits include pre-Columbian gold, plus Spanish armor and weaponry) and the story of the California forty-niners, before moving on to construction of the Panamá railroad; the herculean yet tragic French effort to construct a canal; and that of the U.S. Army Corps of Engineers. The eclectic exhibits also include magnificent models of various ships, such as the steamer SS *Ancón,* which made the first official Canal transit. More contemporary themes are covered on the top level, where you can view commemorative coins and stamps, and a copy of the Torrijos-Carter Treaty of 1977. Alas, signage is in Spanish only, but you can arrange an English-speaking guide in advance, and English-language audio tapes can be purchased.

MUSEO DE CIENCIAS NATURALES

507-225-0645
www.pa/secciones/museo_ciencias
Avenida Cuba between Calle 29 East and Calle 30 East
Tuesday through Saturday 9–3:30
Admission: $1 adults, $0.25 children
Okay, I know. You'd much rather see Panamá's astonishing wildlife in its natural habitat. But failing that, this museum (in a 1930s Art Nouveau building) offers four rooms stuffed with many of the critters you might see in the wild. Monkeys. Big cats. Harpy eagles. Plus a miscellany of beasts from beyond the Neotropics, such as lions, tigers, and rhinos. Also here, sections on marine biology, geology, and paleontology.

Music and Nightlife

Panamá City is abuzz by night, with something for every taste. Seeking a classical concert? Or perhaps a bohemian café as a prelude to letting your hair down in a dance-till-dawn disco? For laid-back bohemian venues, head to Casco Viejo, which is rapidly evolving as an alternative to the shiny shoe parade of Bella Vista. The more upscale nightclubs are mostly found in and around ever-changing Calle Uruguay, chock-full of atmospheric bars and clubs that get in the groove on Wednesday and peak on Friday and Saturday night. The Zona Viva area near the Figali Convention center on Amador Causeway is a hot new venue teeming with bars and nightclubs that sizzle to a South Beach-style *vida loca* vibe. The poshest nightclubs have strict admission policies—you need to look the part to get in.

Here are a few of my favorite nightspots (and faves of others whose taste I might not share):

Los Baños Publicos (Plaza Herrera) Take an old public bathroom and paint it black. Stuff it with tattered couches. Plaster the walls with old vinyl records. Price your beer below the competition. Invite in live rock bands. The result is a grungy garage bar popular with young Goths and rock fans.

Café Havana (507-212-3873; Avenida B and Calle 5, Casco Viejo) A recent addition to Casco Viejo, this trendy epicenter of bohemian life just off Plaza Bolívare is *the* spot to go for a quick drink and, need we say, to smoke a real Cuban stogie. Its *mojitos* are perhaps the best in town, complete with a raw sugarcane garnish.

Guru Clubbing Cult (507-269-6130; www.gurupanama.com; Calle 47, Bella Vista) Shine up your shoes and pack a thick wallet. This posh club is currently the hottest (and one of the snootiest) nightclub in town. Fog machines. Sexy go-go dancers. The best DJs. And the most elite clientele. A stiff dress code and steep cover charge keep the hoi polloi at bay.

Kraze 950 (507-6674-9930; Calle Uruguay, Bella Vista) Reasonably priced for the pricey neon-lit Calle Uruguay zone, this small nightclub has a dance floor. The music aims at an eclectic mix, from rock to reggaeton. The place gets packed for Wild Fridays. If it doesn't work for you, you'll find a dozen or more options within a five-minute stroll.

La Casona de las Brujas (506-211-0740; Plaza Herrera) The former Art Deco Citibank has metamorphosed into a huge art-filled warehouse-style bar. One of the funkiest venues in the city, The House of Witches hosts live music and even late-night techno parties and movies, when a cover is charged.

The Londoner (507-214-4883; Calle Uruguay, Bella Vista) Hankerin' for a pint of ale and game of darts? This wood-paneled venue harks back to the working-class pubs of England, but with a pool table and plasma TVs for the up-to-the-minute sports crowd. Heck, it even has waiter service and valet parking. Brilliant, mate!

Casa Nikki (Avenida Balboa, Punta Paitilla) On the 46th floor of the Nikki Hotel, this super chic and sexy nightclub promises to be the hottest spot in town when it opens around 2010. Dress to impress!

People (507-263-0104; Calle Uruguay, Bella Vista) Fresh from a remodeling, this popular nightclub for the moneyed young has added a VIP floor with its own bar. You can sip at outdoor seating but need to pay for the disco. Bring your earplugs. What is it with the Latin need to overdo the decibels?

Platea (507-228-4011; www.scenaplatea.com; Calle 1ra, Casco Viejo) This bohemian hotspot is ground zero for live jazz. The venue is a refurbished colonial mansion with bare brick walls and modern accouterments for a touch of contemporary chic—a fantastic space! And the *mojitos* are fantastic too.

Nature and Gardens

CINTA COSTERA

Laid out 2007–2009 parallel to Avenida Balboa, this new coastal beltway was built to relieve traffic congestion. It involved reclaiming some 74 acres (30 ha) of land from the sea with landfill along 1.6 miles (2.6 km) of shoreline, and construction of a three-lane highway to carry eastbound traffic (Avenida Balboa is now one-way, westbound). The enhancement includes 62 acres (25 ha) of newly laid-out parkland with a new *malecón,* or promenade, plus an amphitheater, the Monumento Balboa, bicycle paths, a kids' playground, and fountains.

PARQUE NATURAL METROPOLITANO

507-232-5552
www.parquemetropolitano.org
Avenida Juan Pablo II
Daily 6 AM–5 PM
Admission: Free; guides cost $6 per person for groups of five, by prior arrangement

Claiming to be the only true tropical forest reserve within city limits in all Latin America, this hilly 573-acre (232 ha) space lets you don hiking boots or mount your mountain bike and take to the trails like a true Indiana Jones. It's remarkable to think that just minutes from your hotel exists this vast enclave of nature in the raw. The wildlife refuge, established in 1985, protects one of the last pockets of Pacific seasonally dry lowland rain forest in Central America. It provides an invaluable corridor in conjunction with the contiguous Camino de Cruces and Soberanía national parks.

The park teems with animals and birds. Baltimore orioles, blue-crowned motmots, keel-billed toucans, lance-tailed manakins, and piquiblanco parrots are among the 227 bird species to be seen. The 45 species of mammals include agoutis, coatis, Geoffrey's tamarin, and three-toed sloths. And you're sure to see iguanas—among the most prominent of 36 reptile species here.

Geoffrey's tamarin, Panamá

Mono titi (squirrel) monkeys

Wildlife is more easily seen in early morning and during dry season, when many of the trees shed their leaves. Buy a self-guided booklet at the visitor center before setting out, and don't hike alone. Robberies have been reported!

Get your bearings at the park entrance **Visitor Center** (507-232-5516; Camino de la Amistad and Avenida Juan Pablo II), which has maps plus exhibits on the flora and fauna. To get there, take the Corredor Norte, which runs along the park's eastern edge. The center's *orquideario*—orchid garden—is usually full of blossoms.

Easiest of the park's five well-signed trails is the flat, 0.5-mile-long (0.7 km) **Sendero La Momótides,** named for the blue-crowned motmots often seen while hiking. **Sendero Roble** also leads from the Visitor Center to the **Sendero La Cieneguita**, an interpretive nature trail that links with the **Sendero Mono Titi** (named for the squirrel monkey) to form a loop. The Mono Titi trail is actually a former road, perfect for bicycling; it leads to *Mirador Los Trinos,* offering superb views over Panamá City and Miraflores Locks. **Sendero Caobos, 0.7 mile** (1.1 km), also leads to a *mirador.*

Since 2008, visitors are now able to ascend in the **canopy crane** operated by the Smithsonian Institute of Tropical Research (507-212-8233; www.stri.org). Used for research in the upper story of the forest, the revolving 138-foot (42 m) crane has a 167-foot-long (51 m) arm permitting eye-to-eye contact with beasts and birds in one entire hectare (2.5 acres) of forest canopy. **Ancón Expeditions** (507-269-9415; http://anconexpeditions.com; $110 per person) has the exclusive right to take nature enthusiasts up in the gondola at the end of the boom when it is not in use by scientists.

Punta Culebra Nature Center, Panamá City

PUNTA CULEBRA NATURE CENTER

507-212-8793
www.stri.org/english/visit_us/culebra
Isla Naos, Amador Causeway
Tuesday through Friday 1–5, Saturday and
Sunday 10–6
Admission: $2 adults, $1 students and
seniors, $0.50 children
Run as a marine research and education
facility of the Smithsonian Tropical
Research Institute (STRI), this splendid
facility occupies a former military post atop
a rocky headland—Punta Culebra. Trails
wend past a beach and white-mangrove
forest (good for spotting cormorants,
frigatebirds, and blue- and brown-footed
boobies), and through a tiny pocket of
rare Pacific tropical dry forest (good for
spotting birds, iguanas, and sloths). The
highlight, however, is the open-air Marine
Exhibitions Center. Its six aquariums provide insights into marine ecosystems and
species, separated into Caribbean and
Pacific zones. There's a shark pond, a turtle
pond, and a touch pond stocked with
starfish and other harmless invertebrates.

RESERVA NATURAL CERRO ANCÓN

Access via Quarry Road
This steep, freestanding, thickly forested
knoll rises 654 feet high (198 m) over
Balboa (on its west flank) and Ancón (on its
east side). The jungled "island" was protected for its watershed by the U.S. military,
which in 1942 burrowed a bombproof 40-
room command post deep inside the
mountain. The post later served as headquarters of the entire U.S. Southern
Command until 1998. (Today the former
Quarry Heights Military Reservation is
still operated as a secretive communications and intelligence center of Panamá's
Strategic Plan of National Security.) In
2001, the hill was declared an Área
Protegida y Reserva Natural—Protected
Area and Nature Reserve.

A massive Panamanian flag flutters atop
the hill, which is also pinned by broadcast

Calzada de Amador

Fingering the Pacific Ocean, this 3-mile-long (4.5 km) man-made peninsula was built of land-fill excavated during construction of the Canal and forms a breakwater protecting the canal entrance from silt-bearing currents. Completed in 1913, it connects three islands—Culebra, Naos, Perico, and, finally, Flamenco—to the mainland and was guarded by Fort Grant (later Fort Amador) with 14-inch cannon mounted on railway carriages. During WWII, a bombproof strategic command center was built into Isla Flamenco. The peninsula was off-limits to the public until 1996.

Woman skating on Calzada de Amador, Panamá City

Today Fort Amador is the setting for both the **Figali Convention Center** (www.figaliconvention center.com), within the Spanish-Revival-styled Panamá Canal Village (507-314-1414; www.panama canalvillage.com); and the much-anticipated Museo de la Biodiversidad (see separate entry).

The Amador Causeway offers tremendous views over the entrance to the Panamá Canal. A pencil-thin, palm-lined park that extends along much of the western fringe is laced by trails for bicycling, skating, and jogging. It is fast evolving as a trendy nightspot. There's a large marina and yacht club, plus The Smithsonian Tropical Research Institute's Centro de Exhibiciones Marinas (see separate entry).

Sightseeing highlights include several small parks, including **Parque Torrijos-Carter**, where the benevolent dictator-president slumbers beneath the **Monumento Histórico Mausoleo del General Omar Torrijos Herrera**. Nearby, the **Plaza de la Cultura y la Etnia** honors all ethnicities who came to Panamá during the past five centuries. The **Plaza de la Unidad Iberoamericano** honors all the nations of the Americas. And **Pilares a la Patria**, featuring oversize figures (three males and one woman) paying homage beneath the Panamanian flag, honors the indigenous, Afro-Panamanian, and European cultures.

towers. Note the life-sized bronze effigy of Panamanian poet Amelia Denis de Icaza (1836–1911), seated at the flagstaff's base. You can reach the summit by car, or by hiking the serpentine road that snakes up from the **Asociación Nacional para la Conservación de la Naturaleza** (507-314-0060; www.ancon.org; Building 153, Sturgis Road, Quarry Heights), or ANCON, headquarters. Stop in here to learn something about the flora and fauna, including armadillos, coatis, Geoffrey's tamarin, and even deer, that inhabit the forests. The trailhead is just east of B&B La

Estancia, a short distance east of ANCON. Another trail links the summit with Mi Pueblito, at the base of the southeast side. Bring your camera for the awesome 360-degree views from the city's highest point. Don't hike alone, as muggings have been reported. There are usually police at the summit.

Gustavo and Tammy Chan, owners of B&B La Estancia (507-314-1581), lead early morning hikes.

Plans to build a tram to the summit were scrapped by the Supreme Court in July 2009.

Theater, Classical Music, and Concerts

Panamá's performing arts come under the purview of the **Instituto Nacional de Cultura** (507-507-262-3525; www.inac.gob.pa) and **Asociación Nacional de Conciertos** (507-214-7236; www.conciertospanama.org).

The city's two main venues for live concerts are the **Atlapa Convention Center** (507-236-7845 or 226-7000; www.atlapa.gob.pa), which has the 2,800-seat Teatro Anayansi and 500-seat Teatro La Huaca; and the **Figali Convention Center** (506-314-1414; www.figaliconventioncenter.com), on Calzada de Amador.

Concerts are also hosted at the new Amphitheater, on Cinta Costera.

The main theatrical venue is the resplendent **Teatro Nacional** (c/o 507-262-3525; teatronacional@inac.gob.pa), which hosts the **Ballet Nacional de Panamá** (507-269-2375; balletnacional@inac.gob.pa) and **Orquestra Sinfónica Nacional** (507-228-3409; sinfonica @inac.gob.pa), the national symphony orchestra.

My favorite venue is **Teatro Balboa** (507-228-0327; teatrobalboa@inac.gob.pa), a magnificent Art Deco theater that hosts plays and classical performances.

The **Ancón Theater Guild** (507-212-0060; www.anconguild.com), a small English-language theater group that is a legacy of the Canal Zone era, plays at its own tiny theater.

The Smithsonian Tropical Research Institute's **Earl S. Tupper Research and Conference Center** (507-212-8000; Tupper Building, 401 Roosevelt Avenue, Balboa) hosts free twice-weekly seminars on nature and science-related themes in its 176-seat auditorium.

Seasonal Events

The city calendar features several annual events of note, including the four-day **Panamá City Jazz Festival** (www.panamajazzfestival.com) in January. Lovers of classical ballet should time their arrival for October and the **Festival Nacional de Ballet** (507-211-4942).

Panamanians are crazy about beauty contests. The old Miss Panamá contest has been in turmoil in recent years as competing contest organizers battled out for who really had the franchise. The dust seems to have settled in favor of the *Realmente Bella Señorita Panamá* (the Really Beautiful Miss Panamá) contest, with two crowned winners going on to compete in the Miss World and Miss Universe pageants, respectively. However, this is now a TV reality show, with losers being dismissed one by one. There's also the Miss World Panamá contest, which sends winners to the Miss International competition.

RECREATION

Bird-Watching

The parklands bordering the city offer tremendous birding, particularly **Parque Natural Metropolitano** (see *Nature and Gardens*) and the shoreline east of the city around Panamá Viejo.

You can join guided birding tours offered by the **Panamá Audubon Society** (506-232-5977; www.panamaaudubon.org), which also offers monthly lectures on birds, every second Thursday at 7:30 PM.

Biking, Skating, and Running

The palm-lined **Calzada de Amador** is tailor-made for biking and skating. A path wends more or less the full length of the breakwater on the west side, offering tremendous views of the Bridge of the Americas and busy Canal channel. Likewise, the new parks laid out in 2008–9 parallel to the Cinta Costera have biking and skating lanes.

Parque Recreativo Omar (Avenida Belisario Porras and Calle 74), on the northeast side of the city, is Panamá City's second-largest metropolitan park and a great venue for jogging around its 2-mile (3.5 km) path.

Bust of Omar Torrijos, Parque Recreativo Omar, Panamá City

Panamá has a skateboarders association: **Asociación Panameña de Patinaje** (507-260-4652; panamapatin@hot mail.com).

Bowling

You'd imagine that a city blessed (many locals would say cursed) for decades with such a strong U.S. presence would be equally blessed with bowling alleys. **Bolos El Dorado** (507-260-2511; www.bolos eldorado.com; Avenida Ricardo J. Alfaro), in the El Dorado Mall, is a world-class facility with 24 bowling lanes plus pool tables. Likewise, **Albrook Bowling** (507-391-2641; mercadeo@albrookbowling .com; daily 11–11), in Albrook Mall, has 36 lanes and a pro shop.

Aficionados should contact the **Asociación de Boliche de Panamá** (507-236-6830; apabol@hucusa.com).

Fitness Facilities

Most tourist hotels have gyms. **Parque Recreativo Omar** (Avenida Belisario Porras and Calle 74) has a swimming pool, tennis courts, baseball court, and soccer pitch.

Golf

The semi-private **Summit Golf and Resort** (507-232-4653; www.summitgolfpanama .com) has a 6,626-yard, par-72 championship course just a 20-minute drive north of the city on the Gaillard highway.

Your other option is the 72-par layout at **The Tucán Country Club and Resort** (507-211-3472 or 800-456-6016; www.tucancountryclub.com).

Hiking and Horseback Riding

The **Clayton Equestrian Club** (507-232-6272; Friendship Road) offers equestrian training.

Cerro Ancón and **Parque Natural Metropolitano** (see *Nature and Gardens*) have hiking trails.

Racquet Sports

Many hotels have tennis courts. **Club Raqueta de Panamá** (507-260-6884; off Avenida Juan Pablo II, La Loceria; www.clubraquetapanama.com; Monday through Friday 8 AM–10 PM, Saturday 9–6, Sunday 10–4) has three squash and one racquetball courts; short-term memberships are offered. The **Piscina Adan Gordon** swimming pool (507-500-5320; Avenida Cuba and Avenida Justo Arosemena, La Exposición) has tennis courts open to the public.

Water Sports

Sailing trips and sportfishing are offered by **Panamá Yacht Tours** (507-263-5044; www .panamayachtours.com).

Licensed sailors can charter craft at the **Flamenco Yacht Club** (507-314-0665; www .fuerteamador.com) and the **Balboa Yacht Club** (507-228-5794; Calzada de Amador), just south of the Bridge of the Americas.

SHOPPING

The capital city doesn't lack for opportunity, and shopaholics can fill days hunting out bargains. Several markets are dedicated to arts and crafts, from Balboa in the west to Panamá Viejo in the east. Upscale art galleries and clothes boutiques concentrate in Bella Vista, El Cangrejo, and Marbella, where the major shopping malls are also located.

Art

The Bella Vista district is a node for high-stakes galleries. Try **Galería Habitante** (507-264-6470; http://galeriahabitante .com; Calle Uruguay #16, Bella Vista), which sells contemporary works by leading Panamanian and Latin American artists, as does **Galería Imagen** (507-226-8989; imagen@pty.com; Calle 50 and Calle 77, El Dorado).

Books and Music

Your starting point should be **Exedra Books** (506-264-4252; www.exedrabooks.com; Vía España and Vía Brasil), which is well-stocked with both English and Spanish titles.

For a quirky bibliophile's delight, head to **Librería Argosy** (507-223-5344; Vía Argentina and Vía España, El Cangrejo), where dusty antiquarian books rub up against plenty of newer titles. It has scores of books about Panamá.

Shopping Malls

Albrook Mall (507-303-6255; www .albrook mall.com: Avenida Marginal, Corregimiento de Ancón, Ancón; Monday through Thursday 10–8, Friday and Saturday 10–9, Sunday 10:30–8) This mammoth mall takes up nearly 5 million square feet (460,0000 sq m) near Aeropuerto Marcos A Gelabert. More than one hundred stores span the spectrum.

Multicentro Mall (507-208-2500; www .multicentropanama.com.pa; Avenida Balboa, Marbella) Everything from high-end boutiques to stores selling art, perfume, and electronics. Also a casino, multiplex cinema, and 30 restaurants.

Multiplaza Pacific (507-302-5280; www.mallmultiplazapacific.com; Vía Israel, Punta Pacífico) Competes with Multicentral with 52 shops, 7 department stores, and plenty of service facilities.

Tailor of Panamá

When Pierce Brosnan and Geoffrey Rush came to Panamá in 2000 to film the screen version of John le Carré's novel *The Tailor of Panamá* they knew to visit La Fortuna to be fitted with bespoke suits. There's a good reason that autographed photographs of José Abadi posing with Bosnan and Rush are proudly displayed in the store: This tailor's shop is the real-life model for Pendel and Braithwaite Limitada, *El sastre de Panamá* in le Carré's richly textured spy thriller.

In operation since 1925, La Fortuna has been drawing the *panameño* elite for decades. Just as in le Carré's novel, where anybody of importance in the country passes through Harry Pendel's doors, so everyone from General Noriega to Panamanian presidents, U.S. generals, and foreign ambassadors and spies have been dressed by La Fortuna's owner José Abadi and his son, Adán, who now tends the store and its cadre of highly skilled tailors. In fact, late Dictator-President Omar Torrijos supposedly joked that Abadi was the only man he would drop his trousers for. No doubt, La Fortuna's fitting rooms have been privy to more secrets than a priest's confession box.

José Abadi, the "Tailor of Panamá," Panamá City

For maps, head to the **Instituto Geográfico Nacional Tommy Guardía** (507-236-1844; www.ignpanama.gob.pa; Calle 57 Oeste and Avenida 6a. A Norte), on the Universidad de Panamá campus.

Clothing and Accessories

Boutiqe Breebaart (507-264-0159; Calle Abel Bravo #5, Obarrio). Dutch fashion designer Hélène Breebaart melds Kuna *molas* into her contemporary skirts and dresses, which have adorned the likes of Miss Panamá.

La Fortuna (507-263-6434; Vía España, 100 yards east of Via Argentina; Monday through Saturday 9-6) This is *the* place to be fitted out for an off-the-rack shirt or bespoke hand-stitched suit, including a quintessentially Panamanian *guayabera*. For six decades, La Fortuna has been the *sastre* (tailor) of choice for ambassadors, generals, and members of Panamá's *asamblea*. A precisely fitted bespoke suit takes about two weeks and requires two fittings; expect to pay around $500.

Polleras y Artesanias (507-228-8671; hiramcortez@yahoo.es; Avenida A and Calle 8A, Casco Viejo; Monday through Saturday 10–5:30) If you're hankering to buy a hand-made *pollera* (Panamá's exquisite traditional woman's dress) or perhaps a man's traditional *montuño* shirt, then make a beeline for this tiny shop.

Crafts and Jewelry

Centro de Artesanías Internacional, (507-6529-0678; Avenida Arnulfo Arias Madris, Balboa) In the former YMCA building, this indigenous-run market offers a full range of quality crafts, from masks to *molas*.

Esmeralda y Arte Precolombino (507-228-9126; Calle 1, Edificio 844, Casco Viejo) A treasure trove of emerald, gold, and silver jewelry, and raw stones.

Galería de Artes Indígenas (507-228-9557; ero7777@yahoo.com; Plaza de Francia, Casco Viejo) Tucked into Las Bóvedas, it sells a large selection of indigenous crafts, souvenirs, and fine art pieces.

Karavan Gallery (507-228-5161; Calle 3ra and Arco Chato, Casco Viejo) Small it may be, but this well-lit trove is packed with quality *molas*, Panamanian folk art, jewelry, and sculptures.

La Ronda (507-211-1001; souvenirs laronda@yahoo.com; Calle 1ra, Casco Viejo) Specializes in quality indigenous crafts representing the finest of Kuna *molas*, Emberá-Wounaan baskets, Ngöbe jewelry, and *sombreros montuños* and *polleras*).

> **Good to Know About**
> The Office of Casco Antiguo **tourist information office** (507-209-6300; www .cascoantiguo.gob.pa; Bóveda I, Plaza de Francia) is an excellent resource and sells a superb map of the old city ($5).

Casco Antiguo, Panamá City

Mercado de Buhonerías y Artesanias (Avenida 4 Sur and Calle 23 Este, Calidonia; daily 8–6) Mainly indigenous artisans attend this outdoor market selling hammocks, *sombreros montuños*, and crafts. It's tucked just east of Plaza Cinco de Mayo.

Mercado Nacional de Artesanias (Vía Cincuentenario, Panamá Viejo; daily 9–5) This crafts market staffed by indigenous peoples has the usual full complement of Emberá *chaquiras*, Kuna *molas*, and Ngöbe-Buglé jewelry.

Mi Pueblito (Avenida de los Mártires; daily 9–5; admission $1) This contrived shopping complex—My Little Village—at the eastern foot of Cerro Ancón is a triptych featuring three stereotypical villages representing indigenous, Afro-Caribbean, and Spanish-colonial cultures. While ostensibly intended as a museum, including folkloric performances on Friday and Saturday evenings, it's really a hard-core shopping complex where you'll find almost every conceivable craft item made in Panamá.

Museo de la Esmeralda (507-262-1665; Calle 6, Plaza de la Catedral, Casco Viejo) Despite its name and its small museum featuring life-sized recreations of miners at work, this is a commercial jewelry store. Visitors can expect a strong sales pitch.

Reprosa (507-271-0033; www.reprosa.com; Avenida Samuel Loew and Calle 54, Obarrio; daily 9–6) Fine contemporary jewelry including uncut Colombian emeralds and pre-Columbian gold replicas (*huacas*).

Miscellany

Okay, you might not visit here to buy a whole fresh-caught snapper or octopus, but the **Mercado de Mariscos** (Avenida Eloy Alfaro and Calle 15 Este) is worth a visit to watch fishmongers hawking Neptune's larder, brought in by gaily painted fishing boats that tie up at the wharfs at the southern end of the Cinta Costera. You can buy a whole fish and haul it upstairs to the restaurant, which will prepare it for you to your desire.

Photographers are served by **Panafoto** (507-263-0102; Calle 50 and Calle 49A Este, Bella Vista), which stocks cameras, lenses, etc. plus binocular and scopes for the birding crowd.

Isla Taboga

Floating in the Golfo de Panamá, some 11 miles (18 km) south of Panamá City, this laid-back island is a popular destination for day-tripping city folk on weekends and holidays. It has a quasi-Mediterranean feel and is colloquially known as the "island of flowers" due to its abundance of endemic Taboga roses, plus bougainvillea and hibiscus, splashing the landscape with color. Sights are few, but it has some lovely beaches and a laid-back aura conducive to relaxation.

After Pizarro's conquest of the Inca Empire in 1526, the isle became a key transshipment point for Inca treasures and for pearls from the Islas de Perlas. During the French Canal construction effort, in the 1880s, it served as a sanatorium due to its relatively cool and dry climate. French impressionist painter Paul Gauguin (1848–1903) washed up here in 1887 to live "on fish and fruit for nothing . . . without anxiety for the day or for the morrow." Isla Taboga's real estate was already priced at a premium, however, and Gauguin was reduced to laboring on the canal until he earned enough money to sail on. Needless to say, the U.S. military set up shop here during WWI to guard the entrance to the Canal.

Sites

The sole settlement is San Pedro, nestled in a horseshoe-shaped cove backed by forested hills.

The town plaza is anchored by the tiny yet lovely **Iglesia San Pedro**; the church dates back to 1524 and is one of the oldest in the Americas. If possible, time your arrival for July 16 when islanders parade a statue of Nuestra Señora del Carmen; the statue, which normally resides in the church, is borne to the shore and loaded aboard a garlanded boat for a tour around the isle. A stone statue of Carmen may be seen on Calle Francisco Pizzaro.

Fishing boats add metaphorical and literal color to **Playa La Restinga**, the village's sheltered (and somewhat littered) brown sand beach. Low tide exposes a tombolo (sand bar) permitting brief access to **Isla El Morro**. Other beaches can be accessed by water taxi; ask one of the fishing boats to run you out to good snorkeling spots. You can follow the main road (Calle Francisco Pizarro) left from the ferry dock to reach the summit of **Cerro de la Cruz** for fine views of the isle and gulf. En route you'll pass the overgrown ruins of a Spanish cannon embrasure and abandoned WWII bunkers. Beyond the turnoff for Cerro de la Cruz, the road snakes uphill to **Cerro La Vigia** (1,008 feet/307 m)—the isle's highest

---

Hablas español? . . . Say what?

They say that the fastest way to learn a language is to take a lover who speaks no other. Failing that, you can live (even temporarily) in a place where that language is spoken, preferably immersing yourself in a language school for a week, month, or longer. No problem in Panamá, which has several dozen language schools. Here are some to consider:

Habla Ya Panamá Spanish School (507-720-1294; www.hablayapanama.com) Boquete

ILERI Language Institute (507-392-4086; www.ileripanama.com) Panamá City

ILISA Language Institute (507-317-1011; www.ilisa.com/panama) Panamá City

Spanish Panamá (507-213-3121; www.spanishpanama.com) Panamá City

La Lotería

If two hummingbirds fly in a straight line, Panamanians are sure to wager on which will be the winner. They love gambling, as is obvious by the huge number (10,000 nationwide) of licensed lottery-ticket sellers on every street. Twice weekly drawings include a $2,000 first prize, as well as second ($600), and third ($200) prizes. Every last Friday of the month Panamanians hold their breath and pray to win a special drawing called *gordito del zodico* (little fattie of the Zodiac), with a $600,000 grand prize. Meanwhile, the odds are far more favorable to win *los chances*, two-number tickets that cost only 25 cents and pay out meager winnings if the numbers correspond to the last two digits of the winning combination.

So popular are the twice-weekly drawings that they are broadcast live on radio and TV. These protracted *fiesta*-themed affairs draw throngs to La Lotería Nacional de Beneficia (507-207-6800, www.lnb.gob.pa) headquarters, in Parque Victor Julio Gutiérrez, each Wednesday and Sunday afternoon. Traditional folkloric music and dance are featured as local dignitaries gather to watch the four winning lottery balls plucked from a metal cage. The task belongs to three schoolchildren selected for the occasion. Various lottery balls (each containing a single number) are placed in the cage, which is spun by handle for an interminable amount of time before the children step forward to nervously pluck out a ball, which is unscrewed to reveal the winning number. The process is repeated four times to generate the winning combination. (When officials replaced the antiquated spinning cage system in favor of an electronic system, an angry public demanded that the old system be reinstated.)

point; it's a 3-mile (5 km) hike—with U.S. military gun emplacements now forming a *mirador* (lookout).

LODGING AND DINING

Cerrito Tropical B&B and Tropical Apartments (507-390-9999; http://cerritotropical panama.com) Tucked on the hillside above town, this hostelry offers three guest rooms plus four self-catering apartments with Wi-Fi, and views to die for. Units differ but all have delightful furnishings. Run by a Canadian-Dutch couple, Cynthia and Hiddo Mulder. Moderate.

Kool Youth Hostel (507-690-2545; luisveron@hotmail.com) This backpackers hostel, a stone's throw from the pier, has three dorm rooms. It offers free breakfast and has a communal kitchen. Inexpensive.

Hotel Taboga This landmark hotel closed in 2008, but a new development is in the works.

Hotel Vereda Tropical (507-250-2154; www.veredatropicalhotel.com) A lovely Mexican-themed hillside hotel with views over Playa Honda and the gulf. A tinkling fountain, rich ochre, high ceilings, and iron balustrades are highlights. All 12 air-conditioned, individually themed rooms have TVs and balconies, plus irresistibly colorful decor and wrought-iron beds. Myra and Marina are your delightful hosts. A splendid restaurant serves fusion cuisine. Moderate.

Getting There

The *Calypso* Queen (507-314-1730; Monday, Wednesday, and Friday 8:30 AM and 3 PM; Tuesday and Thursday 8:30 AM; and Saturday, Sunday, and holidays 8 AM, 10:30 AM, 4 PM; $10 round-trip, $7 children) departs from the Playita de Amador beach, next to the Smithsonian Tropical Research Institute, on Isla Naos on Calzada de Amador. The journey takes 45 minutes; watch for whales!

You can also hire a water taxi from Balboa Yacht Club.

Scubapanama (507-261-3841; www.scubapanama.com) offers trips to Isla Taboga.

Expect to get around by walking, and be prepared for plenty of hills!

THE CANAL AND COLÓN PROVINCE

"The French had all the will in the world, but it wasn't enough. The timing was off."

—DAVID MCCULLOUGH

This region is perhaps the most diverse of any in Panamá. Within its small compass you can cross the isthmus on a boat excursion on the Canal . . . take a whitewater trip on the Río Chagres . . . visit an indigenous Emberá village . . . go birding in Soberanía . . . hike the ancient Camino Real . . . revisit the ghosts of pirates past in the fortresses of San Lorenzo and Portobelo . . . and snorkel or scuba dive amid the Caribbean's fantastic coral reefs.

Panamá's main tourist draw, of course, is the Panamá Canal, extending 51 miles (80 km) from Panamá City on the Pacific Ocean to Colón on the Caribbean Sea. A feat of remarkable engineering, it draws thousands of visitors daily to view the passage of cargo vessels, cruise ships, and warships. Viewing is easily done from spectator stands at the Miraflores and Gatún locks, while excursion vessels that set out from Panamá City will take you on a mesmerizing passage through the Goliath locks. To ensure an adequate sup-

Panamanian girl in Portobelo, Panamá

ply of freshwater, the forested mountains to either side of the Canal have been protected. These lush hinterlands teem with wildlife, easily seen along trails that snake through rugged rain forest enshrined in national parks—Parque Natural Camino de Cruces, Parque Nacional Chagres, and Parque Nacional Soberanía—that together comprise La Ruta Ecológica Entre dos Océanos (the Ecological Route Between Two Oceans), a biological corridor from sea to sea.

The Caribbean coast is steeped in Afro-Antillean culture, reflected in colorful clapboard houses, a spicy cuisine, and rhythmic dances called *congos*. Colón, at the northern mouth of the Canal, is a melancholic port city that is gateway to Portobelo and Nombre de Dios, fabled treasure ports of the old Spanish Main.

GETTING THERE AND AROUND

By Bus or Público

UltraCopa (507-314-6248; in Colón, 507-447-1763; $2.50) buses depart the Gran Terminal Nacional de Transporte, beside the Corredor Norte in Albrook, for Colón. Buses for Portobelo depart Colón's Terminal de Buses hourly (6:30 am–6 pm, $0.50). Additional buses marked "Costa Arriba" depart Colón for Nombre de Dios on the same schedule ($2.50). Note that the turnoff for Portobelo from the Transístmica is by the Supermercado Rey, at Sabanaitas, 8 miles (14 km) before Colón when traveling from Panamá City; you can catch the Colón-Portobelo bus in Sabana Grande.

By Car

Carretera Gaillard (officially Avenida Omar Torrijos Herrera) leads north from Ancón and parallels the Canal on its eastern side, granting access to Miraflores Locks, Pedro Miguel Locks, and ending at Gamboa. This road also delivers you to Parque Nacional Camino de Cruces and Parque Nacional Soberanía. It also links with the Transístmica (Carretera 2), the main highway linking Panamá City and Colón, on the Caribbean coast. From Colón, Carretera 31 runs east along the Caribbean shore to Portobelo and Nombre de Dios; and Carretera 32 runs west to the Gatún Locks and, beyond, to Parque Nacional San Lorenzo and along the northern shores of Lago Gatún.

By Ship

You can transit the canal aboard cruise ships that include it on their itineraries. The passage is also a highlight of eight-day "Costa Rica and the Panamá Canal" cruise-tours offered by **National Geographic Expeditions** (888-966-8687; www.nationalgeographic expeditions.com), December through May; and similar itineraries by **Cruise West** (888-851-8133; www.cruisewest.com), October through March. I typically escort two or more cruise-tours annually for National Geographic Expeditions. *Please join me!* Dates are listed on my Web site: www.christopherbaker.com.

In Colón, most cruise ships dock at the modern **Colón 2000** (507-447-3197; www.colon 2000.com; Calle El Paseo Gorgas) cruise port. Taxis are available for exploring. A few smaller ships berth at Muelle Cristóbal, near the commercial docks on the opposite side of the city.

By Train

There's no doubt that the best way to travel between the coasts is aboard a train operated by the **Panamá Railway Company** (507-317-6070; www.panarail.com; $22 adults, $15 seniors, $11 children, each way). The train departs Panamá City's Estación de Corazol, in Albrook, for Colón Monday through Friday 7:15 AM; the return train departs Colón at 5:15 PM. Choose from one of five historic wood-paneled coaches or the dome car, with a glass roof. You'll be in view of the Canal and Lago Gatún for virtually the entire way, including a long section that plays hopscotch across bridges that link several isles in the lake. Reservations are not required.

Tour operators offer guided excursions that include train transfers.

By Tours

Most tour operators in Panamá City offer daylong excursions to the Canal, the various national parks, plus Portobelo. Two to consider are **Ancón Expeditions** (507-269-9415; www.anconexpeditions.com) and **Panamá Travel Experts** (507-6671-7923; www.panamatravelexperts.com).

The most thrilling experience of all—a must-do!—is a small boat excursion through the locks. Three companies offer day trips from Panamá City. **Canal and Bay Tours** (507-290-2009; www.canalandbaytours.com) has trips aboard the 400-passenger *Fantasia del Mar* and *Tuira II* and the Prohibition-era *Isla Morada,* departing

Colón 2000 cruiseport sign, Panamá

on Saturday from Balboa. **Panamá Marine** (507-226-8917, www.pmatours.net) offers partial and full-transit trips aboard the *Pacific Queen* every Saturday from Flamenco Marina. **Panamá Yacht Tours** (507-263-5044; www.panamayachtours.com) also departs Flamenco Marina and uses smaller vessels for a more intimate experience. All three companies charge about the same: $115 adult, $60 child, partial transit; $165 adult, $75 child, full transit.

The Canal Zone

The term, the Canal Zone, is politically incorrect in current-day Panamá, where it denotes, to them, the imperialistic U.S.-owned and run 10-mile zone to either side of the Canal during Uncle Sam's tenure (1907–1999). With apologies to Panamanians, I use it here with a *small "c" and small "z"* to encompass the same 2,134-square-mile (552,761 ha) zone administered by the Panamá Canal Authority (Autoridad del Canal de Panamá or ACP; 507-272-1111; www.pancanal.com/eng/index.html) since Panamá gained jurisdiction of the former Canal Zone on December 31, 1999.

For information on Gatún Locks, see the Colón section.

LODGING

AVALON GRAND PANAMA RESORT

800-261-5014
www.avalonvacations.com
Vía Transístmica, Las Cumbres
Moderate
Seemingly at odds with its surroundings, this towering 171-room resort hotel sits on a hill at the edge of Parque Nacional Camino de Cruces. It aims directly at local families with its waterpark. But the huge rooms are tastefully furnished in sober fashion, with tile floors and king beds. Families can opt for any of 41 *casitas* with kitchenettes.

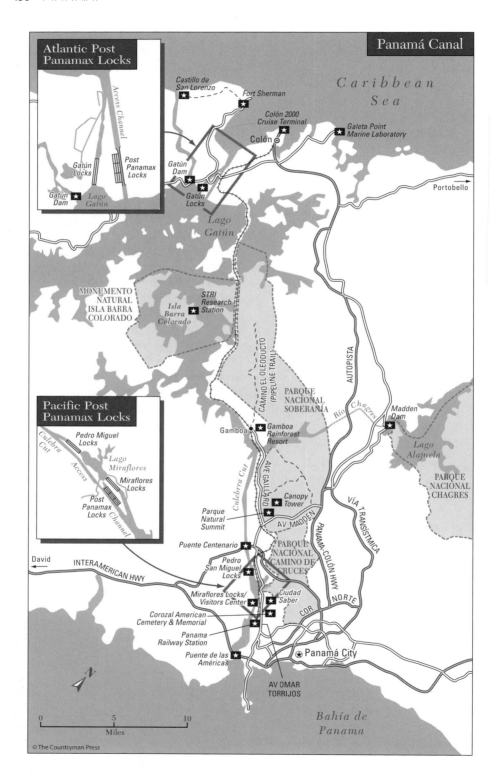

Panamá Canal

Atlantic Post Panamax Locks

Access Channel

Gatún Locks

Post Panamax Locks

Gatún Dam ★

Lago Gatún

Pacific Post Panamax Locks

Culebra Cut

Pedro Miguel Locks

Lago Miraflores

Access

Miraflores Locks

Post Panamax Locks

Channel

Castillo de San Lorenzo ★

Fort Sherman ★

Colón 2000 Cruise Terminal

Colón ○

Galeta Point Marine Laboratory ★

Gatún Dam

Gatún Locks ★

Caribbean Sea

Portobello

Lago Gatún

MONUMENTO NATURAL ISLA BARRA COLORADO

Isla Barra Colorado ★

STRI Research Station

CAMINO EL OLEODUCTO (PIPELINE TRAIL)

AUTOPISTA

PARQUE NACIONAL SOBERANÍA

Río Chagres

Madden Dam ★

Lago Alajuela

PARQUE NACIONAL CHAGRES

Gamboa ● Gamboa Rainforest Resort

Culebra Cut

AVE GAILLARD

Canopy Tower ★

Parque Natural Summit

AV MADDEN

VÍA TRANSÍSTMICA

PANAMÁ-COLÓN HWY

David ←

INTERAMERICAN HWY

Puente Centenario ★

Pedro San Miguel Locks ★

PARQUE NACIONAL CAMINO DE CRUCES

Ciudad Saber

COR.

NORTE

Miraflores Locks/ Visitors Center ★

Corozal American Cemetery & Memorial ★

Panama Railway Station

Puente de las Américas ★

Panamá City ✦

AV OMAR TORRIJOS

Bahía de Panama

0   5   10
Miles

© The Countryman Press

CANOPY TOWER ECOLODGE AND NATURE OBSERVATORY

506-264-5720 or 800-930-3397
www.canopytower.com
Semaphore Hill Road, Parque Nacional Soberanía
Moderate to Expensive

The place par excellence for serious birders, this world-renowned lodge in the thick of Parque Nacional Soberanía is unique in many ways. Start with the octagonal architecture: it used to be a radar tower and still has that hollow warehouse feel, thanks to bare metal walls and beams. First-story rooms are Spartan, share bathrooms, and are a tad pricey. Better by far are the larger more pleasantly furnished, pie-slice-shaped upper-level rooms. Warning: some look out over the parking lot. The rooftop observation platform is a boon for birding. Guests (and day visitors) are offered a range of guided birding options, including aboard modified observation vehicles.

GAMBOA RAINFOREST RESORT

507-206-888 or 877-800-1690
www.gamboaresort.com
Gamboa
Expensive

Truly a resort in the rain forest, this is a perfect base for travelers seeking plenty of comfort and company. Its setting is stunning, with gorgeous views over the vast swimming pool complex toward the Río Chagres and nearby rain forests. Stylish and modern, it has heaps of facilities, including a spa, choice of restaurants and bars, plus organized and self-guided nature activities. The 107 rooms are spacious and pleasingly furnished, and all come with TV, telephone, and balcony with view. Suites have king beds. Families might opt for one of 48 apartments in renovated 1930s Panamá Canal Administration homes.

HOSTAL CASA DE CAMPO COUNTRY INN AND SPA

507-226-0274
www.panamacasadecampo.com
Cerro Azúl, 28 miles (40 km) east of Panamá City
Moderate

This exquisite bed-and-breakfast hotel, close to the eastern entrance to Parque Nacional Chagre, makes a perfect resting place for hikers and birders (guided tours are offered). The owners have decorated the 11 bedrooms in richly colored,

Couple with binoculars atop Canopy Tower, Panamá

old-world fashion, with deep ocher and sienna, and a combination of wicker and antique furniture. It has a spa and swimming pool, and serves home-cooked meals.

HOSTEL LA POSADA DE FERHISSE

507-297-0197
laposadaferhisse@hotmail.com
Calle Domingo Díaz, Cerro Azúl
Inexpensive
For budget travelers. Close to the Parque Nacional Chagres' Cerro Azúl entrance. It has tremendous lake and mountain views, The six accommodations are comfortable but somewhat basic. A high point is the restaurant serving tasty local fare.

PANAMA CANAL FLOATING LODGE

507-832-7679, or 954-678-9990 in North America
www.gatunexplorer.com/panama-canal-floating-lodge.html
Lago Gatún
That's right. Anchored in a cove on Lago Gatún, this rustic two-story wooden houseboat is a terrific, albeit rustic one-of-a-kind experience. It has hammocks on private balconies accessible through screened walls that let in the sounds of screeching monkeys and birds—perfect! Meals are served family-style, alfresco.

SIERRA LLORONA

507-442-8104
www.sierrallorona.com
2.8 miles (4 km) north of Sabanita, 9 miles (15 km) southeast of Colón
Inexpensive to Moderate
This contemporary-styled hotel operates as a "jungle lodge" and is particularly popular with birders and nature lovers keen to spot the region's wealth of wildlife. It sits atop a hill overlooking a 494-acre (200 ha) rain forest reserve laced with trails and observation platforms. It offers pre-dawn birding tours, and a range of nature tours and activities. The eight cross-ventilated rooms and

suite (with Jacuzzi) are a delight, being simply yet tastefully furnished. Each has shuttered, screened windows, plus ceiling fans. Buffet meals are served and it has Internet and a bar. In driving here in wet season, you'll need a 4WD vehicle.

It also has camping facilities with rustic stoves and barbecue pits.

DINING

TOP DECK

507-276-8325
www.pancanal.com
Miraflores Locks Visitor Center, Avenida Omar Torrijos Herrera, 5 miles (8 km) northwest of Albrook
Daily, noon–11
The Miraflores Locks can hold your interest for hours. Fear not when hunger strikes, as the top-floor buffet restaurant is first class. You can dine outside on a shaded terrace overlooking the action. For lighter fare, opt for the ground floor snack bar, selling salads, sandwiches etc.

ATTRACTIONS, PARKS, AND RECREATION

CANOPY TOWER ECOLODGE AND NATURE OBSERVATORY

506-264-5720 or 800-930-3397
www.canopytower.com
Semaphore Hill Road
Atop a hill in the midst of Parque Nacional Soberanía, this world-famous eco-lodge is one of the premier birding sites in the nation. The 12-sided metal tower began life as a U.S. military radar station that pokes above the tropical moist forest canopy. It's not typically open to day visits by your average Joe, but serious birders are usually welcome. It has binoculars and scopes for jaw-dropping vistas from the rooftop. The mile-long access road, Semaphore Hill

Canal Factoids

The failed French effort to build a canal (1879-89) claimed at least 20,000 lives.

The U.S. Army Corps of Engineers oversaw construction (1906–14), which cost $352,000,000.

When completed in 1914, the Panamá Canal was the grandest and most costly human enterprise ever conceived.

5,609 workers died of accidents and disease during U.S. construction (1906–14), averaging about 500 lives per mile.

The canal connects the Caribbean Sea and Pacific Ocean and runs northwest to southeast.

The canal is 50 miles (80 km) long from ocean to ocean.

The canal cuts through the narrowest and lowest saddle in Central America.

56,307 people were employed during construction (1904–14), of which 31,071 were from the West Indies.

The canal has three sets of locks, each with twin chambers side by side; there are 12 chambers in total.

Each chamber is 110 feet (33.5 m) wide by 1,000 feet (305 m) long—the dimensions were intended to accommodate the largest battleships of the day. They average 85 feet (26 m) deep.

The largest vessels allowed are called Panamax ships; they measure 106 feet (32.3 m) wide by 965 feet (294.1 m) long.

There are 46 paired and mitered lock gates, each measuring 65 feet (20 m) wide and 7 feet (2 m) deep. The gates vary in height from 47 to 82 feet (14 to 25 m), depending on their location, with Miraflores having the tallest gates.

The hollow gates float at near negative buoyancy; they are so finely balanced that a single 19-kilowatt electric motor was sufficient to open and close them (a hydraulic system was introduced in 1998).

All upper chambers have double layers of gates to prevent flooding in the event that the first pair is breached.

It takes 52 million gallons (101,000 cubic meters) of fresh water to fill a lock chamber, which can be filled in eight minutes.

The canal accounts for about 60 percent of Panamá's fresh water consumption.

The canal has operated 24/7 only since 1963, when lighting was installed.

Vessels normally pass through both lock chambers in the same direction. Northbound ships transit between midnight and noon; southbound ships transit between noon and midnight. There is a brief period when ships pass in opposite directions.

A typical passage through the canal takes approximately 8–10 hours.

Ships sailing from New York to San Francisco via the canal travel 6,000 miles (9,500 km); the same journey via Cape Horn would require a 14,000-mile (22,500 km) passage.

About 14,000 vessels transit the canal every year, representing about 5 percent of the world's sea traffic.

Tolls are based on vessel type and size, and the type of cargo carried. The most expensive toll charged to date was US$331,200, paid on May 16, 2009, by the *Disney Pearl*.

The lowest toll for passage was 36 cents, paid by Richard Halliburton, who swam the canal in 1928.

Road, from the Gaillard Highway offers tremendous birding, particularly of species that live close to the forest floor, such as antbirds, as well as raptors. And mammals such as agoutis *(ñeques)*, coatis, and howler monkeys, and Geoffrey's tamarin are frequently seen. I highly recommend that you overnight.

CIUDAD DEL SABER

507-317-0111
www.ciudaddelsaber.org
Clayton, 5 miles (8 km) northwest of Balboa
Monday through Friday 8–5
In 1999, the U.S. military handed the former Fort Clayton U.S. Army base to the nation, which turned it into The City of Knowledge. Spanning 297 acres (120 ha), the facility hosts various local and international research organizations, including high-tech companies zoned in the Tecnoparque Internacional de Panamá. Dozens of prestigious entities are based here, including the Organization of American States, Smithsonian Tropical Research Institute, and World Wildlife Fund.

The main draw for visitors is the **Fondo Peregrino Panamá** (Peregrine Fund of Panamá; 507-317-0350; www.fondopere grino.org; Calle Arnoldo Cano, Casa 87, Ciudad del Saber), alias the Neotropical Raptor Center. It breeds harpy eagles for reintroduction into the wild. Call to arrange a visit and to hold a "tame" harpy eagle.

The SACA bus ($0.35) for Clayton departs from beside the Plaza Legislativa, in Panamá City. Taxi Clayton (507-317-0386) operates from the Ciudad del Saber.

COROZAL AMERICAN CEMETERY AND MEMORIAL

507-207-7000
www.abmc.gov/cemeteries/cemeteries/cz.php
abmcpan1@cwpanama.net
Calle Rynicki, off Avenida Omar Torrijos Herrera, Clayton

Panamá Canal pilot boat with Ciudad del Saber behind, Panamá

Daily 9–5, closed December 25 and January 1

This 16-acre military cemetery is under the care of the American Battle Monuments Commission. More than 5,360 U.S. veterans and civilians associated with Canal construction and/or operation are interred here; the oldest grave dates back to 1790. From the Visitors Center, a paved path leads uphill to a small memorial with a rectangular granite obelisk flanked by twin flagpoles flying the U.S. and Panamanian flags.

Gamboa

Gaillard Highway, 20 miles (32 km) northwest of Panamá City. This small community, at the end of the canal road at the mouth of the Río Chagres and at the entrance to the Gaillard Cut, was founded in the 1930s by the Panamá Canal Company to house its Canal Maintenance Division. Originally staffed by U.S. personnel, the community's clapboard architecture is quintessential *yanqui* colonial vernacular. The main sightseeing draws, besides passing ships, are two mammoth floating cranes that are used to haul bulky objects such the 945-ton lock gates. *Hercules* (built in 1914) and *Titan* (1941) were made in Germany.

Pipeline Road, considered Panamá's preeminent birding trail, begins where the paved road ends and snakes into Parque Nacional Soberanía. The Smithsonian Tropical Research Institute's **Gamboa Field Station** (507-212-8082; www.stri.org) is a center for biological research in the park, but is not open to casual visitors. The dock for Barra del Colorado Island is here.

The SACA (507-212-3420) bus departs from in front of the Palacio Legislativo at Plaza Cinco de Mayo.

GAMBOA RAINFOREST RESORT

507-314-5000
www.gamboaresort.com
Gaillard Highway

You don't have to overnight here to participate in the wide range of activities that lure visitors to this luxury hotel and nature-themed adventure center with a scenic setting overlooking the Chagres river. Day visitors are welcome. It offers guided birding hikes as well as an easy 1-mile (1.6 km) self-guided trail. An interpretive park educates you on various local ecosystems, such as the lowland tropical forest. And it has a live butterfly exhibit and nursery; an orchid nursery; and a serpentarium displaying many endemic snake species, from the beautiful finger-thin vine snake to the deadly fer-de-lance. Plus, if you don't make it out to the *real* Emberá village, it has a faux facility here.

Other options include:

Aerial Tram: You can ride in an open cage on a ski-lift-style tram that ascends 367 feet (112 m) through the rain forest. You won't see much wildlife, although the guides assigned to each cage give interesting ecological briefings. At the top, you can climb a 90-foot (27.4 m) *mirador*—lookout tower—for spectacular bird's eye views over the rain forest, Río Chagres, and Gaillard Cut. Departs Tuesday through Sunday 9:15 AM, 10:30 AM, 1:30 PM, 3:00 PM; $50.

Vine snake

Boat and Kayaking Tours: Options include a guided boat tour of Lago Gatún, with an emphasis on wildlife viewing (six tours daily; $35); and a 40-minute tour on the Río Chagres ($15). And who would have thought you could actually kayak on the Canal (three-hours; by demand; $50).

Safari Night: One of my faves is a nocturnal one-hour "Safari Night" tour in search of all the critters that are active after dark. Fascinating! Daily at 7 PM; $40.

Lago Gatún

Sprawling over 166 square miles (423 sq km), this freshwater lake was formed by damming the Río Chagres near the river's mouth at Gatún. The dam was completed in 1910 and it took four years for the lake to fill, forming what was then the largest man-made lake in the world. Dozens of small villages were inundated, as was much of the Panamá Railroad, which was relaid on higher ground. The lake's surface is 85 feet (26 m) above sea level; it is being deepened as part of the Canal expansion. The lake spans half the isthmus; it features lushly clad isles. Along its fringes dead trees protrude like clawing fingers.

Don't swim in the lake. There are crocodiles! The croc population has expanded considerably in recent years, not least in thanks to an abundant supply of peacock bass (*sargento*). Anglers are in their element. **Panamá Fishing and Catching** (507-6622-0212; www.panamafishingandcatching.com) offers fishing tours.

Many of the commercial concessionaires with businesses on the lake have been forced to close in recent years by the ACP. Nonetheless, you can still explore by boat.

Gatun Explorer (507-832-7679; www.gatunexplorer.com) offers a variety of lake tours by canopied motorboat and also by kayak—a great way to get close to anhingas, caimans, monkeys, and sloths. It also has fishing trips. Excursions depart the dock in Gamboa.

Notwithstanding the presence of crocs, **Scubapanama** (507-261-3841; www.scubapanama.com) offers experienced divers a chance to explore a century-old train that lies 52 feet (30 m) down in the murky waters.

MIRAFLORES LOCKS
507-276-8325
www.pancanal.com
cvm@pancanal.com
Avenida Omar Torrijos Herrera, 5 miles (8 km) northwest of Albrook
Daily 9–4:30 (ticket office); 9–5 museum
Admission: $8 adults, $5 students, and children (free under 5 years of age)

The most impressive of the three *esclusas* (locks) by virtue of the superb viewing gallery and museum, this southernmost lock system is a mere 16 miles (25 km) from the city center. No wonder it's Panamá's number one tourist attraction!

Miraflores has two flights that together with the approach channel stretch for 1.1 miles (1.7 km), linking the Pacific Ocean with Miraflores Lake. Because the Pacific tidal variation is far more extreme than that of the Caribbean Sea, the chambers here are deeper than at Pedro Miguel and Gatún, providing a lift varying between 43 feet (13.1 m) and 64.5 feet (19.7 m), depending on the state of the tide. (The lift is fixed at 31 feet/9.45 m at Pedro Miguel, and 85 feet/25.9 m at Gatún.). The steel lock gates here are, logically, also the largest of the three locks and weigh 945 tons apiece. Each transit takes about 10 minutes from the time a vessel enters a chamber. Since there are four chambers here, two in each direction, as many as four Panamax vessels—the maximum size permitted—might be transiting at any one time.

You'll get a grandstand view—literally—from the four-story **Visitor Center** (Centro de Visitantes; www.pancanal.com/eng

Visitor center at Miraflores Locks, Panamá Canal

/anuncios/cvm/index.html), built opposite the control tower and with viewing platforms on each level for an intimate close-to-the-action perspective as cruise ships and supertankers ease past almost within fingertip reach. Bilingual commentators broadcast running commentaries on the operation of the locks and the specifics about each vessel transiting.

Exhibitions: The center has four state-of-the-art exhibition halls with superb presentations that include video presentations, interactive displays, models, and dioramas themed by floor. The History Hall, on the ground floor, profiles the Canal's conception and construction. The second floor Hall of Water educates about the watershed and the role that conservation plays in ensuring the Canal's operation. Above, The Canal in Action takes you inside a culvert and a full-scale pilot-training simulator, while a topographical scale model demonstrates a virtual ocean-to-ocean transit. The fourth floor profiles the Canal's role in world trade. Movies are sometimes shown in a 182-seat theater.

Before entering the Center, note the **Belgian locomotive** near the base of the steps. It was used to haul excavated material to Amador and was restored after being raised from Gatun Lake in 2000. And exit the Center on the canal side to view the **Culebra Cut Rock**, a giant rock inset with a plaque quoting Theodore Roosevelt. It is dedicated TO THE BUILDERS OF THE CANAL.

Getting There: Buses marked Gamboa, Paraíso, and Summit Gardens depart the Gran Terminal Nacional de Transporte, in Albrook. Choose the air-conditioned buses departing 4–7 AM and 2–3:30 PM, as they drop off at the gates to Miraflores. Buses at other times drop you at a stop on the highway, a 10-minute walk away.

A taxi from downtown will cost about $15 one-way.

How the Canal Operates

A SHIP'S PASSAGE

Ships transiting from the Caribbean to the Pacific enter the Canal channel via the Bay of Limón. They then sail 6.2 miles (10 km) to Gatún Locks, which raises the ships 85 feet (26 m) in a three-step lock system. Ships then enter Gatún Lake and sail 23 miles (37.8 km) across the lake—they follow the course of the now-submerged riverbed (the deepest part of the lake)—to enter the Gaillard Cut. This 8.5-mile-long (13.7 km) man-made canyon cuts through the continental divide and is named for Colonel David Gaillard, the engineer in charge of excavation. Ships then arrive at Pedro Miguel, a single-step lock that lowers vessels 31 feet (9.5 m) to Miraflores Lake. A 1-mile (1.6 km) passage across this narrow lake brings vessels to the two-step Miraflores Locks, which lowers them to the level of the Pacific Ocean (the drop varies according to tidal conditions).

Mula at Miraflores Locks, Panamá Canal

All captains (even of military vessels) must relinquish control of their vessel to an ACP pilot for the transit. Ships are guided through the channels and lake by navigational markers. After entering the lock channels, ships are tethered on each side—front and rear—to electric locomotives called *mulas* (mules). These run along tracks parallel to the chambers and serve merely to keep the ships aligned; the vessels move under their own propulsion.

Plaque memorial to Major David Gaillard, Miraflores, Panamá

HOW IT FUNCTIONS

The Canal has operated without a hitch around-the-clock for almost a century—a testament to its genius of simple design and flawless construction. Its operation relies entirely upon a constant flow of fresh water moving under the force of gravity from Lakes Gatún and Miraflores. The lakes are supplied

MONUMENTO NATURAL ISLA BARRO COLORADO

507-212-8026 or 212-8951 reservations
www.stri.org
Lago Gatún
Boat departures from Gamboa: 7:15 AM

Monday through Friday, 8 AM Saturday and Sunday
The 13,800-acre (5,600 ha) Barro Colorado Nature Monument (BCNM) comprises 4,200-acre (1,500 ha) Isla Barra Colorado and five surrounding mainland peninsulas

by water draining in off the surrounding rain forest-clad mountains, principally from the Río Chagres. The entire lock operation was designed to function electrically, with a water spillway and HEP station at Gatún generating the power for the system's 1,500 electric motors. (The system uses only 25 percent of the hydroelectric power produced; the rest is sold to the national grid.)

Water from the lakes also fills the upper chambers and flows from one chamber to the next or to the sea-level channels to raise and lower ships. No pumps are used. Water pours into each chamber via three 22-foot-wide (7 m) culverts: one to each of the massive concrete side walls and a third in the center wall that divides the chambers. The flow of water is controlled by valves at each end of the culverts,

Gaillard Cut rock dedicated to memory of Panamá Canal workers, Miraflores, Panamá

which slide up and down, like windows, on roller bearings. To flood a chamber, valves at the upper end are opened while those at the lower end are closed. Water feeds from each of the main culverts via 10 perpendicular cross culverts (thus, 20 cross culverts per chamber) that run beneath the chambers. Each cross culvert has seven vertical culverts evenly distributed across the chamber floor to minimize turbulence as water boils up under pressure to fill the chamber. The upper valves are closed once the chamber fills. To empty a chamber, the valves at the lower end are opened and gravity does the rest.

Until recently, a locomotive drive-wheel principle was employed to open and close the massive steel gates: A connecting rod affixed to the center of each gate leaf attached at its other end to the outer circumference of a massive horizontal "bull wheel" within the side walls. The wheels were powered by an electric motor as they revolved through 200 degrees. Today, a hydraulic system is employed.

The valves, lock gates, and *mulas* are controlled from a control room, much like an airport control tower, atop the center wall of each set of locks. Today a state-of-the-art computerized hydraulic system using fiber-optic cable has replaced the original electro-mechanical system. (Originally, each control room featured a central control board that was a working scale replica of the locks, with manual switches next to each representation of valves, gates, and other moving components, which mirrored the exact state of the actual lock components in real time. To guard against error, the switches were all linked mechanically and necessitated being operated in correct sequence to function.)

on the southern shores of Lago Gatún. The biological reserve was created in 1923 as a scientific research base for the study of tropical ecosystems. It has been managed since 1946 by the Smithsonian Tropical Research Institute (STRI).

Barro Colorado is the largest island in the Panamá Canal waterway. It is fringed by marshy grasslands and mangroves, while inland comprises primary lowland tropical moist forest. Wildlife abounds. Imagine more than 200 ant species! And almost 400

National Geographic Expeditions passengers birding at Barra Colorado Island, Panamá

species of birds. Plus, its more than 120 mammal species—of which 72 are bat species—include agoutis, coatis, sloths, and 5 monkey species: howler, spider, white-faced, Geoffrey's tamarin, and night monkey. Ocelot, peccaries, and tapirs are also present, though rarely seen by visitors. And jaguars occasionally visit by swimming from the mainland!

Day visitors are welcome by prior request (reserve well in advance). If approved by STRI, your trip includes boat transfers (departing Gamboa Tuesday, Wednesday, and Friday at 7:15 AM, Saturday and Sunday at 8 AM; $70 adult, $40 student), plus a guided three-hour hike and lunch. The Field Research Station has a small visitor center. The laboratories are off-limits to visitors. And only a single 1.5-mile (2.4 km) nature trail is accessible to the public; another 34 miles (56 km) is restricted to scientists. No children under 10.

Some local tour operators offer excursions. And the island is included, uniquely, on **National Geographic Expeditions'** "Costa Rica and the Panama Canal" cruise-tours (888-966-8687; www.national geographicexpeditions.com).

PARQUE MUNICIPAL SUMMIT
507-232-4854
www.summitpanama.org
Gaillard Highway
Daily 9–5
Admission: $1 adult, free to children 11 and under

Managed by the city municipality, Summit Nature Park (formerly Summit Botanical Gardens and Zoo) is a gem. It's the closest thing that you'll find to a zoo in Panamá, and gives a taste of some of the critters you may (or may not) see in the wild, such as tapir, ocelot, peccaries, and the harpy eagle. In fact, this well-maintained facility breeds harpy eagles in huge enclosures that permit these massive birds to fly. It also has a primate enclosure, a crocodile corner, and even "Jaguar World"—reason enough to visit. Summit was established in 1923 as an experimental farm for introduced species; today it is Panamá's national botanical garden, boasting more than 150 species of palms, shrubs, and trees from around the world. Bring the kids and make a picnic of it.

PARQUE NACIONAL CAMINO DE CRUCES

507-229-7885
www.anam.gob.pa
Avenida Omar Torrijos Herrera
Daily 9–5
Admission: Free

Wedged between Parque Natural Metropolitano (to the south) and Parque Nacional Soberanía (to the north), this park is part of the Canal watershed and protects 18 square miles (4,590 ha) of moist forest and, like its neighbors, is a great place for birding and for spotting such mammals as agoutis, coatis, and Geoffrey's tamarin. You can explore along the park's namesake historic treasure trail—the Path of the Crosses—that once linked Panamá City with the Chagres River prior to construction of the Camino Real (which linked to Portobelo). The path is only partially excavated, and the roots of giant ceiba and fig trees snake along the forest floor. *Robberies have occurred in past years. Don't hike alone!*

PARQUE NACIONAL CHAGRES

507-232-7228 or 229-7885
www.anam.gob.pa
Transístmica, Km 40
Daily 8–5
Admission: $3

Enshrining 500 square miles (129,585 ha) of lowland and montane rain forest east of the Transístmica highway, this massive park was created in 1985 to protect the watershed of the Río Chagres basin—the main water source for Panamá City and the Canal. Before construction of the Canal, the mighty river flowed unimpeded into the Caribbean and was a major impediment to the French effort to dig a canal. The U.S. Army Corps of Engineers, however, had the foresight to dam the river to create Gatún Lake and channel the flow. In 1934, they completed Madden Dam to create a second lake—**Lago Alajuela** (previously Madden Lake)—upstream. The lake is good for fishing.

The park spans four different life zones, with elevations ranging from a mere 197 feet (60 m) above sea level to 3,003 feet (1,007 m) atop **Cerro Jefe**, where stunted elfin forest is draped in frequent mists. This peak, and neighboring **Cerro Azul** (2,529 feet/771 m), are in the southeast of the park and are accessed from the Interamerican Highway, about 24 miles (38 km) east of Panamá City; you'll need a 4WD vehicle. They're popular destinations for birders and Indiana Jones-style hikers. The Cerro Azúl ranger station permits camping.

Birding and wildlife viewing are major draws: The park boasts more than 500 bird species. Watch for harpy eagles soaring overhead on the lookout for monkeys or sloths to scoop up from the branches of towering *cedro* and mahogany trees. Wildlife is also encyclopedic. Monkeys are a dime a dozen. Ocelots and jaguars prowl the forests. Capybaras wallow in the swampy lagoons and grasslands. And crocodiles and otters splash around in the rivers.

The park is named for the Indian *cacique* (chief) who ruled the area at the time of the *conquistadores*. Fittingly, two indigenous communities still thrive here on the northern shores of Lago Alajuela (they were actually moved here three decades ago after being displaced by flooding during creation of Lago Bayano, in Darién). Visitors to **Comunidad Emberá Parará Púru** and the more distant and much less visited **Emberá Drua** (507-333-2850 or 6709-1233, www .trail2.com/embera/tourism.htm) are

The Canal Expansion Project

After Panamá gained control of operations in 1999, the ACP invested more than $1 billion to widen, straighten, and modernize the canal, resulting in a 20 percent decrease in transit time and a corresponding increase in shipping volume. Nonetheless, with some 14,000 vessels a year now transiting, the canal is operating at about 95 percent of its potential capacity and is expected to max out by 2012. Moreover, the canal is unable to handle the Goliath "post-Panamax" ships that exceed the current chambers' dimensions. Thus, the Panamá Canal has been losing market share to the Suez Canal.

A national referendum in October 2006 approved the ACP's ambitious decade-long *ampliación* (expansion) plan for construction of a parallel and entirely separate canal and lock system capable of handling "post-Panamax" vessels. The $5.2-billion project, prepared by the U.S. Army Corps of Engineers, consists of the construction of two new sets of locks: one each at the Pacific and Caribbean sides. Each lock will have three chambers measuring 1,400 feet/427 m long by 180 feet/55 m wide by 60 feet/18.3 m deep apiece. Each chamber will be fed from three tiered reservoirs that will recycle the water used. To guarantee sufficient water, the navigation channels are being widened and deepened, and Gatun Lake is also being deepened to increase water depth sufficient for approximately 1,100 additional transits per year. New navigational channels are also being cut.

Fortunately, much of the work had been completed five decades ago. The U.S. Army began cutting its own third set of locks in 1939, but the project was suspended in 1942 when the U.S. entered World War II. The new locks, which will employ rolling gates rather than miter gates, will use a significant portion of these earlier excavations. The project is expected to be completed by 2015.

welcomed with ceremonial dances and demonstrations of traditional Emberá lifestyle. Motorized dugout canoes ($25) will take you to Parará Púru from the lakeside village of Nuevo Vigia; the Panamá City-Colón bus will drop you off at Km 29, from where it's about 2 miles (3 km) to Nuevo Vigia. You'll need a 4WD vehicle to reach Drua via the remote dock of Corotú, where you can take a water taxi (about 45 minutes); see the community Web site for directions. Tour companies such as **Aventuras Panamá** (507-260-0044; www.aventuraspanama.com) and **Ancón Expeditions** (507-269-9415; www.anconexpeditions.com) offer excursions. However, for a more intimate experience, I recommend **Embera Village Tours** (506-6758-7600; www.emberavillagetours.com), run by *gringa* Anne Gordon, whose husband is a member of the Púru. You can overnight in Púru—a very humble experience, as the community has no electricity, and "running water" means a boy with a bucket.

Aventuras Panamá also specializes in one- and two-day whitewater rafting trips on the upper Chagres—a thrilling escapade and escape within an hour or two of Panamá City. And Ancón Expeditions offers guided hikes along the centuries-old *camino real* treasure trail, a partially overgrown and extremely rugged trail that winds through the valleys of the Boquerón and Nombre Azul rivers. You can hike all the way to Nombre de Dios and Portobelo (allow two to three days). *Do not hike this trail alone!*

PARQUE NACIONAL SOBERANÍA

507-232-4291 or 229-7885
www.anam.gob.pa
Avenida Omar Torrijos Herrera, 15.5 miles (25 km) NW of Panamá City
Daily 8–5

Cruise ship and freighter passing in the Gaillard Cut, Panamá Canal

Admission: $3, but the fee is rarely collected

Part of the Canal Zone watershed, this easily accessible park was created in 1980 to protect a 54,597-acre (22,104 ha) swath of lowland rain forest extending inland from the eastern shores of Lago Gatún and the Gaillard Cut and rising to 279 feet (85 m) atop Cerro Calabaza. The dense forest includes massive mahoganies, silk cotton trees, and strangler figs whose crowns form a canopy. It teems with 55 amphibian, 79 reptile, and more than 100 mammal species, including anteater, coatimundis, sloths, tapir, and monkeys such as Geoffrey's tamarin. Soberanía is particularly renowned for superb birding, including the chance to spy bicolored, ocellated, and white-bellied antbirds, and even harpy eagles. In fact, more species of birds have been sighted in a single day—360, set by the Audubon Society in 1996—than anywhere else on earth, along the broad, 10-mile (16 km) Pipeline Road, or **Camino del Oleoducto**. Many early morning hikers report seeing capybaras (the world's largest rodents) in the bogs near the trailhead just outside Gamboa village. **Camino del Plantación** (Plantation Road, 4 miles/6.4 km) is also great for birding.

The trails are all well signed, including the short **Sendero El Charco** (2.5 miles/4 km), which begins roadside about 1.2 miles (2 km) beyond the Summit Botanical Garden. It leads to a waterfall with a pool good for refreshing dips. You'll forever remember a hike along the **Sendero Las Cruces**, a remnant of the 16th-century Camino de Cruces treasure trail, with slippery cobbles underfoot; note the hoof marks etched by mules centuries ago. It extends for about 6.5 miles (10 km) to the banks of the Río Chagres. Here, indigenous members of the **Comunidad Wounaan San Antonio** (507-6706-3031; www.authentic panama.com/wounan.htm) have lived lakeside since 1958 and today welcome visitors, as does the nearby **Comunidad Emberá Ella Purú**.

Recent years have witnessed a series of

Centennial Bridge over Panamá Canal by moonlight

robberies on the trails. Ask the rangers at the ANAM office at the park entrance about current conditions, or book an excursion to Soberanía with a local tour company.

PUENTE CENTENARIO

Opened in 2004, the twin-towered Centennial Bridge spans the Canal at the southern entrance to the Gaillard Cut.

It links Panamá City to the town of Arraiján and today carries the Interamerican Highway. The graceful 3,451-foot (1,052 m) bridge is strung like a harp. The roadway clears the canal by 262 feet (80 m), allowing even the largest vessels to pass beneath. It is illuminated at night and is best admired from vessels on the Canal.

SHOPPING

It always pays dividends to buy from the source, for both buyer and seller. Buying tagua-nut carvings, woven baskets, carved gourds, and bead jewelry is a bonus of any visit to Comunidad **Emberá Parará Púru**, **Emberá Drua**, and **Emberá Púru**, in Parque Nacional Chagres.

For quality crafts and Canal memorabilia, you can't beat the gift shop in the **Miraflores Locks Visitor Center**, at Miraflores Locks.

Colón

To many visitors, this could well be the very definition of a sultry down-at-heels tropical port. The nation's second largest city (population 45,000), at the northern entry to the Panamá Canal, owes its creation in 1850 to construction of the Panamá Railroad to serve argonauts en route to and from the California Gold Rush. (Colón was the Colombian government's name for the town; the *yanquis* called it Aspinwall, after William Henry Aspinwall, the railroad's founder.) Originally it occupied Isla Manzanillo, in the Bahía de

Limón, and was linked to the mainland by a causeway. In ensuing years the watery land between them was filled in and the city expanded: In 1948 the Manzanillo area became a Free Trade Zone—the current lifeblood of the city, along with income from the still-active port.

Much of the town perished in a conflagration on March 31, 1885, during the Colombian civil war. Still, enough centenary structures remain to make this of at least marginal interest for sightseeing. And city fathers have invested considerable money in recent years to spruce up depressed Colón (pronounced *ko-LOAN*). Watch your back when exploring, as Colón has an unenviable reputation for crime.

Colonial wooden home in Colón, Panamá

LODGING

MELIÁ PANAMÁ CANAL

507-470-1100
Fax 507-470-1916
www.meliapanamacanal.com
Antigua Escuela de Las Americas, Lago Gatún, 4 miles (6 km) west of Colón
Expensive

The former headquarters of the U.S. Army's notorious School of the Americas has metamorphosed as a luxury hotel. It enjoys a privileged setting on a headland surrounded on three sides by Lago Gatún. The

Swimming pool of Meliá Panama Canal hotel, Panamá

286 guest rooms are stylish yet conservative and have all mod-cons, except Internet modems or Wi-Fi. Maybe General Noriega or another of the other thuggist right-wing dictators trained by Uncle Sam slept in your very bed! The coup de grace is a multi-level swimming pool. Activities include a zipline, kayaks, and plenty of excursion options.

NEW WASHINGTON HOTEL FIESTA CASINO

507-441-7133
Fax: 507-441-7397
nwh@sinfo.net
Avenida del Frente and Calle Bolívar, Colón
Inexpensive to Moderate

A historic grand dame rejuvenated with gleaming marble in the lobby, with chandeliers. The Fiesta Casino adds a contemporary note but draws a noisy crowd. The 124 guest rooms are comfy and have plenty of amenities, but still feel dowdy.

FOUR POINTS BY SHERATON COLÓN

507-447 1000
www.fourpoints.com/colon
Millennium Plaza, Avenida Ahmad Waked
Moderate

The port of Colón, Panamá

A stylish hotel (themed outside like the prow of a ship, complete with anchor) that is our first choice in town. In fact, this cruise-port hotel will please even the most discerning hipsters with its sophisticated contemporary decor and engaging bar. It has only a café-restaurant, and it charges for Wi-Fi, but the guest rooms have high-speed modems.

RADISSON HOTEL COLÓN

507-446-2000
Fax: 507-446-2001
www.radisson.com/colonpan
Paseo Gorgas and Calle 13
Moderate

In the Colón 200 cruise port terminal, this hotel competes with the Four Points for cruise-passenger business. It's an ugly duckling from afar, but the rooms are graciously appointed in a conservative Edwardian fashion. Pay-per-view TV, high-speed Internet, and luxurious linens are bonuses.

ATTRACTIONS, PARKS, AND RECREATION

The town's main street is tree-shaded **Avenida Paseo del Centenario**, a twin-drag boulevard that locals term "El Paseo." It makes for a pleasant stroll, taking note of numerous monuments and statues, including those of John Stevens (Calle 16), the Chief Engineer of the Canal projects 1905–07; Ferdinand de Lesseps (between Calles 3 and 4); Christopher Columbus (between Calles 2 and 3); and Jesus Christ (Calle 1), shown with outstretched arms and known as El Cristo Redentor (Christ the Redeemer). Creaky clapboard houses in tropical ice cream pastels line the avenue.

A two-block detour west from the Christ the Redeemer statue brings you to the **Hotel Washington**, a venerable centenary grand dame remarkable for its Moorish façade and marble lobby that glistens anew after a recent facelift. It's seen many illustrious guests, including Presidents Howard Taft and Warren Harding. Adjoining the hotel, on its west side, is the old Fort DeLesseps, built in 1911 as part of the Canal defense system. Its **Battery Morgan** has been restored and now displays artillery pieces.

If you have a morbid love for cemeteries, check out **Cemeterio Monte de Esperanza** (507-445-3418), better, and formerly, known as Mt. Hope cemetery; it's on Carretera 32, about 0.6 mile (1 km) west of Colón.

GALETA POINT MARINE LABORATORY

507-212-8191
www.stri.org
galeta@si.edu
Isla Galeta, 3 miles (5 km) northeast of Colón
Tuesday through Sunday 9–3, by reservation only
Admission: $5
This facility of the Smithsonian Tropical Research Institute, on the eastern outskirts of town, offers a richly rewarding educational experience. Created in 1997 on the site of a former U.S. Navy satellite communications center, it includes a science and marine education center welcoming visitors. There's an aquarium, and turtles, stingrays, etc., swim around in marine pools. And you can follow a boardwalk through the mangroves to see shorebirds, waders, etc.

Gatún Locks

Gatún, 8 miles (12 km) southwest of Colón. The longest of the three locks, this three-step lock measures 1.2 miles (1.9 km) long. It has a sheltered spectator stand with a running commentary of the operations broadcast in English and Spanish. Although much simpler, and not as high, as the four-level Visitors Center at Miraflores, this is a treat enough.

You can drive across a narrow swing bridge on the north side of the locks to visit **Gatún Dam**, about 6 miles (10 km) upstream of the Río Chagres' mouth (en route, you pass over the old French canal excavation). This great dam, completed in 1913, spans 1.4 miles (2.3 km) and is 2,100 feet (640 m) broad at its base—the largest earthen dam in the world in its day. Its main feature is a curvilinear concrete spillway topped by 14 gates that can be opened or closed to control the height of the lake. The HEP station that powers the Canal system is here.

The Colón-Achiote bus passes both the locks and dam. Taxis from Colón charge approximately $5 one-way, or $10 round-trip including a one-hour wait.

PARQUE NACIONAL SAN LORENZO

507-442-8346 or 433-1676
www.sanlorenzo.org.pa
Visitors Center El Tucán, Achiote, 9 miles (15 km) west of Gatún Locks
Daily 8–4
Admission: Free
San Lorenzo National Park protects 23,843 acres (9,653 ha) along the shores and inland of the mouth of the Río Chagres. The terrain includes shoreline mangrove forest, floodable cativo forests, plus lowland tropical evergreen forest fed by a whopping 130 inches (330 cm) of rainfall per year. It's perhaps most famous as the setting for the U.S. Army School of the America's Fort Sherman Jungle Operations Training Center (JOTC). Thousands of soldiers, and even astronauts, trained for jungle warfare and/or survival amid the snakes and creepy-crawlies. Today Fort Sherman, adjacent to the northwest entrance to the Panamá Canal, is a node for ecotourism. Meanwhile, the notorious School of the Americas, which trained a generation of Latin American dictators and other thugs, is now a hotel. You still need to show your passport to gain entry!

The **Grupo de Ecoturismo Comunitario Los Rapaces Achiote** (507-6664-2339; http://achiotecoturismo.com), a local community group assisted by USAID, offers

Castillo de San Lorenzo, near Colón, Panamá

guided birding, hiking, and horseback riding. Wildlife viewing excels: bird species top 430, and the 81 species of mammals includes armadillos, coatis, spider monkeys, ocelots, and even jaguars and tapirs. The main trail is **Sendero Achiote**, which begins in the community of Achiote, about 9 miles (15 km) southwest of Gatún Locks and gateway to the remote Costa Abajo section of the Caribbean coast. An alternative is **Sendero El Trogón**. (A bus marked Costa Abajo departs Colón for Achiote hourly 10 AM–8 PM.)

The Smithsonian Institute of Tropical Research operates a **canopy crane** for scientific research in the forest canopy. As yet, visitors don't have access.

Castillo de San Lorenzo el Real de Chagres: This fortress—a UNESCO World Heritage Site—stands atop a high coastal bluff and was first completed in 1597 to guard the mouth of the Chagres river. It was rebuilt in 1680 after a raid by Henry Morgan's pirates. It's a bit of a harpy to get to along a rutted dirt road, but the journey is well rewarded by sturdy albeit timeworn walls and cannon embrasures with rusting cannon in situ.

SHOPPING

Many visitors who've heard or read about Colón's duty-free **Zona Libre** (507-445-2229; www.zonalibredecolon.com.pa; Avenida Roosevelt and Calle) come here to shop. However, the world's second largest free-trade zone after Hong Kong is intended for wholesalers only and primarily sells commercial items. Visitors can request a permit, obtainable at the main gate. Ostensibly, tourists can buy here but cannot leave the zone with a purchase, which must be delivered in-bond to the airport or cruise port.

The **Colón 2000** cruise port (Paseo Gorgas's www.colon2000.com) has duty-free and souvenir stores. For authentic pieces, I recommend a visit to **MUCEC** (507-447-0828; http://mucec.org; Calle 2 and Avenida Amador Guerrida, Colón), a non-profit cooperative workshop for distressed women, who produce pottery, woven items, etc. for sale.

Portobelo and Costa Arriba de Colón

East of Colón the wild Caribbean shore known as the Costa Arriba de Colón (High Coast) is remarkably undeveloped, despite being blessed with beaches and historic gems. During the 16th and 17th centuries, this coast was a crown jewel of the Spanish Main and the port of Portobelo was one of the most prized and well-protected cities in the Americas. Every year the treasures of the region were marshaled here for the arrival of the annual *flota* (the Spanish treasure fleet), drawing pirates such as Sir Francis Drake. Great fortresses were built to stop their predations. Roaming the ruins today you can still hear the clash of cut-

Site of Fuerte de San Fernando, Portobelo, Panamá

lasses and the *BOOM!* of cannon. The region moves to the slow pace of a proud Afro-Antillean culture. Much, if not most, of the populace is black. The regional music, the dialects, the spicy cuisine all hint at a profoundly Caribbean potpourri. Offshore coral reefs and, inevitably, the wrecks of galleons and pirate vessels offer some of the best diving in Panamá. And the annual Black Christ Festival is an unforgettable time to visit.

Cannon at Fuerte de San Jeronimo, Portobelo, Panamá

LODGING

Several families in Portobelo rent rooms. Don't expect anything fancy. These are simple budget accommodations. Places to consider include **Cuartos Josefina** (507-6519-5004); **Hospedaje Antonio Esquina** (507-6713-4516); **Hospedaje La Aduana** (507-448-2925); and **Hospedaje Thamythay** (507-441-7382).

BANANAS VILLAGE RESORT

507-263-9510
www.bananasresort.com
Isla Grande, 13 miles (20 km) east of Portobelo
Moderate
The most "resorty" of hotels along this coast, this venerable and poorly maintained beachfront property is popular with city-folk come to laze by the palm-shaded pool. Its 38 rooms come with CD/DVD players and are modestly comfy. Water sports include beach volleyball and kayaks. A little money and TLC would go a long way to recouping this hotel's faded glory.

COCO PLUM

507-448-2102
www.cocoplum-panama.com
Buena Ventura, Portobelo
Inexpensive
Modest it may be, but this cozy, unpretentious 12-room hotel a five-minute drive west of Portobelo has all the ingredients for an enjoyable Caribbean vacation. The cabins, right on the beach, are splashed with tropical pastels; six are air-conditioned; four have fans. It offers water sports. The open-air Restaurante Las Anclas specializes in seafood and Colombian dishes.

CORAL LODGE

507-232-0300
www.corallodge.com
Santa Isabel
This landlocked eco-lodge is the only upscale option along the entire Costa Arriba. It's made more appealing by its remote location, accessible solely by boat, and by its oh-so-romantic thatched bungalows built directly over the water along a boardwalk pier. It lies at the easternmost extreme of the Costa Arriba, on the doorstep of the San Blas islands (arriving guests are typically transferred by boat after flying into Porvenir). The furnishings can't be termed deluxe, but the air-conditioned octagonal cabins are delightful enough and have high-pitched conical ceilings plus decks. The seafood restaurant is delightful and has a deck. You can even jump in to snorkel right off your deck! It has kayaks, diving, and an infinity-edge pool, and offers a range of activities, including jungle walks.

JIMMY'S CARIBBEAN DIVE RESORT

507-682-9322
www.caribbeanjimmysdiveresort.com
Nombre de Dios
Moderate
Although catering primarily to divers, this no-frills resort 3 miles (5 km) east of Nombre de Dios takes in all comers. It appeals to laid-back types who shun pretense with its five palm-shaded, wood-paneled beachfront cabañas. Offers horseback, fishing, and rain forest excursions, plus dive packages.

SISTER MOON HOTEL

507-236-8489
www.hotelsistermoon.com
Isla Grande, 14 miles (20 km) east of Portobelo
Moderate
Sitting over a rocky and secluded cove with dramatic vistas, this rambling 14-room hotel has some striking features, such as sparsely furnished rooms with loft bed atop natural rock bases; some rooms offer bunks. Nothing fancy here, but it has a bar and small swimming pool. Appeals to luxury-shunning castaways enamored of rusticity.

DINING

Portobelo has a smattering of simple restaurants. For atmosphere, head to **Restaurante Los Cañones** (507-448-2980), overlooking a cove on the approach road into town. This thatched restaurant serves seafoods, such as a delicious house specialty: *pulpo en leche de coco*—octopus in tomato sauce on coconut rice.

ATTRACTIONS, PARKS, AND RECREATION

Beaches

Although lacking the spectacular white-sand beaches of the San Blas islands, farther east, or of the Archipiélago de las Perlas, this coast *does* have some lovely beaches, although resorts and hotels are few. The best, and most developed is **Isla Grande**, 3 miles (5 km) east of Portobelo. It's especially popular with folks who pour in from Panamá City on weekends and holidays. The snorkeling is good.

Water taxis for Isla Grande depart from La Guayra, 13 miles (21 km) east of Portobelo.

Nombre de Dios

15 miles (25 km) east of Portobelo. It's a fabulously scenic drive to reach Nombre de Dios from Portobelo along a potholed rollercoaster road, which peters down to dirt in the town, which straddles an eponymous river. The town's pedigree is ancient: founded in 1510 by *conquistador* Diego de Nicuesa, the port gained rapid import as the assembly point for bullion brought from Nuestra Señora de la Asunción de Panamá via the cobbled *camino de cruces* treasure trail. The marshy harbor was ill-suited to the role of treasure port, being open to attack by pirates and tropical storms. The port was pillaged by Francis Drake in 1572, after which Portobelo superseded Nombre de Dios. The town became a sleepy backwater, as it remains to this day. Most residents make a living from fishing.

In 1998, a shipwreck discovered off Playa Damas was proclaimed (unconvincingly) to be Columbus' *Vizcaina,* which in 1502 sunk hereabouts during his final voyage to the New World. Only cursory recovery efforts have been made to date.

Parque Nacional Portobelo

(507-448-2165) Forming its own great bulwark around the town, this park spans 139 square miles (35,929 ha) of ocean, some 44 miles (70 km) of coastline, and a large range of forested mountains that rise inland. The park abuts Parque Nacional Chagres, forming a biological corridor for wildlife. It encompasses ecosystems from coral reefs and precious mangroves to tropical montane rain forest. At its heart is the town itself, still guarded by fortresses as reminders of a time four centuries ago when this unlikely spot was one of the three prize jewels of the Spanish Main (the others were Cartagena, in Colombia, and Veracruz, in Mexico).

Rivers snake down from the mountains and spill into Portobelo Bay, which is lined on its northern and eastern shores by mangrove, marsh, and moist forest. Safari trips up the **Río Cascajal** and **Río Claro** provide opportunities for spotting anhingas, caiman, crocodiles, sloths, monkeys, crab-eating raccoons, and even river otters. Local operator **Selvaventuras** (507-442-1042 or 6688-6247; selvaventuras@hotmail.com) has guided nature trips, including mountain hikes.

Portobelo

Ruta 31, 28 miles (45 km) east of Colón. Today a sleepy place except for when it bursts into life for the annual Black Christ festival, Portobelo was once a thriving port city. Tucked onto the southern shores of a deep oblong bay framed by sensuously curved hills, its setting is gorgeous. Hence the name: "Beautiful Port." The best views are around sunrise, when fog floats eerily over the vales and waters and you expect a ghost ship to appear through the mist in *Pirates of the Caribbean* fashion. It's a popular destination for yachters.

Portobelo was actually named by Christopher Columbus, who limped into the bay with worm-eaten ships on November 2, 1502, on his fourth and final voyage to the New World. The town, named San Felipe de Puerto Bello, was founded in 1597 after the port town of Nombre de Dios, a few miles farther east, was raided by Francis Drake. Nombre de Dios fell into desuetude and Portobelo, with its better harbor, grew rapidly as the departure point for the *flota* and the most important settlement in the Spanish territory of Nueva Grenada. Its climate was disagreeably humid, however, and the permanent population stabilized at no more than 1,000 people. Nonetheless, the announcement of the approach of the treasure fleet triggered a mass influx of traders, accountants, and military personnel for an annual trade fair, swelling Portobelo's population tenfold. So much gold and silver bullion plundered from Peru and the Islas de Perlas arrived via the *camino real* treasure trail that ingots were actually piled in great mountains on the streets. Portobelo was never walled, but was fortified with batteries of cannons.

In 1597 the town escaped assault by a fleet of 26 pirate ships led by Drake, who sickened and died of dysentery before the attack could take place. The Spanish bulwarked Portobelo with twin huge fortresses—Todo Fierro (Iron Castle) and Fortaleza Santiago de la Gloria—to each side of the harbor entrance. Completed in 1620, they were no match for Welsh pirate Henry Morgan, whose cutthroat army of 450 men overran the fortresses in 1668, resulting in a 14-day barbarous plunder. In 1738, the town fell again, to an English fleet led by Sir Edward Vernon. Before sailing off, he blew up the fortresses. The destruction caused Spain to alter its treasure fleet practice. Although the fortresses were replaced with smaller, second-generation bulwarks, Portobelo never recovered its importance.

The colonial-era military installations, Customs building, church, etc. today form the Conjunto Monumental de Portobelo. The following sights are all must-sees:

Fortresses: Entering the bay from Colón, you pass beneath the **Batería de Santiago**, on the site of the former Fortaleza San Diego (destroyed in 1738). It still has *baluartes* (watchtowers) and cannon in their embrasures, attained by a stepped trail. It was built into the rugged hills on the southern shores to catch passing ships in a crossfire from **Fuerte de San Fernando** across the harbor, on the site of the former Fortaleza San Felipe (a water taxi from the town pier costs about $2.50). Some 218 yards (200 m) east of Batería de Santiago is the meager ruin of the low-slung **Castillo de Santiago de la Gloria**, completed in 1600 but destroyed by Henry Morgan's gang and now mostly overgrown. In town, the harborfront is dominated by the

Baluarte (watchtower) at Fuerte de San Jeronimo, Portobelo, Panamá

ruins of **Fuerte de San Jerónimo**, with its main battery face-on to the harbor entrance. It dates from 1664, although what you see today is the remake in 1758 following Sir Edward Vernon's depredations. It has cannon still in place.

Iglesia de San Felipe: This twee whitewashed church, one block northeast of the town plaza, dating from 1814, has a two-tiered campanile and a simple gilt

> **Good to Know About**
> The **IPAT tourist information office** (507-448-2200; Calle Principal; daily 8:30–4:30), 55 yards (50 m) southwest of the plaza, stocks a map "Costa Arriba y Conjunto Monumental Portobelo."

mahogany altar. Superstitious Panamanians flock to venerate a statue of Jesus painted with black skin, carrying a cross, and dressed in a purple velvet robe; the robe is changed yearly and is given by someone who has earned the honor. According to legend, the statue arrived in the 17th century on a Spanish ship bound for Cartagena, Colombia. The ship tried to leave several times but each time it was beaten back by storms until eventually the crew came to believe that the statue—*El Nazareño*—was to blame and left it behind. Later, the statue was proclaimed responsible for saving Portobelo from a cholera scourge that swept the nation in 1821. A special 11 AM Mass every last Sunday of the month features Afro-based folkloric *congo* music and dance. The Black Christ is the inspiration for the Festival del Nazareno each October 21 (see *Seasonal Events*).

Museo del Cristo Negro de Portobelo: This tiny museum (507-448-2024; daily 8–4; admission $1) is in the **Hospital e Iglesia San Juan de Dios**, next to the Iglesia de San Felipe, which dates from 1801 and stands atop the original, dating from 1598. The museum now displays robes used to adorn the Black Christ statue, and those worn by pilgrim-partyers during the annual festival.

Real Aduana: The twin-story Royal Customs House (507-448-2024; Calle de la Aduana; daily 8–4; admission $1), or "counting house," opening to the plaza in the center of town, was the most important building during Portobelo's heyday. Here, royal accountants kept track of the treasures flowing in and out of town and ensured that the Spanish crown got its cut. It dates from 1630 and was restored in original fashion in 1998, after being badly beaten up by pirates and by an earthquake in 1882. Today it houses a tiny museum with an English-language video on the history of Portobelo, plus maps, 3-D *maquetas* (models) of the castles, and other miscellany on the town's history and folkloric culture.

Taller Portobelo: This workshop and gallery (c/o 507-448-2124 in Panamá City; www.tallerportobelonorte.com) sells works by a local artists cooperative. The artists work in naive styles that reflect the local heritage in vivid color. The **Spelman College Summer Art Colony** (404-270-5455; www.spelman.edu/artcolony), in Atlanta, Georgia, sponsors three-week residency courses for artists.

Scuba Diving

Diving is superb along the Costa Arriba. The **Arrecife Salmadina** reef clasps two Spanish galleons and a Beech C-45 warbird in 75 feet (25 m) of water. Heck, you can even join the search for Sir Francis Drake's lead-weighted coffin, somewhere off **Isla Drake**, where he was laid to rest on January 28, 1596. **Panama Divers** (507-314-0817; www.panamadivers .com) and **Scuba Panamá** (507-261-3841; www.scubapanama.com) offer trips.

The *Real* Jack Sparrow

Fictional character Captain Jack Sparrow, of *Pirates of the Caribbean* fame, is a lovable rascal. A conniving trickster. A deceitful betrayer, even of his friends. Yet almost harmlessly inept, and endearing. Sparrow gives a bad name to pirates. In truth, the vast majority were remorseless cutthroats—the terrorists of their days, eager to torture, murder, and rape without scruple or hesitation. The ruthless sea rovers terrorized the Caribbean and Spanish Main for two centuries. Nowhere was safe. Often they operated in packs of 20 or more ships, sufficient to capture and ransack even the most fortified city. Panamá's history is inseparable from their nefarious deeds.

Almost from the arrival of the first *conquistadores*, Panamá became a major conduit for the vast wealth of the American continent. Stupendous amounts of treasure—Colombian emeralds, Inca silver and gold, pearls from the Archipiélago de las Perlas—were transported overland to the ports of Nombre de Dios and, later, Portobelo to await the arrival of the annual *flota,* or treasure fleet, that would bear the booty to Spain. Pirates, predatory sea-going raiders, arrived in the *conquistadores* wake. At first they acted alone, in single ships; and later as packs, much like wolves. Because Spain possessed most of the Caribbean and mainland America, she became the natural target for foreign pirates, and privateers. Throughout much of the 16th and 17th centuries, Spain warred against England, France, and Holland, which authorized individual captains to attack Spanish ships and cities in the New World as a legitimate form of guerrilla war on the cheap.

Sir Francis Drake (1542–96) was, perhaps, the most famous—and effective—privateer. English myth paints him as a heroic figure, which perhaps he was. But he was also ruthless, and guilty of the most horrendous deeds. Drake started out in 1567 as a slave trader with his cousin John Hawkins. An encounter with the Spanish in 1568 prompted a quest for revenge. Thus, in 1572 he took up piracy against the Spanish Main. In July he raided Nombre de Dios (he succeeded, but retired after being shot); the following year he struck the Camino de Cruces, captured a mule train, and returned home with holds bursting with treasure. Queen Elizabeth granted Drake a privateer's license and sent him

WEEKLY AND ANNUAL EVENTS

In March, head to Portobelo for the **Festival de Diablos y Congos** (507-6714-6550; www .diablosycongos.com), when townsfolk celebrate their long and proud Afro-colonial heritage with traditional carnival-style music and dance.

Portobelo's vibrant art community displays its finest at the annual **Arte Feria** (www.dia blosycongos.com/visitportobeloSite/arteferia.html), every June. The festival includes theater, dance, and poetry, as well as art exhibitions.

The major event is the bi-annual **Festival del Nazareno** (October 21), which draws as many as 40,000 to Portobelo. Many *peregrinos* (pilgrims) arrive barefoot and shaved. Others crawl in on their hands and knees. Most wear an ankle-length, claret-colored velvet toga adorned with gold braid, faux jewels, and sequins. After sunset, the black Christ is taken from its perch in the church and paraded atop a litter. The bearers adopt a military-style sway, side to side, as they take three steps forward and two back—a real pilgrim's progress. The fun begins after midnight, when the statue is returned to the church—signal for a very irreligious bacchanal to begin!

on an expedition. The fleet seemed ill-fated, and five of the original six ships were lost to the elements. Entering the Pacific Ocean via Cape Horn in the *Golden Hinde*, he waylaid a treasure ship, the *Nuestra Señora de la Concepción*. He returned to England westward via Cape Hope to a hero's welcome (he was the first Englishman to circumnavigate the globe; only Magellan's expedition had previously made such a journey). He was knighted by the Queen, who took half the share. After the outbreak of war with Spain, Drake returned to the Americas and ravaged the cities of Santo Domingo and Cartagena. Throughout the Americas, *el draque* became a term of fear. Following his illustrious role in the defeat of the Spanish Armada he pillaged the Iberian ports. In August 1595 he returned to the Caribbean. While preparing to attack Portobelo, he sickened and died (most likely of dysentery) and on January 29, 1597, was buried at sea in a lead-filled coffin.

The mid-17th-century gave birth to an entirely new group of pirates: the "buccaneers." This band of cutthroats had started out innocently enough as a group of international seafaring hobos who had gravitated towards Isla Tortuga, an island off the north coast of Hispaniola. Here they lived relatively peacefully, raising hogs and hunting wild boar to sell as dried meat *(boucan)* to passing ships. The Spanish authorities, however, drove them out. They coalesced again and formed the "Brethren of the Coast"—a band committed to piracy against the Spanish. Their success drew like-minded villains. Soon they were a force to be feared throughout the Caribbean. The English authorities granted them official sanction as privateers, and a base at Port Royal, Jamaica.

They rose to infamy under Henry Morgan (1635–88), a socially privileged Welshman who took to piracy and proved an utterly ruthless and brilliant leader. His predations upon the entire Spanish Main became the stuff of legends, crowned in 1671 when he sacked Panamá City and, in 1688, Portobelo. Although Morgan stood trial for attacking Panamá City (England and Spain had just signed a peace treaty), he was treated as a hero and given a knighthood and eventually named governor of Jamaica. His death signaled the end of an era, affirmed in 1697 when England, France, and Spain signed the Treaty of Ryswick, committing themselves to stamping out piracy.

Children performing an Afro-Caribbean dance, Portobelo, Panamá

5

Kuna Yala

*"It's a cramped, knees-up-to-the-chin, 50-minute flight which ends on a grass
strip right on the water's edge. A short walk and a boat trip to the island of
Uaguinega and the tourist finds he has taken a journey into the past."*
—RICHARD HOLLEDGE

Dazzling sands. Turquoise waters. Postcard-perfect coral cays shaded by palms and sheltered by an offshore coral reef. And an indigenous people dressed in unique, and uniquely colorful, costumes. Even the most jaded and seasoned traveler has a jaw-drop reaction to the first experience of the Kuna Yala. This autonomous *comarca* (region) of the Kuna people is without a doubt the most colorful and fascinating part of the country. It is synonymous with the Archipiélago de San Blas, comprising 365 islands that parallel the coast in a paternoster that ranges from a few hundred yards to 16 miles (25 km) offshore, running from El Porvenir to the Colombian border—a distance of 140 miles (225 km). Only a dozen or so are inhabited. They're populated entirely by the self-governing Kuna, who live in about 40 widely scattered island communities, and in a dozen or so fishing villages and hamlets on the Caribbean mainland. (The comarca was created in 1938 and covers 2,151 square miles/5,570 sq km, taking up the northeast of the country and extending from the continental shelf to the ridgeline of the thickly forested Serranía de San Blas and Serranía de Darién mountains).

While the beauty of the San Blas isles is reason enough to visit (another is the sensational snorkeling; scuba diving is not allowed), the main draw is the Kuna people. Or rather, the Kuna women, who dress in traditional costumes sewn of *molas* (appliqué cloths) in eye-startling colors that reverberate in the incandescent Caribbean sunshine. The fiercely independent women call the shots among this pure-blood pygmyesque people, who are intensely protective of their culture. Tourism is a lifeblood, yet is strictly regulated: Visitors are welcome so long as they play and pay by Kuna rules. Nonetheless, life here is lived very simply and visitors should expect only relatively meager accommodations and services akin to backpacker hostels. A small price to pay for an immersion in one of the most intact indigenous cultures in the world.

The Comarca is neatly divided into three administrative districts that coincidentally accord with the major island clusters: Nibaldid (or Arriba, "Upper"), in the west; Abargined (or Centro, "Center"), in the middle; and Urbalid (or Abajo, "Lower") in the east.

OPPOSITE: *Isla de los Perros, San Blas Islands, Panamá*

Colorful Kuna mola, San Blas Islands, Panamá

Distances between each island group are significant, so pick a single island cluster to visit. Independent travelers must present their passport to Kuna police on each island. There's only one bank, and Kuna Yala is a cash-only society; plan accordingly. Oh, raise your camera and you'll be hit up for $1 per photo. No exceptions! unless you buy a *mola.*

Note that many of the islands go by multiple names, often with no determined spelling. Some names are used for more than one island, such as the two Yandups, miles apart. *And don't go swimming around the populated islands,* where sewage is dumped directly into the sea.

GETTING THERE AND AROUND

By Air
The easiest access is by air. Small airstrips throughout the archipelago are served by **Aeroperlas** (507-315-7500; www.aeroperlas.com) and **Air Panama** (507-316-9000; www.flyairpanama.com). Make reservations well ahead of travel. Flights cost $65 each way to El Porvenir.

By Bus, Público, or Car
A single dirt road contacts the Comarca to "civilization." This rollercoaster, which links the Kuna Yala village of Cartí to the Interamerican Highway (the junction is at El Llano, 11 miles/18 km east of Chepo) via the Serranía de San Blas mountains, is often a bouilla-baisse. In rainy season, usually only the highest-ground clearance vehicles, such as army trucks, can get through (it ate my 4WD jeep for breakfast last time I tried it, leaving my

vehicle trapped thigh-deep in mud). The road has since been upgraded in 2009, but it's still no walk in the park, and extremely lonesome. Plus, there's a river to ford. Maybe you'll make it; maybe you won't. Eventually you emerge at the coast beside the airstrip; water taxis will run you to Cartí or any of the other islands. The government has plans to pave the road, but don't hold your breath.

You have to pay a $6 entry fee upon arrival at Nusagandi, where a "ranger" station marks the boundary of the Comarca.

Private Jeep *públicos* ($25 each way) operate from Panamá City: call Alexis Lam (507-6634-9384 or 6528-5862), Rigoberto González (507-262-4107 or 262-5837), or Urbano González (507-251-3021). And a Jeep leaves daily at 5 AM from Hostel Mamallena (www.mamallena.com).

By Sea

Cruise West (888-851-8133; www.cruisewest.com) features a visit to the San Blas on its nine-day cruise-tours, offered October through March. A few cruise ships also feature a day at anchor close to El Porvenir. Tenders run passengers to the islands. You'll want to avoid visiting during these crowded times.

Yachters can anchor throughout the archipelago ($5 anchorage fee per isle). You'll need good charts, plus a copy of *Cruising Guide to the Isthmus of Panamá* (Nancy and Tom Schwalbe Zydler). The area abounds in reefs.

Cargo craft run between Cartí and Colombia. Many are questionable operations (drug-trafficking is common in the region). You might try to book passage on the *Stahlratte* (507-6536-6032; in Germany 49/030-3700-8748; www.stahlratte.org), a German-run two-masted schooner that occasionally sails between the San Blas and Cartagena.

Local *lanchas* (motor-powered canoes and boats) are the main form of transport between the islands, but it's more fun (albeit considerably slower) to move around with locals in their sleek *ulus* (canoes) with sails.

Airstrip on El Porvenir, San Blas Islands, Panamá

Sailboat in the San Blas Islands, Panamá

By Tours
Many tour operators in Panamá City offer daylong excursions and overnight or multi-day packages that include airfare and accommodation.

Exotics Adventures (507-314-3013; www.panamaexoticsadventures.com) specializes in the San Blas and has a three-day Cartí-El Llano hike and kayak trip.

The Arriba Region
Comprising several discrete clusters of isles, the westernmost region is the most visited part of San Blas. It also has most of the services, concentrated around the small town of Cartí and the pinprick isle of El Porvenir, with one of the two main airstrips. When cruise ships are in, expect to share space with hordes of passengers at the most popular sites around the Golfo de San Blas.

Farther east are two large groupings of islands accessed via the airstrip at Corazón de Jesús, a densely populated island twinned by an arcing steel footbridge to the isle of Narganá (also known as Yandup). Narganá has the only bank in the Comarca, as well as the regional courthouse and police headquarters. Despite, or perhaps because of, its administrative import, it's also the most Westernized place in the San Blas. Most of the Kuna women long ago dropped their traditional garb; the populace lives in concrete houses, eat Western processed foods, and watch TV. More traditional Kuna look with horror at this trend, and the fact that there's no traditional *casa de congreso* and that several evangelical Christian groups work hard here to destroy Kuna culture. Fortunately, it's just a short boat ride to a score of more tranquil and traditional isles that make up the Cayos Odrupuquip. Farther north, a separate and virtually untouched group—the Cayos Holandeses—are among the most pristine isles in all San Blas.

LODGING AND DINING

All the lodgings in San Blas are rustic, some
extremely so; flush toilets are a luxury—at
most you post your derriere over the sea!
And expect to sleep in a hammock, which is
all part of the experience. Most include a
local tour in the room rate (typically $15–35
per night, including meals). Since there's
little to distinguish them from backpackers'
hostels, I've simply listed the options
below. Only those hotels that offer something a little extra are profiled in greater
detail. All are Kuna-owned and operated.
Meals are usually limited to simple seafood
and beans-and-rice variety dishes.

Anbabnega Lodge (507-6780-7002 or
  507-6030-0964; brwn2@hotmail.com)
  Cartí Tupile. A thatched hut with bamboo walls, it has solar power plus flush
  toilets and water faucets. Meals are
  served on a waterfront deck. Run by
  Kuna mother-and-daughter team, Chela
  and Stephanie. A 10-minute boat ride
  from Cartí. Inexpensive.

Cabañas Coco Blanco (507-6715-2223 or
  6700-9427) Ogobsibudup, 2.5 miles
  (7 km) northwest of Narganá. Four
  private cane-walled cabins with wooden
  floors and simple bathrooms with
  flush toilets. Run by the Sánchez family.

Cabañas Dubasenika (507-6540-5478).
  Isla Franklin. One of the original backpackers' hostels, it has cabins on its own
  island.

Cabañas Kuanidup (507-6635-6737 or
  6656-4673; www.kuanidup.8k.com)
  Kuanidup, 2.5 miles (7 km) north of Río
  Sidra. A rustic option with seven basic
  thatch-and-bamboo huts with sand
  floors. Makeshift beds with foam mattresses. Shared toilets.

Cabañas Tigre (507-229-9006). Isla Tigre.
  Cane and thatch huts with hammocks.

Cabañas Yandup (507-261-7229; www
  .yandupisland.com; yandup@cableonda
  .net). Yandup, 0.6 mile (1 km) northeast

of Playón Chico. Fourteen thatched cabins with bamboo walls and patios.
  Shared toilets

Eulogio's. Cartí. A two-story option with
  communal living. Eulogio also has a
  variety of simple cabins on outlying
  islands. Inexpensive.

Hospedaje Corbiski (507-6708-5254;
  http://hospedajecorbiskikunayala.blogs
  pot.com) Isla Corbiski. Owner Elias
  Pérez Martínez plays hospitable host and
  serves delicious seafood dishes. The six
  rooms in cement-block-and-bamboo
  huts are basic.

Hotel El Porvenir (507-229-9000; fax
  507-221-1397; hotelelporvenir@hot
  mail.com) No frills. Cement walls. Tin
  roof. Cold-water showers, but at least
  you get private bathrooms in the 13
  rooms. Inexpensive.

Hotel Noris (507-299-9009 c/o public
  phone) Narganá. Air-conditioned
  rooms! Still, the seven rooms in this
  two-story concrete building are nothing
  to write home about. Shared bathrooms.
  The best is Room #1. It also has a palapa-
  roofed restaurant—Restaurant Nali—with
  sand floor, outdoor seating, and Wi-Fi
  service, but it's a slow connection.
  Imagine! Inexpensive.

Hotel San Blas (507-262-9812; hotelsan
  blas@hotmail.com) Nalunega, 0.6 mile
  (1 km) southwest of El Porvenir. Real
  beds in this otherwise simple place
  with 28 rooms with sand floors, thin
  bamboo room partitions, and basic
  shared cold-water bathrooms. Choose a
  corner room for cross-ventilation.
  Inexpensive.

Nixia's. Cartí. Basic bamboo-and-thatch
  living, with plenty of open lounge space.
  Also basic cabins on outlying islands.
  Inexpensive.

Ukuptupu Hotel (507-6746-5088; www
  .ukuptupu.com; ukuptupu@ukuptupu
  .com) Ukuptupu, 438 yards (400 m)

west of El Porvenir. The former Smithsonian Institute research facility is today a somewhat Spartan hotel with 15 rooms with shared bathrooms, beds with foam mattresses, linoleum floors, and balconies with hammocks.

KUNA NISKUA LODGE

507-259-9136
http://kuna-niskua.com

Wailidup, 0.6 mile (1 km) southwest of El Porvenir

This two-story thatch-and-bamboo lodge is one of my favorites. Kept spic-and-span, it has comfy beds in 12 rooms with woven palm-frond walls. Some rooms have private bathrooms; others share. Private rooms cost about $65 single, $100 double, including food and tours. Solar electricity. In a lovely village.

ATTRACTIONS, PARKS, AND RECREATION

Cartí Sugdup and Vicinity

Lying a few hundred yards off the mainland, the small island of **Cartí Sugdup** (Crab Island) hosts the most developed and commercial settlement in the Comarca. It can be reached by air to the mainland airstrip or by road (mud permitting!); either way, a water taxi ($1.50) will run you from the dock to the isle. Frankly, I find the place a bit of an eyesore. Cruise ships often stop here, when Cartí gets swamped. The only real site of interest is the **Museo Kuna** (507-299-9002; daily 8–4; $2 including a brief guided tour), in the home of a local family; the simple collection explains about Kuna history and culture, such as the all-important puberty ritual for females.

For a true island idyll, take a water taxi out to one of the nearby palm-shaded coral cays, such as **Isla Aguja**.

San Blas Islands at sunrise, Panamá

Cayos Holandéses

Beckoning far out in the briny, this cluster of a score-plus isles lies about 19 miles (30 km) northwest of Narganá, on the periphery of the continental shelf, with waves crashing up against the barrier reef—a deadly passage for vessels. Several Spanish galleons and more modern craft that foundered are clasped to the reef. The Dutchmen's Keys are almost entirely deserted. Hire a boat to take you out (a minimum one-hour run) and take some provisions and snorkeling gear. *Paradise!*

Cayos Los Grullos

Two dozen or so far-flung cays and isles lie scattered in a long line east of Cartí Sugdup, like jewels in a sapphire sea. Most are entirely virgin and tourist facilities are almost non-existent. But these little gems offer some of the finest snorkeling in the entire Central American isthmus. The crystal clear waters are colored in intense Maxfield Parrish blues, and mirror-class calm, too—perfect for yachters.

Planes fly in to the densely populated isle of **Nusadup**, close to the mainland about 9.5 miles (15 km) east of Cartí. Nusadup's twin to the north is **Ursadup** (also known as Río Sidra).

Intriguingly, the fastidiously conservative Kuna culture has a liberal acceptance of homosexuality and of transvestites or transgender males (*omegit*, in Kuna lingo), many of whom count among the finest *mola* artists in the Comarca. If there's one reason to visit Ursadup, it surely is to meet *omegit* Lisa Harris and to buy one of her world-famous works of art, whose designs are much more complex and creative than is the norm. Stunning! Metaphysical masterpieces. They seem to me inspired by Picasso. Lisa has a small museum on *molas* in her home.

Another master *mola*-maker is Venancio Restrepo, who lives on a speck called **Isla Maquina** (2 miles/3 km from Ursadup), the "*mola* makers isle" and a must-visit for anyone serious about buying quality *molas*.

You're spoilt for choice when it comes to picking a Robinson Crusoe-isle where you can leave your Man Friday footprint in pristine sands. Hire a boat to run you the 6 miles (4 km) from Nusadup to Narascandubpipi. Identical in picture postcard beauty, Kuanidup happens to have a small hotel.

El Porvenir and Vicinity

Despite its meager populace and facilities, the tiny isle of **El Porvenir** is the unlikely capital of the Comarca Kuna Yala, as well as the principal gateway to the westernmost group of isles. Locals know it as Gaigirgordup. Floating a mere 1 mile (1.6 km) east of Punta de San Blas, at the extreme west end of the archipelago, it hosts the administrative center, a police station, and the small, community-run **Museo del Nación Kuna** (507-316-1232; http://onmaked.nativeweb.org; koskunkalu@hotmail.com; daily 8–4; $1) displaying musical instruments, household items, crafts, and a replica of a Kuna grave.

El Porvenir is typically used as a jumping off spot to three islands strung in a line to the southwest and mere minutes away by boat. The nearest and, in many ways, the most interesting (and therefore the most popular) is **Wichub-Huala**. The entire island, barely 218 yards (200 m) long and even less wide, is occupied by a densely packed hamlet, mostly made up of humble huts woven of bamboo and palm reeds and jammed one up against the other. Its labyrinthine sandy alleys (barely wide enough for four people side by side) are a veritable non-stop bazaar of Kuna women selling their beautiful *molas*, while young girls

Water taxi on Wichub-Huala, San Blas Islands, Panamá

dressed in their finest traditional garb (and every second one holding a parrot) tether lizards to their headscarves and hawk themselves as photo ops. The downside is that this isle can get jam-packed with tourists, especially when the cruise ships call. And, like almost all Kuna villages, the inhabitants litter their isle with trash—quite disgusting!

Within shouting distance is **Nalunega**, a smaller and but almost identical isle with one of the better hotels around (it was formerly a Smithsonian Tropical Research Institute station, but the Kuna, having full-on paranoia for "foreigners," forced it to close in 1998). Nalunega, which is often called Ukuptupu, is thankfully relatively free of garbage: this due to Juan García (the Kuna owner of the Hotel San Blas with his Kuna wife Albertina), who has educated his neighbors and organized regular clean-up campaigns.

Kuna girls with parakeets on their heads, San Blas Islands, Panamá

A much larger, but relatively sparsely populated, group of some three dozen isles begins about 3 miles (5 km) to the east of El Porvenir. Many of these isles are reef-fringed specks with sublimely talcum-fine beaches. Truly quintessential paradisiacal isles! The most famous is **Isla de los Perros** (Isle of Dogs), known by locals as Achutupbipi. Excursions are popular. It's the perfect idyll for lazing on the beach, or kayaking and snorkeling. As is Kuna custom, the land is communal but a single family owns all the coconut trees. They attend to visitors by preparing meals.

Narganá and Vicinity

While in **Narganá**, note the bronze **statue of Carlos Inaediguine Robinson** in the village square; it honors the leader of the 1925 Kuna Revolution that resulted in autonomy for the Kuna people. Otherwise, Narganá and Corazón de Jesús offer little touristic appeal. You're wise (and well rewarded) to hire a *lancha* or *ulu* to run you to pristine **Isla Tigre** (4.5 miles/7 km east of Narganá), where the triple delights are the blazing white sands, coral-studded gin-clear waters, and a Kuna culture untainted by modern ways. The inhabitants here are a tidy lot, too, and take pains to keep their isle clean. Refreshingly, there's little of the *"Buy . . . Buy . . . Buy!"* mentality that assaults visitors to the westernmost isles. It's a good place, too, to experience traditional festivals.

Numerous other coral cays are well worth a day's visit.

Sign on Isla de los Perros, San Blas Islands, Panamá

Fiddler crab, Isla Iguana, Panamá

SHOPPING

From the minute you arrive in Kuna Yala, you'll be accosted by local women selling brightly colored *molas* (often featured on embroidered blouses and shirts) and beaded bracelets and belts. Women paddle out to yachts to tout their wares. On the islands, there are no shops as such. Vendors simply display their *molas* along the narrow paths. Also look for Pan-style wooden flutes and wooden *nuchunaga* figurines representing spirits. Avoid buying coral and shell jewelry.

The Kuna are aggressive, and tough, salespeople. Feel free to bargain, but don't expect to get prices much below 10 percent discount of the first asking price. *Molas* begin at about $15 and can cost $500 or more for large, quality pieces, identified by a well-balanced design with harmonious colors, smooth edges, evenly spaced lines, and virtually invisible stitches.

Bring lots of small-denomination bills. No credit cards! If you run out of cash, the only bank is in Narganá.

WEEKLY AND ANNUAL EVENTS

Time your visit to Isla Tigre for February 25 to witness a dramatic reenactment of the Kuna Revolt of 1925; or mid-October for a weeklong festival of traditional music and dance. And the folks of Narganá celebrate Carlos Inaegiguine Robinson's birthday each August 20.

Meanwhile, despite the presence of Christian missionaries, the Kuna of Río Azúcar (a coastal hamlet on the mainland, about 2.5 miles/4 km west of Narganá) explodes in carnaval-like bacchanal.

The Centro Region

The central island group comprises several clusters of isles that cling close to the mainland. The necklace of islands that bead the coastline are too remote to reach by boat from the western isles, but regular air service is also offered to Playón Chico, Achutupu, Mamitupu, Ogobsucum, and Tabuala. Nonetheless, they are as beautiful as any in the San Blas, and receive far fewer visitors—reason enough to visit—despite being the most populated islands. The snorkeling here, however, is less exciting due to the rough seas whipped up in the relative absence of an offshore barrier reef. For the same reason, yachters will find the seas here a tad trickier than within the reef-sheltered waters farther west.

Good to Know About

The Comarca's only bank is in Narganá, which has the main hospital. Several other islands have medical clinics. Gardi Sugdup, Río Sidra, and Narganá have basic medical clinics; for any mildly serious issues, you're wise to hop a plane to Panamá City.

Telephone service is very ephemeral and limited. There are public telephones in the main communities, as well as on El Porvenir, Wichubwala, and Gardi Sugdup, and at the Sapibenega Kuna Lodge. Most lodges and hostels have cellphones, and sat-phones are in use in many other locals.

Activities

Most tour operators in Panamá City can arrange custom tours of the San Blas islands. For a truly personal experience, I recommend Kuna freelance guide **Gilberto Alemancia** (507-6688-4623; gilbert04@yahoo.com or galemancia@hotmail.com), bilingual director of the indigenous department of the Panamá Tourism Bureau (IPAT) and a well-known photographer. Gilberto has coordinated expeditions for the BBC, Discovery Channel, and National Geographic, and can organize specialized tours.

The following entities offer or can arrange special-interest activities in Kuna Yala:

BIRDING AND HIKING
Burbayar Lodge 507-261-1679; www.burbayar.com.
Exotics Adventures 507-314-3013 or 6674-5381; www.panamaexoticsadventures.com.

CULTURAL STUDY TOURS
Ancón Expeditions 507-269-9415; www.anconexpeditions.com.

SEA-KAYAKING AND SNORKELING
Exocircuitos 507-317-1279; www.ecocircuitos.com.
Exotics Adventures 507-314-3013 or 6674-5381; www.panamaexoticsadventures.com.
Expediciones Tropicales, telephone/fax 317-1279, www.xtrop.com.

SAILING
San Blas Sailing 507-314-1800; fax 507-314-0735; www.sanblassailing.com.

LODGING

Cabañas Turísticas Waica (507-333-2033; www.geocities.com/mamitupu) Mamitupu. Run by savvy local guide, Pablo Nuñez Perez, this basic thatched accommodation option on a tiny isle is friendly. Inexpensive.

Dad Ibe Island Lodge (507-6487-6239) Achutupu, 1.9 miles (3 km) southeast of Ailigandi. Three simple thatch-and-bamboo huts overhang the waters on this tiny island. Flush toilets and septic tank. Inexpensive.

Yandup Island Lodge (www.yandupisland .com; reservas@yandupisland.com). Yandup, 0.6 mile (1 km) northeast of Playón Chico. On a tiny, private, uninhabited island. Hammocks and outhouse. Inexpensive.

DOLPHIN ISLAND LODGE
507-263-7780
Fax: 225-2521
www.uaguinega.com
Uaguitupo, 437 yards (400 m) east of
Achutupu

A cut above the competition, this hotel on a small private island has 11 thatched, beachfront, concrete-and-wood cabins, plus three junior suites with bamboo-cane walls and hardwood floors. All have private bathrooms with cold-water showers and flush toilets. It even has a bar, the best restaurant for miles, plus satellite Internet feed! Volleyball, plus beach bonfires. Moderate.

SAPIBENEGA KUNA LODGE
507-215-1406
Fax: 507-215-3724
www.sapibenega.com
Iskardup, 3 miles (5 km) west of Playón
Chico
The tiled showers, flush toilets, and solar power (with generator assist) seem almost luxurious at this rustic lodge with 13 duplex cabins on stilts. Plump cushions and batik spreads add lively color. The cabins ring the entire island, which is all of 164 feet (50 m) across. Tiki lamps add a touch of romance to the beachfront, open-air restaurant.

San Blas Islands, Panamá

The Kuna

The Kuna (or Tule, as they refer to themselves) number about 70,000, of which about half occupy the islands of the Archipiélago de San Blas, perhaps another 10,000 live along the Caribbean shores, and another 30,000 are scattered throughout the cities of Panamá.

This fascinating indigenous tribe has inhabited the San Blas islands only within the past few hundred years. They originally inhabited the forests of Darién where, according to oral tradition, conflicts with the Emberá-Wounaan forced them to retreat north into the Serranía de Panamá and Caribbean plains, where they soon came into conflict with Spanish colonists. Finally, they settled the islands. Following Panamá's independence, the government attempted to Westernize the Kuna, who were suppressed. In 1925, they rebelled. After the U.S. government interceded to end the violence, the Kuna gained political autonomy. They have ever since protected their territory (*comarca*) and cul-

ture—including their language, *dulegaya*—with gusto. For example, no non-Kuna may settle or operate a business within the comarca. And any Kuna who marries outside the tribe must leave the comarca. Today the Kuna indigenous culture is one of the most intact and homogeneous in the world. (Land is ostensibly held in common—a vital factor in preventing the division of Kuna society into "haves" and "have-nots.")

Strikingly short, adults average only about 4 feet 10 inches (150 cm), second only to the Pygmies of Africa. Physically, they are also recognizable by their aquiline noses, esteemed within Kuna culture as a sign of beauty. Another hallmark of Kuna culture is albinism—no other group in the

Kuna woman with parrots, San Blas Islands, Panamá

world has such a high incidence (one in every 165, compared to 1:35,000 in the United States). Albinos are revered in Kuna cosmology as "children of the Moon" (they are supposedly born to pregnant women who expose themselves to a full moon) and are considered to possess supernatural powers. Hence, many albinos in Kuna culture rise to become *shamans* and community leaders. Since albinos typically avoid sunlight, male albinos are often raised to fulfill female roles and can often be seen stitching *molas* in the shade.

ATTRACTIONS, PARKS, AND RECREATION

East of Narganá, a 19-mile (30 km) span of ocean is virtually devoid of isles. The western-most cluster in the Comarca Centro is accessed by air to the crowded and relatively modern island community of Playón Chico—a departure point for a handful of exquisite coral cays nearby. **Yandup** (not to be confused with Narganá, nor an isle called Yandup close to Achutupo; see below) and **Iskardup**, two tiny coral-fringed isles close to Playón Chico, each possess hotels and are the most commonly visited local isles. Being so close to the mainland, they're a great base for hikes into the foothills of the Serranía to witness

Forty-nine separate communities comprise the comarca, which is loosely administered by the Congreso General Kuna, which convenes every six months and is headed by three *sahila dummagan* (supreme chiefs) representing each of the comarca's three districts. Each community is headed by an elected *sahila* (chief), who heads a daily *congreso* (congress). Attendance at the all-important Sunday congreso is compulsory for adults. A village *nele* (shaman) and *summaket* (chanter) help maintain traditions, heal the sick, etc., as custodians and practitioners of sacred rites. A surprisingly large bureaucracy exists to enforce regulations, such as issuing permits that are required for individual Kuna to leave the comarca, etc.

Few societies are so matriarchal. The women call the shots. They own most of the real estate, although this typically means simple huts of bamboo-and-thatch with earth floors. There is no "marriage" as such. A male lover simply moves into his girlfriend's hut. She kicks him out to signify divorce. No kowtowing to church or state officials is required. And the women are equally adept as the men in paddling dugout *cayucos* or sail-powered *ulus* (canoes). Female importance has risen as the income derived from sale of *molas* to tourists has increased. Otherwise the Kuna live by fishing, lobstering, and harvesting coconuts, mostly for sale or barter to Colombian schooners, which supply goods in exchange. Although land is communal, individual Kuna members own the palm trees, which are cultivated on islands and in large groves on the mainland coastal strip (otherwise, the land is protected in its natural state). In good years, 30 million coconuts may be harvested. The Congreso General establishes each year's price for coconuts. Many Kuna are sent to Panamá City and elsewhere to earn income.

Irrespective of where they live, Kuna women wear with pride their traditional skirts and blouses adorned with *molas* in blazing primary colors. (The men dress in Western style, with the addition of a de rigueur porkpie or trilby hat.) Females adopt the costume at puberty—the most important time in her life. A girl's coming of age is cause for great celebration involving the entire community, which inhales hallucinogens and imbibes crude *chicha* corn liquor to excess. Her hair is shorn and thereafter she will wear a bloodred *muswe* (shawl) on her head, plus a *saburet* (skirt) worn over a *bicha* (petticoat) tied by a *mudub* (belt). Instead of Max Factor mascara and lipstick, Kuna women paint a black line of *tagua* dye down the length of their nose and daub their cheeks with a pink dye made of *achiote* seeds. No ensemble is complete without multiple necklaces of colored beads, large gold nose rings and earrings, and exquisite multi-colored beaded sleeves decorating their forearms and ankles.

The Kuna are superstitious and revere a spirit world. Every natural thing is believed to be possessed by a guardian spirit. Wooden spiritually alive human figurines called *nuchus* are used to counter *poni* (evil spirits) and to cure human sickness. Although the land and forests are considered sacred, the coral reefs have suffered greatly from overfishing.

a Kuna burial ground, followed by a cooling dip in the Saidap Maar waterfall.

Some 12 miles (20 km) east of Playón Chico, half-moon-shaped **Achutupu** is one of the largest settlements in the San Blas and a key gateway to the eastern isles. Its large thatched community hall is a great place to experience a daily *congreso* (see the sidebar) before hopping a ride southeast to the adjoining and far smaller and more intimate Dolphin Island—**Uaguitupo**—with a hotel, and another good base for tours.

Want to learn *mola* making? A boat from Achutupu will run you the 3 miles (5 km) westward to diminutive **Ailigandi**, a seemingly impossibly crowded isle that's home to almost

Kayakers in the San Blas Islands, Panamá

2,000 Kuna. In the center stands a statue of Simral Colman (a Kuna leader during the 1925 revolt) dressed in a bowler hat and festooned with medals. Visitors are welcomed at the **Hogar Cultura Kuna**, a school for *mola* design, woodcarving, and other traditional skills.

Contrary to reports that islanders on **Mammidup** (0.6 mile/1 km east of Achutupu) are less welcoming to visitors, expect to receive a friendly welcome. A local cooperative here make soap from coconut oil.

Another mini-archipelago is centered on **Ustupo Ogobsucum**, with its own airstrip and a population of some 5,000—by far the most populated isle in the San Blas. It has lots of services but can safely be missed in favor of nearby forested **Isla Pino** (named for its Caribbean pines).

The Abaio Region

You'd think that the more remote islands, close to the Colombian border and the virtually impenetrable jungles of Darién, would be the least populated. In fact, the tiny isle of **Sasardi Muladup** (more commonly known as Mulatupo) is one of the most densely populated of all isles. Its airstrip acts as a stepping-stone for a score of isles (including the three largest in the archipelago) grouped tightly together in a chain to the southeast of Mulatupo.

Tourism to these isles is minimal.

The ruins of Santa María la Antigua del Darién (also known as Aclá, founded by Vasco Núñez de Balboa in 1510) and, nearby

Good to Know About

To request a visit to the Área Silvestre Corregimiento De Narganá, contact the Congreso General Kuna (telephone/fax 507-314-1293 or 314-1513; www.congresogeneral kuna.org; congresokuna@pa.inter.net; Calle Croton, Edificio 820-XB, Balboa).

Doing it Their Way

Visits to the San Blas are strictly regulated, and tourists are subject to local laws and customs, and the hospitality offered varies from isle to isle. Here's a list of regulations:

No scuba diving is permitted. You may snorkel.

Many islands ban alcohol.

Dress modestly off the beach. That means no G-string bikinis in Kuna villages!

Never photograph a person without asking permission. Photographing Kuna individuals does not come free. A rarely waived rule of thumb is $1 per photo. Bring plenty of $1 bills.

at Punta Escosés, the ill-conceived and fated Scottish settlement of New Caledonia (founded in 1698), lie half-buried in the undergrowth at the extreme eastern end of the Kuna Comarca. Exploring this remote region has its risks, due to a presence of Colombian drug traffickers and occasional incursions by guerrillas and paramilitaries.

Bead leg bracelets on a Kuna woman, San Blas Islands, Panamá

Área Silvestre Corregimiento de Narganá

The land portion of the Kuna comarca is enshrined within the Narganá Magisterial Wilderness Area. Spanning 230 square miles (60,000 ha), this forested, mountainous wilderness is purposely protected as a buffer zone that isolates the comarca from loggers and *waga* (outsiders). In fact, it encompasses virtually the entire mainland portion of the comarca between the continental divide and the Caribbean shore, and merges westward into Parque Nacional Chagres. The park is the outgrowth of the ill-fated Proyecto de Estudio para el Manejo de Areas Silvestres de Kuna (Study Project for the Management of the Wildlands of Kuna Yala, aka PEMASKY), initiated in 1983, and is often referred to as the PEMASKY reserve.

With a singular exception, this virtually uninhabited area is purposefully not developed for tourism and is protected as a "spirit sanctuary." The rugged Serranía de San Blas is crossed by a single and dauntingly difficult dirt road, connecting Cartí to the Pan-American Highway (at El Llano) via the park ranger station at Nusagandi (17 miles/27 km from El Llano),

The Darien Scheme

In 1694, a wealthy Scottish merchant and colonialist named William Paterson (1658–1719), founder of the Bank of England, developed what was called the "Darien Scheme" to settle a portion of Darién province and facilitate trade with the Americas and beyond. Having risen to a position of political influence, Paterson elicited the support of the Scottish government for his Scottish Trading Company. He sold Darién as a paradise. Investors flocked. The English government, concerned to protect the commerce of the East India Company, was alarmed by Paterson's intentions and attempted to suppress the scheme. Scottish pride was raised and Scots from all over volunteered to settle the isthmus. A large expedition was outfitted and, joined by Paterson, set sail with 1,200 settlers on July 26, 1698.

On November 3, they landed in Darién and claimed it as "Caledonia" on behalf of Scotland. They established New Edinburgh, guarded by Fort Saint Andrew. Understandably, the Spanish prepared to expel them by force. England's King William III outlawed any assistance to the Caledonia settlers. From the first day, however, the settlement began to rot from within. The gentry refused to do manual labor. The appointed leaders quarreled and feuded. Everyone found the heat, humidity, and diseases such as dysentery, malaria, and yellow fever, too much to bear. Almost one-quarter of the populace died the first year, including Paterson's wife. On June 20, 1699, the settlers abandoned the colony and returned to Scotland carrying barely 400 survivors.

Meanwhile, a second expedition had already set sail for New Edinburgh. In August it found the colony had been abandoned. Nonetheless, a new start was made. Alas, their chief supply ship caught fire and sank, forcing the settlers to set sail for Jamaica while a handful of holdouts remained to await arrival of a third expedition. This duly set sail from Scotland on September 24, 1699, bearing 1,300 settlers and a year of supplies. The arrivistes soon fell victim to the same infighting and diseases as had the first expedition. In February 1700 reinforcements arrived with a newly appointed governor, Captain Alexander Campbell, who swiftly prepared to thwart an impending Spanish attack with a preemptive strike. The Scots (assisted by Indian allies) clashed with a Spanish force comprising mostly press-ganged non-white soldiers at a place called Topocanté. The Spanish were routed. But New Edinburgh's joy was short-lived. On February 25, eleven Spanish ships arrived, accompanied by a land force that surrounded the settlement.

Spanish general and governor, Don Juan Pimienta, sent word that the settlers would be granted 14 days to abandon the settlement with free passage and all their possessions. On April 11, 1700, the Scots, too weakened by disease and hunger to resist, acceded to the Spanish demands. (Many of the colonists perished during the voyage when they shipwrecked during a storm.)

where a $6 entry fee is charged. *Advance request for permission to visit is required.*

The wildlife viewing is superb. More than 550 bird species and 154 mammal species have been identified here. Jaguars and ocelots roam the forests. Monkeys, sloths, coatimundis, tapirs and, of course, snakes abound (a 6-foot/2 m black-as-night serpent emerged from the undergrowth and slithered past me, literally within fingertip reach, as I stood knee-deep in mud while trying to extricate my trapped 4WD).

The best way to explore is to base yourself at relatively easy-to-reach **Burbayar Lodge**, 9 miles (15 km) from El Llano and outside the reserve (therefore requiring no advance permission; see Lodging below); or at the decidedly more rustic **Nusagandi Nature Lodge**. Other than these two places, it's pretty much just you and the jungle.

LODGING

BURBAYAR LODGE

507-390-6674 or 6654-0952
www.burbayar.com
9 miles (14.5 km) north of El Llano
Moderate

This family-run wilderness lodge will delight anyone with even the remotest appreciation of nature. Straddling a ridge at 1,200 feet (375 m) elevation, it combines mild temperatures with great views over surrounding forest comprising a 122-acre (50 ha) rain forest reserve accessed by six trails. The timber lodge has solar power and a small generator and operates according to strict ecological principles. Decor is no-frills. Some rooms have bunks, and the showers and flush toilets are shared. The broad patios with hammocks are great for spotting birds while you laze. Rates include meals, served family-style at candlelit roughhewn tables. Reservations are essential (not least because the gates are locked at 5 PM). It's best to sign up for a two- or three-day package offered by tour agencies in Panamá City.

NUSAGANDI NATURE LODGE

c/o Congreso General Kuna (see Good to Know About)
Nusagandi, 12 miles (20 km) north of El Llano

Perched atop the continental divide, this rustic Kuna-run lodge has spectacular views down the mountains and over the San Blas archipelago. Don't expect frills. It's run-down and has only crude communal outside bathrooms, plus a kitchen (you'll need to bring all your supplies). Hostel-type dorm rooms cost $15 per person per night. The park guards here will be assigned as your guides for hiking the trails.

Molas

These exquisite fabrics are made using an "appliqué" and "reverse appliqué" technique, where several layers of differently colored cloth are stitched together onto the base fabric. Each layer features a cut-out pattern that reveals that of the layer beneath. Underlying layers often follow the same pattern, but narrower.

Kuna mola

The simplest *molas* use two layers and basic, symmetrical geometric patterns, which originated as tagua-nut tattoos and body paintings in days of yore, before the Kuna adopted and evolved their clothing. These basic *molas*, known as *antiguas*, traditionally use layers of black, claret, and orange (artists use their discretion as to the order). *Molas* gradually evolved, with more complex designs, often featuring a "floating" top layer separated from the rest of the upper layers and using additional colors, such as blue, green, pink, and yellow.

Embroidered lines are a recent evolution in many *molas*. So, too, depictions of animals—especially parrots, fish, and turtles—usually matched in pairs to maintain all-important symmetry. Some contemporary *molas* even depict scenes of Kuna life or mythology.

6

DARIÉN

"Darien begins just beyond the suburbs of Panama City and sprawls east, thickening as it goes, until it has erased all roads, all telephone lines, all signs of civilization, turning the landscape into one solid band of unruly vegetation filled with jaguars, deadly bushmasters, and other exotic wildlife."

—BEN RYDER HOWE

Panamá's eastern extreme is indeed a world of extremes. The name Darién is synonymous with impenetrable jungle. Famously, the Interamerican Highway (the sole road access) peters down to a muddy track, then halts altogether at Yaviza, many miles from the Colombian border. No road whatsoever penetrates the dense rain forests that sweep east into Colombia and form the largest tract of primary rain forest in all Central America. Hence, the untamed region is known as the "Darien Gap." As such, the 2,236-square-mile (579,000 ha) Parque Nacional Darién is a teeming hothouse of tropical biota offering wildlife encounters and Indiana Jones-style experiences nowhere excelled in the nation.

Welcome to Darién sign, Darién, Panamá

Darién province curls south and takes up fully one-half of the nation, yet is sparsely populated. Until recent decades, the rain forests extended almost to Panamá City's borders. In 1977, completion of the Interamerican Highway spawned an invasion of settlers. Much of the newly accessible forest was felled for cattle. And villages and tiny towns dot the route. Fortunately, beyond Yaviza the forests remain almost entirely pristine. Access is via a few airstrips or by *cayucos*—motorized dugout canoes that ply the dark, muddy rivers, linking remote communities of Emberá and Wounaan indigenous people. This welcoming and fascinating "Amazonian" tribe (actually two closely related tribes, yet each with its own language) has traditionally lived by nomadic, slash-and-burn agriculture and by hunting using *boroqueras* (blow guns) and poison-tipped darts. In recent years, they have increasingly settled into permanent communities that derive a living from forestry and the tourist trade. A visit to a traditional village is a highlight of any Panamanian vacation. These people are welcoming to a fault.

OPPOSITE: *Red-eyed tree frog*

And it's a fascinating and illuminating entrée into a primitive way of life that is at one with Mother Nature. Heck, go the whole hog and have your body "tattooed" with tagua-nut juice, in true Emberá-Wounaan fashion. The Emberá-Wounaan domain is split into two semi-autonomous districts, the Comarca Emberá Cemaco and Comarca Emberá Sambú.

Tourist facilities are few and far between, and with only a few exceptions, travelers should lower their expectations with regard to accommodations and food. *Large tracts are a no-man's-land in which ultra-violent Colombian drug barons, left-wing FARC guerrillas, and right-wing paramilitary death squads operate with frightening freedom (the 180-mile-long/286 km Colombian border is unguarded), notwithstanding a significant Panamanian military presence. The rain forest of Darién is one place you don't want to be exploring alone.* You must carry your passport at all times, and report to local police upon arrival. They can advise of current conditions.

Darién is separated from the Caribbean coast by the pencil-thin Comarca Kuna Yala. Darién extends from the continental divide along the rugged Serranía del Darién to the Pacific Coast. Two equally rugged coastal mountain ranges—the Serranía de Majé in the north and Serranía del Sapo in the south—rise from a narrow and thinly populated coastal strip facing onto the Golfo de Panamá. The Archipiélago de las Perlas studs the gulf, 20 miles (35 km) from shore. Well-named, these gorgeous islands are well developed for tourism thanks to their blazing white beaches and pristine coral reefs. Whales abound in the warm shallow waters.

If birding or hiking, waterproof lightweight boots are advised, as you're going to get wet. Locals use rubber boots, which have the advantage of guarding against snakebites (the deadly and aggressive fer-de-lance is common in Darién); you may be able to buy a pair in local *tiendas* (shops) in La Palma and other towns.

Fer-de-lance

Getting There and Around

By Air

Aeroperlas (507-315-7500; www.tacaregional.com) flies from Panamá City's Albrook airport to Bahía Piña and Jaqué on Saturday. **Air Panama** (507-316-9000; www.flyair panama.com) flies from Panamá City's Albrook airport to Garachiné and Sambú (Tuesday and Thursday), Jaqué (Monday, Wednesday, and Friday), and La Palma (Tuesday and Saturday).

You can charter planes to fly you to other airstrips, including Cana and Punta Patiño Field Stations, both of which are run by Ancon Expeditions, which makes charter flight arrangements for guests.

By Bus or Público

Buses depart Panamá City daily every hour on the hour starting 5 AM to 5 PM from the Gran Terminal Nacional de Transporte, beside the Corredor Norte in Albrook (about $12 each way to Metetí; allow six to nine hours). Buses end their journey at Metetí, from where you can catch a twice-daily bus, or more numerous *chivas* (pick-up trucks) to Yaviza and Puerto Quimba.

By Car

The Interamerican Highway is the only road into and through Darién, connecting Panamá City with Yaviza. Don't be misled by the term highway (the Central American portion of the Pan-American Highway stretching from Alaska to Tierra del Fuego). This is no freeway. In fact, east of Panamá City it's almost entirely one lane in each direction. At Metetí, about 140 miles (225 km) east of Panamá City, it deteriorates markedly and 4WD is essential for the final 31 miles (50 km) to Yaviza, where it peters out at the riverside dock. This latter section is often so muddy that even buses get stuck up to and beyond their axles. (The Darien Gap is the only incomplete section of the 16,000-mile/25,800 km highway between Alaska and the southern tip of Argentina.)

By Ship and River Transport

The main form of transport in eastern Darién is by *cayuco* (paddle-powered dugout canoe) and *piraguas* (motorized canoes) along the Río Tuira and Río Chucunaque and their myriad tributaries. If you arrive under your own steam in

Emberá girl and baby boy, Darién, Panamá

Yaviza, boat is the only way forward: however, the police may give you a lengthy examination before permitting you to leave (or not). *Piraguas* typically cost about $50 per day with driver (gasoline costs extra, about $3.75 a gallon). Water taxis (every 30 minutes for the 20-minute journey) serve the capital of La Palma from Puerto Quimba, which is linked to the Interamerican Highway.

Cruise West (888-851-8133; www.cruisewest.com) includes the remote Emberá coastal community of Playa de Muerte on its eight-day cruise-tours of Panamá and Costa Rica.

By Tours
Many tour operators in Panamá City offers multi-day guided trips to the region. However, the standout company is **Ancón Expeditions** (507-269-9415; www.anconexpeditions .com), which specializes in birding and nature trips with an adventure component. **Panama Exotic Adventures** (507-673-5381; www.panamaexoticadventures.com) offers three- to eight-day trips, specializing in stays with Emberá and Wounaan communities. **Exocircuitos** (507-314-1586; www.ecocircuitos.com) has a three-day "Darien Ethnic Expedition" that includes Mogue.

Along the Interamerican Highway
The Interamerican Highway runs through the intermontane basin, with the Serranía de San Blas and, later, Serranía de Darién to the north and the Serranía de Majé to the south. Gateway to Darién is the town of **Chepo**, 33 miles (53 km) east of Panamá City. (The town is actually 1.2 miles [2 km] south of the highway and the turnoff is easy to miss; turn south at the statue of St. Christopher on the highway). Until the early 1970s, this was the end of the road! Although it's in eastern Panamá province (Darién province actually begins 76 miles/122 km farther east, at Aguas Frías), but locals consider this to be where Darién begins. South of town, the Río Chepo snakes through a swampy mangrove forest good for birding, including the largest colony of cattle egrets in Panamá. You can hire boats at the dock at **Puerto Coquira**, about 3 miles (5 km) south of Chepo.

Tropical flower, Panamá

There are very few places or sites of interest along the route to Yaviza, gateway to Parque Nacional Darién. Still, the Istmo de Darién (Darien Isthmus) contains several semi-autonomous indigenous *comarcas* that offer an entrée into the lives of Kuna (centered on Ipetí, 53 miles/86 km east of Chepa) and Emberá and Wounaan communities. Much of the virgin rain forest that clad the vale has been cut in the decades since completion of the Interamerican Highway (with good reason, the Panamanian government is resisting lobbying by logging and cattle ranching interests, who want to see the highway pushed all the way into Colombia). You'll pass mile after mile of relatively recent cattle pasture.

Happy visitor with Emberá at Playa de Muerte, Darién, Panamá

About 32 miles (50 km) east of Ipetí, you might divert 1.8 miles (3 km) from the high-way for **Santa Fe**, on the east bank of the Río Sabaná. Here you can visit **Finca Sonia** (507-299-6951 or 299-6529, Spanish only), an agro-forestry and community development project where locals grow fruits and make soaps and medicinal products from all-natural ingredients. Water taxis will run you 5 miles (8 km) down the Río Sabana to the Wounaan community of **Boca de Lara** (you can also reach it by 4WD via a turnoff from the highway, 1.2 miles (2 km) south of the turnoff for Sante Fe). A sign designates this as a place to *VISIT AND LIVE WITH THE WOUNAAN INDIANS AND EXPERIENCE THEIR LIFE*. **Panama Exotic Adventures** (507-673-5381; www.panamaexoticadventures.com) includes Boca de Lara on its trips.

The largest settlement in the area is **Metetí**, an administrative and commercial center, 110 miles (177 km) east of Chepo. Beyond here the going gets tougher. You can turn west at Metetí for the funky little port of **Puerto Quimba**, which bustles with the watercraft head-ing to and from the Golfo de San Miguel and La Palma, the provincial capital, (pick-up truck *colectivos* leave Meteti for Puerto Quimba hourly, 6 AM to 6 PM; 45 minutes, $1.50). You can get a foretaste of the Darién rain forest at two private reserves: **Agroforestal Salina** (507-299-6070; feliciano.salina@gmail.com) and nearby **Colegio Agroforestal Tierra Nueva** (507-214-6945), both of which have forest trails good for spotting monkeys, poi-son-dart frogs, and birds.

Finally you arrive in **Yaviza**, the end of the road (literally and metaphorically); you'll need to register at the heavily fortified police station upon arrival. The sole site of inter-est—and surely not worth the drive!—is the overgrown and meager ruins of 18th-century **Fuerte San Jerónimo de Yaviza**, rising over the Río Chicunaque. Otherwise, this dour riverside village has few redeeming qualities and is unmistakably a rowdy frontier town where staring too long into the eyes of pimped-up drug-dealer types in the bar is *not* a wise move. You are strongly advised against exploring beyond Yaviza except with a guide or tour group.

LODGING AND DINING

The numerous barebones hostelries ($5–10) include **Pensión y Restaurante Tres Hermanos Ortiz** (no telephone), and **Hotel y Restaurante Felicidad** (507-299-6188), both in Metetí; and **Hospedaje Las Narishas** (507-299-6393), outside Puerto Quimba. If you arrive late in the day in Yaviza, your options are pretty much limited to the grim **Hotel 3 Américas**, adjoining a raucous bar. In nearby El Real, the **Hotel Mazareno** is equally dour.

Dosi Lodge (c/o Panamá Expeditions, 507-314-3013 or 6747-6096; www.panamaexotic adventures.com) Near Boca de Lara. A lodge in a Wounaan village, this makes the most of traditional Wounaan architecture, with simple bamboo-reed walls and palm-thatch roof, this simple stilt-legged lodge is basic yet stylish. It has three rooms with polished hardwood floors; even the private bathrooms with showers have sinks carved of hardwoods. You dine in a communal setting with local villagers. Moderate.

Filo del Tallo Lodge (c/o Panamá Expeditions, 507-314-3013 or 6747-6096; www.panama exoticadventures.com) 1.8 miles (3 km) west of Metetí. In a Wounaan village, this hilltop retreat has the nicest lodging for miles. Despite the palm-thatch roofs and thin bamboo-reed walls, the three simple rooms here are exquisitely furnished in a trendy fashion. Dining is in a soaring circular *palenque,* doubling as a lounge with poured concrete sofas. Stylish! Horseback riding, kayaking, and guided birding and hikes are offered. Moderate.

Pensión Casa de Hospedaje Tortí (507-640-1500) Tortí, 60 miles (100 km) east of Chepo. Primarily a truckers' lodging on the Interamerican Highway, this no-frills *pensión* has 25 air-conditioned rooms with shared bathrooms. Inexpensive.

ATTRACTIONS, PARKS, AND RECREATION

Lago Bayano

Bayano, 24 miles (38 km) east of Chepo. This huge 135-square-mile (35,000 ha) manmade lake was created in 1975 when the Río Bayano was dammed. Locals swear that the waters harbor a Loch Ness-like monster. Don't let that put you off hiring a boat at the dock at Bayano—there are many to choose from—for the 40-minute ride to Cuevas Bayano. These riverine caverns boast fabulous dripstone formations, and bats, while the lake itself is a breeding habitat for heron and Neotropical cormorant. The eastern portion of the lake extends into the Comarca de Kuna de Madugandi.

Panama Outdoors (506-261-5043 or 507-6430-2824; www.panamaoutdoors.com /cuevas_bayano.html) offers guided tours of the caves from Panamá City.

Comarca de Kuna de Madugandi

This semi-autonomous district of a Kuna subgroup is distinct from the Comarca de Kuna Yala and occupies 800 square miles (2,073 sq km) at the *western* base of the Serranía de San Blas. Some 5,000 Kuna live in 12 communities, and there are also Emberá

Lago Bayano, Darién, Panamá

communities, several of which are easily visited off the highway near Ipetí. The almost contiguous villages of **Ipetí Kuna** and neighboring **Ipetí Emberá**, (0.9 mile/1.5 km north and 0.6 mile/1 km south of the highway, respectively) welcome visitors with ceremonial dances and give craft demonstrations. **Panamá City Tours** (507-263-8918; www.panama citytours.com) includes the villages on cultural excursions from Panamá City—a fascinating chance to learn about *two* distinct indigenous groups living almost within shouting distance of one another.

Some 6.5 miles (10 km) east of Ipetí, the village of **Tortí** is a famous center for saddle making; you can stop at roadside *talabarterías* (leather workshops).

WEEKLY AND ANNUAL EVENTS

Two agricultural fairs bring the Interamerican Highway to a crawling halt, when the **Feria Agropecuario de Tanara-Chepo** (January) is held in Chepo, and the **Feria de Santa Fé** (March) in Santa Fé.

Saddle maker near Playa Santa Catalina, Panamá

Good to Know About

You must carry your passport to present at the numerous militarized police checkpoints. Even at Metetí, a full 31 miles (50 km) before arriving at Yaviza, police may tell you that they can no longer vouch for the safety of travelers continuing on.

Set out from Panamá City with a full tank of gas! Metetí has a gas station and a bank, opposite the main police station (507-299-0612) in the region. Yaviza has a basic hospital.

Soldier guarding the Emberá village of Playa de Muerte, Darién, Panamá

Golfo de San Miguel

The scores of rivers that drain the Darién region merge into the Río Tiura, which builds to a width of 3 miles (5 km) where it pours into the Golfo de San Miguel, an inlet of the Golfo de Panamá. The funky town of **La Palma**, capital of Darién province, occupies a peninsula at the marsh-fringed mouth of the river. It's not much more than a one-street town! Many homes—often of simple lumber and corrugated steel sheets—rise on stilts over the water and mud banks. It was hereabouts that Vasco Nuñez de Balboa became the first European to sight the Pacific Ocean, on September 25, 1513; he supposedly waded into the ocean still wearing his armor. Soon thereafter, with the discovery of the gold mines at Cana, the settlement became a strategic transshipment point guarded by a fort—**Fuerte San Carlos**—whose ruins are slowly succumbing to the surrounding jungle. It stands on **Isla Boca Chica**, in the middle of the river.

La Palma is a gateway for exploring inland the **Comarca Emberá Sambú**, to the west. Sambú offers fascinating cultural immersions, plus sensational birding on river explorations. A *colectivo* water taxi from La Palma to Sambú takes two hours ($20).

Closer to La Palma is the Emberá community of **Mogue**, just 3 miles (5 km) inland of the Golfo de San Miguel via the Río Mogue, midway between La Palma and Punta Patiño. Mogue is the setting for the **Pajaro Jai Foundation** (207-460-4184; www.pajarojai.org; 420 Post Road West #202, Westport, CT 06880), which promotes ecologically sustainable lifestyle intended to integrate Darién's indigenous communities into the contemporary world while preserving their traditional culture. Its success includes small-scale furniture factories (a single hardwood tree can produce income equivalent to 40 acres cleared for cattle) and, most notably, the Mogue community's construction—a 15-year labor!—of a 92-foot-long oceangoing ketch, the *Pajaro Jai* (Enchanted Bird).

LODGING AND DINING

Many locals rent out rooms for about $10 a night. Ask around. In Sambú, try Father Hector Quinteros (hequirosq@hotmail.com), who has rooms. Most Emberá communities have basic facilities similar to those described below.

Hotel Biaquirú Bagará (507-299-6224) La Palma. There's not much to choose from in La Palma, but this 13-room riverfront hotel run by the Ramady family is the nicest option. Rooms vary: only two have air-conditioning and private bathrooms. It has a TV lounge.

Hotel Emberá (507-299-6083 or 649-6686 c/o Ricardo Cabrera) La Chunga. Slightly more upscale than most *tambos* hereabouts, these four twin-room, stilt-legged cabins of bamboo and thatch have foam-mattress beds with mosquito nets, plus flush toilets and cold-water showers.

Mama Grajales' (507-299-6428, c/o Gisela de Olmedo, in Guarachiné) Playa de Muerto. You'll sleep like a true Emberá in two basic bamboo reed-and-thatch huts atop stilts in this remote coastal village. You can also pitch your own tent atop a stilt-legged platform. Matriarch "Mama" Grajales keeps shared outdoor bathrooms spic and span, and serves filling meals. Inexpensive.

Punta Patiño (c/o 507-269-9415, Ancon Expeditions; www.anconexpeditions.com) Situated atop a bluff with fine views over the Gulf of San Miguel and, beyond, the Gulf of Panamá, this nature lodge has 10 modestly furnished cabins with loft bedrooms and private hot-water bathrooms. Six cabins have air-conditioning; the others have fans. It specializes in guided birding and hikes. Dining is family style.

SambuHause (507-268-6905, 6766-5102 or 6627-2135; http://sambuhausedarien panama.com, sambuhause @yahoo.com) Sambú. Run by Michael Harrington, a U.S. transplant, and his Panamanian sister-in-law, Maria, these are the nicest digs for miles. Gosh! You even get air-conditioning in the traditional bamboo-and-thatch structure with four rooms, one with private bathroom. There's a communal kitchen and dining area, plus BBQ. Michael is extremely knowledgeable about this region, and eager to help. Expensive.

An Emberá family at Playa de Muerte, Darién, Panamá

Tambo **Mogue** (no telephone) Mogue. In the middle of this Emberá community, this thatched *tambo* (stilt house) is open-walled. You can pitch a tent atop the platform reached by a notched log staircase, or simply snuggle into a hammock. It has a basic latrine and cold-water shower. Locals serve hearty fare, such as chicken, and beans n' rice.

Werará Purú Lodge (507-299-6090) Werará Purú, 2 miles (3 km) west of Sambú. Another *tambo* high off the ground, this open-air, two-room thatch-and-bamboo lodge is basic but gives you a taste for indigenous life.

ATTRACTIONS, PARKS, AND RECREATION

Playa de Muerto

9 miles (15 km) south of Punta Garachiné. Visitors are few and far between to this remote unique Emberá coastal community, on the east shore of the Golfo de Panamá. I will always treasure arriving here while participating in a 10-day adventure cruise aboard M/V *Pacific Explorer* (**Cruise West**; 1-888-851-8133; www.cruisewest.com). Alternately, you can hire a boat in Garachiné (2.5 hours; about $200 round-trip); you need to register with the police before departing. Be sure to rent a life-preserver from Gisela de Olmedo, owner of the Hotel Guarinche; call the public phone (507-299-6428 or 299-6477) and make arrangements in advance. And a small freight-ship, the *Amparo,* departs Panamá City once a week for Jagua, stopping at Playa de Muerto.

You'll step ashore through the surf to an authentic indigenous village beneath thick palms at the base of the Serranía del Sapo coast range. This is a great place to hang loose for a few days, get your skin tattooed with tagua, and learn about how this community is transitioning to 21st-century life. Community members hire out as guides for about $20 a day.

RESERVA NATURAL PUNTA PATIÑO

c/o 506-269-9415 Ancon Expeditions
Fax: 507-264-3713
www.anconexpeditions.com
Reserva Natural Punta Patiño, 9 miles (15 km) southwest of La Palma

A 45-minute flight from Panamá City or boat ride from La Palma delivers you to this nature reserve on a headland that encloses the northern side of the Enseñada de Garachiné (Garachiné Bay). A lighthouse sits on the point. The reserve is operated by ANCON (Asociación para la Conservación de la Naturaleza) and protects 117 square miles (30,263 ha) of varied habitat—including tropical moist lowland forest, coastal wetlands, and mangroves—much of it reclaimed from a former cattle ranch and coconut plantation. Small it may be, but this is one of the nation's prime birding and wildlife-viewing locales, boasting an astounding 10 percent of the nation's bird and animal species. You have a high possibility of spying harpy eagles, and even Baird's tapir and the big cats. Macaws soar overhead. Monkeys cavort in the treetops. Poison-dart frogs hop around underfoot. And capybaras are virtually guaranteed to be there, chomping on the marsh grasslands near the lodge.

Emberá tattooed with tagua at Playa de Muerte, Darién, Panamá

Emberá members perform a traditional dance at Playa de Muerte, Darién, Panamá

Reservations are handled by **Ancon Expeditions**, which has three- and four-day excursions.

Sambú and Comarca Emberá Sambú

The Enseñada de Garachiné enfolds the estuarine mouth of the Río Sambú, which rises in the southernmost mountains of Parque Nacional Darién and flows north through a broad valley hemmed by the Serranía de Bagre (to the east) and Serranía del Sapo, or coast range. The village of **Sambú** is intriguing for its black population of *darientes*. Descended from African slaves who once worked the Cana gold mines, these communities maintain age-old musical and other cultural traditions, which includes *bullerengue*, a sensual dance that hails from the Batá region of Africa's Spanish Guinea. To experience *dariente* life, head to the fishing hamlet of **Punta Alegre**, 3 miles (5 km) north of Patiño.

Sambú is the gateway to the 502-Square-mile (1,300 sq km) Comarca Emberá Sambú, occupying the river basin and surrounding hills to the east, west, and south. Many of the comarca's dozen or so heavily guarded (by militarized police units) indigenous communities welcome visitors with ceremonial dances etc., plus basic accommodations. You can travel up the snaking river—a chance to spy caiman, crocodiles, monkeys, river otters, and fabulous birdlife—but must utilize an Emberá guide. However, as of mid-2009 the upper reaches of the valley, around **Pavarando** (the easternmost Emberá village) were put off-limits due to infiltration by FARC guerrillas. No worries: some of the most authentic Emberá villages in the region are around Sambú itself.

Sambú is connected by a rickety footbridge to **Puerto Indio**, an Emberá community where you pay your $10 per person fee to enter the Comarca (it's a fascinating transition, notable in the change from squat concrete cabins in Sambú and the thatched stilt-legged

Speckled caiman

tambo across the river) Nearby, **Werará Purú** is known for its artisans' workshop. And in Sambú, you can hire a guide (again, ask around) and *piragua* to take you downriver to **Chunga**, which can also be reached via the only road in this part of Darién—it's an arcing road connecting two small ports (Taimati and Garachiné, respectively, at the north and south ends of the bay).

You can fly into Sambú with Air Panama (about $50 each way), departing Albrook airport in Panamá City. Alternately, water taxis depart La Palma; scheduled service operates at 5 AM on Monday, Wednesday, and Friday ($15, around 90-minutes), but you can also hire private water taxis.

Parque Nacional Darién and Vicinity

While commonly equated with virtually impenetrable lowland swamps and rain forest, this 2,236-square-mile (5,790 square km) national park—the largest in Central America—extends from sea level to 6,152 feet (1,875 m) atop Cerro Tacarcuna, where eerie mists shroud temperate montane cloud forests. In fact, the park has five distinct life zones, including coastal mangrove systems. Almost uniquely pristine, it's a precious repository for healthy populations of jaguars and other big cats. The chattering and screeching of monkeys fills the forest, where tapirs, capybaras, sloths, and anteaters abound. Five species of macaws flap raucously overhead, while harpy eagles soar silently above the forest canopy, their keen eyes and fist-sized,

Good to Know About
La Palma has a bank and basic hospital. There's a basic medical post in Sambú.

razor-sharp talons ever-ready to seize an unwary sloth or monkey for lunch. In all, more than 450 bird species have been sighted, including the rare golden-headed quetzal in the higher cloud-forest elevations.

The region, which was declared a UNESCO World Heritage Site in 1981, is drenched year-round by heavy rains, feeding tempestuous rivers that crash down from the mountains to lazily snake across the lowland *llanuras* (plains) and eventually pour their muddy waters into the Golfo de San Miguel. It is hard to conceive that five centuries ago, Vasco Nuñez de Balboa and other gold-besotted and half-deranged *conquistadores* prevailed against the arduous odds of crocodile-infested swamps, extreme humidity, venomous snakes and spiders, and hostile natives to conquer the jungle for Spain, conjuring images of Werner Herzog's *Aguirre: Wrath of God*. The first Spanish colonial settlements in Panamá were established here. So, too, early gold mines, deep in the interior at Cana; and fortresses along the rivers along which the treasure was ferried for transit to Nuestra Señora de la Asunción de Panamá and thence by mule to Nombre de Díos and Portobelo.

Tamandua anteater on a tree

Today's treasure is counted in bird and animal sightings. Indeed Cana, where the bird count exceeds 400 species, is one of only two lodges within this vast park. For reasons of safety, it is highly recommended that you explore these zones through a reputable tour company and/or accompanied by an accredited guide. (This is one place you do not want to get injured or lost while hiking alone!) I recommend flying in with Ancon Expeditions. If you choose to boat in, the gateway is the rugged frontier community of **El Real de Santa María**, on the Río Tuira 3 miles (5 km) downriver of Yaviza and 40 miles (65 km) upriver from La Palma. Here visitors heading to Parque Nacional Darién must register with ANAM (507-299-6965). It has an airstrip.

Eyelash vipers

LODGING AND DINING

CANA FIELD STATION

c/o 507-269-9415, Ancon Expeditions
Fax: 507-264-3715
www.anconexpeditions.com
Moderate
This cozy albeit simple lodge in the heart of
the rain forest caters to birders and wildlife
enthusiasts, the majority of whom come in
on package excursions (Ancón Expeditions
has exclusive use). It has 10 bedrooms,
most with two single beds and basic furnishings, including portable battery-
powered lamps for when the generator
shuts off at night. You'll share bathrooms
with solar-heated water. Meals are served
family-style in the main lodge, with a large
balcony overlooking the river.

You can opt to stay in the high-elevation
Pirre Tent Camp; included in some Ancon
Expedition packages, it has two-person
screened tents under a thatch shelter. It's a
five-hour uphill hike. You must pack your
own gear, although porters carry supplies
and cater to guests.

ATTRACTIONS, PARKS, AND RECREATION

CANA

c/o 507-269-9415, Ancon Expeditions
www.anconexpeditions.com
Moderate
At 1,500 feet (457 m) elevation on the
southeastern flank of Cerro Pirre, this
isolated biological station is renowned
worldwide as a phenomenal birding site.
Remarkable for its truly remote location, an
important Spanish settlement—Santa Cruz
de Cana—evolved here in the early 16th
century around the Espíritu Santo gold
mines, worked by slave labor. It was abandoned in 1727. Rusting locomotives and
railcars are a legacy of a brief resurrection
in the mines in the late 19th century,
prompting sensations of a *Heart of Darkness*
experience. The relatively short and easy
Sendero Maquina leads to the locomotives.
More adventurous souls might hike the 6-
mile-long (9 km) **Sendero Cerro Pirre**,
which climbs into cloud forest. You can
even overnight at a tent camp.

The station is administered by ANCON
and is easily visited with **Ancon
Expeditions**, which operates the eco-lodge
here. The company's four- to eight-day
Darién trips fly you in. If you plan on boating, check with Ancon Expeditions as to
current conditions. At time of writing, the
now virtually abandoned gateway river port
of **Boca de Cupe** was off-limits due to guerrilla activity in the area.

*Emberá woman with child at Playa de Muerte,
Darién, Panamá*

Comarca Emberá Cémaco

Much of the national park lies within the eastern portion of the autonomous Comarca Emberá-Wounaan, created in 1983 and which is divided into the Comarca Emberá Cémaco and the Comarca Emberá Sambú, in the west of Darién. Together the twin *comarcas* occupy one-quarter of Darién and are home to about 17,000 Emberá and Wounaan people. Comarca Emberá Cémaco comprises 28 native communities and takes up 1,112 square miles (2,880 sq km), from the foothills to the continental divide of the Altos de Puna and Altos de Limón (the ridgeline is also the Colombian border). Access is by boat from Yaviza. You must register at every police checkpoint along the route. However, at time of writing boat access was restricted due to guerrilla infiltration.

Good to Know About
The **ANAM headquarters** (507-299-6579 or 299-6373; www.anam.gob.pa) is at El Real de Santa María. You need to register at the police station (507-299-6137) upon arrival.

Pirre

This biological station run by ANAM, the governmental agency in charge of national parks, is on the banks of the Río Perensico, on the northeast flanks of Cerro Pirre, in the heart of Darién's lowland rain forest. You must first get a permit ($3) from the ANAM office in El Real. It takes about one hour by boat (about $50) from El Real to reach Piji Baisal, from where it's another one hour on foot to Pirre, which offers simple dorm accommodation ($10) and a basic kitchen, but has no electricity. Alternately, with a guide, you can hike direct from El Real—allow four hours.

It's relatively cool at this elevation. Several trails offer fabulous birding and wildlife viewing, including **Sendero Cerro Pirre**, which ascends the mountain for spectacular views over Darién. You cannot hike from Pirre to Cana, as there are no trails.

Archipiélago de las Perlas

Floating in the middle of the Golfo de Panamá, this archipelago of 100 or so isles is a tropical paradise lying 40 miles (65 km) southeast of Panamá City and a similar distance west of Punta Patiño. Ringed by stunning sugar-white sands dissolving into jade turquoise waters, they tempt beach lovers who hop 20-minute flights from Panamá City. Two isles are well developed with tourist facilities and are renowned retreats of the rich and famous, including singer Julio Iglesias and fashion designer Christian Dior, who have villas here alongside those of Panamá's own elite. The rest of the isles are home to tiny fishing communities, several of which earn an income from pearling (principally on Isla Casaya and Isla Casayita). The isles were a prize possession of early Spanish *conquistadores*, due to the large natural oyster beds. Hence the name: the Pearl Islands. The Spanish developed a significant pearling industry in the 16th century. And Isla Contadora (Bookkeeper Isle) is supposedly named for the role it once played in tallying booty as an obligatory way stop for treasure ships from Peru.

Many of the isles are ringed by spectacular coral reefs. The warm ocean waters also draw several species of whales, commonly sighted year-round, but most prominently in winter.

Jaqué and Bahía Piña

The southernmost (and perhaps the most isolated) community in Panamá, the coastal community of **Jaqué**, midway between Punta Garachiné and the Colombian border, boasts a sensational setting. Thick emerald rain forest sweeps inland and up the slopes of the mist-shrouded Sierra de Jungurudó Mountains. North of town, waves crash against rocky promontories that pincer Bahía Piña, a sheltered warm-water bay that draws humpback whales and is the locale of Panamá's premier sportfishing lodge—Tropic Star Lodge—near the Emberá community of **Puerto Piña**. You can hike a mountain trail that deposits you at **Playa Blanca**, named for its gorgeous white sands (take snorkeling gear, as the reef-protected waters shelter a lagoon full of tropical fishes); most sands hereabouts are black. And the Emberá and Wounaan hamlets of **Lucas and El Coco,** and **El Mamey** and **Biroquera**, respectively, can be visited with a guide. Don't venture alone (four Spanish citizens were kidnapped by guerrillas in January 2006 inland of Biroquera)

In Jaqué, take time to visit the women's cooperative sponsored by **Bridges Across Borders** (352-485-2594; www.bridgesacrossborders.org) and which makes cards from recycled paper and natural fibers. It serves refugees forced out of the Colombian town of Choco by massacres. Bridges Across Borders also has a leatherback turtle preservation project.

Lodging: The upscale **Tropic Star Lodge** (407-423-9931 or 1-800-682-3424; fax 407-839-3637; www.tropicstar.com), nestled within Bahia de Piña, specializes in sportfishing using 31-foot Bertrams. The main fishing ground is the world-acclaimed Zane Grey Reef, an underwater mountain 15 miles (25 km) from shore. It began life as the private villa of a Texas oil tycoon. Today it offers 18 cabins and rooms with colonial-themed furnishings. Some have king beds. You can also rent the original hilltop villa—El Palacio—accessed by steep stairs (a funicular is provided for the infirm). Dining is family style. A one-week minimum stay is mandatory in high season

Many of the islands—notably Isla del Rey, the largest island—are thickly forested, and patient hikers might see sloths, anteaters, and white-brocket deer.

Although virtually unknown to foreigners (almost all the visitors are Panamanians), the archipelago was given a boost in 2003 when the TV "reality" show *Survivor* was filmed here.

GETTING THERE AND AROUND

By Air

Most visitors arrive by air. **Aeroperlas** (507-315-7500; www.tacaregional.com) has two flights on Saturday only from Panamá City's Albrook airport to Isla Contadora ($35). **Air Panama** (507-316-9000; www.flyairpanama.com) flies daily from Panamá City's Albrook airport to Isla Contadora ($35 each way) and on Tuesday, Thursday, and Saturday to Isla San Miguel ($30.50).

By Sea

National Tours (507-314-0571 or 6615-1392; www.nationaltourspanama.com) has ferry service, departing Panamá City from the Balboa Yacht Club, on Amador Causeway, at 7:30 AM and 2:30 PM , and departing Contadora at 9 AM and 4 PM ($40 each way; approximately

75 minutes); however, departure times keep changing, so check ahead. At the time of writing, **Panama Pearl Marine Group** (507-6784-3564; www.panamapearl.com) had suspended its daily ferry service to Isla Contadora from Las Brisas Marina, on Amador Causeway in Panamá City. However, it had plans to reinstate service in 2010.

By Golf Cart

The locals get around on golf carts, which most hotels provide for free or for rent. You can also rent from the Perla Real Inn (about $45 daily); and **Coral Dreams** (507-6536-1776; www.coral-dreams.com) and **Waterland Adventures** (507-6673-3020; mozartlee@cableonda.net) rent ATVs.

LODGING

The 326-room **Hotel Contadora Beach Resort**, on Playa Larga, Isla Contadora, once exuded grandeur but hit skid row a few years back and at this writing had closed and was being stripped bare by locals. Rumor has it that new owners will tear it down and build a new resort.

CABAÑAS DE CONTADORA

507-394-0307 or 250-2514
http://cabanasdecontadora.com
Isla Contadora
Inexpensive
If you don't mind cooking for yourself, this fully contained three-bedroom house may fit the bill, although it's one of the least elegant properties on the isle. There are also four studios. Furnishings are simple, almost ascetic. Nonetheless, it has some high points, namely ocean views from the shaded coralstone deck. And the rates are as low as $45 for studios in low season.

CASA DEL SOL B&B

507-250-4212
http://panama-isla-contadora.com

Dolphins in Golfo de Panamá, Panamá

Isla Contadora
Inexpensive
On the west side of the isle, this small, air-conditioned studio apartment is set in a twee garden and has equally quaint furniture, including wrought-iron seats and a mint green and maroon color scheme. It's intended as a self-catering unit, but a breakfast is prepared. It has ceiling fans.

CONTADORA ISLAND INN

507-6699-4614
www.contadoraislandinn.com
Isla Contadora
Moderate
This bed-and-breakfast, which opened in 2006, is a lovely option, combining intimacy and class. It has two houses: the original has six rooms, the second has three rooms and a suite. All rooms are air-conditioned and have ceiling fans and safes. These one-story properties each have spacious decks to fore and rear and are very homey. Guests come together in the TV lounge with DVD library. They're perfect for families to rent in entirety.

HACIENDA DEL MAR

507-269-6634
Fax: 507-264-1787
www.haciendadelmar.net
Isla San José
For luxurious indulgence this is the stand-out property in the Pearl Islands. It clings to a headland with fabulous ocean views. Its oval, slate-lined swimming pool overhangs the ocean, as do the 17 wooden cliff-side cabins on stilts. Albeit rustic—they're lined inside with bamboo reeds—they're infused with romance. Each has a balcony, ceiling fan, and air-conditioning. You can also go upscale with the graciously appointed junior suites or two-room "VIP *cabaña*" with king-sized beds. There are no phones in the rooms, nor TVs. The coup de grace is the open-air dining room beneath a soaring bamboo roof. This Clubhouse also has a games room and TV, and there's a gym. Whales can often be seen while you laze in the sun with cocktail in hand. Choose from activities such as sea kayaking, ATV tours, and sportfishing. It bills itself as an eco-resort—a ridiculous notion when it has noisy Jet-Skis!

HOTEL PUNTA GALEON RESORT

507-250-4134
Fax: 507-250-4135
www.puntagaleonhotel.com
Isla Contadora
Moderate
There's nothing remarkable about this somewhat staid property, but it has lovely gardens and a fine location over a white-sand beach. The 48 air-conditioned rooms are simply appointed, and beds are atop poured concrete bases. It has a swimming pool and open-air beachfront restaurant.

PERLA REAL INN

507-250-4095 or 949-228-8851
www.perlareal.com
Isla Contadora
Moderate

The most gracious property on Isla Contadora, this is my preferred place to rest my head. It's run by a California couple, who graced it with Spanish colonial decor. With just six rooms (two are suites with kitchens), it is lent a romantic intimacy by its exquisite wrought-iron, heavy wooden furniture, terra-cotta floors and hand-painted blue-and-white tiles. It has a courtyard with fountain. There's no restaurant or pool, but a beach and restaurants are mere minutes away, and it rents golf carts.

VILLA ROMÁNTICA

507-250-4067
www.contadora-villa-romantica.com
Playa Cacique, Isla Contadora
Moderate
This lovely looking Austrian-owned villa property is either quaintly kitschy or simply lacking in good taste, depending on your point of view. At least the location above gorgeous Playa Cacique earns rave reviews, and the restaurant is the island's best. The spacious air-conditioned rooms—each with wall murals of Panamanian themes—have huge glass doors opening to balconies, but decor in some rooms has a sickly Vegas love-motel tackiness, exemplified by the Honeymoon Suite, with its king bed with bloodred velvet spread and Corinthian column posts. And a mini-golf course? What was the owner thinking?

VIVEROS RESORT

507-264-3900
www.islaviveros.com
Isla Viveros
Expensive
Still under construction at this writing, this residential resort complex promises to bring true luxury to the archipelago. Based around a Jack Nicklaus-designed 18-hole golf course and 300-slip marina, it will have rental villas and, eventually, two 5-star hotels. An eight-room cottage was slated to open in 2010.

DINING

El Suizo (507-6560-3824; elsuizorestau-rant@gmail.com) Isla Contadora. Enjoy views over the golf course from this thatched hilltop grill (formerly Restaurante Gerald's) with an eclectic menu ranging from local seafood dishes, including jumbo shrimp in beer batter,

to pork chops, beef Stroganoff, and bratwurst. Open: Monday through Friday 11 AM–3 PM and 6–midnight, Saturday and Sunday 11 AM–midnight. Inexpensive to Moderate.

Restaurante Sagitario (507-250-4091) Isla Contadora. This is the preferred spot of locals, who refer to it as "Matilde's" for the owner, who specializes in fresh seafood such as ceviche and delicious jumbo shrimp. She also does Panamanian staples, such as stews and chicken with rice and beans. Open: Sunday through Thursday 7 AM–9 PM, Friday and Saturday 7 AM–10 PM. Inexpensive to Moderate.

Restaurante Romántica (507-250-4067) Isla Contadora. In the Villa Romántica. Come for the ocean views at this outdoor restaurant known for its seafood dishes, fondues, and hot-stone dinners. It also serves salads, pastas, and steaks. Begin or end with cocktails at Beachbar Hawaii. Open: Daily 7 AM–10 PM. Inexpensive to Moderate.

ATTRACTIONS, PARKS, AND RECREATION

Isla Contadora

Despite its small size, "Countinghouse Isle" is the most developed isle in the chain. It has a dozen stunning beaches tucked into coves on the north, east, and south shores; many are overlooked by multi-million dollar vacation villas perched on the cliffs. **Playa Larga**, on the east coast, is the largest beach and is easily accessed from the several hotels found here. Panamá's only nude beach, **Playa de las Suecas** (Swedes' Beach), is here, too, on the southeast corner and just over a headland from Playa Larga; the snorkeling is good right off the beach. There's even a nine-hole golf course. A noteworthy historical tidbit: deposed

La Peregrina

Perhaps the most famous pearl in the world, the Pilgrim Pearl was culled from the waters around the Archipiélago de las Perlas in the 16th century. Over the centuries this huge pearl has passed through many illustrious hands. Vasco Nuñez de Balboa supposedly gave it to King Ferdinand V of Spain. Phillip II (1556–1598) gave it to his bride-to-be, the brief-reigning Queen Mary I, the loyally Catholic daughter of Henry VIII. When she died in 1585, the pearl returned to Spain, where it remained until carted off to France by Joseph Bonaparte in 1508, earning it its current moniker. Charles Louis Bonaparte (Napoleon III) later sold it to the Duke of Abercorn, in whose family it remained until actor Richard Burton bought it in 1969 for $37,000 as a gift for his wife, Elizabeth Taylor. Today the teardrop-shaped pearl is a pendant on Taylor's exorbitant diamond, pearl, and ruby necklace, designed by Cartier.

Poison-dart Frogs

It's remarkable to think that such tiny and beautiful creatures can be so deadly. Yet, for sure, you don't want to pick up *Phyllobates terribilis*, an inch-long neon-yellow frog that can kill you on contact, thanks to its unique neurotoxin 250 times more deadly than strychnine. This tiny critter, found only in Darién and the Choco region of northern Colombia, is by far the most lethal of the 170 or so species of "poison-dart frogs" that inhabit the warm moist Neotropical forests. Choco tribes, such as Panamá's Emberá-Wounaan, need simply wipe their blow-darts along the frog's back—the toxin-tipped darts will remain deadly to monkeys and other game for up to a year!

Poison-dart frogs

Two cousins of *Phyllobates terribilis* also produce batrachotoxin—from *batrachos*, the Greek word for frog—that are among the deadliest neurotoxins in the natural world. Together the triptych comprise the Phyllobates genera, after which the entire family takes its colloquial name.

Poison-dart frogs belong to the Dendrobatidae family, of which two-thirds of the "poison-dart" frog family are non-toxic. When these frogs feel threatened or stressed, mucous glands beneath their skin produce bitter-tasting alkaloid compounds that cause predators to instantly gag. It's no good advertising your toxicity *after* being eaten. Hence, these frogs, most of which are no bigger than a thumbnail, advertise their deadly nature through vivid coloration that serves as a warning. Thus they hop about the forest floor in broad daylight, secure in their Day-glo liveries, like enameled porcelain figurines. Each species is highly endemic: The frogs of Isla Cerro Brujo are dark blue. Those of neighboring Isla Bastimentos are strawberry red, but yellow with black dots on nearby Isla Bocas.

The frog's toxins are actually a result of their diets. Much as DDT, mercury, and other chemicals become more concentrated as they move up a predatory food chain, poison-dart frogs sequester neurotoxins possessed by their prey, such as batrachotoxin-rich tiny beetles of the Choresine genus favored by the Phyllobates. Poison-dart frogs kept in captivity and fed a non-Choresine diet soon lose their toxicity.

Persian shah, Mohammad Reza Pahlavi, arrived in 1980 and lived briefly on Contadora before departing for Egypt, where he died a few months later.

A sizeable black population is descended from African slaves brought here in early colonial days to harvest pearls. Most live on **Isla Saboga**, about a 10-minute boat ride due west of Contadora.

Isla del Rey

(Isla San Miguel) The most southeasterly of the Pearl Islands is also by far the largest, measuring 93 square miles (240 sq km). San Miguel, the largest settlement in the archipelago, is also here on the north shore. Locals live off the sea: shrimping is the main industry. Although accommodations and tourists services are limited, Isla del Rey is a base for some of the best scuba diving and sportfishing to be enjoyed in Panamá. A long-touted residential resort complex, Kingfisher Bay, seems to have died a death.

Isla San José

This rugged island, the most southwesterly isle, is forest-festooned and ringed by 50-some beaches, from white to black. It's also a setting for active adventures, based out of the Hacienda del Mar hotel. Options include ATV tours, mountain biking, kayaking and, alas, noisy Jet-Skis. There are caves to explore, with caution! The Hacienda has a Sea Turtle Conservation Program, which protects marine turtles' nests and typically releases more than 1,000 baby turtles to the sea every year.

Isla San Telmo

This speck in the ocean, 0.6 mile (1 km) to the southeast of Isla del Rey, is a protected nesting site for boobies, cormorants, frigatebirds, and pelicans. It's protected as a nature reserve overseen by the Asociación Nacional para la Conservación de la Naturaleza (ANCON, 507-314-0060; www.ancon.org), as is similarly uninhabited **Isla Pacheca**, north of Contadora. The intertidal zone of San Telmo clasps the rusting wreck of a prototype U.S. submarine from the 1870s (it was used for pearl diving).

Isla Viveros

This private island, to the northwest of Isla San José, is currently being developed to become a major residential tourist facility. At this writing, Grupo Viveros (www.islaviveros .com) had completed the first nine holes of a Jack Nicklaus-designed championship golf course, and two hotels plus a 300-slip marina with scuba center are planned. Many of the deluxe villas will be available for rent.

Water Sports

Coral Dreams (507-6536-1776; www.coral-dreams.com), a scuba operation, will take you snorkeling to Isla Mogo Mogo (setting for *Survivor*) and offers PADI certification, plus trips for certified divers. It has a well-stocked dive shop.

Las Perlas Sailing (507-6413-7128; www.lasperlassailing.es.tl) offers day excursions aboard a 38-foot catamaran, including whale-watching trips. Snorkeling is included in the $75 per person fare. It also offers sportfishing with 26- and 36-foot Biminis.

7

CENTRAL PANAMÁ

"Birdcalls awaken you. Wisps of fog arise from Cerro Gaitán across the stream."
—FROM THE CANOPY LODGE WEB SITE

To the west of Panamá City, a narrow coastal littoral is framed hard up to the coast by a mountain massif—the Altos de Campaña—in whose folds is tucked a sensationally beautiful alpine valley. This coast, just a one-hour drive or so from the city, is the setting for the nation's premier beach resorts, including large-scale all-inclusives drawing the capital's moneyed middle-classes (albeit few foreigners up to now). Westward, the mountain range merges with that of the even more rugged Cordillera Central, while the coastal plain broadens into a fertile valley cusped between the thickly forested mountains and the Azuero peninsula and spanning the two provinces, Coclé and (to the west) Veragua, that make up Central Panamá.

This region boasts some of the best hiking and mountain biking terrain in the country. The refreshingly temperate alpine settlement of El Valle de Ancón is one of my favorite destinations in the entire country, and a perfect venue for horseback rides and mountain exploratories from quaint bed-and-breakfast hotels as your base. Parque Nacional Altos de Campaña is unsung, yet a fabulous venue for hikers, as is the Parque Nacional Omar Torrijos—a crown jewel of montane rain forest biota. The highland hamlet of Santa Fe is a center of coffee production, and an acclaimed venue for birders. There are even some pre-

Isla Coiba, Panamá

Columbian sites near Penonomé, one of several towns (such as Natá and Santiago) that retain pockets of colonial charm. Natá claims to have the oldest Catholic church in the Western hemisphere. Panamá's most important pre-Columbian site is at nearby El Cano. And the bustling city of Santiago has a fine colonial core that includes a museum brim-full of dusty antiques. Farther west, the Golfo de Montijo is a sportfishing base and also draws surfers seeking the next big wave.

OPPOSITE: *National Geographic Expeditions passengers exploring mangroves, Panamá*

And all this is just a one- to three-hour drive from the capital city.

The Interamerican Highway runs east and west through the heart of the region, making access a cinch.

GETTING THERE AND AROUND

By Air

You can charter a small plane for flights into the small Ruben Cantu Airport at Santiago (SYP).

By Bus or Público

The region is easily accessible by public bus from Panamá City's Gran Terminal, with dozens of buses daily plying the Pan-American Highway.

By Car

The well-maintained Interamerican Highway grants easy access and runs inland of the shore then slices due west through the middle of the region, linking Panamá City with the town of Santiago.

Spur roads lead north and south off the highway to all the major sights. East of Santiago, the highway is two lanes in each direction; westward, however, it's one lane, with danger-ously fast traffic (including big rigs) pressing hard up your rear as the highway snakes up over the mountain pass that's the gateway to Chiriquí province. There's no shortage of traf-fic cops, especially east of Penonomé. However, there are few settlements, gas stations, restaurants, or lodgings west of Santiago—plan accordingly.

By Taxi

Taxis await custom at bus stops along the highway, doing a brisk business ferrying passen-gers to and from the various beach resorts (typically about $3).

By Tours

Pesantez Tours (507-263-7577; www.pesantaz-tours.com) offers scheduled transfers between Panamá City and the beaches.

Golfo de Panamá Beaches

Panamá's hot-spot beach resorts begin less than one hour west of Panamá City and line the coast of Panamá and Coclé provinces for about 37 miles (60 km) between Chame and Playa Juan Hombrón. The area is part of "The Dry Arc," so-called for its comfortably dry climate most of the year. The Interamerican Highway runs parallel to the shore between 0.6 mile and 3 miles (1 and 5 km) inland, granting access via spur roads.

There is no Cancún equivalent, however. Nor even a town by the shore; they lie inland, along the highway. Most beachfront communities are really agglomerations of second homes for Panamá City's middle classes, although you can still find simple fishing villages. Hotels concentrate at Playa Coronado and at Playas Farallon and Blanca, the westernmost (and prettiest) of the beaches. Elsewhere, self-catering rental villas are the name of the game.

The international crowd has suddenly wised up to this coast's allure, as demonstrated by the opening in 2009 of a SuperClubs all-inclusive and the much-anticipated oh-so-chic Nikki Beach Playa Blanca resort for sexy Miami-type fashionistas. And in December 2008, the Hard Rock chain announced plans for a 500-room Hard Rock Hotel with swim-in rooms at Playa Blanca. True, Playa Blanca is named for its white(ish) sands. But this isn't Cancún or Punta Cana. Most beaches are of varying shades of gray. If it's *gorgeous* beaches you're seeking, fly out to the Archipiélago de las Perlas or to the San Blas Islands.

LODGING AND DINING

Punta Chame has just one restaurant—a traditional thatched fisherman's hangout serving great garlic lobster and fresh fish dishes. If you're self-catering you can stock up on fresh shrimp at the local shrimp bar, and on groceries at the local store; being run by Chinese, it keeps late-night hours.

Seeking a self-catering villa? Try **Tropical Escapes Panama** (507-6550-6302; www.tropicalescapespanama.com).

BAY VIEW RESORT
507-240-9621
www.bayviewelpalmar.com
Playa El Palmar
Inexpensive to Moderate
This family-friendly budget hotel for unfussy travelers has 30 minimally furnished air-conditioned rooms set in lush grounds with redbrick pathways edging up to the narrow beach. You can even camp. It has a pool, and activities include volleyball and a surf school. The restaurant has Wi-Fi.

BREEZES PANAMA RESORT AND SPA
1-877-273-3937
www.breezes.com/resorts/breezes-panama
Playa Blanca
Expensive
The class act along this coast, this family-friendly resort opened in 2009 and is a total break for this Jamaica's all-inclusive chain. First, it's the company's first property in Central America. It also breaks the mold with its super contemporary motif, which plays on a Caribbean plantation

theme. It features four blocks rising six stories behind the beach and has 294 air-conditioned, tastefully furnished guest rooms and suites. Choose Panamanian, Italian, or Japanese restaurants. And it has all the water sports, activities, and nocturnal entertainment, including a nightclub, you'd expect of SuperClubs.

CASA DE LAS ORQUIDEAS
c/o 425-391-8210
www.casadelasorquideas.com
Calle O, Punta Chame
Inexpensive
Tucked behind bright blue gates near the tip of Punta Chame, is a delightful spot with five air-conditioned cabins, each painted in lively pastels, set in an orchid garden. Though simply furnished, each cabin is exquisitely maintained. Join your fellow guests in the thatched lounge-bar with TV and DVDs. It has a shaded pool.

CLUB GAVIOTA
507-224-9053
gaviota@turistaintl.com
Paseo George Smith, Playa Coronado
Inexpensive
A motel-style building with nine air-conditioned rooms, this place offers value-for-money budget accommodations at about $35–40 double, but the best deal is to take an inclusive package with meals ($65–80). Avoid the two dingy original rooms here; the seven more modern additions are far better, although none offer ocean views. All have TVs and safes.

CORONADO GOLF AND BEACH RESORT

507-264-3164

www.coronadoresort.com

Avenida Punta Prieta, Coronado

Moderate to Expensive

Most suited to families and conservative travelers, this resort commands much of the Playa Coronado beachfront and likes to promote its all-inclusive packages (although the package is far from that, so expect plenty of extra costs). It boasts a wish list of amenities, from the Olympic-sized pool and Tom and George Fazio-designed championship golf course to an equestrian club (Saturday only), tennis courts, water sports, and kids' club, plus five restaurants and a casino. The spacious rooms are nicely furnished, without winning prizes. The Royal Suites and Residential Suites sleep six people—ideal for families. That said, it's a lackluster property compared to the all-inclusives of, say, Jamaica or the Dominican Republic.

COROWALK INN

507-240-1516

Avenida Roberto Eisenmann, Playa Coronado

www.hostalesdelpacifico.com

Inexpensive to Moderate

No prizes for the location: right on the Pan-Am Highway, next to El Rey shopping plaza. But this hotel is stylish and well run, with handsome enough rooms: 14 in all, furnished in upscale U.S. motel fashion with an eye to the passing business market. Check a few, as they vary, and you'd be wise to be as far from the highway as possible.

EL LITORAL

507-332-6416 or 6658-1143 (cellular)

Lot 12 Punta Prieta, Coronado

www.litoralpanama.com

Moderate

French owners Anne-Marie and René Bergeron run this five-bedroom, non-smoking bed-and-breakfast by the beach. Three rooms have private bathrooms; two others share. All have cool tile floors, and simple but tasteful decor, including wrought-iron beds in some rooms. It has a swimming pool, plus Wi-Fi. Occasional yoga classes are hosted.

HOTEL CANADIAN

507- 240-6066, in Canada 867-536-2272

www.hotelcanadianpanama.com

Off the Interamerican Highway, Chame

Inexpensive

Word of mouth brings a steady flow of mostly foreign backpacking tourists to this Canadian-run guesthouse close to Playa Gorgona. With its hilltop roost, it gets the breezes, best enjoyed by the pool. It has seven rooms, including two family-sized units. Katie and Ralph Grunow, the owners, fuss over guests in the restaurant and bar.

HOTEL PUNTA CHAME

507-264-7560

Punta Chame

Inexpensive

This simple spot is the only place in Chame to lay your head. Hence, the owners charge monopolistic prices for the six simple air-conditioned cabanas ($40–60). It also has a camping area with water and electricity, and there's a thatched restaurant and, in dry season (November through April), the Machete Kitesurfing school is based here.

ISLA TABORCILLO |JOHN WAYNE VILLAGE

507-264-2708

www.isla-taborcillo.com

Isla Taborcillo

Moderate to Expensive

If you can get beyond the ridiculous and hokey John Wayne motif, this could be actually a pleasant spot to rest your head for a few days, at least if you have bored kids in tow (there's even a small zoo among the Wild West buildings). The 27 rooms come with free DVDs, and pleasant albeit minimal furnishings. Thatched umbrellas festoon the palm-shaded lawns, with both freshwater and saltwater pool. It has horseback riding and—yuk!—noisy Jet Skis.

LAS SIRENAS
507-993-3235 or 6747-1772
www.lasirenas.com
Playa Santa Clara
Moderate
Run by a delightful Panamanian couple, this calming place has a hillside setting over the beach. Choose spacious individual self-catering cottages with cable TV and Wi-Fi, or smaller rooms closer to the beach with downstairs and loft beds. Furnishings are a bit spare, but bougainvillea bowers add heaps of color and cottages have their own barbecue pits and patios with poured-concrete sofas. There's a seafood restaurant a few minutes' walk along the beach. You're pretty much on your own here, as maids appear about once in three days.

NIKKI BEACH PLAYA BLANCA
c/o 786-515-1130
http://nikkibeachhotels.com/playablanca
Playa Blanca
Very expensive
Playa Blanca's "wow!" factor will soar when (and if) the Nikki Beach Playa Beach opens some time in 2010–11 to serve high-energy fashionistas and an otherwise sexy young crowd. The original and now infamous Nikki Beach Miami was chosen by the Travel Channel as the World's Sexiest Beach Bar in 2009. This copycat tropical version will feature Nikki's signature broad-daylight disco, over-the-top parties, and king-sized Ali Baba beds laid out on platinum sands. Female waitstaff in navel-revealing tube tops and drawstring pants set the sexy tone. The 220 chic and spacious rooms and suites include 83 two-bedroom suites, 7 two-bedroom Penthouses, and 20 ultra-luxury three-bedroom Penthouses, all with floor-to-ceiling windows, 42-inch HD plasma TVs, Wi-Fi, and super chic decor.

All that said, I attended the opening party at Nikki Beach Turks and Caicos in 2008. A year later it closed due to financial problems. So don't hold your breath for Nikki Beach Playa Blanca to actually open, although construction was well advanced in late 2009.

PLAYA BLANCA RESORT, SPA & RESIDENCES
1-888-790-5264
www.playablancaresort.com
Playa Blanca
Moderate
This mid-market all-inclusive opened in 2003 and has 219 rooms, three suites, and a penthouse, and gets mixed reviews from past guests, although I like the stylish decor and it is less impersonal than the nearby Decameron. The positives include a huge pool complex, and its dining options include a sushi restaurant and a huge thatched open-air buffet restaurant. Entertainment includes a nightly show and beach party. It has a kids' club and kids' entertainment. The negatives? The hotel feels a bit long in the tooth and some rooms are said to suffer from mildew.

RANCHO BONITO
507-240-6513
www.hotelranchobonito.com
Playa Gorgona
Inexpensive to Moderate
With a lovely garden setting, this hotel is popular with Panamanian families, although furnishings in the 15 rooms are a bit barebones, and the place can get noisy with kids. It has a restaurant, simple bar, a pool, and children's playground.

XS MEMORIES
507-993-3069
www.xsmemories.com
On the north side of the Interamerican

Highway, Playa Santa Clara
Inexpensive to Moderate
Now here's a winner! RVing? Then you won't want to miss this *yanqui*-owned RV park run by Dennis and Sheila Parsick. It has 22 motor home hookups, with water, electricity, and septic-tank service, all for a fair $10 daily. You can also trade your motor home for a night in one of three air-conditioned cabins with ceiling fans ($55). And it also has a campsite for tents. There's a swimming pool, a bar with TV, and a charming stone-lined restaurant (Monday through Thursday 8–8, and Friday through Sunday 8 AM–10 PM). And Kayak Panama is here.

ATTRACTIONS, PARKS, AND RECREATION

The beaches (playas) are presented here in order, as approached southward from Panamá City.

Punta Chame

Arriving from Panamá City, the beaches begin around **Chame**, a nondescript town that is gateway to **Punta Chame** (buses run hourly from Bejuco, the turnoff on the Pan-Am Highway). This fishing village, at the tip of a 6-mile-long (10 km) sand spit whipped by constant trade winds, draws windsurfers and kiteboarders to the country's capital of wind-sport action. It's a beautiful drive (despite the horrendous potholes) along the roller-coaster spit, with views north across **Bahía de Chame**, where dolphins are often seen frolicking in the jade-colored waters. Much of the bay shore is lined with mangroves (good for birding), and with shrimp farms. A tan-colored beach unspools along the ocean side of the peninsula and is pristine enough that three species of marine turtles nest here. Swimming, however, requires caution due to riptides.

Two caring locals, Ramón and Vilma Morales, run **Fundación de Amigos de las Tortugas Marinas** (FATmar, 507-227-5091), with hatcheries where turtle eggs are incubated and the hatchlings released to the sea. You can bunk with the Moraleses in simple cabins with cold-water showers.

There are big plans for Punta Chame. If it is finally built, the Portones del Mar Yacht Club and Resort will host the only marina between Panamá City and Chiriquí province, along with a tennis center and condo hotel.

Floating at the entrance to the bay, boomerang-shaped **Isla Taborcillo** is another great birding site—in fact, one of the region's most important nesting sites for tricolored heron and yellow-crowned night-heron. Once owned by actor John Wayne (and known colloquially as "Isla de John Wayne"), it's also a kind of Disneyland, as the owners operate their hotel as a sort of Western theme park, with staff dressed in cowboy gear, a sheriff's house with prison cells, etc. See the *Lodging* section.

Kite-boarding: This is *the* hot new water sport. Imagine strapping yourself onto a modified surfboard and into a harness attached to a giant kite, or wind foil, then skimming over the ocean at a helluva speed. Talk about an adrenaline rush! Experienced kite-boarders are capable of performing spectacular leaps 30 feet (9 m) above the water. Yes, the sport is potentially dangerous. But like every sport, you learn to walk before you try to run. Novices should aim to be out at midday, when winds rarely exceed 10 knots. In early morning and toward sundown the winds crank up to 30 knots. The season is November through April.

The lead operator is **Machete Kiteboarding** (507-674-7772; www.machetekites.com), at Hotel Punta Chame, run by veteran kite-surfing champion, Itzick Lalo. It's usually open only in dry season.

Isla Boná, Estivá, and Otoque

These three islands, about 9 miles (15 km) southeast of Punta Chame, are important nesting sites for brown pelicans, magnificent frigatebirds, and brown and blue-footed boobies. The nutrient-rich currents that well up around the islands teem with fish and provide a ready-at-hand food source for the birds. Fishermen set out from Chame and from a hamlet on Otoque to work the waters. Snorkeling around the Otoque islands is risky due to strong currents.

You can hire a boat and fisherman to take you out, but be warned: these waters can be choppy. **National Geographic Expeditions** (1-888-966-8687; http://nationalgeographic expeditions.com) includes a visit on its eight-day "Costa Rica and Panama Canal" cruise-tours.

Playa Gorgona

This beach, south of the mangrove and *salinas* (salt ponds) of Chame peninsula, is dark gray. Almost black. You'll need sandals for walking the sizzling hot sands. That doesn't stop Panamanian families (most impecunious) pouring in on weekends and holidays.

Playa Coronado

The yin to Gorgona's yang is this middling grayish beach, 31 miles (50 km) southwest of Panamá City and which Panamá's moneyed class has made a major second-residence zone.

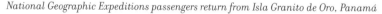

National Geographic Expeditions passengers return from Isla Granito de Oro, Panamá

Those without homes here like to flash their money around at the **Coronado Golf and Beach Resort**. The community is gated, but if you say you are staying at the Coronado Beach Resort, you'll usually be let in (bring ID).

Arriving by bus, you alight on the Pan-Am Highway by the Texaco gas station at the turnoff for Coronado. *Colectivo* minivans await custom here 6 AM–7:30 PM. Hop aboard for the short trip to the beach (50 cents).

> **Good to Know About**
> The **Panamanian Tourist Board** (IPAT, 507-993-3241) has a small information bureau at Playa Farallón, 400 yards (365 m) south of the Interamerican Highway. It had only a bare minimum of literature when I last called in. Open Monday through Friday 8–5.

Playa San Carlos to Playa Santa Clara

About 3 miles (5 km) south of Coronado, Playa Santa Carlos still clings (barely) to its traditions as a fishing village. It merges south into Playa El Palmar, which is known as a great surfing destination, with 10-foot-tall (3 m) waves pushed ashore by the winds. Hotels here with surf schools include **Bay View Resort**.

Next up are Playas Río Mar, Playa Corona, and then one of my favorite beaches hereabouts, Playa Santa Clara: Pretty, and well served with hotels and restaurants.

Playa Farallón

At the farthest reach comes the most developed of the beach resorts. Playa Farallón is the setting, since 2000, of the all-inclusive Royal Decameron Beach Resort and Casino. You can purchase a day-pass to make the most of this mega-resort, which isn't my thing at all. But Panamá City's middle classes seem to love it, despite the lackluster gray sands. They come for the casino, I suppose. Believe it or not, a small fishing community clings to its impoverished existence within a stone's throw of the Decameron's high walls, providing an opportunity to commune with real downtown folks as they tend their fishing nets and colorful *piraguas* drawn up on the sands.

Pipa's Bar and Restaurante (507-233-0945; www.pipasbeach.com), a 15-minute stroll from Decameron, is just the kind of funky beach bar that I love to hang out at, with a chilled beer and my bare feet stretched out in the sands. It serves lobster and fresh garlic shrimp. Speaking of which, **Bubba Shrimp Fishing Tours** (507-993-2740; bubashrimp@cwpanama.net) lets passengers play the part of Forrest Gump as you go shrimping at sea. Part working vessel, part party boat, it has a bar and lively sound system.

The turnoff for Playa Farallón is between the towns of Santa Clara and Río Hato. A former U.S. airfield that also sits between the two towns took a plastering on December 20, 1989, courtesy of AC-130 Specter gunships during Operation Just Cause to oust General Manuel Noriega. "Pineapple face" had a beach home near the Decameron. U.S. Army Rangers dropped from the sky and took that out too. You can still see the bullet holes.

Playa Blanca

The attractive tan sands of Playa Blanca, about 3 miles (5 km) west of Farallon, received a boost in 2009 when Jamaica's SuperClubs opened its Breezes all-inclusive resort. There are several other resorts here, and the beach is slated to receive the sexiest hotel of all—the Nikki Beach Playa Blanca—in 2010.

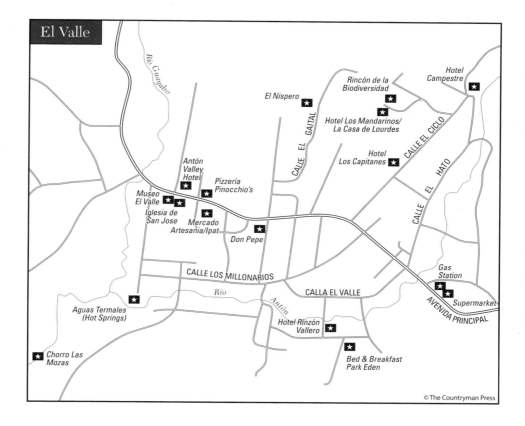

Altos de Campaña and Valle de Antón

The first time I saw the Altos de Campaña massif, which rises about 30 miles (50 km) west of Panamá City, I did a double take. The tan-colored landscape reminded me more of the craggy Welsh highlands than the jungle-clad slopes one hour's drive east, such as Chagres. The first sight is misleading, however. While much of the lower slopes close to the Interamerican Highway have been denuded, the upper slopes and Caribbean-facing northern slopes are rain-soaked and lushly forested. You can experience four distinct ecosystems.

The Parque Nacional Altos de Campaña, on the northeast slopes, offers splendid birding and hiking opportunities and will also thrill botany enthusiasts: These upper slopes are renowned for their endemic orchids and other flora (pines are typical on the Pacific slopes, while the Caribbean side is bottle-green lush). On its western side, the massif rises to 3,888 feet (1,185 m) atop Cerro Gaitál, spectacularly framing the Valle de Antón, one of the most delightful settings in Panamá. Basking in springlike temperatures year-round, it's justifiably a popular weekend escape from the lowland heat, and a center for active adventures—from horseback riding to zipline rides.

LODGING

ANTON VALLEY HOTEL

507-983-6097
www.antonvalleyhotel.com
Avenida Principal, El Valle de Antón
Inexpensive to Moderate

Right in the heart of the village, this lovely little hotel is run by a gringo couple, Les and Earle, and feels like a cozy, impeccably clean bed and breakfast. Like most hotels hereabouts, it is set in lovely gardens. Rooms vary, so check a few. None are air-conditioned. It's not needed, anyway, and the ceiling fans work a treat. Hearty gringo breakfasts are served on the patio. You can practice your Spanish with Coconut, the talking bird.

BED & BREAKFAST PARK EDEN

507-983-6167
www.parkeden.com
Calle Espave 7, El Valle de Antón
Moderate

Another lovely stone-and-timber lodge, this bed and breakfast is set in 2 acres (0.8 ha) of lush gardens great for birding. Lionel Alemán Toledano and his delightful wife, Monica, are your hosts, and they run Park Eden with a loving touch reflected in the filling breakfast and the afternoon tea, English fashion, served on the porch. There's a quaint and romantic old-world touch to the eight air-conditioned rooms, all with cable TV and DVD player, coffeemaker, and mini-fridge plus ceiling fan. Two rooms are family-sized suites.

CANOPY LODGE

507-264-5720 or 800-930-3397
www.canopylodge.com
1.2 miles (2 km) northwest of El Valle de Antón
Moderate to Expensive

Beloved of birding groups, the Canopy Lodge is a true eco-lodge combining a superb location hard up against a forested mountainside with superior facilities and comfort. Slide back your French doors and you can relax on your veranda and spot the birds, and maybe a monkey and sloth or two. Meals are served family style on an open-air, stone-lined veranda dining room. There are comfy open-air lounges, and the eight spacious rooms have stone floors and blazing white walls to set off eye-pleasing contemporary hardwood furnishings. It doubles as an activity center; the zipline tour is here, for example, and it has world-class birding guides and tours.

HOSTAL HACIENDA DOÑA VICTORIA

507-263-4593 or 6618-8370
http://hostalvictoriapanama.com
Campana, 2 miles (3 km) W of Capira
Inexpensive

You'd be forgiven, at first sight, for thinking that "hostal" doesn't do justice to this intimate old Spanish hacienda set in a beautiful garden in the eastern foothills of the Altos de Campana. Approached by a stone courtyard with fountain, the exterior exudes charm thanks to terra-cotta patios, red-tile roof, and wrought-iron grills. However, the eight bedrooms are a huge letdown, with barebones furnishings and a students'-dorm feel. Swimming pool. Games room. Camping permitted.

HOTEL CAMPESTRE

507-983-6146
www.hotelcampestre.com
Calle El Hato, El Valle de Antón
Moderate

Looking suitably alpine, this low-slung lodge squats at the base of forested mountains. The interior of this 1920s hotel, with its beamed restaurant and large fireplace, is timeworn, but 2010 hopefully will see completion of a drawn-out reconstruction meant to replace the termite-ridden structure with a more contemporary brick and steel vogue.

HOTEL LOS CAPITANES
507-983-6080
www.los-capitanes.com
Calle de la Cooperativa, El Valle de Antón
Moderate
Run by a retired and amiable German sea
dog, Manfred Koch, this hotel floats amid a
sea of gorgeous greenery. Buildings feature
red tin roofs. The 10 bedrooms are sparsely
furnished and the mood is a bit dowdy;
some have loft bedrooms; others are
equipped for handicapped travelers. Sr.
Koch serves up the likes of German pancakes, meatloaves, and pork chops and
sauerkraut, plus barbecues on weekends.

HOTEL LOS MANDARINOS
507-983-6645, or toll-free 888-281-8413
(in the U.S.)
www.losmandarinos.com
218 yards (200 m) west of Escuela Primero
Ciclo, off Calle El Ciclo, El Valle de Antón
Expensive
Looking like a piece of Tuscany transplanted, this deluxe boutique hotel owned
by Pedro Fábrega, is the region's finest.
Faced with river stones and Romanesque
columns, it cuts a striking figure against the
mountain backdrop. Most of the 31 rooms
are in villas. All feature sleigh beds and
heavy drapes, plus French doors opening to
large balconies for enjoying the gorgeous
views. The acclaimed La Casa de Lourdes
gourmet restaurant is overseen by Pedro's
sister, Lourdes Fábrega de Ward, and opens
to a striking pool with Jacuzzi. There's even
a games room with Wi-Fi for kids, an Irish
pub for adults, and a top-class spa.

HOTEL RINCÓN VALLERO
507-983-6175
www.hotelrinconvallero.com
Calle Espave, El Valle de Antón
Moderate
This hacienda-style hotel in lush grounds
with flower-ringed pond and a stream is a
peaceful recluse. Most of the cabins are

lovely junior suites and suites, but many of
the rooms in the hotel proper are mere
cubbyholes. Mosaic-lined sunken showers
and bamboo-lined ceilings make amends.
The El Pez de Oro restaurant serves an
eclectic menu.

TANGLEWOOD WELLNESS CENTER
6-671-9965 or 301-637-4657
www.tanglewoodwellnesscenter.com
Sorá, 9 miles (15 km) NW of Bejuco
Expensive
The mountain setting is appropriate for
this health-and-fasting-retreat. Festooned
with bougainvillea and trailing vines, it has
seven cabins that stairstep the slopes.
Guests socialize in a library-lounge furnished with wicker. One-week minimum.

DINING

CASA DE LOURDES
507-983-6450
www.lacasadelourdes.net
218 yards (200 m) west of Escuela Primero
Ciclo, off Calle El Ciclo, El Valle de Antón
Cuisine: Nouvelle Panamanian
It doesn't get any better than this! Housed
in an Italianate villa, this is one of the top
five restaurants outside Panamá City in my
book, and is the very epitome of romance.
Red-tile roofs. Lush formal gardens with
Roman fountains. And antique furnishings,
sumptuous leather couches, and timber
ceiling beams. All combine to grace this
beautiful villa, with a dining terrace
beneath a portico opening onto a swimming pool courtyard. Lourdes Fábrega de
Ward's acclaimed cooking (she studied with
Paul Prudhomme and Martha Stewart) is
worth the drive from Panamá City in its
own right. Treats might include langosta
Grand Marnier, blackened fish in
tamarindo sauce, and a killer fruit and ice
cream sundae. Open: Monday, Wednesday,
and Thursday 7:30 AM–9 PM, Friday-

Saturday 7:30 AM–10:30 PM. Expensive to Very Expensive.

DON PEPE

507-983-6425
Avenida Principal, El Valle de Antón
Cuisine: Panamanian
A perfectly unpretentious place to enjoy local fare, this diner-style restaurant offers an eclectic menu that includes burgers, veggie items, and even Chinese dishes alongside good ol' Panamanian *ropa vieja* (braised beef with rice and beans). No reservations. Open: Monday through Thursday 7 AM–9 PM; Friday through Sunday 7 AM–11 PM. Inexpensive to Expensive.

EL VALLE GOURMET AND COFFEE SHOP

507-6715-5785
Avenida Principal, El Valle de Antón
Cuisine: Delicatessen
On weekends, this is the place to pick up sandwiches, cold cuts, cheeses, tinned goods, and gourmet coffees, including cappuccinos and espressos. Open: Friday noon–9 PM, Saturday 9 AM–10:30 PM, and Sunday 9 AM–6 PM. Inexpensive.

PIZZERÍA PINOCCHIO'S

507-983-6715
Avenida Principal, El Valle de Antón
Cuisine: Panamanian
Catercorner to the church, on the main drag, this simple refectory-style Italian restaurant serves tremendous thin-crust pizzas baked in a wood oven, although you'll also find spaghetti, lasagne, etc. No credit cards. Open: Friday 4–9 PM; Saturday and Sunday noon–9 PM. Inexpensive to Moderate.

Iglesia San Jose, El Valle de Antón, Panamá

ATTRACTIONS, PARKS, AND RECREATION

PARQUE NACIONAL Y RESERVA BIOLÓGICA ALTOS DE CAMPANA

507-244-0092
www.anam.gob.pa

This 12,170-acre (4,925 ha) national park was the nation's first when created in 1966. Although taking up only a fraction of the massif, it features attractions unique in the country, not least dramatic volcanic formations that include lava fields and huge freestanding boulders known as tors. With a 4WD vehicle, you can exit the Interamerican Highway at Capira to access the eastern side of the park and to a steep, slippery trail to the summit of **Cerro Trinidad** 3,176 feet (968 m). The highest point is Cerro Chame (3,304 feet/1,007 m), which is accessed from an exit off the highway about 2 miles (3 km) west of Capira. The snaking road is a real scenic stunner. There's a lookout *(mirador)* just beyond the ranger station with a great perspective of the plains far below. The trails include **Sendero La Cruz**, a relatively easy and well-maintained trail that begins 3 miles (5 km) above the ranger station and leads you to the top of **Cerro Campaña**. For a more rugged hike, choose the **Sendero Cerro Campaña**. Bring your binoculars to help identify the 267 bird species so far identified here. Hopefully, too, you might see coatis, sloths, howler monkeys, Geoffrey's tamarin, and poison-dart frogs.

El Valle de Antón

This fabled vale, in the heart of the Altos de Campaña, is actually a former lake bed within the crater of a now (hopefully) extinct volcano. The flat-as-can-be valley floor is at 1,975 feet (600 m), surrounded by a thickly forested mountain meniscus. Scenic beauty astounds. Likewise, the eternal springlike climate. And the air is scented with a piney fragrance. Reason enough, then, to explain the vale's popularity as a weekend retreat for Panamá City's moneyed folk, many of whom have built villas. Many are in Swiss alpine style. Others are Tuscan themed. Still others, Modernist inspirations. Add to the mix a couple of dozen cozy bed-and-breakfast hotels tucked behind white-picket fences, bougainvillea bowers, and topiary hedgerows. The result is a delightfully peaceful and colorful village that is second only to Boquete (in Chiriquí province) as a center for eco-adventures: hikes, horseback riding, and even an exhilarating zipline ride. And the birding around here is world-class.

El Valle village is laid out in a rough grid on the east bank of the Río Antón. Simply walking the tree-shaded lanes is reward enough.

Canopy Adventure: Fancy whizzing between treetops, Tarzan style? Actually, Tarzan could never have conceived of a zipline—a meta cable slung between trees.

Squirrel monkeys

It's the new rage for exploring the canopy, but don't expect to see much, if any, wildlife. It's all about the adrenaline rush as you *whizzzz* downhill in a harness attached to the cable. It's offered by the Canopy Lodge (507-264-5720; www.canopy lodge.com; Calle Cerro Macho, 2 miles (3 km) northwest of town; open 6 AM–5 PM; $50 full tour, or $15 short tour).

Good to Know About
In El Valle de Antón, there's an IPAT **tourist information bureau** (507-983-6474; open Tuesday and Thursday through Sunday 7:30–3:30) in the Mercado Artesanal.

Birding and Hiking: The north side of the vale is framed by Cerro Gaitál (3,888 feet/1,185 m). The mountain lies at the heart of the 827-acre (337 ha) **Monumento Natural Cerro Gaitál**, created to protect the only habitat of the highly endangered *rana dorado* (golden toad), endemic to this area. A modestly steep and moderately challenging trail (three hours; open 6 AM–6 PM; $3) begins at the north end of Calle El Gaitál and has a *mirador* (lookout) halfway, offering sensational views over the valley and even, on clear days, to the Pacific and Caribbean. You can join guided hikes offered by the **Panamá Explorers Club** (507-215-2330; Vía Ranita Dorada; www.pexclub.com; $20 from El Valle, $60 from Panamá City), which follows a trail to the summit of **Cerro La Indian Dormida** (Sleeping Indian Woman), named for its clearly discernible form.

Some of the best birding and easiest hiking is on the trails of the **Canopy Lodge**. These include the **Chorro Macho**, leading to a 150-foot (45 m) waterfall, and short **Riverside Trail**. Expect to see such species as rufous motmot, chestnut-backed antbird, and even the rare sunbird. Sloths are also commonly seen.

A short and somewhat overgrown trail to the right (south side) of the Hotel Campestre leads to a copse of *arboles cuadradas* (square trees). Yes, *square* trunks! Or so they say. I had difficulty discerning any such thing.

Sites: The yellow-and-black *rana dorado* can be seen at a rather pathetic zoo and plant nursery—El Nispero (507-983-6142 or 6566-2220; E-mail: zoonispero@gmail.com; Calle Carlos Arosemena; open daily 8–5; $2). The critters displayed here (in far-too-small cages) include kinkajous, monkeys, and ocelots, as well as native and exotic bird species. There are even ostriches here! Most of the animals were illegal pets confiscated from their owners by government authorities; the tapirs once belonged to former Dictator Manuel Noriega. Refrain from following the awful habit of Panamanians, who feed the animals! Here, the **El Valle Amphibian Conservation Center**, funded by the Smithsonian Institute, breeds and studies the *rana dorado* to save it from total demise at the hand of a fungus (*Batrachochytrium dendrobatidis*) that has wiped it, and many of its cousins, out in the wild.

To learn about wriggly reptiles, head to the **Serpentario** (507-983-6680; Avenida Principal; variable hours; entrance $1), a small snake exhibit with 15 local species.

Rincón de la Biodiversidad (507-6706-1271; daily 7–6; free), fronting Hotel Los Mandarinos, welcomes visitors to this organic farm, where you can even pick your own veggies.

The town's **Iglesia San José** is a tiny footnote. Next door, the yet tinier **Museo El Valle** displays folkloric costumes plus pre-Columbian relics, including petroglyphs (Saturday and Sunday, 9–5). A far more impressive pre-Columbian site is **Piedra Pintada**—a massive boulder etched with ancient symbols; it's at the far west end of town, off the road to the Canopy Lodge. Local youngsters will be ready at the parking lot to guide you and give you a basic spiel for a tip. Don't leave *anything* in your car, as break-ins have been reported.

SHOPPING

Sunday holds added appeal, when Ngöbe-Buglé Indians come to El Valle de Antón to sell their crafts in the open-air **Mercado Artesanal** (artisans' market; daily 8–6; free), on Avenida Central—look for ceramic figurines of *ranas doradas* (golden frogs). This is a great time to meet Ngobe-Buglé people (and even some Emberá) selling their exotic baskets, jewelry, and clothing, etc. You'll also find orchids and ceramics. A smaller version is held daily. And you can find wonderful indigenous items for sale at **Tienda Artesanía Don Pepe** (507-983-6425; daily 8–6), next to the market.

Penonomé and Vicinity

On the western side of the Altos de Campaña, the prosperous yet small provincial capital of Penonomé has a colonial pedigree dating back to 1581, when it was born as a forced reset-tlement colony (a *reducción de indios*) for indigenous slave laborers. In fact, the town is named for the execution (*penó*) of an indigenous chief, Nomé. In the late 17th century it briefly served as the region's capital. Today, the whitewashed town bustles as an agricul-tural center and as gateway to the Cordillera Central.

The mountains to the north and east of Penonomé are among the most scenic in the nation and made more so by flat-topped *mesas* (such as Cerro Ororari), sugarloaf-shaped *mogotes* (such as Cerro Chiquiralí), and other dramatic limestone and volcanic formations that stud the landscape. These highlands are frequently shrouded in clouds and tendril-like mists that feed the lush forests.

Bust of Arnulfo Arias, Penonome, Panamá

LODGING AND DINING

POSADA CERRO LA VIEJA ECO-HOTEL & SPA

507-983-8905
Fax: 507-983-8900
www.posadalavieja.com
Chiquirí Arriba, 17 miles (27 km) NE of Penonomé

Posada Cerro La Vieja Eco-Hotel & Spa, Panamá

Moderate
Formerly Trinidad Spa and Lodge, this hacienda-style hilltop eco-lodge boasts a sensational location with marvelous views. It sits in lush gardens enfolded by a macadamia farm and lush forest. Most of the 22 rooms are in spacious fourplex cabins with terra-cotta floors and modest furnishings, including comfortable king-sized beds. You can soak in healing mineral waters in stone-walled spa rooms. Walls of glass open to verandas with hammocks. The rustic dining room exudes charm. Games room.

LA IGUANA ECO-RESORT

507-991-0879 or 6785-7550
www.laiguanaresort.com
Churuquita Grande, 9 miles (14.5 km) NE of Penonomé
Inexpensive
No frills at this thatched, riverside eco-lodge with eight rooms. Some have loft bedrooms, and bathrooms lack hot water. It has trails for guided hikes and horseback rides, plus a mini-zoo and playground, and swimming pool.

ATTRACTIONS, PARKS, AND RECREATION

The town's few sites revolve around **Parque 8 de Diciembre**, the main plaza, ablaze in summer with African flame trees. It is centered on a gazebo and pinned on its south side by a life-sized bronze **statue of Simón Bolívar**. On the park's north side, the **Iglesia San Juan Bautista** has a lovely baroque façade and exquisite stained-glass windows. To the west side, a medieval-style police station abuts the *gobernación* (municipal government building). The park opens to the northeast to a boomerang-shaped *plazuela* studded with busts and monuments of Panamanian presidents born in Penonomé, most famously ill-fated three-time President Arnulfo Arias (1901–88).

Nearby, the small **Museo de Penonomé** (Calle San Antonio; 507-997-8490; open Monday through Saturday 9 AM–12:30 PM and 1:30–4 PM, Sunday 9:30 AM–1 PM; entrance $1) is spread among four red-tile-roofed, colonial homes. It displays pre-Columbian relics, colonial religious icons, and other exhibits pertaining to local history.

La Pintada

15 miles (24 km) northwest of Penonomé. This hamlet makes for a scenic excursion. It lies in the foothills of the Cordillera Central and is centered on a pine-fringed plaza hosting

the colonial-era **Iglesia de Candelaria**. Its main call to fame is **Cigarros Joyas de Panamá** (507-6729-4978; joyapan@yahoo.com; open daily 7 AM–8 PM), a tiny cigar factory where 12 types of *puros* are rolled from Cuban-seed tobacco, including oddities such as a cigar shaped like a baseball bat. Reservations are advisable.

PARQUE NACIONAL OMAR TORRIJOS

507-997-9089, or 997-9805 in Penonomé
997-7538
www.anam.gob.pa
30 miles (50 km) NW of Penonomé via
El Copé

Protecting 62,455 acres (25,275 ha) of montane cloud forest in the Cordillera Central, this park was created in 1986 and named in honor of Major General Omar Torrijos, Panamá's populist military leader, who was killed when his plane crashed here on July 31, 1983. Colloquially called Parque El Copé (for the *el copé* tree), it straddles the continental divide. Birders and hikers never had it so good, as the U.S. Peace Corps maintains a latticework of trails.

The rugged, rain-soaked park teems with wildlife. All six cat species stalk tapir and smaller game. The bare-necked umbrellabird, red-fronted parrotlet, and immaculate antbird are among the commonly seen, yet rare, bird species. Poison-dart frogs hop about underfoot. And monkeys are a dime a dozen. Hummingbirds buzz around the **ANAM ranger station**, about 0.8-mile (0.5 km) before the ridgetop **Alto del Calavario Visitor Center**, where you can look out toward the Caribbean Sea. From here you can tackle short self-guided trails and longer, more rugged trails that lead to the summits of Cerro Marta and Cerro Peña Blanca. You can even hike to see remnants of the Torrijos wreck—a five-hour hike from the ranger station—and, for experienced hikers with full provisions, all the way downhill to the Caribbean coast. The Asociación de Guías, in Barrigón, offers guide services ($5–10 per person).

You'll need a 4WD to reach the park beyond the hamlet of Barrigón (a 60-minute hike from the park), where families rent rooms to hikers. The visitor center also rents a simple dorm with kitchen, and you can camp. It gets cold up here at night; pack accordingly.

Parque Nacional Omar Torrijos visitor center, Panamá

Red-eyed tree frog

Serranía del Escaliche

This mountain group, about 12 miles (20 km) east of Penonomé town, is studded with soaring limestone cones. The forests are alive with the calls of three-wattled bellbirds, toucans, oropendolas, and a veritable encyclopedia of other birds. With luck you might spy monkeys, sloths, poison-dart frogs, and perhaps even a wild cat, such as an ocelot.

The best base for exploring is the Posada Cerro La Vieja Eco-Hotel & Spa, named for **Cerro La Vieja**, a huge sugarloaf-like mountain. The hotel offers horseback rides and guided hikes, including to **Cascada Tavida**, a 98-foot-tall (30 m) waterfall. It even has its own trails, including the 0.6-mile-long (1 km) **Sendero Pozo Azul**, which leads to a *pozo azul* (blue well), where you can soak in invigorating mineral waters.

SHOPPING

Penonomé is famous for its *sombreros pintados* (straw hats). Expect to pay up to $200 for a quality hat at the **Mercado de Artesanías Coclé**, beside the Interamerican Highway at the entrance to town. Most, though, are of lesser quality and thereby much cheaper.

La Pintada also has its **Mercado de Artesanías de La Pintada** (507-983-0313; open Tuesday through Sunday 9 AM–5 PM) selling *sombreros pintados* and *muñequitas* (dolls) dressed in *polleras*. To see the hats being made, head to the neighboring hamlet of Pedregosa.

Ildaura Saavedra de Espino sewing a lace pollera, *Guararé, Panamá*

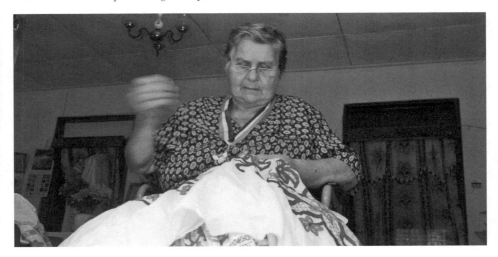

Aguadulce and Vicinity

West of Penonomé, the Interamerican Highway slices through a broadening valley planted with sugarcane and in whose heart the town of Aguadulce ("sweet water") acts as an agricultural center and industrial node. To the east, a huge swamp and mangrove forest lines the Bahía de Parita—migratory waterfowl abound in the coastal wetlands. Last century, Aguadulce had a thriving salt and sugar industry.

LODGING AND DINING

HOTEL CARISABEL

507-997-3800
www.hotelcarisabel.com
Interamerican Highway at Calle Alejandro Escobar, Aguadulce
The nicest hotel in town, this centrally located option wins no prizes for beauty or decor, but at least it has Wi-Fi plus a beat-the-heat swimming pool, and the staff are friendly. Its 19 air-conditioned rooms are modestly, almost functionally, furnished.

EL JARDIN DE SAN JUAN

507-997-2849
Plaza 19 de Octubre, Aguadulce
Choose the refreshing air-conditioned interior or the courtyard terrace at this simple restaurant, run by friendly owner Nelva Real. I enjoyed a delicious sea bass fillet with mushroom sauce and mashed potatoes, washed down with sangría. Open: 7 AM–3 PM and 6–10 PM.

ATTRACTIONS, PARKS, AND RECREATION

The few sites of interest in Aguadulce surround **Plaza de 19 de Octubre**, the main square with the rather austere **Iglesia de San Juan Bautista** on its north side. The square's main draw is the **Museo Regionales Stella Sierra** (507-997-4280; Calle Fábrica Final; Tuesday through Saturday 9–5; admission $1), principally dedicated to telling the history of the local salt and shrimping industries. Housed in a two-story mansion (1925), it also has pre-Columbian artifacts, a small *trapiche* (sugar press), plus military paraphernalia relating to the Colombian civil war (1899–1903).

Birders should head southeast to the wharf on the **Bahía de Parita**. En route, you'll pass abandoned salt pans *(salinas)* and still-active brine pools where shrimp are farmed. The coastal wetlands hereabouts are a habitat for shore and marsh birds, including such waders as heron, roseate spoonbill, and even wood stork.

Ingenio de Azúcar Santa Rosa (Santa Rosa Sugar Refinery; 507-987-8101; El Roble, 9 miles (15 km) west of Aguadulce) operates around the clock during the December through April sugar harvest, when the air for miles around carries the unmistakable smell of molasses. You can tour the facility, including the original mill-owner's home, displaying 19th-century furniture. Monday through Saturday by 24-hour prior appointment.

Natá de Los Caballeros

6 miles (10 km) N of Aguadulce. This small town, on the Interamerican Highway, has one of Panamá's most endearing churches. The **Basilica Menor de Santiago Apostól**, on the tree-shaded main square, dates back to 1522 and claims to be the oldest surviving church in the Americas. It has an impressive baroque façade (suggesting that the church has a

Basilica Menor de Santiago Apostól, Nata, Panamá

later provenance), a statue of the patron saint carrying a Spanish flag, plus a wooden altar carved with fruits, flowers, and feathered serpents. The town itself was founded in 1517 and is named for a local *cacique* (Indian chief).

A local produce company, **Hermann Gnaegi S.A.** (507-993-5546 or 6617-3500; info@agroturismopanama.com), offers tours of its various enterprises, including a fruit processing plant, turf plantation, cashew nut farm, dairy farm, and the Gnaegi family Swiss-style villa.

PARQUE Y MUSEO ARQUEOLÓGICO DEL CAÑO

507-987-9352
http://ciudad.latinol.com/chicasusma
5 miles (9 km) NE of Natá
Open: Tuesday through Saturday 9 AM–4 PM, Sunday 9 AM–1 PM
Admission: $1

The nation's most important pre-Columbian site spans 20 acres (8 ha) and displays relics unearthed since its discovery in 1924. Dating back about 5,000 years, the ancient ceremonial center and burial ground most prominently features stone stelae jutting up from pasture. You can also view petroglyphs plus five skeletons curled in fetal positions and stuffed into jars, in ancient burial fashion. Various artifacts are displayed in a small museum (the most important relics were shipped abroad, while others reside in the Museo Antropológico Reina Torres de Araúz, in Panamá City). It's 2 miles (3 km) north of the Interamerican Highway.

WEEKLY AND ANNUAL EVENTS

Every mid-October Aguadulce bursts to life for the annual festival celebrating the city's founding, with everything from *topes* (displays of horsemanship) and folkloric music to beauty pageants and live music.

Santiago de Veraguas and Vicinity

The largest settlement between Panamá City and David, near the Costa Rican border, Santiago de Veraguas serves as the main administrative and commercial center of the region. It occupies the heart of a rich agricultural lowland vale and is a crossroads granting access northward to the delightful mountain hamlet of Santa Fe, in the Cordillera Central; and southward to the mangroves and surfing-and-sportfishing resorts of the Golfo de Montijo.

LODGING AND DINING

HOTEL GRAN DAVID
507-998-4510
Interamerican Highway
Inexpensive
Comfy yet unremarkable air-conditioned rooms at this hotel just off the Interamerican Highway serve impecunious travelers with minimal expectations and have cable TV and phones. It has a swimming pool, restaurant, and Internet.

HOTEL AND RESTAURANT LA HACIENDA
507-958-8580
Fax: 958-8579
Interamerican Highway, 2 miles (3 km) W of Santiago de Veragua
Inexpensive
As you might expect by its name, Santiago's nicest and most colorful hotel is Mexican-themed. The place is adorned with ceramic sun and moon smiley faces, echoing those of the friendly staff. The 42 bedrooms surround a courtyard and are furnished in traditional hacienda fashion; some rooms have king beds, and the orthopedic mattresses are firm. The restaurant has wisely shifted from Mexican fare (my meal was a real letdown) to Italian. Swimming pool. Wi-Fi.

HOSTAL LA QHIA GUEST HOUSE
507-954-0903
www.panamamountainhouse.com
Santa Fe
Inexpensive
A wealthy Panamanian businessman's former alpine retreat has metamorphosed as a gorgeous Swiss-style lodge set in a riotously colorful garden and now run by a Belgian-Argentine couple. Rooms are a medley, including an eight-person dorm and three upstairs "matrimonial" rooms. However, they have only minimal furnishings and are far too Spartan given the expectations that the exterior instills. You can rent the entire facility May through November.

HOTEL SANTA FE
597-954-0941 or 954-0881
santafeexplorer@hotmail.com
Carretera Santiago-Santa Fe, Santa Fe
Inexpensive
This timeworn, U-shaped hotel has a porch with valley views. Budget hounds will be pleased to find 21 cozy rooms, albeit meagerly furnished and with tepid water in the showers. Some rooms have TV and are air-conditioned, but it seems superfluous at this elevation. It offers guided hikes and horseback tours. The tiny restaurant serves excellent dishes, including seafood.

HOTEL SOL DE SANTA FE

507-954-0941
www.hotelsolsantafe.com
Santa Fe
Inexpensive
New in 2009, and stair-stepping a hillside on the outskirts of Santa Fe, this 20-room hotel is just the ticket for hikers and birders seeking an unpretentious budget base at low prices. It shows movies and has a library, bar, and simple restaurant. Rooms sleep from two to five people. Campers can pitch their tents.

HOTEL VISTA LAGO ECORESORT

507-954-9916
www.hotelvistalago.net
Interamerican Highway, Km 258, Santiago de Veragua
Moderate
Sitting over a lake a 10-minute drive outside town, this hotel is surprisingly stylish for an "eco-resort," at least in the public arenas, where minimalist contemporary furnishings bring this newcomer to life. The 24 air-conditioned rooms aren't quite so en-vogue; furnishings are, in fact, a bit sparse. Nouvelle dishes are served in what the owners claim to be a gourmet restaurant. It has a swimming pool and trails.

ATTRACTIONS, PARKS, AND RECREATION

Although Santiago was founded in 1632, relatively little of its colonial heritage remains. Nonetheless it's worth a detour when traveling the Interamerican Highway, not least to admire **La Escuela Normal Superior Juan Demostenes Arosemena** (507-998-4862; Calle 6ta). Erected in the 1920s, this teacher training college is justifiably a national historic monument. The highlight features are its plateresque façade adorned with nymphs; and, inside, murals by acclaimed Panamanian artist Roberto Lewis depicting major events in ancient history.

Then, head to **Parque Juan Demostenes Arosemena**, the main plaza named for the homeboy politician and man of letters who died in 1936 mere months after being elected president of Panamá. A bas-relief monument of Arosemena pins the plaza, on the south

Ceramic dolls and Iglesia Santiago Apostól, Santiago de Veraguas, Panamá

Worker roasting coffee beans at Café El Tute, Santa Fé, Panamá

side of which stands the austere **Iglesia Santiago Apóstol**. One block away, the **Museo Regional de Veraguas** (507-988-4543; Calle 2da and Avenida Juan Demóstenes Arosemena; Monday through Friday 7:30 AM–3:30 PM; $1) occupies a replica of the town's former jail. The eclectic displays range from prehistoric beasts (!) and pre-Columbian jewelry to musical instruments and a collection of *sombreros montuños,* the locally made straw hats. You can pick up a *sombrero* at the lively **Mercado Artesanal de la Peña** on Avenida Central, which branches from the Interamerican Highway and runs west 1.2 miles (2 km) to the main plaza.

Ecclesiastics on a busman's holiday might head north 10 miles (16 km) to **San Francisco de la Montaña**, a sleepy village that boasts its own national historic monument—the **Iglesia San Francisco de la Montaña**. Completed in 1727, remodeled in 1937, and recently restored, it features a Romanesque bell tower and a baroque cedar altar remarkable for its fusion of Indian folkloric elements with scriptural scenes.

Santa Fe

32 miles (52 km) N of Santiago. To beat the lowland heat, follow the rollercoaster Carretera 91 that leads due north from Santiago via San Francisco de la Montaña into the Cordillera Central, ending at the sleepy mountain village of **Santa Fe**, at 1,500 feet (450 m) elevation. It's a perfect spot to relax in crisp air scented by pines and by the aroma of coffee being roasted at **Café El Tute** (507-954-0801; daily 8–5). This small *beneficio* (roasting plant), run as a local *campesino* (peasant) cooperative, sits amid coffee fields on the north side of the village; you can visit to learn about coffee cultivation and processing. Ngöbe-Buglé Indian women in bright hand-stitched dresses can be seen picking beans alongside their children during harvest season (October through January). The **Mercado Agríola y Artesanal Santa Fe**, on the west side of the plaza, is a venue for Ngöbe-Buglé artisans to sell their *chacaras* (woven bags) and other handicrafts.

Orchid

Orchids: Santa Fe is a paradise for botanists, especially lovers of orchids. Many a local garden is adorned with these epiphytes. More than 300 species grow locally. Many are endemics. The most substantial garden is **Orquideário y Cultivos Las Fragrancias de Santa Fe** (507-954-0910; no set hours; by donation), lovingly tended by Berta Castrellón, Santa Fe's former mayor and erstwhile president of the Asociación de Orquideologia de Panamá. Time your visit for mid-summer, when the orchids are in full bloom and the village hosts an annual three-day orchid show.

Tubing: The village sits above the Río Bulabá, which has calm pools for swimming and is perfect for tube floats. William Abrego (507-6583-5944) rents tubes for $5 and will even accompany you on the hour-long trip.

Hiking and Birding: More than 280 square miles (72,636 ha) of these mountains are enshrined within **Parque Nacional Santa Fe de Veraguas**, established in 2001 to guard the habitat of fabulous wildlife species, including anteaters, monkeys, tapirs, jaguars, and more than 400 bird species. Santa Fe lies beneath the gaze of **Cerro Tute**, a heavily forested mountain that in 1959 was the setting for a short-lived leftist guerrilla insurrection intent on overthrowing the Omar Torrijos regime. Clouds drift around the mountain summit. The trail begins about 1 mile (1.6 km) south of the village. Another trail (follow the sign in town) leads 3 miles (5 km) to the triple waterfalls of **Alto de Piedra**, passing *cafetales*—coffee farms—en route. Above, you enter pristine forest that echoes with a calliope of birdcalls: Rufous-winged woodpecker. Pygmy owl. Great potoo. Crimson-collared tanager. Toucans. Local guides, dedicated birder Berta Castrellón (507-954-0910), and Cesar Miranda (507-954-0807 or 6792-0571; aventurascesamo@hotmail.com;. http://aventurascesamo.blogspot.com) can be hired; he also has his own orchid farm. And the **Panamá Audubon Society** (507-232-5977; www.panamaaudubon.org) runs birding trips.

Getting There: Buses depart Santiago every 30 minutes, 5 AM–6 PM ($2.50).

RESERVA FORESTAL LA LAGUNA DE LA YEGUADA

40 miles (65 km) NE of Santiago, via Pedrogoso
www.ecoviajerospanama.com/yeguada.htm
Pine trees abound in this 17,000-acre (70 sq km) upland forest reserve centered on a man-made lake, created within an extinct volcanic crater to feed a hydroelectric plant. Some 4,900 acres (2,000 ha) of pines have been planted in a reforestation project. Trails lead to a cascade that tumbles 100 feet (30 m), perfect for waterfall rappels during dry season (in wet season the water volume is dangerous).

Golfo de Montijo

This huge gulf indents the coast of Veraguas province. The San Pedro and San Pablo rivers drain from the Cordillera Central and snake to a slow crawl at the head of the gulf, which is accessed at Puerto Mutis, a small port 20 miles (35 km) southwest of Santiago. Communities of Ngöbe-Buglé are interspersed with ramshackle fishing villages. Isles stud the gulf, whose west-facing shores receive crashing waves—nirvana to surfers, whose capital of cool is the small fishing village of **Santa Catalina**, at the end of the road on the west shore of the gulf. Santa Catalina is booming as a newfound frontier for developers who spy the next big resort, and realtors' signs have sprouted like mushrooms on a damp log. The first planned luxury oceanfront development—**Big World Villas**—has already broken ground.

> **Good to Know About**
> Santiago has an IPAT **tourist information bureau** (507-994-7313; facing Hotel Gran David, on the Interamerican Highway in Santiago; open Monday through Friday 8–4).
> A local tourism cooperative (507-954-0737) arranges tours.

Much of the shore is lined with wetland and mangroves that form a habitat for countless waterfowl and wading birds—many of them migratory shorebirds (black-bellied whistling ducks and Muscovy ducks; whimbrels and willets)—plus caimans and crocodiles and other reptiles, and no shortage of mammals. The **Humedal Golfo de Montijo** (Gulf of Montijo Wetlands) protects 541 square miles (140,000 ha) of coastal ecosystems, including mudflats and gulf waters. Frigatebirds, pelicans, and boobies inhabit some of the gulf islands.

An all-weather road runs the length of the east shore (the western shore of the Azuero Peninsula), rising and dipping and ending at the small fishing hamlet of **El Varadero**.

Getting There: Buses from Santiago to Santa Catalina travel to Soná four times daily (90 minutes; $4).

Pacific Ocean view from Playa Santa Catalina, Panamá

LODGING

Santa Catalina has more than one dozen surf camps. One of the best is **Blue Zone Surf and Dive Camp** (in the U.S., 760-723-4787; www.bluezonepanama.com). The five rooms at this well-run oceanfront surf camp share two bathrooms. It has a shared kitchen plus laundry, and has board rental and surfing lessons. For the truly impecunious, **Campin'** (507-6579-1504), on the road to Playa Estero, is run by a local family that welcome surfers and backpackers. You'll share a rustic outhouse.

ART LODGE LAND ART
507-6517-1618
www.artlodgepanama.com
Isla Gobernadora, 6 miles (10 km) SE of Santa Catalina
Moderate
Established and run by two French artists, Valerie and Yves, this exquisite back-to-nature option looks like a yesteryear hippy commune that has metamorphosed into the kind of rustic yet trendy digs that Hollywood stars might gravitate to. Its entire essence is focused on ecological sensitivity. Accommodations are in open-air thatched A-frames with "rain forest showers" featuring exquisite and artsy mosaics. You'll sleep beneath mosquito nets on platform beds and dine on wholesome organic meals. The lodge has its own boat. Yoga and surf packages can be arranged.

LA BUENA VIDA
507-6635-1895
www.labuenavida.biz
Santa Catalina
Moderate
The three colorful, air-conditioned villas at this lovingly cared for (by U.S. escapees Michelle and Mike) hotel are each distinct. Butterfly Villa sleeps five people in one bedroom and has a bunk. The bi-level, two-bedroom Bird Villa has two bedrooms

American crocodiles

and a shaded porch with hammock. Gecko Villa has one bedroom and a patio. Health-conscious breakfasts and lunches, such as pancakes and huevos rancheros, are served alfresco daily, 7 AM–2 PM.

CASA DOS PALMAS
507-6614-3868
www.dospalmascatalina.com
Santa Catalina
Moderate
The closest thing to a true hotel in these parts, this whitewashed two-story, hilltop structure sits amid tree-shaded lawns with ocean views. The rooms are meagerly appointed but have TVs, Wi-Fi, and telephones. It specializes in surf packages.

HIBISCUS GARDEN
507-6615-6097
www.hibiscusgarden.com
Playa Lagartero, Santa Catalina
Inexpensive
This former German-run hotel now in the hands of Mike and Ollie, from California, is perhaps the classiest in Santa Catalina, with its stylishly minimalist rooms adorned with seashells. All guest rooms are spacious and air-conditioned and have fans and patios or balconies. This is a budget option with class, more so for its excellent food and the ability to spy caimans, herons, and other wildlife in the river to one side. The hotel

sits above a gray-sand beach in a tranquil bay. Shared kitchen.

OASIS SURF CAMP
507-6588-7077
www.oasissurfcamp.com
surfoasis@hotmail.com
Playa Estero, 1 mile (1.6 km) E of Playa Santa Catalina
Bring your tent to pitch on the cliff top, or opt for one of eight colorful, simply appointed, tree-shaded *cabañas* with batik spreads, and hammocks slung on the porches. Owners David and Sylvia prepare filling breakfasts and Italian meals served in an open-air thatched *rancho* with hammocks and a TV. It also has a volleyball court, and surf lessons ($25 hourly). You need to ford a small river that can be tricky at high tide.

DINING

Most of the hotels and surf camps serve meals. Most other restaurants open mid- or late afternoon. For a break try **Pizzería Jammin'** (no telephone; open daily 4–10 PM only), between Playa Santa Catalina and Punta Brava, and which opens in the evening to serve thin-crust pizzas fired in a brick oven. No frills here: you eat alfresco at bench tables. It has hammocks.

For local fare, you can't beat **Donde Viancka's** (daily 2–10 PM low season, 10 AM–10 PM high season), on the dirt road to Playa Estero and named for the charming owner. Viancka—once a local surfing champion—dishes up tasty fresh seafood and vegetarian dishes ($5–8).

ATTRACTIONS, PARKS, AND RECREATION

Santa Catalina is all about water sports, but it does have a series of lovely dark sand beaches. The two principal beaches are **Playa Santa Catalina**, at the end of the paved road in town; and more secluded and peaceful **Playa El Estero**, to the east and reached by dirt road. The beaches vary in length and accessibility according to tide levels, which here can vary as much as 20 feet (6.5 m).

Water Sports

Santa Catalina is abuzz with water-bound activities above and below the waves and every year sees one or more new operators open shop. **Santa Catalina Boat tours** (507-6481-3401; www.santacatalinaboattours.com) specializes in trips to Isla Coiba and other islands; it runs surfers to remote spots. It also has surfing and snorkeling tours.

Sea-Kayaking: Michael and Javier, the Canadian-California owners of **Fluid Adventures Panama** (Calle Principal; 507-6560-6558; www.fluidadventurespanama.com), offer sea kayaking trips (from $45 half-day at Isla Coiba to $239 for an overnight trip at Coiba). You can also rent kayaks by the hour, day, or week.

Scuba Diving and Snorkeling: Santa Catalina is considered one of Panamá's premium scuba diving bases. Two local outfitters run dive trips as far out as Isla Coiba, where the coral reefs and pelagics astound. It's not unusual to see marine turtles, huge schools of rays (especially prolific October through December) or sharks (including whale sharks February through July). Humpbacks calve in these waters June through October, but pilot

Parque Nacional Isla Coiba

Comprising the huge (194-square-mile/50,315 ha) ox-jaw-shaped island of Isla Coiba, 39 satellite islands, and the marine waters that surround them, this the largest marine park in Central America. The park extends about 55 miles (88 km) east and west and an equal distance north and south. Isla Coiba is clad in dense tropical rain forest and rises to 1,365 feet (416 m) atop Cerro La Torre. Of the isle's 147 bird species, more than 20 are endemics, such as the brown-and-white Coiba spinetail. The stars of the show are the scarlet macaws: Isla Coiba has Panamá's largest population. It's also the last refuge in Panamá for the endangered crested eagle. Monkeys abound, including an endemic sub-species of spider monkey.

Offshore, the warm nutrient-rich waters are a breeding and calving area for humpback, minke, and pilot whales, while large pelagics—tuna, sharks, etc.—abound, and the healthy coral reefs and underwater lava rock formations act as condominiums for a zebra-striped, piebald-dappled, polka-dotted, multi-hued array of fish.

Parque Nacional Isla Coiba, Panamá

Between 1918 and 1991, Isla Coiba—the largest island in Panamá—served as a convenient colony for the nation's worst criminals. Although the free-range prison (it had 14 separate penal camps) was closed in 1991, rumor has it that a few dozen prisoners still live wild.

Access is by permit only. Visitors must first check in at the **ANAM ranger station** (507-998-4271 or 998-3829; park entrance costs $20) in a cove on the northeast of Isla Coiba, a 90-minute boat ride from Santa Catalina. The station has a small yet excellent natural history exhibit (including the skeleton of a humpback whale) and doubles as a biological research station. You can laze in hammocks and swim in the warm waters. You can rent duplex cabins ($20 per person). There's a communal kitchen for self-catering.

Nature-oriented cruises offered by **Cruise West** (1-888-851-8133; www.cruisewest.com) and **National Geographic Expeditions** (1-888-966-8687; www.nationalgeographicexpeditions.com) include Isla Coiba and Granito de Oro on their itineraries.

TRAILS: Hiking is restricted to short trails that begin at the ranger station. The short (20 minutes) **Sendero del Observatorio** trail leads uphill to a mirador, with views north toward Isla Coabita. The **Sendero de los Monos** (Monkey Trail) requires a short boat ride from the ranger station; the 2-mile (3 km) loop trail is named for the howler, spider, and white-faced monkeys commonly seen while hiking.

DIVING AND SNORKELING: The volcanic outcrop that forms **Isla Granito de Oro**, to the northeast of the main island, features a gorgeous white-sand beach shelving into turquoise waters where the snorkeling is superb. Moray eels poke up between submerged rocks. And harmless nurse sharks and large green and hawksbill turtles are almost always around in the warm waters, while needlefish, parrotfish, and angelfish are among the dozens of smaller fry species.

Divers like to head to the **Bahía Damas** reef, spread over 334 acres (135 ha) and thereby the largest in Pacific Central America. Underwater pinnacles pierce the coral formations, providing a dramatic backdrop for sighting sharks (hammerheads, nurse, tiger, white-tip, and massive whale sharks), manta rays, and even whales.

Coiba Dive Center (507-6565-7200; www.coibadivecenter.com) and **Scuba Coiba** (507-6575-0122; www.scubacoiba.com) offer snorkeling and scuba trips out of Santa Catalina.

Woman donning snorkel gear at Isla Granito de Oro, Panamá

and minke whales are commonly seen. Many of the Isla Coiba dives are best suited to experienced divers, while beginners should opt for inshore dives.

Canadian Glenn Massingham's **Coiba Dive Center** (507-6565-7200; www.coibadive center.com) offers snorkeling at Isla Coiba ($55) plus two-tank dives from $65, and PADI certification ($365). **Scuba Coiba** (507-6575-0122; www.scubacoiba.com; open 8 AM–6 PM), run by Austrian Herbie Sunk, charges from $100 for a full-day trip to Coiba, with a two-person minimum. Non-divers can join the trip for $60. And weeklong dive trips are offered aboard the **M/V** *Coral Star* (985-845-0113 or 866-924-2837; www.coralstar.com). **Sportfishing:** Sportfishers are gleeful about the bonito and billfish to be hooked in these waters. **Santa Catalina Boat tours** (507-6481-3401; www.santacatalinaboattours.com), **Pesca Panamá** (507-6614-5850, in the U.S. 1-800-946-3474; www.pescapanama.com), and **Coiba Adventure Sportfishing** (507-999-8108 or 1-800-800-0907, www.coibadven tures.com) arrange trips deep-sea fishing, plus inshore trips for snapper, roosterfish, etc., off the east coast of Isla Coiba (a $50 per boat fishing permit is required, valid for one week; fishing is catch and release). The island is just a few miles from the edge of the continental shelf, where the waters plummet to the inky black depths. No restrictions apply for fishing these offshore waters of the Hannibal Bank, west of Isla Coiba. You can book multi-day fishing trips aboard the **M/V** *Coral Star* (985-845-0113 or 866-924-2837; www.coralstar.com).

The **Cebaco Bay Sport Fishing Club** (507-317-6670; www.cebacobay.com) is a 110-foot-long floating hotel operated by Captain Jim Wiese. Moored at Isla Cebaco, the club has a 47-foot Buddy Davis boat, plus *pangas* rigged for cast fishing.

Surfing: Surfing is the big enchilada around Santa Catalina, which is renowned for its consistent and powerful, easy to line up, hollows that break both left and right on a lava-rock reef. Most of the surf camps offer lessons. Mike and Javier of **Fluid Adventures Panama** (see above) run a three-day surf camp (from $369 per person), offer hourly lessons, rent boards, and run surf trips. Why not sign up for a three-in-one, six-day "Surf, Sea Kayak & Snorkel Extravaganza" ($989)? Awesome!

8

AZUERO PENINSULA

"Panamá is a little country that has regional cultures, cuisines and dialects. The Azuero Peninsula, which is more arid than the rest of the country, is the heartland of the cultura típica."

—ALLAN HAWKINS

My favorite region of Panamá, oblong-shaped Azuero is one of the nation's unsung treasures and is unique in several ways. First, the nation's folkloric traditions—its music, dance, and dress—hail from here, and the region is ground-zero for artisanal crafts and folkloric festivals. Plus, the peninsula is studded with well-preserved colonial cities, pickled in aspic at their cores. The peninsula's eastern shore, facing onto the Bahía de Parita, is lined with wetlands comprising a series of nature reserves offering spectacular birding; and with gorgeous beaches—as yet undeveloped for tourism—where marine turtles come ashore to lay eggs. The wave-washed south-facing shore of Azuero is nirvana to surfers. And the Tuna Coast along the south-facing shore gives sport-fishers thrills, with prize-winning catches from amberjack to yellowfin tuna.

Hermit crabs at Isla Granito de Oro, Panamá

Remarkably, for all this, the peninsula remains virtually unknown to tourists, although Panamanians flock there each Lent for the country's most vibrant carnivals.

Despite being surrounded by water, this is Panamá's dry quarter. None of the stifling humidity of Panamá City here! In pre-colonial times, the region was covered with tropical dry deciduous forest. The Spanish cut most of it down to farm cattle (Parque Nacional Sarigua, in the

OPPOSITE: *Iglesia de San Altanacio in Villa de los Santos, Azuero, Panamá*

235

Sombrero montuños *(straw hats)*, *Panamá*

extreme northeast, is a barren desert testifying to the ravaging long-term effects). Cowboys dominate the landscape atop their *Paso Fino* horses. Most of the land is a kind of savanna shaded by stands of deciduous trees that burst into riotous bloom each spring and summer. On Azuero's west side, a mountain backbone forms a north-south spine along the length of the peninsula, protecting rare swaths of forest (the western slopes and coastal littoral belong to Veraguas province and are as divorced from Azuero as Mars is from the Moon).

The Spanish heritage is much stronger here than elsewhere in Panamá (the populace is almost exclusively white or mestizo). Many males still wear locally made *sombrero montuño* (the traditional straw hat of the region, and a component of Panamá's national costume), which principally hail from Ocú. Guararé and San José keep alive the traditions of *pollera* lace-making. La Arena is a center for pottery, made the old-fashioned way.

Hotels, restaurants, and other tourist services are few in number.

GETTING THERE AND AROUND

By Air
You can charter a plane to Aeropuerto Valderrama at Chitré (CTD). **Aeroperlas** (507-315-7500; www.aeroperlas.com) flies between Panamá City and Pedasí on Monday and Friday ($55 each way).

By Bus or Público

Tuasa (507-996-2661) and **Transportes Inazun** (507-996-1794) compete with hourly service between Panamá City and Chitré (6 AM–6 PM; four hours; $7), where the Terminal de Transportes de Herrera (506-996-6426) is 0.75 mile (1 km) south of downtown, near the ring-road (*circunvalación*). Local buses and *públicos* link Chitré with Divisa (at the junction of the Interamericana) and other towns in Azuero.

By Car

You can loop around the peninsula along the two main roads that link Azuero to the Interamerican Highway The main highway—Carretera 3 (aka Vía Nacional)—begins at Divisa and runs inland of Azuero's eastern shore, linking all the towns of importance.

Chitré and Vicinity

Chitré, about 25 miles (40 km) southeast of Divisa and the Interamericana, is the largest town in Azuero. Its core struggles to retain its 19th-century colonial charm amid the whirligig of commercialism that surrounds it. Nonetheless, twirled-wood window grills and iron-studded doors still grace the heart-of-the-city streets. Chitré lies a mere 3 miles (5 km) inland of the shore, lined with beaches of modest appeal and the setting for a fistful of wildlife reserves.

Catedral de San Juan Bautista, Chitre, Panamá

LODGING AND DINING

HOTEL BALI PANAMA

507-996-4620
www.balipanama.com
Avenida Herrera, Chitré
Inexpensive

Formerly the Hotel Prado, this budget hotel literally a stone's throw north of the cathedral is now run by a Panamanian-Indonesian couple. It offers a solid bargain. All rooms are air-conditioned, clean, and have cable TV, although the decor is soulless. Wi-Fi.

HOTEL LOS GUAYACANES

507-996-9758
Fax: 507-996-9759
www.losguayacanes.com
Vía Circunvalación, Chitré
Moderate

On the outskirts of town, this Germanic-styled hotel in beautifully landscaped grounds is by far the nicest around. It overlooks a pond with cascade. The 64 rooms include 8 suites, all decked out in heavy timber furniture. You'll dine alfresco in the Restaurante Las Brisas.

HOTEL VERSALLES

507-996-4422
Fax: 996-2090
www.hotelversalles.com
Paseo Enrique Geenzier, Chitré

Catering principally to business folk, this visually unexciting modern option on the outskirts of town is clean and has the basic comforts travelers require. The 60 bedrooms are spacious and pleasantly furnished. You can exercise in a lap pool, and the hotel has Internet.

RESTAURANTE EL PRADO

507-996-4620
Avenida Herrera, Chitré

In the Hotel Bali Panamá, so no surprise that it serves an eclectic mix of Panamanian and Indonesian dishes, including a classic *sate ayam* (chicken kebabs with peanut sauce; US$4). The restaurant is squeaky clean. Open: daily 7 AM–8 PM. No credit cards.

ATTRACTIONS, PARKS, AND RECREATION

Chitre

Chitré's main sights are centered on **Parque Unión** (Avenida Herrera and Avenida Central). Walk the square to peruse the various busts of local heroes before popping inside the **Catedral de San Juan Bautista**—completed in 1910—to admire its gilt altar and stained-glass windows. Chitré's former post office today houses the **Museo de Herrera** (507-996-0077; Calle Manuel María Correa and Avenida Julio Arjona; open Tuesday through Saturday 8–4; $1), on Plaza de las Banderas, two blocks west of Parque Unión. Its miscellany spans the eons, from a mammoth fossil to the region's famous *polleras* and devil costumes.

Villa de Los Santos

2.5 miles (3.5 km) SE of Chitré. Virtually a suburb of its larger sibling city to the north, Los Santos was founded in 1577 and retains much of its yesteryear ambience.

Los Santos was the setting for the *grita de la villa* ("Scream of Los Santos"), on November 10, 1821, which launched the movement for independence from Spain. Panamá's president flies in each year to celebrate the anniversary. **Iglesia de San**

Museo de Herrera, Azuero, Azuero, Panamá

Altanacio, completed in 1782, stands over **Plaza Simón Bolívar**, proudly displaying a bust of the namesake "South American liberator." The church boasts impressive rococo *reredos* (altar screens).

The town's highlight—the **Museo de la Nacionalidad** (507-966-8419; Calle José Vallarino)—is one of Panamá's most endearing museums. The venue, a gabled 18th-century townhome, features original terra-cotta floors, walls of adobe and reed, and a courtyard displaying a replica of a typical yesteryear country kitchen. Its main theme is Panamá's quest for independence and early republican history, with a suitably impressive collection of colonial-era weaponry.

Colonial street scene in La Parita, Azuero, Azuero, Panamá

La Parita

6 miles (10 km) NW of Chitré. The most intact of Azuero's colonial towns, La Parita exudes a charm rapidly being subsumed by modernity in neighboring towns. While it lacks a grand central plaza, the 18th-century **Iglesia de Santo Domingo de**

Man in sombrero montuño *at Museo de la Nacionalidad, Los Santos, Panamá*

Guzmán literally shines thanks to its steeple overlain with twinkling mother-of-pearl. Its baroque altar crawls with carved serpents. The chapel doubles as the **Museo de Arte Religioso Colonial**, displaying religious icons.

Parque Nacional Sarigua
(507-996-8216) 6 miles (10 km) N of Chitré; it is signed off Carretera 3. You'll be forgiven for doing a double-take upon first site of this desert-dry park, which encompasses 19,768 acres (8,000 ha), of which about half is marine environment extending about 6 miles (9.5 km) to sea. The barren landscape is locally called *albina,* signifying bleached to the bone by slash-and-burn agriculture for cattle farming. Over decades, the thin tropical soil was stripped of vegetation. Then the winds and rains went to work, washing away the topsoil and leaving a Sahara-like wasteland of gullies, bare rock, and dunes. Rare stands of dry forest provide pockets of shade.

More than 160 species of bird can be seen, principally in the shoreline marshes, mangroves, and inshore lagoons. A lookout *(mirador)* beside the **ANAM ranger station** gives a great vantage.

Wildlife Sites
Birders will have a field day exploring the shoreline of the Bahía de Parita, northeast of Chitré. Start at **Playa El Agallito**, 4 miles (7 km) north of Chitré; a bus serves the beach from town. Here, low tide reveals vast mudflats picked upon by spoonbills, stilts, and a dizzying array of other shorebird species. Inland pond-pocked salt marshes deliver tasty tidbits for the birds at high tide. You can hire a guide at Estación Biológica Alejandro von Humboldt (507-996-1725).

The **Ciénaga Las Macanas** wetlands, about 15 miles (25 km) north of Chitré, are the only known breeding site in Panamá for fulvous whistling duck; the **Ciénaga del Rey**, immediately west of Las Macanas—is the only known breeding site in Panamá for the glossy ibis. And **Refugio de Vida Silvestre Cenegón del Mangle**, between Las Macanas and Parque Nacional Sarigua (turn east off Carretera 3 at Paris), has boardwalks for more easily spotting crocodile and scores of bird species; the refuge also has a pre-Columbian shell midden, **Cerro Mangote**, some 7,000 years old.

> **Good to Know About**
> **IPAT** has tourist offices in Chitré (507974-4532; Carretera 3, Barrio La Arena; open Monday through Friday 8 AM–4 PM) and Los Santos (507-966-8013; Calle 19 de Octubre, Chitré; Calle José Vallarino.
>
> **Hospital Cecilio Castillero** (507-996 4444; 24 hours) is on Carretera 3, 1 mile (1.6 km) east of town.

And the 58-square-mile (15,000 ha) **Refugio de Vida Silvestre Peñon de la Honda**, 5 miles (8 km) southeast of Chitré, is a great place to spot magnificent frigatebird and blue-footed boobies, as well as marine turtles, which nest here.

SHOPPING

If you're seeking to buy a devil mask, as used during carnival celebrations, you *must* visit the studio of **Dario López** (507-974-2015 or 6534-1958; Carretera 3), opposite the Shell gas station in Parita, 5 miles (8 km) north of Chitré. Sr. López is Panamá's most famous maker of papier-mâché masks.

The colonial village of **La Arena**, between Parita and Chitré, is lined with artisan stores selling ceramics, from tiny pre-Columbian whistles to huge vases, all cast in traditional fashion and fired in earthen kilns to the rear of the studios.

Blue-footed boobies at Isla Bona, Panamá

Dario López with one of his devil masks, in La Parita, Azuero, Panamá

WEEKLY AND ANNUAL EVENTS

Villa de Los Santos kicks off the festive season with its two-weeklong Corpus Christi festival in early June, when celebrants don costumes. On June 24, Chitré explodes into revelry during the Fiesta Patronal de San Juan. July brings Panamanians from all over the country for Los Santos' Festival de la Pollera. And each November 10 Los Santos celebrates the "Grito de la Villa"—a national independence holiday with parades.

Las Tablas and Vicinity

Ground zero of Panamanian folklore, Las Tablas, 16 miles (28 km) southeast of Chitré, and neighboring villages such as Guararé, are considered the main center for traditional lace making, notably of *polleras*—the national dress. Not surprisingly, the national Festival de la Pollera is held in Las Tablas, the capital of Los Santos province. So, too, the country's most colorful carnival.

Museo de la Nacionalidad, Los Santos, Panamá

Lodging and Dining

CASA DEL PUERTO

507-994-4982
www.panamacasadelpuerto.com
Puerto Rio Guararé

Gorgeous views of the gulf are a selling point at this simple bed-and-breakfast near the mouth of the Rio Guararé. The furnishings in the four guestrooms are functional, rather than eye pleasing, but at least you get heaps of natural light plus spacious terraces with hammocks. It has a small kitchen, and simple restaurants are a few minutes stroll away. It's run by Bonnie Birker, a former U.S. Peace Corps volunteer who settled after her stint of duty.

HOTEL RESIDENCIAL LA MEJORANA

507-994-5794
Fax: 507-994-5796
Carretera 3, Guararé
Inexpensive

Devil masks adorn the walls at this tiny, functional, no-frills, 22-room hotel that has the best restaurant around—the main reason to stay here. It serves burgers ($3 with fries and salad), plus seafood (including lobster for $12), chicken and pork dishes, and even filet mignon ($11), with filling portions.

POSADA DE MAR

507-394-2049 or 6675-6882
www.posadadelmar.com
Playa Uverito, 6 miles (10 km) E of
Las Tablas
Moderate

Run as a beachfront guesthouse, this nonsmoking hotel is by far the nicest for miles. The owners display good taste with their classy furnishings. One room has a king bed (four others have queens); all have air-conditioning and Wi-Fi. Hop into a two-seater kayak, or into a hammock on the shaded sundeck kissed by ocean breezes.

Polleras

Panamá's beautiful national dress is a source of great pride to women and an instantly recognizable symbol of Panamá. What is a *pollera*, you ask? It's a white, two-piece, frilly skirt made of cambric or linen used for festive occasions. It comprises a short-sleeved blouse worn off the shoulders, with ruffled sleeves and neckline edged with colored lace; and a two-tiered full-length skirt with petticoat, often embroidered with floral designs. The ruffles feature hand-sewn appliqué motifs, such as flowers or birds. A waist band, also ruffled to the sides, is hung with *cabestrillos* (chains of gold coins) and of ribbons at front and back, while matching pom-poms hang from the blouse, front and back (sometimes waist-length *cabestrillos* also hang from the neck). A choker and a silk purse hung from the waist complete the ensemble, while heel-less satin slippers are de rigueur.

The dress derives from simple Spanish Gypsy dress introduced to South America with the *conquistadores* by maids and servants. Being lightweight and perfect for Panamá's tropical climate, it was soon adopted by society ladies, who embroidered and elaborated. Special occasions called for use of large, lavish hairpins in age-old Spanish tradition. In Panamá, they evolved as *templeques* (tremblers) made of pendulous pearls, tortoiseshell, and gold.

There are several regional variations.

Polleras, *Panamá*

ATTRACTIONS, PARKS, AND RECREATION

In Las Tablas, the most interesting site is **Iglesia de Santa Librada**, on **Parque Porras**, the main square. The church is barely half-a-century old and is a replica of the original, dating from 1789, destroyed by fire in 1950. If interested in local history, visit **Museo Belisario Porras** (507-994-6326; Avenida Belisario Porras, Parque Central, Las Tablas; Tuesday through Sunday; $1), tracing the life of the three-time president of Panamá between 1912 and 1924; and **Casa Museo El Pausilipo** (507-994-6290 or 994-6326; Las Tablas Abajo; Tuesday through Sunday; $1), Porras' former country estate.

Casa-Museo Manuel Zarate, Guararé, Panamá

To see *polleras* being hand-made, head north 4 miles (7 km) to the sleepy village of **Guararé**, the country's main center for production of these exquisite dresses and of Panamá's five-string guitar—the *mejorana*. The tiny **Casa-Museo Manuel F. Zárate** (507-994-5644; Calle 21 Enero, Guararé; Tuesday through Saturday; $1) displays *polleras, mejoranas,* and devil masks.

WEEKLY AND ANNUAL EVENTS

The hottest *carnaval* in Panamá is considered to be that of Los Tablas during the four days preceding Ash Wednesday. Uniquely, the town divides into two sections, each of which selects a beauty queen and tries to outdo the other with music and dance. Brazilian-style parades with floats *(carrozas)* and sexy, scantily clad women contrast with lasses and ladies more conservatively *empollerada* (dressed in *polleras*), while fireworks burst over town.

The **Festival de la Mejorana**, held in Guararé each September 24, is the most important of Panamá's festivals for traditional folkloric music. It includes a parade of traditional oxcarts bearing females dressed in *polleras.*

Pedasi To Tonosí

Carretera 3 runs as far as the fishing village of Pedasi, from where a series of dirt roads fan out to the southeast tip of the peninsula at Punta Mala. The cape—Bad Point—is well-named, as the seas offshore can be rough, and waves crash ashore along the south-facing shore of Azuero to the west of Pedasi. The majority of locals live from the sea: the shore is called "The Tuna Coast" for a reason. But things they are a'changing. This is the new frontier for tourism in Panamá. Surfers have discovered the allure and several surf camps have sprouted, while upscale hotels and residential resort complexes are rising behind the sands. Marine turtles also come ashore here, notably Ridley turtles, which nest en masse at the Isla Cañas Wildlife Refuge.

Lodging and Dining

CASA DE CAMPO
507-6780-5280
http://casacampopedasi.com
400 yards (366 m) S of the gas station, Pedasi
Moderate to Expensive
A newcomer for 2009, this hacienda-style property in Pedasi town is set in 2 acres (0.8 ha) of leafy grounds. The four guestrooms have a stylish panache, from the poured concrete floors to the wood ceilings and modern fixtures. Highlights include a palm-fringed swimming pool, thatched open-air bar, thatched open-air billiard room, and massage alfresco.

CASITA MARGARITA BOUTIQUE INN
507-995-2898
www.pedasihotel.com
Calle Principal, Pedasi
Moderate
Just five guest rooms at this heart-of-Pedasi hotel, also new in 2009. The elegantly understated furnishings make the most of local hardwoods and come as a pleasant surprise. Hammocks are slung on the balconies. Ceiling fans are a nice touch, and all have Wi-Fi and satellite TV. Charming stone-lined dining room.

POSADA LOS DESTILADEROS
507-995-2771
www.panamabambu.net
7 miles (12 km) SW of Pedasi
Moderate
With 12 timber and thatch Jungle Jane-style beachfront cabins, this rustic option exudes charm. A lap pool is set in a wooden sundeck, and it has a cozy library lounge, plus Adirondack chairs strategically placed for enjoying the views. The French owner doubles as chef. Cash only.

VILLA CAMILA
507-232-0171 or 6670-6721
www.villacamillahotel.com
6 miles (10 km) SW of Pedasi
Very expensive
This is the only truly deluxe option in Azuero. In fact, it's one of the most deluxe boutique hotels in the nation. Commanding a hilltop, this contemporary take on a Spanish hacienda of burnt sienna with red-tile roofs is the creation of French designer Gilles Saint-Gilles and his Parisian wife Camille. The lounge opens to a lap pool framed by columns and palms. The seven guest rooms are a statement in simple elegance. Gourmet meals are served, with an emphasis on fresh seafood; the restaurant is open to non-guests for lunch and dinner ($35).

Attractions, Parks, and Recreation

Beaches
Tuna fishermen set out from **Playa Punta Mala**, the easternmost beach, 4 miles (7 km) south of Pedasi. To the west, surf crashes ashore at gorgeous palm-shaded **Playa Los Destiladores**. The main surfers' beach is **Playa Venado**, about 18 miles (30 km)

Surfers at Playa Venado, Azuero, Panamá

southwest of Pedasi. International surf competitions are often held in this sweeping half-moon bay.

Immediately south of Playa Venado, the headland above flask-shaped **Playa Achotines** is the setting for **Laboratorio Achotines** (507-995-8166; achotine@cwp.net.pa; guided tours by appointment Monday through Friday 8:30–noon and 1–4), a laboratory where scientists study tuna ecology.

Beyond Achotines, the road swings inland around the Refugio de Vida Silvestre Isla de Cañas (Cane Island Wildlife Refuge) and at the village of Tonosí turns south to reconnect with the coast at **Playa Guánico** and (at the end of the road) **Playa Cambutal**, about 55 miles (90 km) west of Pedasi. West of Cambutal, a 30-mile (48 km) stretch of coast is hemmed hard to the shore by rugged mountains; access to remote communities and beaches is by boat or by trails that require river fordings.

Refugio de Vida Silvestre Isla de Cañas

(507-995-2734) c/o ANAM, Calle Marciana Batista corner Calle José Carrasquilla, Pedasí. This 98 square-mile (25,433 ha) refuge, between the mouths of the Cañas and Tonosí rivers, protects Panamá's most important marine turtle nesting site, including ocean waters. Five species (hawksbills, leatherback, loggerhead, olive Ridley, and Pacific green) nest on the isle's 9-mile-long (14 km) sands. The stars of the show are the Ridley turtles, which storm ashore in mass nestings called *arribadas* (arrivals) involving tens of thousands of turtles who come ashore over the course of three or four days. August through November is the peak nesting season.

Ridley turtles

The inshore side of the island is a vast tangle of mangrove forest that also extends inland on the mainland north of the isle. Caimans and crocodiles lurk in the estuarine waters. And ibis, frigatebirds, herons, and dozens of species of waterfowl are guaranteed to thrill birders.

The lagoon that separates the isle from the mainland contains billions of microscopic dinoflagellates that glow with an effulgent bioluminescence when disturbed.

The refuge is accessed via the hamlet of Agua Buena, 15 miles (22 km) west of Playa Venado. A boat will run you to the barrier isle.

Refugio de Vida Silvestre Isla Iguana

3 miles (4.3 km) offshore, 6 miles (10 km) N of Pedasí. You'll need to hire a local boatman (about $55 round-trip) to take you out to this remote island. But the effort is well rewarded. You'll put ashore at a small white-sand beach—**Playa El Cirial**—with a ranger station (c/o 507-995-2734) from where a loop trail leads to a frigatebird colony on the wind-whipped eastern shore. Mid-winter is the best time to visit, when the males inflate their bloodred gular sacs to woo the females, who sail overhead. The loop continues around **Playa El Faro** (at high tide it might not be accessible, as you need to scramble over wave-battered rocks).

The refuge protects 131 acres (53 ha) that includes ocean waters surrounding the isle. Humpback whales are often seen close to shore June through December. And five species of marine turtles nest here (mostly April through September). Bring your snorkel gear to explore the fabulous coral reefs.

You can camp at the ranger station, but you'll need to be entirely self-sufficient.

National Geographic Expeditions passengers coming ashore at Isla Iguana, Panamá

Water Sports

Buzos de Azuero (507-995-2405; www.dive-n-fishpanama.com), in Pedasi, offers fishing and scuba diving tours. **Panama Fishing Experts** (507-314-0829; www.panamafishing experts.com; from $500 half-day) is the big fish in town. **Mario Espino** (507-678-7272; www.islaiguana.com) offers trips to Isla Iguana, including scuba and snorkeling trips.

A sportfishing marina is slated for the **Los Buzos** (www.losbuzos.net) resort development at Cambutal, where horseback riding and sea-kayaking is also offered.

Happy kayakers at Isla Granito de Oro, Panamá

Western Azuero

The entire western half of the Azuero peninsula is dominated by a relatively inaccessible mountain massif with fabulous wildlife to view. The rugged coastline draws surfers in search of the next undiscovered killer wave. A paved highway runs along the eastern foothills, linking Tonosí to the Interamericana via the charming colonial village of Ocú.

LODGING AND DINING

HOTEL PLAYA CAMBUTAL

507-832-0948
http://hotelplayacambutal.com
Expensive

"Boutique lodge" and "affordable luxury" claim the owners. Well, the 10 spacious air-conditioned bedrooms are so thinly furnished as to be almost ascetic, and unduly so given the hotel's price. Still, the bathrooms are lovely, and for this neck of the woods, locals probably do think it's a luxury option. Non-smoking. Lunch and dinner served Monday through Saturday noon–8:30.

PANAMAGIC FARM-TO-FOREST PROJECT

507-6715-7471
www.tanagertourism.com
Palmilla, 38 miles (60 km) S of Santiago.
Inexpensive

Tanager Tourism offers luxury camping safari-style, beneath thatch atop stilt platforms. The spacious tents come with two camp beds with mattresses, and the decks

Devil Dancers

The Corpus Christi festivals of Azuero are famous for their *baile de los diablos* (dance of the devils) in which dancers dressed as *diablos blancos* (white devils) do battle against *diablos sucios* (dirty devils). It's a classic tale of good versus evil. The *diablos sucios* sure look the part in their red-and-black-striped satin jumpsuits, red capes, and grotesque demonic face masks, often adorned with multiple horns and macaw feathers.

have hammocks. You can participate in reforestation projects at this Dutch-run eco-sustainable project; the lovely stone-floored rain forest bathrooms and showers provide compost and gray water for plants. You can pitch your own tent or hammock. A four-room hotel and self-catering cottages were being added, as are solar panels. The owners, biologists Loes Roos and Kees Groenendijk, lead birding, hiking, and kayaking trips.

ATTRACTIONS, PARKS, AND RECREATION

Many residents of **Ocú** make a living weaving *sombreros ocueños* (the village's trademark straw hats), traditional *montuño* shirts of white-and-red cotton, and *espinquita* lace items, including *polleras ocueñas* denoted by a distinct *punta de la cruz* (point of the cross) embroidered stitch.

Pesé, 15 miles (24 km) east of Ocú, stands amid sugarcane fields—a fitting surround for the **Destilería Seco Herrerano** (507-974-9491; www.varelahermanos.com; Monday through Saturday; free), a rum distillery that offers tours January through March with one-week's notice.

Parque Nacional Cerro Hoya

ANAM ranger stations: 507-998-4271 (Restingue), 995-8180 (Tonosí). The rugged, mountainous extreme southwest of Azuero is a densely forested oasis that stands in sharp contrast to the otherwise heavily deforested peninsula. The mountains, of volcanic origin, rise to 5,115 feet (1,559 m) atop **Cerro Hoya**. The park also enshrines coastal mangroves, and coral reefs. Thus, the elevational range is reflected in varying ecosystems, including cloud forest at highest elevations. The almost 100 bird species to be seen include scarlet

Epiphytes growing on a tree

macaws and painted parakeets. Monkeys, sloths, agoutis, and other mammals abound, and marine turtles nest on the beaches.

The ANAM administrative centers are at Tonosí and at Restingue (in Veraguas province, on the Golfo de Montijo; most visitors enter from the west via Santiago and Restingue). From the east, access is via Jobero (16 miles/22 km west of Tonosi) and **Reserva Forestal La Tronosa**, a forest reserve adjoining the park. Buses for Tonosí depart from Panamá City's Albrook terminal at 7:45 AM and PM; and from Las Tablas at 8 AM and hourly until 5:30 PM.

Dutch-run **Tanager Tourism** (507-6715-7471; www.tanagertourism.com), in Palmilla (aka Malena) on the western Azuero coast, specializes in eco-tours, including Cerro Hoya National Park. It also has guided entomological tours, turtle-watching, kayaking, birding, and boat and snorkeling tours.

The **Azuero Earth Project** (631-907-9040; http://azueroearthproject.org; 962 Springs Fireplace Road, East Hampton, NY 11937) works to foster eco-sensitive lifestyle and refor-estation on the peninsula.

Chiriquí

*"In the middle of the day in the highland town of Boquete a misty rain
descends from the skies. It's as slight as a hand held atomiser and it drops gently
from the heavens just as the day threatens to become too warm."*
—Richard Holledge, *The Times*

White-sand beaches. Mangroves and wetlands. Cloud-draped volcanoes. It's all packed
into Panamá's southwesternmost province. In fact, Chiriquí delivers as much tourist punch
as any other region of the country, with a full week barely enough to sample its wares. It's
really a two-part world. Call it parallel worlds: the Pacific coastal plain and, to the north,
the rugged Cordillera Tabasará mountain chain, which rises to 11,400 feet (3,475 m) atop
Volcán Barú. The gateway is David, Panamá's third largest city. Its location dead center in
the province and astride the Interamericana is a boon for travelers, who can fly in for hub-
and-spoke exploration (the town offers little in its own right and can be stifling hot).

The rivers that pour from the mountains feed Central America's largest mangrove and
coastal wetlands—vital habitats for migratory waterfowl and other birds. The beaches here
are ho-hum from a touristic viewpoint, although viewing marine turtles in nesting season
is a draw, and surfers rave about the waves that break onto gray-sand beaches. Sportfishers
are gung-ho about the marlin, tuna, wahoo, and other gamefish that swim offshore. A
cluster of isles in the Golfo de Chiriquí forms the nucleus of wildlife-rich Parque Nacional
Marino Golfo de Chiriquí.

West of David, the land curls around and tapers to Punta Baruco, Panamá's most westerly tip. The flatlands hereabouts are given over to sugarcane and banana plantations,
although the peninsula is a remote refuge for Ngobe-Buglé, the region's indigenous people,
who exist in large numbers in the highlands. Ah, yes . . . the highlands! A 40-minute drive
north from David delivers you at Boquete, the nation's most important tourist center, in
the heart of a valley at the eastern base of Volcán Barú. With its alpine airs (and Swiss-
influenced architecture), it's a delightful base for exploring the cloud forests of nearby
Parque Nacional Volcán Barú and Parque Internacional La Amistad. Birders flock here for
almost-guaranteed sightings of the resplendent quetzal. Boquete is also coffee country,
and many estates can be toured. It's also an activity center, with ziplines and whitewater
rafting, plus some of the most exquisite hotels in the country.

OPPOSITE: *Los Quetzales Ecolodge cabins in Parque Internacional La Amistad, Panamá*

Marker for Comarca Ngöbe-Buglé, Chiriquí province, Panamá

Higher still, on the western flank of Volcán Barú, is Cerro Punta, a less-developed yet enchanting base for hikes and horseback rides and for exploring orchid farms and stud farms.

GETTING THERE AND AROUND

By Air
Aeroperlas (507-315-7500; www.aeroperlas.com) flies to David from Panamá City (three times daily, $80 each way), and Changuinola and Bocas del Toro. **Air Panama** (507-316-9000; www.flyairpanama.com) also flies thrice daily from Panamá City ($80) and daily to/from San José, Costa Rica ($125).

By Bus or Público
Express buses for David (six hours, $15) leave the Albrook Terminal in Panamá City at 10:45 PM and midnight; regular buses (eight hours, $12.50) depart more or less hourly, 5:30 AM–8 PM. Several companies compete using modern air-conditioned buses with reclining seats. Crowded old-fashioned school buses run to Boquete every 30 minutes (6 AM–9:30 PM; $1.45) and elsewhere from the chaotic regional section of the David bus terminal (507-775-2923).

By Car
David is a six-hour drive from Panamá City (290 miles/470 km) on the Interamericana, which continues westward to the Costa Rican border, at Paso Canoas.

Museo de Historia y de Arte, David, Panamá

David and Vicinity

Founded in 1602, David (population 125,000) is today a bustling commercial and agricultural center with limited visual and touristic appeal. However, since you'll most likely be passing through here en route to other places in Chiriquí province, you might want to peruse its fistful of historic sites, concentrated in Barrio Bolívar, immediately south of the main square. The city can be hot as Hades. It lies in a rain shadow and the climate is relatively dry (cattle *fincas* surround the city).

David lies only a few miles inland of the Golfo de Chiriquí, with its surfing beaches, mangrove-lined shores teeming with birdlife, and its islands and coral reefs easily accessed from the sportfishing center of Boca Chica.

LODGING

GONE FISHING PANAMA
507-851-0104, in the U.S. 786-393-5882
www.gonefishingpanama.com
2 miles (3 km) S of Boca Chica
Moderate
The nicest of the Boca Chica lodgings, this U.S.-owned and operated lodge enjoys bay views from its hilltop perch, flush with bougainvillea. The three guest rooms are cozy and homey, with lively murals. The infinity pool has a bar. Sign up for a whale-watching or sportfishing excursion. Open-air bar-restaurant.

GRAN HOTEL NACIONAL
507-775-2222
Fax: 507-775-7729
www.hotelnacionalpanama.com
Calle Central and Avenida 1 Este, David
Moderate

A banking district hotel catering to business folk. Almost gauche in its furnishings and surfeit of shiny marbles, this contemporary-themed hotel has been at least partially refurbished with more tasteful soft goods and hardwood pieces. Small bathrooms. Casino and swimming pool.

ISLAS SECAS RESORT

805-729-2737 in North America
www.islassecas.com
Isla Cavada, Islas Secas group
Expensive
Perched atop a woodsy cliff overlooking white sands and turquoise waters, this deluxe eco-resort defines "true escape." Forget phones, radios, and even TVs. There aren't any. It operates as an all-inclusive. The seven wood-framed yurt-style cabins are tastefully furnished, combining simplicity with modern comforts. Meals are served in a thatched beachside *rancho*.

PANAMA BIG GAME FISHING CLUB

507-6674-4824, in North America 866-281-1225
www.panamabiggamefishingclub.com

Isla Boca Brava, 0.6 Miles (1 km) NE of Boca Chica
Expensive
A U.S.-run sportfishing lodge specializing in fishing the waters of the Hannibal Bank and around Isla Coiba and Isla Montuosa. The four spacious six-person cabins are modestly furnished and overpriced for non-fishers. Tasty seafood meals are cooked up by the owners, who also run restaurants in Florida.

PURPLE HOUSE HOSTEL

507-774-4059
www.purplehousehostel.com
Calle C Sur and Avenida 6 Oeste, David
Inexpensive
Budget-priced digs for backpackers and other penny-pinching travelers. Yes, everything here *is* purple. It has dorms, plus private rooms (some air-conditioned, cable TV, and private bathrooms). Shared bathrooms are kept spic and span. The biggest plug here is the friendly owner, ex-Peace Corps volunteer, Andrea Aster, who fusses over her hostel and guests. Lovely garden setting with hammocks and communal

Island in Parque Nacional Isla Coiba, Panamá

area, plus lockers and a communal kitchen. Free Wi-Fi.

DINING

PANAMA BILL'S AMERICAN BAR & GRILL

507-774-4686
panamavill@cwpanama.net
Avenida Domingo Díaz and Calle C Norte
American
A gringo-run joint for gringos, who gather in very un-Panamanian Hawaiian shirts. Unsurprisingly, the menu serves up down-

home favorites, from Buffalo wings and burgers to prime rib. Paella served on Tuesday nights. Live music. Open: Daily 10 AM–11PM.

RESTAURANTE EL FOGÓN

507-775-7091
Avenida 2da Oeste and Calle D Norte
International
Looking quite Mexican in its design and decor, this large and lively restaurant actually specializes in seafood and international dishes. Open-sided. Open: Monday through Saturday noon–midnight, Sunday 5 PM–midnight.

ATTRACTIONS, PARKS, AND RECREATION

David's central square is the recently remodeled **Parque Cervantes**, with an unpretentious 19th-century **Iglesia de la Sagrada Familia** on its west side. The city's main site, the **Museo de História y de Arte José de Obaldía** (507-775-1217; Avenida 8A Este, between Calle A Norte and Calle Central; open Tuesday through Saturday 9–5; $1), in Barrio Bolívar, occupies a creaky 19th-century mansion stuffed with period furniture. The miscellany here recalls the colonial epoch, with everything from pre-Columbian culture to swords and pistols and even *ropaje litúrgico* (religious clothing). The museum stands next door to the equally intriguing **Fundación C. Gallegos Culturama**, a research library, also with eclectic exhibits.

Pre-Columbian ceramic at Fundacion C. Gallegos Culturama, David, Panamá

If you're fascinated by rum and intrigued to learn about its production, head to the **Central Industrial Chiricana** rum factory (507-772-7073; www.cartaviejapanama.com; Monday through Friday 9–5 by appointment), in the village of El Tejar, about 12 miles (20 km) west of David. It manufactures the *Carta Vieja* labels.

Golfo de Chiriquí

The 120-mile-wide (200 km) Gulf of Chiriquí is fringed by long gray sand beaches and by mangrove and wetland ecosystems at the mouths of the main rivers that wash down from the *cordillera*. Beginning immediately south of the city, the nation's largest mangrove system—the **Manglares de David**—covers 100 square

> **Good to Know About**
> **IPAT** has a tourism office in David (507-775-2839; Edificio Galherma, Avenida Domingo Díaz between Calle 5ta. and 6ta.).

miles (26,600 ha), in a huge delta system fed by the Chiriquí, Chico, and David rivers. The Minotaur's maze of creeks and lagoons shelter a wealth of wildlife. For a foretaste, head to **Playa Barqueta**, 13 miles (20 km) southwest of David. This wave-washed beach is gateway to **Refugio de Vida Silvestre Playa de la Barqueta Agrícola**, a wildlife refuge good for spotting ibis, herons, frigatebirds, etc., as well as the nesting sites of marine turtles.

You can rent boats and water taxis for excursions at the wharf at **Pedregal**, 3 miles (5 km) south of David; and at the fishing village and burgeoning resort center of **Boca Chica**,

Playa Barqueta, Chiriquí province, Panamá

about 30 miles (50 km) southeast of David. Boca Chica is a few minutes' water-taxi ride from **Isla Boca Brava**, where monkeys are easily seen while you hike rain forest trails.

Parque Nacional Marino Golfo de Chiriquí

(507-774-3163) c/o ANAM, Avenida 4 Este, David. Extending seaward south of Boca Chica, this marine park protects 57 square miles (14,740 ha) of marine ecosystem that includes the **Archipiélago de las Islas Parides**, comprising about two dozen isles. White sand beaches shelve into turquoise waters with some of Panamá's most pristine coral reefs; the waters surrounding **Isla San José** are considered prime for snorkeling.

The main isle, **Isla Parida** is shrouded in rain forest (home to parrots) and fringed by mangroves, where frigatebirds number in the thousands. Howler monkeys frequent the forests; if you don't see them, you'll surely hear them. And marine turtles, including endangered leatherbacks, crawl ashore to lay eggs.

The marina-hotels in Boca Chica offer tours.

About 25 miles (40 km) southeast of the park boundary, floating on their lonesome in the gulf, are the **Islas Secas** group of half-a-dozen small islands fringed with white sands and coral reefs.

Water Sports and Whale-Watching

Boca Chica is one of Panamá's premier gateways for sportfishing and whale-watching. Billfish, tuna, and other game fish stream through the Golfo de Chiriquí and the nutrient-rich waters of the Hannibal Bank, while the warm waters also lure humpbacks and other whale species to breed and calve. Book excursions through **Gone Fishing Panamá** (507-851-0104; www.gonefishingpanama.com) and **Panamá Big Game Fishing Club** (507-6674-4824; www.panamabiggamefishingclub.com) or **Marina Boca Chica** (507-757-9242; www.marinabocachica.com).

Rey Sánchez of **Golden Frog Scuba** (507-6414-5322; www.goldenfrogscuba.com) can take you diving. And **Panamá Surf Tours** (507-6671-7777; www.panamasurftours.com) knows all the best surf breaks.

Boquete and Vicinity

At 4,200 feet (1,280 m) elevation, this mountain resort town, 25-mile (40 km) north of David, boasts an agreeably temperate alpine climate. For this reason, a century ago it attracted immigrants from Switzerland, Germany, and other Central European regions, all of whom stitched their cultures and architectural styles on Panamá's mountain terrain.

Astride a river on the coffee-clad eastern foothills of Volcán Barú, Boquete is acclaimed as an activity center, notably for birding and hiking in nearby forest parks. Whitewater rafting is also big, as is horseback riding. The region abounds in lush, formally tended gardens (a local obsession), and is the setting for Panamá's most important annual flower and orchid show. Add in the charming and colorful presence of Ngöbe-Buglé peoples, especially during the winter coffee-picking season; plus, the most varied, and most appealing, lodgings and restaurants in the nation outside Panamá City. The result is a decade-long tourism (and real estate) boom that has firmly established Boquete as the nation's number one destination for foreign visitors.

In 2008, major floods and mudslides swept through town, causing considerable damage.

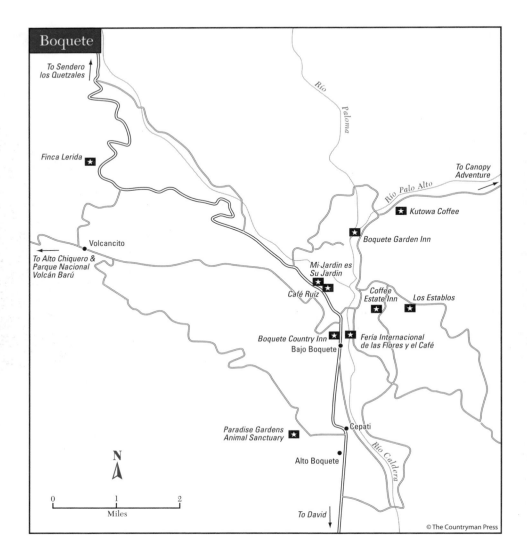

Boquete

To Sendero
los Quetzales

Río Paloma

Finca Lerida ★

To Canopy
Adventure

Río Palo Alto

★ Kutowa Coffee

★ Boquete Garden Inn

Volcancito

To Alto Chiquero &
Parque Nacional
Volcán Barú

Mi Jardin es
Su Jardin
★ ★

Coffee
Estate Inn
★   ★ Los Establos

Café Ruíz

Boquete Country Inn ★ ★ Fería Internacional
de las Flores y el Café
Bajo Boquete

Paradise Gardens ★
Animal Sanctuary

Cepati

Río Caldera

N

Alto Boquete

0   1   2
Miles

To David

© The Countryman Press

LODGING

BOQUETE GARDEN INN

507-720-2376
Palo Alto, Boquete
www.boquetegardeninn.com
Moderate
One of the nation's finest bed and breakfast
inns, this Canadian-owned hotel sits in
lovingly tended gardens beside the Río Palo
Alto. The 10 guest rooms are in two-story
octagonal cabins with stylish, plantation-
style furnishings and top-quality linens.
Nice! Many have king beds. Free Wi-Fi.

THE COFFEE ESTATE INN

507-720-2211
Fax: 507-720-2211
www.coffeeestateinn.com
Jaramillo Arriba, Boquete
Moderate
Another lovely bed-and-breakfast set in a

Boquete, Panamá

lush tropical garden with volcano views and trails through the inn's garden, forest, and coffee estate. I love staying here, not least for the attentive care of Canadian owners, Jane and Barry, who prepare candlelit gourmet dinners to be enjoyed on your balcony. Accommodations are in cozy bungalows with deluxe mattresses, flat-screen cable TVs, Wi-Fi, and kitchenettes. Boxed lunches prepared.

FINCA LÉRIDA BED & BREAKFAST
507-720-2285
www.fincalerida.com
Alto Quiel, 6 miles (10 km) NW of Boquete
An atmospheric wooden lodge in the midst of a coffee *finca* surrounded by forest, this 16-room inn offers two types of accommodation: wood-paneled rooms in the venerable family home, or cottages (both are furnished with antiques), or 11 rooms in a modern "eco-lodge." The cozy lounge in the home is warmed by a log fire in a stone hearth. Birding is a hotel specialty; quetzals are frequently sighted.

LOS ESTABLOS
507-720-2685
www.losestablos.net
Jaramillo Arriba, Boquete
Expensive
With its dramatic mountainside location, this deluxe *hacienda*-style hotel (converted from a stable) makes quite an initial impression; views of the volcano don't get any better than this. Graciously furnished, it has just six rooms, so consider it an intimate home-away-from-home, combining antiques and antique reproduction furnishings, and state-of-the-art fixtures such as flat-screen TVs.

Coffee Estate Inn, Boquete, Panamá

Finca Lérida, Boquete, Panamá

PANAMONTE INN AND SPA

507-720-1324
Fax: 507-720-2055
www.panamonteinnandspa.com
Avenida Central, Boquete
Moderate to Expensive
In the heart of town, this centenary gem has a quintessential charm. The owner, Inga Collins, took advantage of the 2008 floods to remodel. The result is a superlative of good taste and refinement. The lounge, with its hearth, has all the warmth and ambience of a classic English country house hotel, while guest rooms are thoroughly up-to-date and all you could wish for. Gorgeous gardens and a gourmet restaurant complete the picture.

DINING

BISTRO BOQUETE

507-720-1017
http://bistroboquete.com
Avenida Central and Calle 1ra Sur
Deli fare
Colorado-raised owner Lauretta knows how to run a relaxed deli restaurant, with all the American favorites (from artichoke dip, burgers, and BLT sandwiches to filet mignon). Local dishes include grilled trout fresh from the streams. Leave room for cheesecake. Open: Tuesday through Sunday 7 AM–10 PM.

DELICIAS DEL PERÚ

507-720-1966
Avenida Los Fundadores and Calle 2da
Peruvian
This is *the* place in town to savor fresh seafoods, Peruvian style. Start with shellfish soup or ceviche. Not just any ceviche. It comes several ways. I recommend the tongue-tingling ceviche with *ají chombo* (yellow habanero peppers). My favorite entrée? Sea bass stuffed with shrimp. Wash your meal down with a classic pisco sour. Open: Daily noon–11 PM

PANAMONTE INN AND SPA

507-720-1324
www.panamonteinnandspa.com
Avenida Central, Boquete
When you want to splurge on the best meal in town, this is the hands-down choice. First, the romantic candlelit ambience can't be beat. And Chef Charlie Collins' fusion dishes make the most of local ingredients, such as fresh trout—the restaurant's signature dish. The seasonal menu might feature such mouthwatering delicacies as pork chops with onion ragout, and veal stock and wine sauce. For a more relaxed ambience, opt to dine beside the fire in the cozy lounge-bar. Go on Sunday for the special brunch. Open: Daily 7–9:30 AM, 12:30–3 PM, and 6–10 PM.

ATTRACTIONS, PARKS, AND RECREATION

Arriving in town from David, your first view of Boquete is from the **Centro de Información Turística** (CEFATI) coffee shop and info bureau at Alto Boquete (High Boquete). It perches atop a bluff called **Mirador de la Virgen de la Gruta** overlooking the valley of the Río Caldera.

The town (Bajo Boquete), on the west bank of the river, slopes gently northward for more than a mile but is barely four blocks wide. The pine-studded square **Parque Domingo Médica** is a good place to relax and savor the lazy pace of life. An antique railroad car to one side recalls the defunct service that once served Boquete.

Garden enthusiasts should visit **Mi Jardín es Su Jardín** (open daily dawn to dusk; free), on the main street just 0.6-mile (1 km) northwest of the town center. Here the González

Psychedelic cow, Mi Jardin es su Jardin, Boquete, Panamá

family has created an orderly garden adorned with eclectic sculptures, such as psychedelic cows—the result of three decades of work.

Set amid landscaped gardens, **Paradise Gardens Animal Sanctuary** (507-6615-6618; www.paradisegardenspanama.com; Thursday through Tuesday 10–4; $5 donation), the only licensed animal sanctuary in Panamá, is a great place to see many of the animals you'd like to see in the wild—armadillos and kinkajous, ocelots and margays, capuchin and howler monkeys, etc. This is no zoo. Most animals were orphaned or injured; others are being raised for release to the wild. It also has a butterfly house, plus the largest aviary in Panamá. And the gardens are simply sensational.

Boquete Mountain Safari (507-6627-8829; www.boquetemountainsafaritours.com) specializes in orientation tours by Jeep, but also has hiking tours, horseback rides, and more.

Boquete acquired an 18-hole championship golf course in 2009, at **Cielo Paraíso** (507-720-2431; www.cieloparaiso.com), 5 miles (8 km) S of Boquete. It's a private course.

Take a thrilling zipline tour between treetops with the three-hour **Boquete Tree Trek** (507-720-1635; www.aventurist.com). The same company also offers a three-hour **Boquete Mountain Bike Tour** plus guided hikes (daily 7 AM and 1 PM; $25).

Whitewater Rafting

The Ríos Chiriquí and Chiriquí Viejo cascade down the slopes of Volcán Barú, providing perfect conditions for rafting. Although capable of being run year-round, the most exhilarating rides are May through December. Your journey will alternate between tranquil stretches and adrenaline-charged runs through rapids. Contact **Chiriquí River Rafting** (507-720-1505; www.panama-rafting.com), which has trips from relatively calm Class II to challenging Class IV runs on six rivers.

Coffee Tours

Aaaahhhh! . . . Redolent aromas of fresh-roasted coffee waft over town, for Boquete is Panamá's main center of coffee production. The slopes above town are corduroyed in neat rows of dark green coffee bushes. A tour of one or more *beneficios* (coffee mills) is usually fun and fascinating. Here are three excellent venues:

Ngöbe-Buglé women picking coffee, Boquete, Panamá

Beneficio Cafetelero Café Ruíz (507-720-1392 or 1-800-CAFE; www.caferuiz.com; Alto Boquete; by appointment): Lets you tour the coffee fields and *beneficio*. Ends with a tasting.

Finca Lérida (507-720-2285; www.fincalerida.com; Alto Quiel, 7 miles/11 km NW of Boquete; by appointment): One of Boquete's oldest coffee estates (since 1922) enjoys a sensational location and includes 640 acres (259 ha) of cloud forest with trails. The original *beneficio* is today a coffee museum, which is visited on an in-depth interactive coffee tour.

Kotowa Coffee Tour (507-720-3852; www.kotowacoffee.com; Palo Alto, 3 miles/5 km NE of Boquete; Monday through Saturday 2 PM; $28.50): Panamá's oldest coffee mill doubles as a cupping (tasting) room on this tour, which explains the whole process from the coffee bean to the cup.

Volcán Barú, Panamá

Parque Nacional Volcán Barú

(507-775-2055) 1 mile (1.6 km) N of Volcancito. Panamá's only volcano 11,398-foot (3,474 m) Barú towers over Boquete, luring hikers and birders for an experienced unsurpassed in the country. Dormant for at least 500 years, it is easily accessed by trails that begin within minutes of town.

The 8.5-mile-long (13.5 km) **summit trail** (five hours) begins at the ANAM ranger station above Volcancito (5 miles/8 km) northwest of Boquete; getting to the station requires a high-ground-clearance Jeep or a 40-minute hike from Volcancito. At the top you'll find seven craters surrounded by dwarf forest, stunted by cold winds and mists. On sunny days the 360-degree views are to be seen to be believed. An early morning start is recommended, as clouds often move in by mid-morning.

Monkeys, agoutis, and sloths are among the most common mammals you can expect to see. And the birding is fabulous. Listen for the metallic clang of the endangered three-wattled bellbird. Quetzals—named for the Holy Grail of Neotropical birds—are numerous, and frequently seen; you'll be wise to hike with a qualified guide if you want to spot the well-hidden wildlife.

Lower down, the 12-mile (19 km) **Sendero Los Quetzales** swings around the northern flank of **Volcán Barú**. It begins at the ANAM ranger station at **Alto Chiquero** and leads uphill to **El Respingo**, near Cerro Punta, on the west side of Barú.

The 55 square-mile (14,322 ha) park is contiguous with Parque Internacional La Amistad, to the north.

Good to Know About

The well-stocked **CEFATI** (507-720-4060; daily 9–6) tourist information center is at Alto Boquete, on the right as you enter Boquete. It has a delightful café and a lookout with views.

Quetzals

The quetzal could well be the most sought sighting of the Neotropics by avid birders. Officially known as the resplendent trogon, this pigeon-sized bird is known for its spectacular plumage. The male's iridescent emerald feathers, including twin trailing trail feathers (with a crimson belly and a white undertail), were so prized by Mayans that the bird was revered in the form of their most important god—Quetzalcoatl, or Plumed Serpent. The mountain-dwelling quetzal occupies cloud forest from southern Mexico to Panamá at elevations of between 3,500–7,000 feet (1,000–2,000 m). In spring mating season, the male can be seen in plummeting rise-and-dive flight. The birds nest in tree-trunk hollows and feed almost exclusively on the fruit of the *aguacatillo*, which it swallows whole.

WEEKLY AND ANNUAL EVENTS

The **Fería Internacional de las Flores y el Café** (507-720-1466; www.feriadeboquete.com; florescaf@cwpanama.net) is held each January, when the Flower and Coffee Fair brings thousands to Boquete.

Volcán and Cerro Punta

The mountain community of Volcán, 40 miles (58 km) northwest of David, is surrounded by boulders on a plateau on the western flank of Barú. It's reached via Carretera 41 from La Concepción, on the Interamericana, 16 miles (26 km) west of David. The village is an adventure center for hikers, kayakers, and white-water rafters. Coffee estates line Carretera 42, which runs west from Volcán to the Costa Rican border. It's also the gateway to Cerro Punta, an alpine community that is a breadbasket for Panamá, and a horse-breeding and flower-growing center at the gateway to both Parque Nacional Volcán Barú and Parque Internacional La Amistad.

Sendero Los Quetzales, Cerro Punta, Panamá

LODGING AND DINING

CASA GRANDE BAMBITO RESORT

507-771-5126
www.casagrandebambito.com
Bambito, 5 miles (8 km) N of Volcán
Moderate to Expensive
The former El Manantial Spa and Resort
recently metamorphosed as a deluxe boutique hotel in the mountains. The 20
wooden cabin suites are all graced with
stylish contemporary furnishings, fluffy
down duvets, and state-of-the-art electronics such as plasma TVs. The lush
grounds merge into forest. You can bathe in
thermal baths, and healing treatments are
offered in its luxury spa. And the Blue
Garden Restaurant sets the standards for
miles around.

CERRO BRUJO GOURMET

507-6669-9196
Volcán
This is true gourmet dining! Owner artist
Patricia Miranda Allen concocts some creative dishes such as chicken with green
curry, or the herbed rabbit, served with
French fried yuca chips and artfully presented. All entrées come with soup (such as
creamy yellow split pea) or salad. Best yet is
the setting: a quaint cottage in a lovely garden where you can dine on the porch.
Open: Daily noon–9 PM. Moderate to Very
Expensive.

HOTEL BAMBITO RESORT

507-771-4373
Fax: 507-771-4207
www.hotelbambito.com
Bambito, 3 miles (5 km) S of Cerro Punta
Moderate
Another recently upgraded property, this
lovely alpine lodge overlooks its own ponds
and gardens to the fore, and thick forest
behind. Its 47 pleasantly furnished rooms
each feature rattan furniture, plus cable TV,
minibar, coffeemaker, and Internet
modems. Heated indoor swimming pool.
Horseback riding and guided hikes are
offered. The restaurant specializes in trout
dishes.

HOTEL DOS RÍOS

507-771-5555
Fax: 507-771-5794
www.dosrios.com.pa
Volcán
Moderate
The best of few options in Volcán, this two-
story, wood-paneled hotel is a slightly
decaying, no-frills option. It has 18 fairly
simply furnished rooms that verge on
basic; take a suite, and avoid downstairs
rooms due to squeaky floors above. The
dowdy Barriles Bar is lively on weekends,
and the Estrella Volcanera Restaurant
focuses on ho-hum Italian dishes. A high
point is the lovely garden.

LOS QUETZALES ECOLODGE & SPA

507-771-2291
Fax: 507-771-2226
www.losquetzales.com
Guadalupe, 2 miles (3 km) NE of Cerro
Punta
Inexpensive to Moderate
At 7,260 feet (2,200 m) above sea level, it's
the highest hotel in the country. Reason
enough for guests to gather around the log-
burning hearth centered in a cozy and rustic upstairs lounge. Choose from simple yet
comfy dorms and hotel rooms to more spacious suites and chalets, or (for the ultimate
nature experience) five spacious yet simple
wooden cabins in the heart of the forest on
the boundary of Parque Nacional La
Amistad, where quetzals can be seen from
the balconies. Wi-Fi. The restaurant delivers tasty dishes (including local trout)
using crisp veggies fresh from the surrounding fields.

RESTAURANTE ACROPOLIS
507-771-5184
Avenida Central, Volcán
Greek
It causes a double take at first sight to see this Greek restaurant in the midst of the volcanic highlands. Greek owner George Babos (a former skipper) wed his Panamanian wife, Elizabeth, and put down roots here. Together they cook up a mean moussaka, plus souvlaki, baklava, and other Hellenic faves, alongside burgers and pastas, and trout in garlic and lemon butter. Open: Tuesday through Sunday noon–10 PM. Moderate to Expensive

ATTRACTIONS, PARKS, AND RECREATION

Around Volcán

A tour of local coffee estates is always interesting. You can explore **La Torcaza Estate** (507-771-4306 or 1-866-316-9052; www.estatecoffee.com or www.jansoncoffee.com; Monday through Friday 8–4:30, Saturday 8:30–1:30; $10) coffee farm and *beneficio,* where the Janson family has been producing gourmet organic coffee for decades. The hour-long tour is in Spanish and English and ends with a coffee tasting at their Janson's Coffee House. The estate is signed on the Vía Aeropuerto (airport road).

    Finca Hartmann (507-6450-1853; www.fincahartmann.com; Carretera 42, 17 miles/28 km W of Volcán; by 24 hours appointment; $10 coffee tour) is a coffee farm in two parts. The main facility—Ojo de Agua—has a tiny coffee museum that also has pre-Columbian

Finca Hartmann coffee, Volcán, Panamá

Ngöbe-Buglé picking vegetables at Cerro Punta, Panamá

Kayaking and Whitewater Rafting

Volcán is a center for whitewater fun on the tempestuous Ríos Macho de Monte and Gariche, which tear down the mountain slopes and offer boulder-strewn runs. For kayakers, a highlight of the Macho de Monte is the sheer-walled **Cañon Macho de Monte**. You can stop beneath waterfalls and swim in exhilaratingly chilly pools.

Chiriqui River Rafting (507-720-1505; www.panama-rafting.com) has Class II and III runs on the Gariche June through November.

and entomological exhibits. Its Palo Verde locale draws birders and hikers with 3 miles (5 km) of self-guided trails through a 12-acre (5 ha) forest reserve teeming with animals and birds.

Birders should hire a guide for viewing migratory waterfowl at the **Lagunas de Volcán**, west of Volcán.

Sitio Barriles (507-575-2121; 4 miles (6 km) W of Volcán; daily 7 AM—6 PM; by donation) is another small coffee farm open to the public, although the main draw here is its collection of pre-Columbian artifacts and an ancient tomb and rocks carved with petroglyphs.

Around Cerro Punta

A 20-minute drive north from Volcán delivers you in a mountain bowl at 6,463 feet (1,970 m) enfolded to the east by Volcán Barú, to the north by Cerro Punta (7,792 feet/2,375 m), and to the west by Cerro Picacho (9,797 feet/2,986 m). The bowl is actually an extinct

Rainbow over Parque Internacional La Amistad, Panamá

Thoroughbred horse at Haras Cerro Punta, Panamá

volcanic crater. The road—lined with impatiens—loops around the bowl, connecting the alpine farming communities of **Cerro Punta** and **Guadalupe**. Strawberries, flowers, and vegetables are intensively grown, while the area is also the nation's foremost center for breeding thoroughbred horses. The **Haras Cerro Punta** (507-771-2057; www.harascerro punta.com) stud farm raises championship racehorses and French Percheron drays and offers tours by appointment.

Orchid-lovers will thrill to **Finca Dracula** (507-771-2070; www.fincadracula.com; Monday through Friday 8–11:30 AM and 1–5 PM; $5 entrance, $10 guided tour), just outside Guadalupe, where 2200 orchid species grow on 22 acres (10 ha). The farm is dedicated to the conservation of orchids and other tropical ornamental plant species. It is named for the orchid genus *Dracula,* which consists of 123 species.

Midway between Volcán and Cerro Punta, you pass through the communities of **Bambito** and **Nueva Suiza**, founded a century ago by Swiss immigrants and looking like a Tyrolean landscape transplanted.

Hiking and Birding: Cerro Punta is literally at the doorstep of both **Parque Internacional Volcán Barú** and **Parque Internacional La Amistad**, a mammoth 799-square-mile (207,000 ha) swath of pristine mountain terrain—much of it unexplored—that extends north to the Caribbean lowlands and west into Costa Rica.

The **Sendero Los Quetzales** begins at Bajo Grande (3 miles/5 km northeast of Cerro Punta) and swings around the north side of Volcán Barú and descends to Boquete.

Parque Internacional La Amistad is accessed from the **ANAM ranger station** (which has a small nature exhibition center) at Las Nubes (4 miles/7 km NW of Cerro Punta). From here, the easy **Sendero La Cascada** leads 1 mile (1.6 km) to a waterfall, while the moderate **Sendero El Retoño** and more demanding **Sendero La Montaña** ascend into the cloud forest. Shorter trails within the park are accessed from the private reserve of Los Quetzales Lodge & Spa, which offers guided birding and hikes.

SHOPPING

Local artist José de la Cruz has his studio-store—**Artesanías Cruz Volcán** (507-6622-1502; Monday through Saturday 8 AM–noon and 1–5 PM)—on Carretera 41 just before entering Volcán. Although principally a woodcarver, José also produces stained-glass pieces. He does custom pieces to order, and will handle shipping.

You can buy gorgeous orchids in export-ready sealed vials at **Finca Dracula Orchid Sanctuary** (507-771-2070; www.fincadracula.com).

10

BOCAS DEL TORO

"This Caribbean archipelago on Panamá's north coast is tropical paradise by day and party central by night."

—LAURA SICILIANO-ROSEN, *New York Magazine*

The hip, happenin' spot for backpackers and counter-culture travelers, Bocas del Toro is often conceived as being a group of small Caribbean islands in Panamá's extreme north-west. This mini-archipelago—the country's most popular vacation destination for non-Panamanians—is actually just a small part of an eponymous province that extends inland uphill to the Continental Divide. The vast majority is mountainous and thickly forested. Much lies within the vast Parque Internacional La Amistad (and adjacent Bosque Protector Palo Seco). La Amistad offers some of the most challenging hiking in the country—a virtu-ally unexplored final frontier for jaguar, tapir, and a wealth of other wildlife, although access is very limited from the lowlands, where the only town of consequence is Changuinola—a center for banana companies, whose plantations smother the lowlands.

Few visitors explore beyond "Bocas" (the island group, although the term usually denotes Bocas Town, on Isla Colón), where hotels perch over the water and the funky beauty lies in its tumbledown bars and pool halls and a somnolent Afro-Caribbean laissez-faire atmosphere. Water taxis will whisk you to prime surfers' beaches, pristine sands that dou-ble as nesting grounds for marine turtles, and to neighboring isles laced with trails where colorful poison-dart frogs (each isle has its own species) hop about under-foot. Never seen a manatee? A sighting is virtually guaranteed at San San Pond Sak, a wetland reserve hard up against the Costa Rican border.

Bocas has gone more upscale, more mainstream, in recent years, with accom-modations for every budget. The word got

Parque Internacional La Amistad, Panamá

OPPOSITE: *Rainstorm over Bosque Proctector Palo Seco, Panamá*

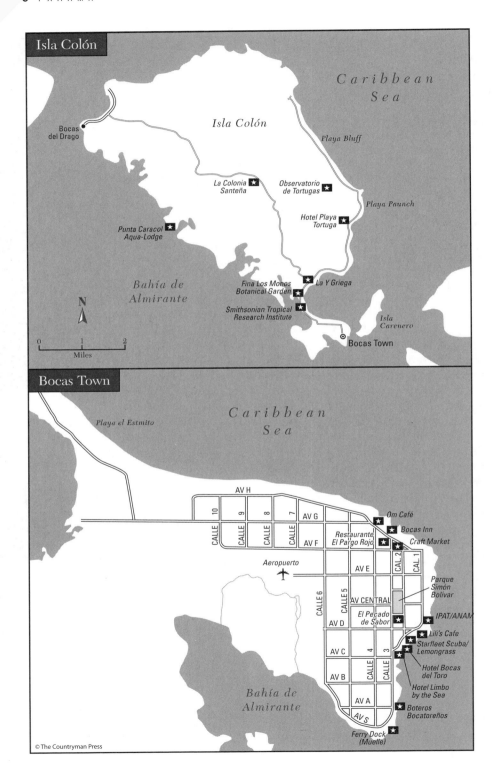

Isla Colón

Caribbean Sea

Isla Colón

Bocas del Drago

Playa Bluff

La Colonia Santeña

Observatorio de Tortugas

Playa Paunch

Punta Caracol Aqua-Lodge

Hotel Playa Tortuga

Bahía de Almirante

N

Fina Los Monos Botanical Garden

La Y Griega

Smithsonian Tropical Research Institute

Isla Carenero

0   1   2
Miles

Bocas Town

Bocas Town

Caribbean Sea

Playa el Estmito

AV H

CALLE 10
CALLE 9
CALLE 8
CALLE 7

AV G

Om Café

Bocas Inn

AV F

Restaurante El Pargo Rojo

Craft Market

CAL 2
CAL 1

AV E

Aeropuerto

CALLE 6
CALLE 5

Parque Simón Bolívar

AV CENTRAL

El Pecado de Sabor

IPAT/ANAM

AV D

Lili's Cafe

Starfleet Scuba/ Lemongrass

AV C

CALLE 4
CALLE 3

Hotel Bocas del Toro

Hotel Limbo by the Sea

AV B

Bahía de Almirante

AV A

AV S

Boteros Bocatoreños

Ferry Dock (Muelle)

© The Countryman Press

Young woman in window, Bocas Town, Bocas del Toro, Panamá

out long ago. The bulldozers have arrived and huge swaths of forest are falling for ever bigger resorts. Go now!

GETTING THERE AND AROUND

By Air
Aeroperlas (507-757-9236; www.aeroperlas.com) flies to Bocas del Toro from Panamá City's Albrook airport ($8) and Changuinola ($8) twice daily, and from David (daily, $36). **Air Panama** (507-316-9000; www.flyairpanama.com) also flies twice daily from Panamá City ($80). Nature Air (506-2299-6000 or 800-235-9272; www.natureair.com) flies to Bocas from San José, Costa Rica, five times weekly ($139).

By Bus and Water Taxi
Express buses (507-232-5803) for Almirante (10 hours, $25) and Changuinola leave the Albrook Terminal in Panamá City. Buses travel via David, from the "David-Almirante Coaster" (three hours, $6) leaves hourly to Almirate.

You need to take the water taxi from Almirante (a funky banana-loading port 18 miles/30 km SE of Changuinola) to Bocas Town (15 minutes, $4), hourly 6 AM–6:30 PM. Two companies compete: **Bocas Marine Tours** (507-757-9033 in Bocas, Calle 3 and

Water taxi crossing from Isla Carinero to Bocas del Toro, Panamá

Avenida C; 507-758-4085 in Almirante; www.bocasmarinetours.com) and **Taxi 25** (507-757-9028; Calle 1 and Avenida Central). Water taxis are the only way of getting between islands of the archipelago. Several freelance operators compete with Bocas Marine Tours and Taxi 25. And numerous freelance boat guides can be hired in Bocas Town for exploring the isles; **Gallardo Livingstone** (507-757-9388) is recommended.

By Car

Bocas is a two-hour drive from Chiriquí (on the Interamericana, 8 miles/14 km southeast of David) on Carretera 4 via Gualaca and the continental divide. You'll need to park your car in a secure lot by the Almirante wharfs, from where water taxis leave for Bocas. A car ferry runs from Almirante daily at 8 AM ($15–30), but there is no need for a vehicle on Bocas.

In the winter of 2009, torrential rains caused landslides on Carretera 4, and severe flooding and road damage throughout the lowlands. All road transportation leading to Bocas de Toro was shut down for a week. Check conditions ahead.

From Costa Rica

You can cross into Panamá from Sixaola, in Costa Rica. The community on the Panamanian side of the border is Guabito, about 9 miles (16 km) west of Changuinola, from where buses and taxis ($12) run to Almirante. Water taxis also run direct to Bocas from Finca 60, near Changuinola ($7). Transporte Bocatoreño buses depart Changuinola at 10 AM for Guabito.

Far easier is to take the **Caribe Shuttle** (506-2750-0626 in Costa Rica; 507-757-7048 in Bocas Town; http://caribeshuttle.com; $34 adult, $25 child one-way), a boat shuttle between Cahuita, Puerto Viejo, and Manzanillo (in Costa Rica) and Bocas del Toro.

Carretera 4 and the Cordillera

From the Interamericana at Chiriquí (8 miles/14 km southeast of David), Carretera 4 snakes up and over the cloud-draped *cordillera* and coils down to the Caribbean coast. It's supremely scenic. But be prepared for fog and potential landslides.

LODGING AND DINING

FINCA LA SUIZA JUNGLE LODGE
507-6615-3774
www.panama.net.tc
Carretera 4, 26 miles (42 km) N of Chiriquí
Inexpensive
A Swiss-run mountain lodge high in the *cordillera* near La Fortuna forest reserve. It has its own 494-acre (200 ha) cloud forest with challenging trails, and the mountain views (you can see all the way to the Pacific Ocean) are sublime from the three cozy cottages. Organic meals are served. Closed June, September, and October. Two-night minimum. No credit cards.

LOST AND FOUND LODGE
507-6581-9223
www.lostandfoundlodge.com
Carretera 4, 26 miles (42 km) N of Chiriquí
Inexpensive
Billing itself as "Panamá's only fully functioning eco-hostel inside the cloud forest," Lost and Found Lodge truly is a backpackers' dream. Choose from dorms or private rooms, all colorfully painted-up in Egyptian hieroglyphics and pointillist dots. You'll need to hike uphill after alighting the bus at the Km 42 marker (look for the yellow-painted rocks). It has stunning views down the mountain from wooden decks. Long-term guests get free board for volunteer duties, including community development projects.

Storm over Bosque Protector Palo Seco, Panamá

ATTRACTIONS, PARKS, AND RECREATION

Reserva Forestal Fortuna protects 75 square miles (19,500 ha) of montane cloud forest—a fitting environment for a Smithsonian Tropical Research Institute research center (closed to the public). The easiest hiking is at **Finca La Suiza** (507-615-3774; www.panama.net.tc; $8 entrance, 7–10 AM), at Km 42; its private forest reserve has well-marked trails that include a challenging all-day adventure to the top of Cerro Hornito.

Man-made **Lago Fortuna** was created by the **Presa Edwin Fabrega**, a dam where the roadside visitor center has excellent nature exhibits. A short distance north you'll cross the continental divide, where the road begins its serpentine descent through the valley of the Río Guarumo and the village of **Punta Peña**, surrounded by pineapple fincas.

Changuinola and Vicinity

West of Punta Peña, Carretera 11 parallels the coast and runs northwest to the regional center of Changuinola and, beyond, the Costa Rican border. Changuinola (and the valley of the Río Sixaola) is Panamá's most important center of banana production and a gateway to Parque Internacional La Amistad (to the west) and San San Pond Sak, a coastal wetland reserve protecting manatees and aquatic birds.

Nature exhibits at Presa Edwin Fabrega, Panamá

LODGING AND DINING

SOPOSO

507-6631-2222
www.soposo.com
5 miles (8 km) W of Changuinola
Inexpensive
A chance to immerse yourself in the Naso indigenous culture. For now accommodations are limited to two thatched huts (one with a single bedroom; the second with four rooms) with mosquito nets, porches with hammocks, and solar lanterns. You'll share a composting latrine and shower. Naso women prepare hearty meals on a wood-fired stove.

WEKSO ECOLODGE

507-620-0192
turismonaso_odesen@hotmail.com
12 miles (20 km) W of Changuinola
Inexpensive
Run by the Naso indigenous community, this eco-lodge is built on the site of a former U.S. Army jungle training camp and is the closest base to Parque Internacional La Amistad. The three thatched, stilt-legged, four-person cabins are simple, if not basic, yet cozy. Cold-water showers. Reached by an hour-long boat ride.

ATTRACTIONS, PARKS, AND RECREATION

San San Pond Sak

c/o 507-758-6794; or ANAM, 507-758-6603 in Changuinola; 3 miles (5 km) N of Changuinola. This precious coastal wetland covers 39,845 acres (16,125 ha) stretching from the Río Sixaola to the Bahía de Almirante. Its multiple ecosystems include marshes, mangroves, and seasonally flooded orey forest. Although a wealth of wildlife exists here, from sloths and monkeys to river otters and crocodiles, San San's claim to fame is its large population of manatees. The rare tucuxi freshwater dolphin is also found here. And green, hawksbill, and leatherback turtles nest on the beaches; a boardwalk (often flooded) leads from the ANAM ranger station.

Starfleet Scuba (507-757-9630; www.starfleetscuba.com), in Bocas Town, offers a full-day excursion by dugout canoe (7 AM–5 PM). Other tour operators in Bocas del Toro offer excursions.

Naso Comarca

5 miles (8 km) W of Changuinola. Looking for a remote adventure? Head up the Río Teribe to **Soposo**, home to the Naso indigenous people (aka the Teribe), who number about 3,000 individuals in 27 communities led by a king. A visit offers a chance to interact with (and learn from) the Naso, who strive to preserve a traditional lifestyle in harmony with their rain forest environment. They are also fighting to have their territory designated an autonomous *comarca*. **Soposo Rainforest Adventures** (507-6631-2222; www.soposo.com; $90–500) offers one- to seven-day trips from Bocas del Toro. Community members lead

---

Manatees

Looking like swollen wine-sacs, or tuskless walruses, manatees are gentle herbivorous mammals that have adapted completely to a life in warm water. *Manatís* (the word is a native Taíno word for "breast") inhabit shallow tropical coastal waters and are particularly fond of river estuaries, but they move freely between fresh and saline waters.

These highly intelligent animals lack hind limbs entirely. Instead, they propel themselves gracefully with a single spatulate tail that surely gave rise to the myth of the mermaid. Adult manatees average about 1,000 pounds and 9 feet (2.7 m) in length, although much larger individuals have been sighted. Females are slightly larger than males and reach sexual maturity at about four years old. They have tough gray skin, tiny beady eyes, and fleshy and pendulous upper lips like a shortened trunk similar to the elephant, to which they are closely related. This they use to gather vegetation. Opportunistic, non-territorial feeders, they are capable of chomping up to 75 pounds or more of sea grasses, water hyacinths, and other aquatic vegetation daily. Uniquely among mammals, they have only six pairs of dentures—all molars and premolars—that are constantly replaced throughout life.

Males gather to compete to mate with ovulating females, who give birth to a single calf (and occasional twins) only once every two to five years. While males contribute no parental care, mother and calf remain together for up to two years throughout weaning. Manatees can live to be 60 years old. The West Indian manatee is now an endangered species following centuries of being hunted for meat, disturbance of its habitats, entanglement with fishing gear and, increasingly, collisions with speeding boats. However, they are easy to spot in the sheltered waters of San San Pond Sak.

Main drag in Bocas Town, Bocas del Toro, Panamá

trips to **Seiyik**, their capital "city," plus hikes into the adjoining Parque Internacional La Amistad. Getting there requires a 30-minute boat journey from El Silencio, 2 miles (3 km) W of Changuinola).

An alternative 7 miles (12 km) upriver is **Centro Ecotúristico Wekso** (507-758-9137; turismonaso_odesen@hotmail.com), where the Naso run an ecotourism project—Proyecto ODESEN (Organization for the Sustainable Development of Naso Ecotourism)—at an eco-lodge converted from Pana Jungla, a former military jungle survival school. The **Sendero Los Heliconias** offers an easy loop for visitors wishing to spot monkeys, sloths, etc. without too much exertion. Tour companies in Bocas Town offer one- to three-day excursions.

Bocas del Toro Archipelago

The Bocas archipelago comprises six main islands in Bahía de Almirante (Admiral's Bay, named for the visit by Christopher Columbus, in 1502), with Isla Colón, the westernmost and most populous and important. The airport and sole town—Bocas Town—are here. Founded in 1826 as a logging center, Bocas Town really harks back to 1889 when it became the local headquarters for the United Fruit Company, which established banana planta-tions on the mainland, drawing laborers from Jamaica and from San Andrés and Providencia, Colombia. The town's pastel-painted clapboard buildings with gingerbread trim recall the era. Many have metamorphosed into hotels suspended on stilts above the water. Although Bocas Town has seen a tourism boom within the past decade, it retains its uniquely offbeat tropical lassitude and is the kind of place you'll want to simply laze the days away in a hammock with a good book and chilled beer.

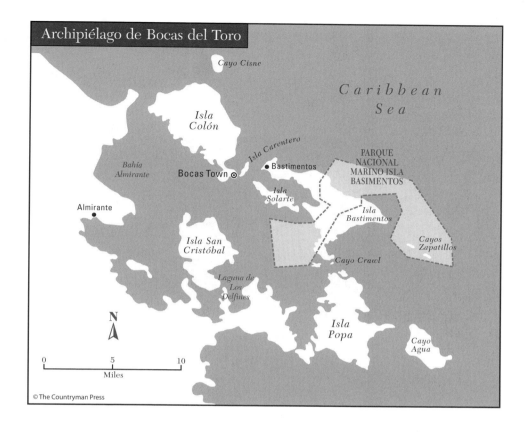

Isla Colón has great surfers' beaches. And there's rain forest. However, the most exhilarating wilderness experiences are to be had on neighboring isles, where snorkeling amid coral reefs is also superb. There are gorgeous beaches, too—most are reached by boat—drawing marine turtles to nest at night. However, riptides along the windward shores make swimming risky. Leave the ocean to the surfers.

LODGING

Bocas del Toro has more than two dozen hotels to choose from. Most are concentrated in Bocas Town, where they cling to the waterfront. More recent large-scale resorts have opened, with more to follow, further afield. Here's my pick of the litter.

BOCAS INN

507-757-9600 or 269-9415
www.anconexpeditions.com
Calle 3 and Ave G, Bocas Town
Inexpensive to Moderate
Operated by Ancón Expeditions, this unpretentious yet highly regarded waterfront two-story lodge is a perfect spot to laze back in a hammock or rocker on broad verandas. Six spacious rooms are modestly furnished. It has a small bar and breakfasts are served.

Lazing in a hammock in Bocas Town, Bocas del Toro, Panamá

CAREENING CAY RESORT

507-757-9157
www.careeningcay.com
Isla Carenero
Moderate
This waterfront lodge is a two-minute boat ride from Bocas Town. It's known for its over-the-water Cosmic Crab Café serving such delights as seafood lasagna and banana leaf-wrapped baked grouper or mahi-mahi. Colorful yet simple decor makes good use of hardwoods in bungalows, in various styles. Some have kitchenettes. Wi-Fi.

HOTEL BOCAS DEL TORO

507-757-9018
www.hotelbocasdeltoro.com
Calle W, Bocas Town
Moderate
Perhaps the nicest boutique hotel in town, this charmer combines a fabulous waterfront setting with simple elegance in its 12 spacious air-conditioned rooms, including attics. All have flat-screen cable TVs, Wi-Fi, coffeemakers, and sexy-to-the-touch 400-thread-count cotton sheets. You can dine alfresco on the waterfront deck, and the open-air bar is a popular local venue. Ocean kayak rentals and in-room massage.

HOTEL EL LIMBO BY THE SEA

507-757-9062
www.ellimbo.com
Calles 1ra and 2da, Bocas Town
Moderate to Expensive
A tremendous waterfront option, this three-story hotel has 15 rooms, some with balconies, and all with plasma TVs and Wi-Fi. You can rent sea kayaks. Open-air bar-restaurant, plus deck with lounge chairs.

HOTEL PLAYA TORTUGA

507-757-9050
www.hotelplayatortuga.com
Isla Colón
Expensive to Very Expensive

Bocas Town waterfront, Bocas del Toro, Panamá

The only true beach resort on Isla Colón, this low-rise newcomer set a new tone when it opened in 2009. If you like minimalist contemporary styling, you'll love the 74 standard rooms, 40 junior suites, and 3 suites, all oozing luxury with their chocolate-and-white decor and divinely comfortable linens. The bi-level swimming pool features inset lounge chairs.

LA LOMA JUNGLE LODGE
507-6592-5162
www.thejunglelodge.com
Bahía Honda, 6 Miles (10 km) E of Old Bank, Isla Bastimentos
Expensive
On the mangrove-fringed shores of southern Isla Bastimentos, adjoining the national park, this intimate and remote lodge has three open-walled *ranchos* of bamboo and thatch. Decor is ultimately romantic. Mattresses beneath mosquito nets rest atop tree-trunk logs on glazed hardwood floors. It's a stiff five-minute climb to two of the cabins. Canopy tree house doubles as a bird-watching blind.

PUNTA CARACOL ACQUA-LODGE
507-6612-1088
www.puntacaracol.com
Punta Caracol, Isla Colón
Very expensive
Imagine, your very own thatched stilt-legged, one- or two-story suite-cabin suspended above turquoise ocean. This ecologically sustainable eco-lodge's nine huts are all connected by a long boardwalk to the public areas on *terra firma*. They're exquisitely appointed with king-sized four-poster beds and calming pastels. Gourmet cuisine in the dining room.

HOTEL TRANQUILO BAY
507-380-0721, in North America 713-589-6952
www.tranquilobay.com
Cayo Crawl, Isla Bastimentos
Moderate

An eco-lodge with its own forest reserve and trails. Six air-conditioned hardwood, tin-roofed cabins look over the forests, with views and wildlife viewing enjoyed from hammocks and Adirondack chairs on your veranda. Relax at night in the lodge's TV lounge.

DINING

Bocas Town is a veritable gourmands' nirvana, with everything from local seafood dives to restaurants specializing in Indian and Thai dishes. All of the hotels above offer meals, and many have restaurants open to the public.

EL PARGO ROJO

507-6597-0296
Calle 3 and Avenida H, Bocas Town
International

A popular Iranian-owned restaurant on a corner at the west end of town, it offers a hip, romantic open-air ambience beneath whirring fans. Some of the best dishes around include killer breakfasts, such as omelets; plus salads, blue-cheese burgers, pizzas; while my faves off the dinner menu include Thai soup and a delicious shrimp in coco and curry sauce. Open: Tuesday through Sunday 7–10 PM. Moderate to Expensive.

LEMONGRASS

507-757-9630
Calle 2, Bocas Town
Seafood
Above Starfleet Scuba, this place has an enviable second-floor location in an aged wooden building perched over the Caribbean. Mike Thompson, the English owner, couldn't resist adding fish-and-

Waitress in window, Bocas Town, Bocas del Toro, Panamá

chips to the menu, but mostly marries fresh seafood to Southeast Asian inspiration. Start with spicy crab cakes followed, perhaps, by a curry or fresh trout glazed in chile and ginger, with a decadent cappuccino tiramisu sundae to close. Expensive. Open: Friday through Wednesday noon–3 and 5–10 PM. Moderate to Very Expensive.

LILI'S CAFE
507-6560-8777
www.kodiakbocas.com/lilis
Calle 1, Bocas del Toro
Cheery local cook Lili always has a smile for guests at this tiny restaurant on a waterfront deck. It's a great lunch spot for veggie quiche, sandwiches made with home-baked bread, or some classic local dishes spiced up with Lili's very own Killin' Me Man pepper sauce. Open: Monday through Saturday 7 AM–5 PM, Sunday 7 AM–1 PM.

OM CAFÉ
507-6624-0898
Avenida E and Calle 2, Bocas del Toro
Indian
A cozy little place is tucked above a surf shop in a creaky old wooden building. You'd expect an Asian-inspired menu from a restaurant owned by a Canadian-Punjabi, and Sunandra Mehra delivers in spades. Even the breakfast menu includes spicy eggs vindaloo in roti wrap accompanied by a mango lassi. For lunch or dinner, you can't go wrong with chicken tikka masala, prawn vindaloo, or a veggie dish. Groovy music. Open: Thursday through Tuesday 8–noon and 5:30–10 PM.

EL PECADO DE SABOR
507-6597-0296
Calle 3 and Parque Bolívar, Bocas Town
Eclectic
Bohemian upstairs restaurant a stone's throw from the park. French-Canadian Chef Stefan spans the globe with his eclectic menu that includes Panamanian favorites, Thai-inspired dishes, and even Mexican fare, plus lots of fresh seafood dishes. Suggestions? Beef tenderloin with Dijon mustard sauce, or tuna fried in a crunchy herb breading. Be warned, the sagging balcony gives you an unnerving "this could collapse at any moment" feel. Open: Tuesday through Saturday 5–10 PM; closed May through June.

ATTRACTIONS, PARKS, AND RECREATION

Isla Colón

The archipelago's main isle measures 24 square-mile (61 sq km)—small enough to explore entirely by bicycle if you're fit. Many visitors are happy simply to laze in **Bocas Town**, where the pleasure is to be had in wandering the streets. Otherwise, the only site of interest (the town measures just eight blocks long by four wide) is **Parque Simón Bolívar** (Calle 3 and Avenida Central), where a bronze bust of the "Great South American Liberator," Simón Bolívar, presides. The town beach is **Playa El Istmico**, a narrow sliver of sand at the west end of town.

The beach runs along a tombolo (narrow sand spit) that separates Bocas Town from the rest of the island. Occupying the spit, the **Smithsonian Tropical Research Institute** (STRI) scientific research station (507-212-8564; www.stri.org; open Thursday and Friday 3–5, free) can be visited: a chance to learn about coral reefs and the local marine environment.

Isla Colón's prize attraction is surely **Finca Los Monos Botanical Garden** (507-757 9461; http://www.bocasdeltorobotanicalgarden.com; open Monday at 1 PM, Friday at

Bust of Simón Bolívar, Parque Simón Bolívar, Bocas Town, Panamá

8:30 AM, and other times by appointment; two-hour tours $10), a magnificent 20-acre (8 ha) hilltop garden just beyond the STRI station. Tenderly cared for by creators, David and Lin Gillingham, the garden is a riot of colorful heliconias, gingers, flowering trees, fruits, spices, and ornamentals.

West from town, a dirt road runs along the windward shore to two prime surfing beaches—**Playa Paunch** and **Playa Bluff** (5 miles/8 km from town; a taxi will cost about $10 each way)—where Hawaii-scale waves offer a radical challenge. These miles-long beaches are backed by thick jungle good for spotting parrots, toucans, and monkeys.

For swimming, head to the sheltered, albeit tiny, beach at **Bocas de Drago**, at the far west end of the isle ($25 by taxi, round-trip), 8 miles (14 km) from Bocas Town. Nearby **Starfish Beach** is named for the zillion starfish that crawl on the seabed in crystal-clear waters. A dirt road leads through the center of the island via the hamlet of La Colonia Santeña. Cyclists be warned: there are hills! And the going is tough after rains. You can divert at La Colonia Santeña to visit **La Gruta** cavern, full of dripstone formations and bats; it's also a religious sanctuary and pilgrimage site each third Sunday in July.

Transporte Boca del Drago (507-774-9065; Monday through Friday at 6:45 AM, 10 AM, noon, 3 PM, and 6 PM) operates a minibus between Bocas del Toro to Bocas del Drago.

Water taxis will run you to Bocas del Drago ($10). The journey is best combined with a visit to **Swan Cay**, a rocky palisade rising from the ocean 1 mile (1.6 km) off Playa Bluff. Birders will thrill to the nesting boobies and other seabirds, including red-billed tropic birds. This is a protected wildlife reserve: *You may not step ashore!* Instead, step ashore on **Cayo Carenero**, a two-minute boat ride north of Bocas Town and a sleepier, smaller twin known for its superb surfers' reef break off the north shore.

Isla Bastimentos

Take your pick. Hikes in search of straw-berry-red poison-dart frogs. Hanging 10 on Hawaii-sized waves off Playa Red Frog. Shooting sloths with your camera. Or learning *guari-guari* (the local creole dialect) as you slap down dominoes with locals in a funky community bar.

A 10-minute boat ride southeast of Bocas Town, this 20-square-mile (52 sq km) island has a thriving Afro-Antillean culture centered on **Old Bank**, a one-street waterfront settlement. Try to visit on Mondays, when you can linger at night to jive to calypso jam sessions with the world-famous Bastimentos Beach Boys.

Bastimentos has the best beaches in the archipelago; high surf and riptides preclude swimming. A track through the rain forest leads from the village to, in order, **Wizard's Beach**, **Red Frog Beach**, and **Playa Larga**. These gorgeous, miles-long white sands are all favored by marine turtles as nest sites. From Playa Larga, trails turn inland to explore **Parque Nacional Marino Isla Bastimentos**. The park covers 51 square miles (13,226 ha), including coastal mangrove forest, bay waters, coral reefs, and cays. Riotous with birdcalls (including red-lored Amazons and blue-headed parrots), the dense tropical forests abound with critters: agoutis, howler monkeys, sloths, and caimans, plus the island's endemic bloodred poison-dart frogs. You're guaranteed to see these porcelain-like creatures while hiking the **Sendero del Rana Rojo** trail, which leads south from Red Frog Beach to the humble Ngöbe-Buglé community of **Bahía Honda**.

The twin tiny isles of **Cayos Zapatillos**, about 5 miles (8 km) east of Isla Bastimentos, are well worth the 15-minute journey: these beach-fringed, palm-shaded isles are ringed

Good to Know About

IPAT (507-757-9642; www.ipat.gob.pa; open Monday through Friday 8–5) has a tourist information booth on Calle I at Avenida D. **ANAM** (507-758-6802 or 757-9244; Calle I and Avenida E; Monday through Friday 8–4), the national parks agency, has an office one block north.

Panamanian playing banjo in Bocas Town, Panamá

Nocturnal Monkeys?

For sure! Bocas' endemic Northern Night monkey—*Aotus trivergatus*—belongs to a monkey genus that inhabits vine-draped coastal rain forest from Panamá to Brazil and is the only truly nocturnal primate on the planet. With a cute round face and orange brown eyes as big as twin saucers, it resembles a loris or bush baby. It has a long, non-prehensile tail for better balance when leaping from branch to branch. These omnivores snooze among thick foliage by day and emerge after dusk to forage. Full moon nights are the best time to see them, as they are most active then.

by turquoise waters. A postcard perfect scene! The coral reefs here are among the best in Panamá, drawing day-tripper snorkelers and divers.

Isla Solarte

This 3-mile long by half-mile wide (6.5 km by 1 km) slender isle, a several-minute boat ride east from Bocas Town, is occupied by Ngöbe-Buglé people, who eke a living from fishing. **Punta Hospital**, at the western tip, is one of the best snorkeling and diving sites in the archipelago. **Bocas Water Sports** (507-757-9541; www.bocaswatersports.com) offers dive trips from Bocas Town.

Water Sports and Excursions

The new U.S. owners of **Bocas Water Sports** (see the Isla Solarte entry, above) offer diving (including night dives), snorkeling ($17–20), kayaking ($3 hourly, $10 half-day), plus dolphin-spotting and birding trips. **Starfleet Scuba** (507-757-9630; www.starfleetscuba.com; Calle 1A, Bocas Town) gives first-timers an introductory "Discover Scuba" dive ($75–95), but also has certification and advanced specialty courses.

Fancy a thrilling ride on a luxury catamaran? Call **Panamá Sailing & Diving Adventures** (507-6668-6849; www.panamasailing.com), which offers one- to seven-day cruises around the archipelago. Skipper Daniel Ayora also teaches sailing. **Catamaran Sailing Adventures** (507-757-9710 or 6625-8610; www.bocassailing.com) competes. For a more prosaic experience with local boatmen, hook up with **Boteros Bocatoreños** (507-757-9760; boterosbocas@yahoo.com), a local boatmen's cooperative providing custom tours.

Sign for JJ Transporte Boat Tours, Bocas Town, Bocas del Toro, Panamá

Jim Kimball and Jay Viola, at **Hotel Tranquilo Bay** (507-380-0721, in North America 713-589-6952; www.tranquilobay.com) are fly-fishing experts. They'll take you out in their 25- and 27-foot fishing boats to hook tarpon, snook, snapper, jacks, and the like.

Bocas del Toro archipelago is Panamá's rising surfing star, with huge, uncrowded waves. Surf season

Woman selling Kuna molas in Bocas Town, Bocas del Toro, Panamá

is December through April, with June and July also good. **Del Toro Surfing** (507-6570-8277; deltorosurf@yahoo.com.ar) and **Rancho Paraíso** (507-757-9415; www.rancho paraiso.biz) offer surf lessons and board rentals, plus multiple-day packages

SHOPPING

Molas and Ngöbe-Buglé crafts astound at **Artesanías Bribrí Emanuel** (507-757-9652; Calle 3 and Avenida B; open Monday through Saturday 10 AM–8 PM). I bought a fabulous, oversized hammock at the **open-air crafts market** (Calle 3 and Avenida H), where you'll also find *molas* and indigenous crafts.

Surfers can get outfitted with the coolest duds at **Tropix Surf Shop** (507-757-9297; Calle 3 between Avenida Central and D).

WEEKLY AND ANNUAL EVENTS

Bocas is a lively place, with something happening most months. Three big events stand out:

Each July 16, the **Día de la Virgen del Carmen**, devout Catholics come to town for a pilgrimage to La Gruta, the cave containing a shrine of the Virgin Mary.

The five-day **Fería Internacional del Mar** (International Festival of the Sea), during the second week of September, is the big enchilada, with everything from folkloric dances to the crowning of the Sea Fair Queen.

Townsfolk celebrate the **Fundación de la Provincia de Bocas del Toro** (Founding Day) each November 16 with street parties and parades.

11

If Time is Short

Hopefully your visit to Panamá will be long enough to make the most of many of the attractions listed in the regional chapters. But if your time is limited and you're scratching your head over so many options, then why not follow an itinerary that samples my personal favorites? Not everyone might pick these particular spots, but I feel confident that you won't go home disappointed.

Places to Stay

Bocas Inn (507-757-9600 or 269-9415; www.anconexpeditions.com; Bocas Town, Bocas del Toro) This inexpensive option is all you need to settle into the laid-back, no-frills Caribbean laissez-faire attitude of Bocas. Rooms are simply furnished, and it serves only breakfasts, but the broad waterfront balcony with hammocks and rockers does the trick.

Canal House (507-228-1907; www.canalhousepanama.com; Casco Viejo; Panamá City) There's a reason Daniel Craig slept here while filming *Quantum of Solace*. Perhaps the finest boutique hotel in the city, it combines intimacy (there are only three suites) with super sophistication and an unbeatable location.

Coffee Estate Inn (507-720-2211; www.coffeeestateinn.com; Boquete) Lovingly run by an erudite and attentive Canadian expat couple, this hillside hotel is set in gorgeous gardens on a coffee estate with views of Volcán Barú. Plus, it has all the comforts of home.

Cultural Attractions: Day

Boat Excursion through the Canal (Panamá Canal). It's one thing to *see* the Canal in operation. It's quite another to pass through it, which is easily done on full-day small-boat excursions departing Balboa or Flamenco Marina, in Panamá City, on weekends. Contact Canal and Bay Tours (507-290-2009; www.canalandbaytours.com) or Panamá Marine (507-226-8917, www.pmatours.net).

Casco Viejo (Panamá City) It's hard to single out one item in the city's colonial core, so spend a full day (at least) walking the cobbled streets, being sure to visit the Plaza Bolívar, Plaza de la Francia, and the Plaza de la Catedral with its Museo del Canal Interoceánico. The old city is also full of art galleries and great restaurants.

El Porvenir and Vicinity (Kuna Yala). It's hard to imagine just one day visiting the Kuna indigenous peoples, but visiting Panamá without a trip to these exquisite islands—easily reached by plane from Panamá City—would be like visiting France without tasting the wine. Explore Wichub-Huala, and go snorkeling at Isla de los Perros. Bring lots of dollar bills for photography, and larger bills to buy yourself a fabulous *mola* at the source.

CULTURAL ATTRACTIONS: NIGHT

Café Havana (507-212-3873; Avenida B and Calle 5, Casco Viejo, Panamá City) As its name suggests, this sophisticated nightspot appeals to hip bohemians whose idea of a good time is to relish smoking a Cuban (or Panamanian) cigar with a divine *mojito* cocktail. Its setting in the heart of the old city is icing on the cake.

Platea (507-228-4011; www.scenaplatea.com; Calle 1ra, Casco Viejo, Panamá City) Set in a restored colonial mansion in the heart of the old city, this venue draws urban sophisticates to enjoy live jazz. You're surrounded by bare brick walls, although Platea exudes 21st-century style. Plus, it has one of the best restaurants in town.

Teatro Nacional (c/o 507-262-3525; teatronacional@inac.gob.pa; Casco Viejo, Panamá City) Culture vultures should keep their eye out for classical or operatic concerts, or even ballet, at this gorgeous historic theater. You'll want to dress to the nines for a performance by the Ballet Nacional de Panamá or Orquestra Sinfónica Nacional, the national symphony orchestra.

RESTAURANTS

Madame Chang (507-269-1313; madamechange@cableonda.net; Calle 48, Bella Vista, Panamá City) This world-renowned Oriental restaurant is one of the finest in Central America. The elegant decor is a match for mouthwatering dishes melding local ingredients with Asian spices and flavors. The divine seafood dishes include róbalo (snook) steamed with ginger and green onions.

Niko's Café Balboa (507-228-8888; www.nikoscafe.com; Steven's Circle, Balboa) Perfect for a break when exploring the former U.S. colonial town of Balboa, or when you want a bargain-priced buffet any time of day or night. The eclectic menu includes Greek dishes, a paean to its founder. Historic prints of the Canal add historic intrigue.

Panamonte Inn & Spa (507-720-1324; www.panamonteinnandspa.com; Avenida Central, Boquete) Exuding an old-world English elegance, this exquisite restaurant is one of Panamá's finest. Dine by candlelight, or in cozy comfort in the lounge-bar. Chef Charlie Collins' fusion dishes include local trout straight from the stream.

RECREATION

Coiba Dive Center (507-6565-7200; www.coibadivecenter.com; Santa Catalina, Veraguas) This professional scuba diving outfit specializes in dives of Parque Nacional Marino Isla Coiba, with fantastic coral formations plus the chance to encounter sharks and even whales.

National Geographic Expeditions (1-888-966-8687; http://nationalgeographicexpeditions.com) A weeklong adventure cruise aboard the M/V *Sea Lion* packs in hiking and

Woman sunbathing on Isla de los Perros, San Blas Islands, Panamá

wildlife viewing at otherwise hard-to-visit Isla Barra del Colorado; birding at Isla Boná, Estivá, and Otoque; snorkeling and kayaking at Isla Granito de Oro; and even a passage of the Panamá Canal. It doesn't get any more complete than this!

Panamá Surf Tours (507-6671-7777; www.panamasurftours.com) These guys are the experts when it comes to finding the best surf breaks. Newbies can learn to ride boards, and the professionals who run the company have more advanced tuition.

Parque Natural Metropolitano (507-232-5552; www.parquemetropolitano.org; Avenida Juan Pablo II, Panamá City) You don't need to leave the city to go hiking and wildlife viewing. This metropolitan park, on the northern outskirts, has well-manicured trails and teems with bird and animal life. Expect to see agoutis, coatis, Geoffrey's tamarin, and three-toed sloths.

Parque Nacional Darién/Cana Field Station (c/o 507-269-9415; www.anconexpeditions .com; Ancon Expeditions) Have Ancon Expeditions arrange a guide and lodgings, or join one of their group tours, to explore one of the premier birding and wildlife viewing sites in the country. Here, you're deep in the heart of the Darién rain forest.

Recommended Reading

Coffee-table

Friar, William. *Portrait of the Panama Canal: From Construction to the Twenty-First Century.* Portland, OR: Graphic Arts Center Publishing Company, 2003. 80 pages. Large-format. Black-and-white and color plates.

Keller, Uhlich. *The Building of the Panama Canal in Historic Photographs.* Mineola, NY: Dover Publications, 1984. 176 pages. A fascinating photographic study.

Perrin, Michel. *Magnificent Molas: The Art of the Kuna Indians.* Flammarion, 2000. 208 pages. Exquisitely illustrated look at more than 300 fabric "paintings" made and worn by the women of the Kuna.

Culture, History, Economics, and Politics

Buckley, Kevin. *Panamá.* New York: Touchstone, 1998. 304 pages. A former *Newsweek* correspondent vividly recounts the CIA's sponsoring of Noriega and events leading up to "Operation Just Cause" in Panamá.

Díaz Espino, Ovidio. *How Wall Street Created a Nation: J.P. Morgan, Teddy Roosevelt, and the Panama Canal.* New York: Basic Books, 2003. 276 pages. Financial speculation, fraud, and international conspiracy are unveiled in this historical account that castigates Wall Street banks.

Dinges, John. *Our Man in Panamá: How General Noriega Used the United States—and Made Millions in Drugs and Arms.* New York: Random House, 1970. 4092 pages. An excellent and disheartening account of the rise and fall of Noriega and the sordid part played by the U.S. government in supporting this unscrupulous thug.

Earle, Peter. *The Sack of Panama: Captain Morgan and the Battle for the Caribbean.* New York: Thomas Dunne Books, 2007. 304 pages. Historian Peter Earle's vivid and thoroughly researched account of the seminal pirate raid on Panamá.

Eisner, Peter. *America's Prisoner: The Memoirs of Manuel Noriega.* New York: Random House, 1997. 293 pages. Noriega's own account of his life reveals lots of dirty laundry.

Greene, Julie. *The Canal Builders: Making America's Empire at the Panama Canal.* New York: Penguin Press, 2009. 496 pages. The oft-neglected story of the workers who made the Canal possible is paramount in this engaging historical treatise.

Harris, David. *Shooting the Moon: The True Story of an American Manhunt Unlike Any Other, Ever.* Boston, MA: Back Bay Books, 2002. 400 pages. Medellín's cocaine cartels, the Iran-Contra Affair, CIA incursions. It's all here, distilled into a fascinating tale about the taking down of Noriega.

The Independent Commission of Inquiry on the U.S. Invasion of Panama. *The U.S. Invasion of Panama: The Truth Behind Operational 'Just Cause.'* Cambridge, MA: South End Press, 1999. 144 pages. A disquieting volume of speeches and testimonials comprising an official account of the invasion that toppled Noriega.

McCullough, David. *The Path Between the Seas: The Creation of the Panama Canal.* New York: Simon & Schuster, 1978. 704 pages. A sensational read, this Pulitzer Prize-winning text tells the fascinating story of the construction of the Panamá Canal.

McGinnis, Aims. *Path of Empire: Panama and the California Gold Rush*. New York: Cornell University Press, 2009. 264 pages. The intertwined histories of the California Gold Rush and the rise of U.S. hegemony form the background to this historical text.

Parker, Matthew. *Panama Fever: The Epic Story of the Building of the Panama Canal*. New York: Anchor, 2009. 576 pages. An epic tale about the construction of the Canal. Rivals McCullough's classic book in stature.

Seales Soley, La Verne M. *Culture and Customs of Panama*. Santa Barbara, CA: Greenwood Press, 2008. 148 pages. An exploration of contemporary Panamanian culture.

Literature

Le Carré, John. *The Tailor of Panamá*. New York: Ballantine Books, 1997. 416 pages. A smashing tale of espionage and deceit as the Chinese manipulate a toehold to control the Canal. Hints of Graham Greene's *Our Man in Havana*.

Zencey, Eric. *Panama: A Novel*. Berkley Trade, 2001. 400 pages. An unusual thriller sets Henry Adams amid the Panama Canal scandal of the 1880s. A Book-of-the-Month choice.

Natural History

Angehr, George R,. Dodge Engleman, and Lorna Engleman. *A Bird-finding Guide to Panama*. Ithaca, NY: Comstock, 2008. 391 pages. An essential new bird-watcher guide in association with the Panama Audubon Society.

Ridgely, Robert S. and John A. Gwynne, Jr. *A Guide to the Birds of Panamá*. Princeton, NJ: Princeton University Press, 1992. 412 pages. Beautifully illustrated guidebook considered the bible for birders heading to Panamá.

Recreation and Travel

Crowther, Heloise. *Panama Culture Smart! A Quick Guide to Customs and Etiquette*. London: Kuperard, 2006. 168 pages. A pocket-sized prodigy packed with essential information on attitudes, beliefs, and behavior.

DuFord, Darrin. *Is There a Hole in the Boat? Tales of Travel in Panama without a Car*. Booklocker.com, 2006. 196 pages. A personal account of travel writer Darrin DuFord's sometimes irreverent travels around Panamá.

Henderson, Malcolm. *Don't Kill the Cow Too Quick: An Englishman's Adventures Homesteading in Panama*. iUniverse, 2004. 250 pages. A self-published account of six years as a gringo facing the trials and tribulations of a life in Panamá.

Howard, Christopher. *Living and Investing in Panama*. 2004. San Jose, Costa Rica: Costa Rica Books, 2004. 312 pages. Almost everything you need to know to live, retire, and make money in Panamá.

Hutchins, William G. *Choose Panama . . . the Perfect Retirement Haven*. San Francisco: Mission Bay Publishing, 207. 172 pages. A worthy guide to giving it all up for a life in the tropical sun.

Mitchinson, Michael. *The Darien Gap: Travels in the Rainforest of Panama*. Bainbridge Island, WA: Harbour Pub Co., 2008. 284 pages. A U.S. travel writer's sometimes harrowing account of a personal 18-month journey through the dangerous Darién rain forests.

Parker, Clive. *Pedaling to Panamá*. AuthorHouse, 2008. 368 pages. An Englishman's personal account of a 7,000-kilometer journey by bicycle from Mexico to the end of the road.

Snyder, Sandra T. *Living in Panama*. Panama: TanToes, S.A, 2007. 360 pages. An exceptional guide for people thinking of retiring or otherwise moving to Panamá.

Index

Isla San Telmo, 63, 203

Isla Solarte, 290

Isla Taboga, 63, 131–33; dining, 132; ferries, 51, 133; lodging, 132

Isla Taborcillo, 208–9, 210

Isla Tigre, 173; events, 173; lodging, 169

Isla Viveros, 203; lodging, 200

Islas Secas, 259

Islas Secas Resort, 256

J

Jaqué, 198

Jeep tours, 56

jewelry stores, in Panamá City, 129–30

Jimmy's Caribbean Dive Resort (Nombre de Dios), 60, 158

John Wayne Village (Isla Taborcillo), 208–9, 210

Joyas De Panamá Cigars (La Pintada), 72, 221

K

Karavan Gallery (Panamá City), 130

kayaking, 62; Bocas del Toro, 290; Boquete, 174, 271; Kuna Yala, 174; Lago Gatún, 144; San Blas, 61, 168; Santa Catalina, 231, 233; Volcán, 271

Kinomaxx (Panamá City), 109

kiteboarding, 61, 210–11

Kool Youth Hostel (Isla Taboga), 132

Kotowa Coffee Tour (Palo Alto), 265

Kraze 950 (Panamá City), 121

Kuanidup, 171; lodging, 169

Kuna Indians, 37, 41, 176–77; etiquette, 179

Kuna Niskua Lodge (Wailidup), 170

Kuna Revolt (1925), 73, 173, 178

Kuna Yala, 165–81; Abaio Region, 178–81; Arriba Region, 168–74; Centro Region, 174–78; tours, 168; transportation, 166–68. See also specific destinations

L

La Amistad International Park, 66, 272–73; lodging, 280

La Arena: information, 241; shopping, 241

La Buena Vida (Santa Catalina), 230

La Casona de las Brujas (Panamá City), 121

La Dulce Colmena B&B (Panamá City), 93

La Escuela Normal Superior Juan Demostenes Arosemena (Santiago de Veraguas), 226

La Estancia B&B (Panamá City), 91–92, 125

La Exposición (Panamá City), 86, 87; architecture, 101; casinos, 108; historic sites, 111; lodging, 93

La Fortuna (Panamá City), 129

La Gruta: events, 291

La Gruta Cavern, 288

La Iguana Eco-Resort (Churuquita Grande), 220

La Loma Jungle Lodge (Bahía Honda), 285

La Lotería, 132

La Palma, 190, 194; lodging, 191; tourist information, 81

La Parita, 239–40; event, 74; shopping, 241

La Peregrina, 201

La Pintada, 220–21; shopping, 222

La Ronda (Panamá City), 130

La Torcaza Estate (Volcán), 269

Laboratorio Achotines (Playa Achotines), 247

Lago Alajuela, 149–50

Lago Bayano, 188

Lago Fortuna, 280

Lago Gatún, 60, 144–48; lodging, 140

Lagunas de Volcán, 67, 271

language schools, 131

Las Perlas Sailing, 203

Las Sirenas (Playa Santa Clara), 209

Las Tablas, 242–45; dining, 243; events, 74, 245; lodging, 243; sights/activities, 244–45

Las Tinajas (Panamá City), 100

Lemongrass (Bocas Town), 286–87

libraries, in Panamá City, 116

Librería Argosy (Panamá City), 128

Lili's Cafe (Bocas Town), 287

Limoncillo Pony Club (Panamá City), 98

Lindblad Expeditions, 49

lizards, 25

lodging, 293; price codes, 11, 70; Abaio